Brief Menu

More →

Rules *for* WRITERS

Ninth Edition

Rules
for

Diana Hacker

Nancy Sommers
Harvard University

Contributing ESL Specialist

Kimberli Huster
Robert Morris University

bedford/st.martin's
Macmillan Learning

Boston | New York

For Bedford/St. Martin's

Vice President, Editorial, Macmillan Learning Humanities: Edwin Hill
Executive Program Director for English: Leasa Burton
Executive Program Manager: Stacey Purviance
Director of Content Development: Jane Knetzger
Senior Executive Development Editor: Michelle M. Clark
Senior Media Editor: Barbara G. Flanagan
Associate Editors: Cara Kaufman, Melissa Rostek
Assistant Editor: Julia Domenicucci
Editorial Assistant: Aislyn Fredsall
Marketing Manager: Vivian Garcia
Senior Content Project Manager: Gregory Erb
Senior Workflow Project Manager: Jennifer Wetzel
Production Supervisor: Brianna Lester
Senior Media Project Manager: Allison Hart
Project Management and Editorial Services: Lifland et al., Bookmakers
Indexer: Ellen Kuhl Repetto
Composition: Lumina Datamatics, Inc.
Photo Editor: Angela Boehler
Permissions Editor: Kalina Ingham
Design Director, Content Management: Diana Blume
Text Design: Claire Seng-Niemoeller
Cover Design: William Boardman
Printing and Binding: RR Donnelley

1 2 3 4 5 6   25 24 23 22 21 20

For information, write: Bedford/St. Martin's, 75 Arlington Street, Boston, MA 02116

ISBN   978-1-319-36781-7   (Student Edition, APA Update, Paperback)
ISBN   978-1-319-36130-3   (Student Edition, APA Update)
ISBN   978-1-319-16226-9   (Instructor's Edition)
ISBN   978-1-319-36132-7   (Student Edition with Writing about Literature, APA Update)

Acknowledgments

Adler, Jonathan H., excerpt from "Little Green Lies: The Environmental Miseducation of America's Children," *Policy Review,* Summer 1992. Copyright © 1992. Reprinted by permission of the Heritage Foundation.

Berger, Michelle, excerpt from "Volunteer Army," *Audubon Magazine,* November–December 2010. Copyright © 2010 by the National Audubon Society. Reprinted by permission.

Rothman, Joshua, "What Amazon's Purchase of Whole Foods Really Means," *New Yorker,* June 24, 2017. Copyright © 2017 Condé Nast. Reprinted by permission.

Rudloe, Jack, and Anne Rudloe, excerpt from "Electric Warfare: The Fish That Kill with Thunderbolts," *Smithsonian,* vol. 24, no. 5, 95–105. Copyright © 1993 by Jack and Anne Rudloe. Reprinted by permission of Jack Rudloe.

Taylor, Betsy, "Big Box Stores Are Bad for Main Street," from David Masci, "The Consumer Culture," *CQ Researcher,* vol. 9, no. 44, November 19, 1999. Copyright © 1999 by CQ Press Researcher. Reprinted by permission of CQ Press Researcher, an imprint of SAGE Publications, Inc.; permission conveyed through Copyright Clearance Center, Inc.

Art acknowledgments and copyrights appear on the same page as the art selections they cover; these acknowledgments and copyrights constitute an extension of the copyright page.

Contents

Preface for Instructors

Dear Colleagues:

Welcome to the ninth edition of *Rules for Writers*. When you assign *Rules for Writers*, you send an important message to your students: Writing is worth studying and practicing. And you make it easy for students to find answers to their writing questions quickly and efficiently. The more comfortable students become using their handbook, the more confident and successful they become as college writers.

As I developed the ninth edition, I listened to students talk about the new expectations and new freedoms of college writing. Students quickly learn that they are expected to experiment with new genres and structures, take positions in academic arguments, learn how to use MLA in humanities classes and APA in social science and health science classes, read and respond critically to multimodal texts, and move away from formulaic rules. What became clear in all my conversations with students is that having a handbook — a trusted resource with guidance for answering questions — helps students meet the new expectations of college writing and gives them the confidence to experiment and succeed as college writers.

I worked with my editors at Bedford/St. Martin's to learn as much as I could from students about the ways in which they use textbooks and handbooks. That research — small student focus groups and surveys — informed our thinking about terminology and about the placement of certain navigational aids. For example, in response to student feedback, we moved the lists of documentation models so that they are easier to find, and we've included references to these critical research tools right on the inside front cover of the book. We made this change in response to your feedback as well; many instructors told us in reviews and in surveys that the research and documentation materials were among the most frequently used sections of the handbook.

Rules for Writers is designed to be a student's companion throughout the writing and researching processes, of course, but it is also designed for you so that all your students are on the same page, with access to the same trusted answers to common questions and practical solutions to common problems. You and your students will also have access to practice tools in LaunchPad Solo; instructors tell me they find LearningCurve, the research exercises, and the writing prompts especially valuable. What's more, I've developed a series of new video tutorials to help you teach common assignments such as argument, analysis, and annotated bibliography — but also to help you teach MLA and APA citation. These are conveniently located in LaunchPad Solo.

I tell my students — *Everything you need to become a successful writer in any college course is in* Rules for Writers. *Buy it, and become friends with it.* I am eager to share the ninth edition with you, confident that you will find everything here that you and your students trust and value about *Rules for Writers.*

Acknowledgments

I am grateful for the expertise, enthusiasm, and classroom experience that so many individuals brought to the ninth edition.

Reviewers

Nasreen Abbas, The George Washington University; Rian Acklin, Los Angeles Trade Technical College; Cameron Bentley, Augusta Technical College; Suzanne Biedenbach, Georgia Gwinnett College; Victoria Bowman, Camden County College; Jennifer Boyle, Davidson County Community College; Frances Burt, Hill College; Cathy Chaney, Northern Virginia Community College; Jonathan Cook, Durham Technical Community College; Dana Crotwell, El Camino College; Hugh Culik, Macomb Community College; Jill Darley-Vanis, Clark College; Crystal Edmonds, Robeson Community College; Bonnie Feeser, Hutchinson Community College; Wendy Fields, Robeson Community College; Ulanda Forbes, North Lake College; Lisa Ford, Tompkins Cortland Community College; Jacqueline Goffe-McNish, Dutchess Community College; Robert Goldberg, Prince George's Community College; Sherry Goodyear, Luna Community College; Sarah Gottschall, Prince George's Community College; Odile Harter, Harvard University; Anne Helms, Alamance Community College; Sara Hillin, Lamar University; Laura Jeffries, Florida State College at Jacksonville; Geri Lawson, California State University, Long Beach; Rebecca Lorenz-Schumacher, University of Wisconsin–Stevens Point; Harry Manos, Los Angeles City College; Carol McCarthy, Delgado Community College; Duygu Minton, Augusta University; Kylowna Moton, Los Angeles City College; Danielle Nielsen, Murray State University; Ellen Olmstead, Montgomery College; Jeanne Purtell, Harrisburg Area Community

College; Rosalie Roberts, Clark College; Art Schuhart, Northern Virginia Community College–Annandale; Rashidah Shakir, Los Angeles Trade Technical College; KT Shaver, California State University, Long Beach; Katherine Silvester, Indiana University; Jenny Simon, El Camino College; Susan Slavicz, Florida State College at Jacksonville; Nancy Staub, Lamar University; Anthony Stevens, Los Angeles Trade Technical College; Gail Upchurch, Dutchess Community College; Lykourgos Vasileiou, LaGuardia Community College; Erin Whitford, Howard College; Natasha Whitton, Southeastern Louisiana University; Debbie Williams, Abilene Christian University.

Contributors

I am grateful for contributions from the following individuals, all fellow teachers of writing: Kimberli Huster, ESL specialist at Duquesne University and Robert Morris University, for her work on content for multilingual writers; Sara McCurry, who teaches at Shasta College, for her contributions to *Teaching with Hacker Handbooks*; and Margaret Price, associate professor of English at The Ohio State University, and Rosalie Roberts, adjunct instructor of English at Clark College, for helping me to think about new content on pronouns, gender, and audience awareness.

Students

For participating in focus groups related to handbook usability, I thank Amy Shea's composition students at Massachusetts College of Pharmacy and Health Sciences and Linda Sutliff's composition students at Bunker Hill Community College. I also thank recent grads Aislyn Fredsall (Northeastern University) and Paola Garcia-Muniz (Fairfield University) for helping to shape our understanding of how students navigate handbooks and their content. Finally, I extend my gratitude to the following students for letting us adapt their work as models: Sophie Harba, Sam Jacobs, Michelle Nguyen, Emilia Sanchez, and April Bo Wang.

Bedford/St. Martin's and beyond

A handbook is a collaborative writing project, and it is my pleasure to acknowledge the enormously talented Bedford/St. Martin's editorial team, whose focus on students informs each new feature of *Rules for Writers*. Edwin Hill, vice president for humanities editorial, and Leasa Burton, executive program director for English, generously offer their deep knowledge of the field of composition. Stacey Purviance, executive program manager, brings her creative energy and enormous talents to *Rules for Writers*. I am grateful for her devotion to designing new ways to pair print and digital content. Much thanks to Bedford colleagues Joy Fisher Williams and Vivian Garcia, who, like me, spend many hours on the road and in faculty offices, for their treasured advice. Doug Silver, product manager for English, helps us to reimagine writers' and teachers' opportunities with digital tools.

Michelle Clark, senior executive editor, is the editor every author dreams of having. She manages to be exacting and endearing all at once — a treasured friend and colleague and an endless source of creativity. Michelle combines imagination with practicality and hard work with good cheer. Barbara Flanagan, senior media editor, brings unrivaled expertise in documentation and manages content development for LaunchPad Solo for Hacker Handbooks. It is a wonderful pleasure to work with Barbara and to have her good sense on important details. Thanks to Cara Kaufman, associate editor, whose clear-headed thinking and editorial eye have significantly influenced the ninth edition. Cara's editorial talents are evident throughout the handbook and in our digital content — streamlining manuscript, developing video tutorials, leading student focus groups, and developing the *Working with Sources* research exercises. Thanks to Julia Domenicucci, assistant editor, for expertly conducting reviews and surveys, leading student focus groups, and developing the popular *Developmental Exercises,* and to Aislyn Fredsall, editorial assistant, for lending her youthful eye to the cover design effort. Many thanks to the media production team — Michelle Camisa and Allison Hart — for delivering engaging handbook tools, including new e-books, for students in the digital age.

Many thanks to Gregory Erb, senior content project manager, for a careful eye and smart management of our schedule. And thanks to Sally Lifland and Quica Ostrander, copyeditors, for thoroughness and attention to detail; to Claire Seng-Niemoeller, text designer, who crafted a clean and more navigable ninth edition; and to Billy Boardman, senior design manager, who has introduced a striking new cover.

Last, but never least, I offer thanks to my own students who, over many years, have shaped my teaching and helped me understand their challenges. Thanks to my friends and colleagues Jenny Doggett, Joan Feinberg, Suzanne Lane, Maxine

Rodburg, Laura Saltz, and Kerry Walk for sustaining conversations about the teaching of writing. And thanks to my family: to Joshua Alper, an attentive reader of life and literature, for his steadfastness across the drafts; to my parents, Walter and Louise Sommers, who encouraged me to write and set me forth on a career of writing and teaching; to my extended family, Ron, Charles Mary, Alexander, Demian, Devin, Liz, Kate, Sam, Terry, Steve, and Yuval, for their good humor and good cheer; and to Rachel and Curran, Alexandra and Brian, world-class listeners, witty and wise beyond measure, always generous with their instruction and inspiration in all things that matter. They share my thrill when they hold this handbook in their hands. And to my grandchildren, Lailah and Oren, thanks for the joy and sweetness you bring to life.

Nancy Sommers

Nancy Sommers
nancy_sommers@harvard.edu

Welcome to the Ninth Edition

Rules for Writers offers the clear guidance and comprehensive content that student writers need to become confident, successful writers. Students may want to turn to popular search engines for quick answers, but the real shortcut is right in their hands. *Rules for Writers* provides trustworthy advice that's easy to understand and apply. No guesswork involved.

What's new?

Better navigational help.   Based on usability research with students from two- and four-year colleges, we have made the book even easier to navigate. A new *How to use this book* page orients students to the major avenues for quick help, and a new scavenger hunt offers a useful activity-based introduction to the book. Menus, contents, and lists of documentation models are in more accessible locations.

A more practical *how-to* approach. New step-by-step instruction will help students apply writing advice and transfer skills to many different kinds of writing assignments. Fifteen new *How-to* pages deliver the straightforward help that instructors and students want — how to go beyond a Google search, how to give better peer review comments, and more.

New help designed for beginning academic writers. The ninth edition offers stronger, more useful advice for students just beginning to write with sources and develop an academic voice.

- New *sentence guides* help students with the most basic academic scenario: presenting and responding to the views of others. Fill-in sentence starters provide useful models for participating in academic discourse and writing research essays (see 55c).

> **Using sentence guides to integrate sources**
>
> You build you credibility (*ethos*) by accurately representing the views of others and by integrating these views into your paper. An important way to present the views of others before agreeing or disagreeing with them is to use sentence guides. These guides act as academic sentence starters; they show you how to use signal phrases in sentences to make clear to your reader whose ideas you're presenting — your own or those you have encountered in a source.
>
> **Presenting others' views.** As an academic writer, you will be exp[ected] to demonstrate your understanding of a source by summarizin[g the] views or arguments of its author. The following language will h[elp] you to do so:
>
> X argues that _____.
>
> X and Y emphasize the need for _____.
>
> _____, according to X, is most the critical cause of _____
>
> **Presenting direct quotations.** To introduce the exact words of a source because their accuracy and authority are important for [your] argument, you might try phrases like these:
>
> X describes the problem this way: ". . ."
>
> X argues strongly in favor of the policy, pointing out that ". [. ."]
>
> According to X, _____ is defined as ". . ."
>
> **Presenting alternative views.** At times, you will have to synthesi[ze] views of multiple sources before you introduce your own.
>
> While X and Y have supported these findings, new research[er] Z suggests that _____.

- New coverage guides students as they learn *how to detect fake and misleading news* as they search for sources (see 52c).

> **HOW TO**
>
> ## Detect fake news and misleading sources
>
> Fake news and fabricated sources distort information or spread misinformation by taking information out of context or by promoting opinions as facts. As you evaluate sources, determine the authenticity of information and its source: Can the information be verified? Is the source reliable? If you are researching a controversial issue, verify facts and quotations by reading multiple sources and gathering a variety of perspectives. Because information and misinformation live side by side on the web, you need to read critically to determine the truth.
>
> **1** Consider the source.
>
> Ask: Is more than one source covering the topic? Is the author anonymous or named? What can you learn about the author's credentials and the mission of the source from checking the "About Us" tab? Does the site present only one side of an issue? Be skeptical if the source is the only one reporting the story.
>
> **2** Examine the source's language and visual clues.
>
> Does the headline use sensational shocking or emotional language? Is the language of the source offensive? Is the screen cluttered with ALL CAPS and unprofessional web design?
>
> **3** Question the seriousness of the source.
>
> Is it possible that the source is satirical and humorous and is not intended to be read as factual?
>
> **4** Pay attention to the URL.
>
> Established news organizations have standard domain names. Fake sites often u~~~~ ~~~es that imitate

- Four new "*Writing for an audience*" boxes help students keep their readers in mind as they make decisions about how to develop their ideas. See 50b for one example.

- Revised notes about *using sources responsibly* develop good academic citizenship among beginning college writers.

Engaging video tutorials that support common writing assignments. Twenty-four new video tutorials for writing and citation support students as they learn difficult academic concepts. These tools combine brief, lively videos with scorable practice items to help students with common first-year writing assignments, such as argument, analysis, and annotated bibliography, and with using MLA and APA style. The following video tutorials appear in LaunchPad Solo for Hacker Handbooks:

Analytical essay
What is an analytical essay?
How to read critically
How to draft an analytical thesis
How to balance summary and analysis

Annotated bibliography
What is an annotated bibliography?
How to enter a research conversation
How to evaluate a source
How to write an annotation

Researched argument
What is a researched argument?
How to ask a research question
How to develop an argumentative thesis
How to acknowledge counterarguments

MLA
MLA documentation style (Overview)
How to cite a selection from an anthology in MLA style
How to cite an article in MLA style
How to cite a book in MLA style
How to cite an article from a database in MLA style
How to cite a work from a website in MLA style
How to format a paper in MLA style

APA
APA documentation style (Overview)
How to cite an article in APA style
How to cite an article from a database in APA style
How to cite a book in APA style
How to cite a work from a website in APA style

A new supplemental workbook for students in paired/co-requisite sections. *A Student's Companion to Hacker Handbooks*, designed specifically to help under-prepared students succeed in their first-year writing course or sequence, provides a wide range of activities and strategies to help students practice the skills and habits they need to be successful academic writers. The text includes coverage of important college success strategies including time management and planning. A variety of activities and templates help students improve their reading and writing performance; graphic organizers help visual learners, exercises for thesis statements and topic sentences help writers with little academic writing experience, and grammar and research exercises help strengthen students' work at the sentence level. *A Student's Companion to Hacker Handbooks* is available in print workbook format or online within LaunchPad Solo.

What hasn't changed

Rules for Writers, Ninth Edition, still includes **writing guides** for common assignments because you told us how useful these are in your classes. The new edition still emphasizes **critical reading and academic writing**. The book will feel familiar to you because it offers comprehensive coverage of the topics you teach and the reference material your students need — especially when they cite sources in **MLA and APA** style. And, since we know how much you value the practice **exercises and activities** that help with grammar, style, and punctuation topics, we've added a few new ones to the book — with many more online.

Rules for Writers is still available in two versions — **a spiral-bound classic version** and a **tabbed version with Writing about Literature**.

Ordering information for *Rules for Writers*, Ninth Edition

Classic (APA Update)	ISBN 978-1-319-36130-3
Tabbed with Writing about Literature (APA Update)	ISBN 978-1-319-36132-7

For packaging information and ISBNs, please contact your Bedford/St. Martin's sales representative.

What's online for *Rules for Writers*?

⚏ LaunchPad Solo for Hacker Handbooks.   This digital companion provides engaging online content and new ways to get the most out of your course — with practice activities, adaptive quizzing, video content, and models for student writers.

- **New:** 24 engaging **video tutorials** support students as they do the most difficult work of the course — write analysis papers, arguments, and annotated bibliographies and cite sources. See the list on p. xxvii.

- **New:** 150 Grammar Girl **podcasts** offer engaging, accessible mini-lessons on grammar and style.

- 300 interactive **exercises**, most of which are auto-scored, cover writing, grammar, and research topics.

- 44 **writing prompts** help students apply the lessons of the handbook to their own writing.

- 33 **LearningCurve** adaptive, game-like quizzes help students focus on the topic areas in which they need help in a low-stakes environment.

- 13 complete **models of student writing** are annotated to show effective writing and proper format.

- Easy functionality makes **assigning** a breeze, and a **powerful gradebook** helps you track student progress.

What else? *we're all in*. As always.

Bedford/St. Martin's is as passionately committed to the discipline of English as ever, working hard to provide support and services that make it easier for you to teach your course your way.

Find community support at the Bedford/St. Martin's English Community (community.macmillan.com), where you can follow our Bits blog for new teaching ideas, download titles from our professional resource series, access *Teaching with Hacker Handbooks*, and review projects in the pipeline.

Choose curriculum solutions that offer flexible custom options, combining our carefully developed print and digital resources, acclaimed works from Macmillan's trade imprints, and your own course or program materials to provide the exact resources your students need. Our approach to customization makes it possible to create a project uniquely suited for your students and, based on your enrollment size, return money to your department. We can also help you raise your institutional profile with a high-impact author visit through the Macmillan Author Program ("MAP"). Visit **macmillanlearning.com /curriculumsolutions**.

Rely on outstanding service from your Bedford/St. Martin's sales representative and editorial team. Contact us or visit **macmillanlearning.com** to learn more about convenient, high-quality options for your course and your program.

SCAVENGER HUNT

Learning to use *Rules for Writers*

Using one of the five paths described on the inside front cover of this book, practice locating the help that writers typically need in college. Knowing how the book works and being able to find answers quickly means you get more for your money. Answers appear at the back of the book.

🔍 Finding answers to common writing questions

1 Your first assignment requires an effective thesis statement. This section of *Rules for Writers* covers drafting and revising a thesis statement.

_____
Book section numbers
(4a, 12d, for example)

2 You have been asked to format your essay in MLA style. Where in *Rules for Writers* can you find an example showing MLA format?

_____

3 You are writing a research paper and want to cite a short article from a website in your APA references list. Where will you find a model that shows you how?

_____

4 Where in the book will you find a two-page writing guide on how to write an argument essay?

_____

5 Where in *Rules for Writers* will you find advice that will help you to detect fake or misleading news?

_____

6 Locate the box that gives you advice on how to write better peer review comments.

_____

Q Using the Brief Menu, Contents, or Glossary of usage

Each of the following sentences includes an error. Identify the number of the section in *Rules for Writers* that includes advice that will help you edit the sentence. As a bonus, try to edit each of the following sentences correctly!

7 A verb have to agree with its subject.

_____
Book section numbers
(4a, 12d, for example)

8 Commas are useful, but are generally overused.

_____

9 About sentence fragments. Academic writers should avoid them.

_____

10 I plan to lay down for a nap before my shift begins.

_____

11 Professor, will you except late papers?

_____

12 The city felt the affects of the hurricane for months afterward.

_____

A PROCESS FOR WRITING

One of the pleasures of college writing is exploring ideas and discovering what you think about a subject. You may find that the process leads you in unexpected directions — the more you read about a topic, the more questions you formulate; new questions may lead you to challenge your initial assumptions. It is in the *process* of writing — thinking in depth about ideas — that you learn what's interesting in a subject and why you care about it.

1 Exploring, planning, and drafting

Academic writing is a process of figuring out what you think, not a matter of recording already developed thoughts. Since it's not possible to think about everything all at once, most experienced writers handle a piece of writing in stages — planning, drafting, revising, and editing. As you discover what you want to say, you'll often find yourself circling back to earlier stages to develop your ideas.

Before composing a first draft, spend some time generating ideas. Consider these questions: What do you find puzzling or interesting about your subject? What would you like to know more about? Be curious and open to new ideas and different points of view. Explore questions you don't have answers to.

1a Assess the writing situation.

Begin by taking a look at your writing situation. Consider your subject, your purpose, your audience, available sources of information, and any assignment requirements related to genre, length, document design, and deadlines (see the chart in this section).

Process for assessing the writing situation

Subject

- Assigned or free choice?
- Why is your subject worth writing about? What questions will you explore?
- Do you need to narrow your subject to a more specific topic?

Purpose and audience

- Why are you writing: To inform readers? Persuade them? Call them to action? Some combination of purposes?
- Who are your readers? How well informed are they about the subject?
- Will your readers resist your ideas? What objections will you anticipate and counter?

Genre (type of writing)

- What genre is required: Essay? Letter? Report? Proposal?
- Expectations of your assigned genre? For instance, what type of evidence is typically used?
- Does the genre require a specific format or organization?

Sources of information

- Where will your information come from: Reading? Research? Direct observation? Interviews? Questionnaires?
- What type of evidence suits your subject, purpose, audience, and genre?

Length and format

- Length requirements?
- Format requirements?
- Do you have guidelines or examples?
- MLA, APA, or other style?
- Would visuals help? Are they allowed?

Deadlines

- Rough draft due date? Final due date?
- How to submit writing: Print, post, email, or share?

Academic English What counts as good writing varies from culture to culture. In some situations, you will need to become familiar with the writing styles — such as direct or indirect, personal or impersonal, plain or embellished — that are valued by the culture in which you are writing.

Subject

Frequently your subject will be given to you, but when you are free to choose your own subject, let your curiosity focus your choice. If your interest in a subject stems from personal experience, you will want to ask what it is about your experience that would interest your audience and why. Make sure that you can reasonably investigate your subject in the space you have. If you are limited to a few pages, for example, you could not do justice to a broad subject, but you could focus on one aspect of the subject.

Purpose

In many writing situations, part of your challenge will be discovering your purpose or reason for writing. The wording of an assignment may suggest its purpose. If no guidelines are given, you may need to ask yourself, "What is my goal?" or "What do I want to accomplish?" Identify which one or more of the following aims you hope to accomplish.

to inform	to analyze
to explain	to synthesize
to summarize	to propose
to persuade/argue	to call readers to action
to evaluate	to reflect

Audience

Take time to ask questions about your readers and their expectations: Who will be reading your draft? What is your relationship to your readers? What information will your audience need to understand your ideas? Questions about audience should guide your writing, whether you are writing in college or in a professional or public context. The choices you make as you write will tell readers who you think they are (novices or experts, for example) and will show respect for your readers' values and perspectives.

In college writing, considerations of audience can be more complex than they seem at first. Your instructor will read your essay, of course, but most instructors play multiple roles while reading. Their first and most obvious roles are as coach and evaluator; but they are also intelligent and objective readers, the kind of people who might be informed or called to action by what you have to say and who want to learn from your insights and ideas.

When you are writing in a job or internship, keep in mind that you might often write for multiple audiences — a client and a supervisor, for example. And in public contexts, where you may be familiar with the readers' views, you can think very specifically about how to engage your audience.

For help with audience when composing email messages, see the following chart.

Considering audience when writing email messages

When you write an email message to an instructor, a classmate, or a potential employer, show readers that you value their time. Here are some strategies for writing effective emails:

- Use a concise, meaningful subject line.
- State your main point at the beginning.
- Keep paragraphs brief and focused.
- Proofread for typos and errors.

You will want to follow conventions of etiquette and academic integrity. Here are some strategies for writing responsible emails:

- Do not write anything that you wouldn't feel comfortable saying directly to your reader.
- Avoid forwarding another person's message without permission.
- Choose your words carefully because email messages, without facial expressions and tone of voice, can easily be misread.
- If you include someone else's words, let your reader know the source.

Genre

Pay close attention to the genre, or type of writing, assigned. Each genre is a category of writing meant for a specific purpose and audience, with its own set of agreed-upon expectations and conventions for style, structure, and format. Sometimes an assignment specifies the genre — an essay in a writing class, a lab report or research proposal in a biology class, a policy memo in a criminal justice class, or a slide presentation in a business class. Sometimes the genre is yours to choose, and you need to decide if a particular genre will help you communicate your purpose and reach readers.

Exercise 1–1 Narrow three of the following subjects into topics that would be manageable for an essay of two to five pages.

1. The minimum wage
2. Immigration
3. Cyberbullying
4. The cost of a college education
5. Internet privacy

Exercise 1–2 Suggest a purpose and an audience for three of the following subjects.

1. Medical experimentation using animals
2. Government housing for military veterans
3. Genetically modified foods
4. Working with special needs children
5. Alternative sentencing for first offenders

1b Explore your subject.

Experiment with techniques for exploring your subject and discovering your purpose: talking and listening; reading and annotating texts; asking questions; brainstorming and freewriting; keeping a journal or blog. Whatever technique you use, the goal is the same: to generate ideas that will lead you to a question or topic that you want to explore further.

Talking and listening

Talking about your ideas can help you develop them before writing a first draft. By talking and listening to others, you can hear yourself think aloud and also discover what your listeners find interesting, what they are curious about, and where they disagree with you. If you are writing an argument, you can try it out on listeners with other points of view.

Reading and annotating texts

Reading is an important way to deepen your understanding of a topic, learn from the insights and research of others, and expand your perspective. Annotating a text encourages you to read actively — to highlight key concepts, to note possible contradictions in an argument, or to raise questions for further research and investigation.

Asking questions

Asking questions is a productive way to get started on a piece of writing. You might try asking *Who? What? When? Where? Why?* and *How?* If you were writing about a negative reaction to a film, for instance, you might want to ask *who* objected to the film and *why? What* were the objections and *when* were they voiced? Such questions will help you discover important facts.

If you are writing in a particular discipline, try to find out which questions its scholars typically explore. Look for clues in assigned readings and class discussions to understand how a discipline's questions help you identify its concerns.

Brainstorming and freewriting

Brainstorming and freewriting are good ways to figure out what you know and what questions you have. Write (in list form or sentence form) whatever comes to mind without pausing to think about word choice, spelling, or even meaning. The goal is to write quickly and freely to discover what questions are on your mind and what directions you might pursue.

Keeping a journal or a blog

A journal is a collection of informal or exploratory writing. In a journal, often meant for your eyes only, you can experiment. You might freewrite, pose questions, comment on an interesting idea, or keep a list of questions that occur to you while reading. You might imagine a conversation between yourself and your readers or stage a debate to understand opposing positions.

Although a blog is a type of journal, it is a public rather than a private writing space. In a blog, you can explore an idea for a paper by writing posts from different angles. Since most blogs allow commenting, you can start a conversation by inviting readers to give you feedback in the form of questions, counterarguments, or links to other sources on a topic.

1c Draft and revise a working thesis statement.

For many types of writing, you will be able to state your central idea in a sentence or two. Such a statement, which ordinarily appears in the opening paragraph, is called a *thesis*.

Understanding what makes an effective thesis statement

An effective thesis statement is a central idea that conveys your purpose, or reason for writing, and that requires support. An effective thesis should

- state a position that needs to be explained and supported
- use concrete language and be sharply focused
- let your readers know what to expect
- be appropriate for the length requirements of the assignment, not too broad or too narrow
- stand up to the "So what?" test (see p. 9)

Drafting a working thesis

As you explore your topic, you will begin to see possible ways to focus your material. At this point, try to settle on a *tentative* central idea, or working thesis statement, to narrow your topic. You'll need to revisit your working thesis as your ideas develop, to see if it presents the position you want to take and if it can be supported by the sources of evidence you have collected.

You'll find that the process of answering a question you have posed, resolving a problem you have identified, or taking a position on a debatable topic will focus your thinking and lead you to develop a working thesis. Here, for example, are one student's efforts to pose a question and draft a working thesis for an essay in his ethics course.

QUESTION

Should athletes who enhance their performance through biotechnology be banned from athletic competition?

WORKING THESIS

Athletes who boost their performance through biotechnology should be banned from athletic competition.

The working thesis offers a useful place to start writing, a way to limit the topic and focus a first draft; but it doesn't respond to readers who will ask "Why?" and "So what?" The student has taken a position — athletes who use performance enhancers should be banned — but he hasn't explained *why* athletes should be banned. To fully answer his own question, he might push his own thinking with the word *because*.

STRONGER WORKING THESIS

Athletes who boost their performance through biotechnology should be banned from athletic competition *because* biotechnology gives them an unfair advantage and disrupts the sense of fair play.

Revising a working thesis

As you move toward a clearer and more specific position you want to take, you'll start to see ways to revise your working thesis. You may find that the evidence you collected supports a different thesis; or you may find that your position has changed as you learned more about your topic.

Revision is ongoing; as your ideas evolve, your working thesis will evolve, too. One effective way to revise a working thesis is to put it to the "So what?" test. Such questions help you keep audience and purpose in mind as you revise.

Putting your working thesis to the "So what?" test

Use the following questions to help you revise your working thesis.

- Why would readers want to read an essay with this thesis? How will you respond to a reader who hears your thesis and asks "So what?" or "Why does it matter?"
- Will any readers disagree with this thesis? If so, how might you revise in response?
- Is the thesis too obvious? If you cannot come up with counterpositions that oppose your own, consider revising your thesis.

HOW TO

Solve five common problems with thesis statements

Revising a working thesis is easier if you have a method or an approach. The following problem/solution approach can help you recognize and solve common thesis problems.

1 **Common problem: The thesis is a statement of fact.**

Solution: Enter a debate by posing a question about your topic that has more than one possible answer. For example: Should the polygraph be used by private employers? Your thesis should be your answer to the question.

Working thesis: *The first polygraph was developed by Dr. John Larson in 1921.*

Revised: *Because the polygraph has not been proved reliable, even under controlled conditions, its use by private employers should be banned.*

2 **Common problem: The thesis is a question.**

Solution: Take a position on your topic by answering the question you have posed. Your thesis statement should be your answer to the question.

Working thesis: *Would President John F. Kennedy have continued to escalate the war in Vietnam if he had lived?*

Revised: *Although President John F. Kennedy sent the first American troops to Vietnam before he died, an analysis of his foreign policy suggests that he would not have escalated the war if he had lived.*

3 **Common problem: The thesis is too broad.**

Solution: Focus on a subtopic of your original topic. Once you have chosen a subtopic, take a position in an ongoing debate and pose a question that has more than one answer. For example: Should people be tested for genetic diseases? Your thesis should be your answer to the question.

Working thesis: *Mapping the human genome has many implications for health and science.*

Revised: *Although scientists can now detect genetic predisposition for specific diseases, policymakers should establish clear guidelines about whom to test and under what circumstances.*

4 Common problem: The thesis is too narrow.

Solution: Identify challenging questions that readers might ask about your topic. Then pose a question that has more than one answer. For example: Do the risks of genetic testing outweigh its usefulness? Your thesis should be your answer to the question.

Working thesis: *A person who carries a genetic mutation linked to a particular disease might or might not develop that disease.*

Revised: *Though positive results in a genetic test do not guarantee that the disease will develop, such results can cause psychological trauma; genetic testing should therefore be avoided if possible.*

5 Common problem: The thesis is vague.

Solution: Focus your thesis with concrete language and clues about where the essay is headed. Pose a question about the topic that has more than one answer. For example: How does the physical structure of the Vietnam Veterans Memorial shape the experience of the visitors? Your thesis — your answer to the question — should use specific language.

Working thesis: *The Vietnam Veterans Memorial is an interesting structure.*

Revised: *By inviting visitors to see their own reflections in the wall, the Vietnam Veterans Memorial creates a link between the present and the past.*

Exercise 1–3 In each of the following pairs, which sentence might work well as a thesis for a short paper? What is the problem with the other one? Is it too factual? Too broad? Too vague? Use the problem/solution approach presented above to evaluate each thesis.

1. a. Many drivers use their cell phones irresponsibly while driving.
   b. Current state laws are inadequate to punish drivers who use their cell phones irresponsibly to text, read email, or perform other distracting activities.

2. a. Although Facebook was designed to help people keep in touch, it actually keeps them apart by discouraging face-to-face interactions and creating an illusion of intimacy.
   b. Facebook was designed to make it easier for people to keep in touch.

3. a. As we search to define the intelligence of animals, we run the risk of imposing our own understanding of intelligence on animals.

   b. How does the field of animal psychology help humans define intelligence?

4. a. The high cost of college needs to be reduced because it affects students and their families.

   b. To reduce the high cost of college, more students should be offered opportunities for dual-enrollment courses and a three-year college degree.

5. a. Anorexia nervosa is a dangerous and sometimes deadly eating disorder occurring mainly in young, upper-middle-class teens.

   b. The eating disorder anorexia nervosa is rarely cured by one treatment alone; only by combining drug therapy with psychotherapy and family therapy can the client begin the long journey to wellness.

1d Draft a plan.

Listing and organizing supporting ideas can help you figure out how to develop your thesis. Creating outlines, whether informal or formal, is a way to make sure your writing is focused and logical and can help you identify any gaps in your support.

When to use an informal outline

You might want to sketch an informal outline to see how you will support your thesis and to figure out a tentative structure for your ideas. Informal outlines can take many forms. Perhaps the most common is simply the thesis followed by a list of major ideas.

INFORMAL OUTLINE

Working thesis: Animal testing should be banned because it is bad science and doesn't contribute to biomedical advances.

- Most animals don't serve as good models for the human body.
- Drug therapies can have vastly different effects on different species; 92 percent of all drugs shown to be effective in animal tests fail in human trials.
- Some of the most important biomedical discoveries were made without the use of animal testing.

- The most effective biomedical research methods — tissue engineering and computer modeling — don't use animals.
- Animal studies are not scientifically necessary.

If you began by brainstorming a list of ideas, you can turn the list into a rough outline by crossing out some ideas, adding others, and putting the ideas in a logical order.

When to use a formal outline

Early in the writing process, rough outlines have certain advantages over formal outlines: They can be produced quickly, they are tentative, and they can be revised easily. However, a formal outline may be useful later in the writing process, after you have written a rough draft, especially if your topic is complex. A formal outline can help you see whether the parts of your draft work together and whether your draft's structure is logical.

The following formal outline brought order to the research paper that appears in 57b. The student's thesis is an important part of the outline. Everything else in the outline supports the thesis, directly or indirectly.

FORMAL OUTLINE

Thesis: In the name of public health and safety, state governments have the responsibility to shape public health policies and to regulate healthy eating choices, especially since doing so offers a potentially large social benefit for a relatively small cost.

I. Debates surrounding food regulation have a long history in the United States.

    A. The 1906 Pure Food and Drug Act guarantees inspection of meat and dairy products.

    B. Such regulations are considered reasonable because consumers are protected from harm with little cost.

    C. Consumers consider reasonable regulations to be an important government function to stop harmful items from entering the marketplace.

II. Even though food meets safety standards, there is a need for further regulation.

    A. The typical American diet — processed sugars, fats, and refined flours — is damaging over time.

    B. Related health risks are diabetes, cancer, and heart problems.

    C. Passing chronic-disease-related legislation is our single most important public health challenge.

III. Food legislation is not a popular solution for most Americans.

    A. A proposed New York City regulation banning the sale of soft drinks greater than twelve ounces failed in 2012, and in California, a proposed soda tax failed in 2011.

    B. Many consumers find such laws to be unreasonable restrictions on freedom of choice.

    C. Opposition to food and beverage regulation is similar to the opposition to early tobacco legislation; the public views the issue as one of personal responsibility.

    D. Counterpoint: Freedom of "choice" is a myth; our choices are heavily influenced by marketing.

IV. The United States has a history of regulations to discourage unhealthy behaviors.

    A. Tobacco-related restrictions faced opposition.

    B. Seat belt laws are a useful analogy.

    C. The public seems to support laws that have a good cost-benefit ratio; the cost of food/beverage regulations is low, and most people agree that the benefits would be high.

V. Americans believe that personal choice is lost when regulations such as taxes and bans are instituted.

    A. Regulations open up the door to excessive control and interfere with cultural and religious traditions.

    B. Counterpoint: Burdens on individual liberty are a reasonable price to pay for large social health benefits.

VI. Public opposition continues to stand in the way of food regulation to promote healthier eating. We must consider whether to allow the costly trend of rising chronic disease to continue in the name of personal choice, or whether we are willing to support the legal changes and public health policies that will reverse that trend.

1e Draft an introduction.

Generally, the introduction to a piece of writing announces the main point; the body develops it; and the conclusion drives it home. You can begin drafting, however, at any point. If you find it difficult to introduce a paper that you have not yet written, try drafting the body first and saving the introduction for later.

Your introduction will usually be a paragraph of 50 to 150 words (in a longer paper, it may be more than one paragraph). A common strategy is to open with a few sentences that engage, or hook, the reader and that establish your purpose for writing and your central idea, or thesis. In the following introduction, the thesis is highlighted.

> As the United States industrialized in the nineteenth century, using immigrant labor, social concerns took a backseat to the task of building a prosperous nation. The government did not regulate industries and did not provide an effective safety net for the poor or for those who became sick or injured on the job. Immigrants and the poor did have a few advocates, however. Settlement houses such as Hull-House in Chicago provided information, services, and a place for reform-minded individuals to gather and work to improve the conditions of the urban poor. Alice Hamilton was one of these reformers. Her work at Hull-House spanned twenty-two years and later expanded throughout the nation. Hamilton's efforts helped to improve the lives of immigrants and drew attention and respect to the problems and people that until then had been ignored.
>
> — Laurie McDonough, student

Whether you are writing for an academic audience or a more general audience, you cannot assume your readers' interest in the topic. The sentences leading to your thesis should hook readers by sparking their curiosity, drawing them into your essay, and giving them a reason to continue reading.

For more examples of effective introductions, see the model essays in 5d, 7h, and 57b.

Strategies for drafting an introduction

Whether you are composing a traditional essay or a multimodal work such as a slide presentation or a video, the following strategies can hook readers and focus their attention on your work:

- Offer a surprising statistic or an unusual fact
- Ask a question
- Introduce a quotation or a bit of dialogue
- Provide historical background
- Define a term or concept
- Point out a problem, contradiction, or dilemma
- Use a vivid example or image
- Develop an analogy
- Relate an anecdote (story)

Academic English If you come from a culture that prefers an indirect approach in writing, you may feel that asserting a thesis early in an essay sounds unrefined and even rude. In the United States, however, readers appreciate a direct approach, which shows that you understand your topic and value your readers' time.

1f Draft the body.

The body of your essay develops support for your thesis, so it's important to have at least a working thesis before you start writing. What does your thesis promise readers? What question are you trying to answer? What is your position on the topic? Keep asking these questions as you draft the body of your essay.

Asking questions as you draft

You may already have written an introduction that includes your working thesis. If not, as long as you have a draft thesis, you can begin developing the body and return later to the introduction. If your working thesis suggests a plan or if you have sketched a preliminary outline, try to organize your paragraphs accordingly.

Draft the body of your essay by writing at least one paragraph about each supporting point you listed in the planning stage. If you do not have a plan, pause for a few moments to sketch one.

As you draft the body, keep asking questions; keep anticipating what your readers may need to know.

At times, you might not know what you want to say until you have written a draft. It is possible to begin without a plan — assuming you are prepared to treat your first attempt as a "discovery draft" that you will need to revise. Whether or not you have a plan when you begin drafting, you can often figure out a workable order for your ideas by stopping each time you start a new paragraph to think about what your readers will need to know to follow your train of thought.

For more detailed help with drafting and developing paragraphs, see 3.

★ **Using sources responsibly**   As you draft, keep notes about sources you read and consult (see 51). If you quote, paraphrase, or summarize a source, include a citation, even in your draft. You will save time and avoid plagiarism if you do so.

Adding visuals as you draft

As you draft, you may decide that some of the support for your thesis could come from one or more visuals. Visuals can convey information concisely and powerfully. Graphs and tables, for example, can simplify complex numerical information, and images often express ideas vividly. Keep in mind that if you download a visual or use published information to create your own visual, you must credit your source. Also, be sure to choose visuals to supplement your writing, not to substitute for it.

Always consider how a visual supports your purpose and how your audience might respond to it. For example, in writing about the shift from print to online news, student writer Sam Jacobs used a screen shot of a link embedded in a news article to illustrate his argument (see 7h).

The chart in this section describes eight types of visuals and their purposes.

★ **Using sources responsibly**   If you create a chart or graph using information from your research, cite the source of the information even though the visual is your own. If you download a photograph from the web, credit the person or organization that created it.

Choosing visuals to suit your purpose

Pie chart

Pie charts compare a part or parts to the whole. Segments of the pie represent percentages of the whole (and always total 100 percent).

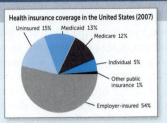

Health insurance coverage in the United States (2007)

Uninsured 15% Medicaid 13%
Medicare 12%
Individual 5%
Other public insurance 1%
Employer-insured 54%

Bar graph (or line graph)

Bar graphs highlight trends over a period of time or compare numerical data. Line graphs display the same data as bar graphs; the data are graphed as points, and the points are connected with lines.

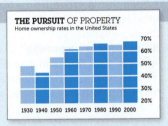

THE PURSUIT OF PROPERTY
Home ownership rates in the United States

70%
60%
50%
40%
30%
20%

1930 1940 1950 1960 1970 1980 1990 2000

Infographic

An infographic presents data in a visually engaging form. The data are usually numerical, as in bar graphs or line graphs, but they are represented by a graphic element rather than bars or lines.

Just 8% of kids growing up in low-income communities graduate from college by age 24.

Table

Tables display numbers and words in columns and rows. They can be used to organize complicated numerical information into an easily understood format.

Information from "Millennials after 2016: Post-Election Poll Analysis," published by the Center for Information and Research on Civic Learning and Engagement at Tufts University, March 7, 2017.

Millennials after 2016: How They Want to Stay Engaged

Type of Engagement	Trump Voters		Clinton Voters	
	Have done	Would with opportunity	Have done	Would with opportunity
Volunteer for a community organization on a regular basis	32%	26%	35%	40%
Vote in local elections	73%	15%	74%	16%
Help raise money for a cause or an organization	34%	19%	45%	30%
Donate money for a cause or an organization	47%	16%	55%	22%
Participate in demonstration or protest	7%	11%	19%	32%
Display sticker or sign supporting candidate or a cause	20%	16%	22%	29%

Photograph

Photographs vividly depict people, scenes, or objects discussed in a text.

Library of Congress, Prints & Photographs Division, Reproduction Number LC-DIG-highsm-04024.

Diagram

Diagrams, useful in scientific and technical writing, concisely illustrate processes, structures, or interactions.

National Institutes of Health.

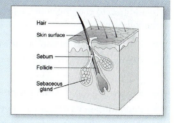

Flowchart

Flowcharts show structures (the hierarchy of employees at a company, for example) or steps in a process and their relation to one another. (See also p. 127 for another example.)

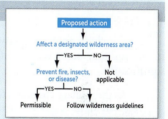

Map

Maps illustrate distances, historical information, or demographics and often use symbols for geographic features and points of interest.

From *The Making of the West: People and Cultures*, 5e, by Lynn Hunt et al. Copyright 2016 by Bedford/St. Martin's. All rights reserved. Used by permission of the publisher Macmillan Learning.

1g Draft a conclusion.

A conclusion should remind readers of the essay's main idea without repeating it. By the end of the essay, readers should already understand your main idea; your conclusion reinforces your thesis and, perhaps, gives readers something more to consider or proposes a course of action.

Strategies for drafting a conclusion

In addition to echoing your main idea, a conclusion might do any of the following:

- Briefly summarize your essay's key points
- Propose a course of action
- Offer a recommendation
- Suggest the topic's wider significance or implications
- Redefine a key term or concept
- Pose a question for future study

To conclude an essay analyzing the shifting roles of women in the military services, one student suggests her topic's wider significance.

> As the military continues to train women in jobs formerly reserved for men, our understanding of women's roles in society will no doubt continue to change. And as news reports of women training for and taking part in combat operations become commonplace, reports of women becoming CEOs, police chiefs, and even president of the United States will cease to surprise us. Or perhaps we have already reached this point.
>
> — Rosa Broderick, student

To make the conclusion memorable and to give a sense of completion, you might bring readers full circle by returning to the thesis or including a detail from the introduction. To conclude his argument essay about the shift from print to online news, student writer Sam Jacobs returns to the phrase "fit to print" from his introduction and echoes his thesis to show the broader importance of his argument. (See pp. 99–104.)

> The Internet has enabled consumers to participate in a new way in reading, questioning, interpreting, and reporting the news. Decisions about appropriate content and coverage are no longer

exclusively in the hands of news editors. Ordinary citizens now have a meaningful voice in the conversation — a hand in deciding what's "fit to print." Some skeptics worry about the apparent free-for-all and loss of tradition. But the expanding definition of news provides opportunities for consumers to be more engaged with events in their communities, their nations, and the world.

To see more examples of effective conclusions, see the model essays in 5d, 7h, and 57b.

Whatever concluding strategy you choose, keep in mind that an effective conclusion is decisive and unapologetic. Avoid introducing completely new ideas at the end of an essay. And because the conclusion is closely tied to the rest of the essay in both content and tone, be prepared to rewrite it as you revise your draft.

2 Revising, editing, and reflecting

Revising is rarely a one-step process. Global matters such as thesis, purpose, content, organization, and overall strategy generally receive attention first because global revisions involve big changes, including rewrites of paragraphs or whole sections of a paper. Revising at the sentence level gives you a chance to reconsider whether a particular point could be stronger or clearer or if a certain word or phrase sends the message you intended.

Editing involves identifying errors or patterns of errors, such as failure to use commas and quotation marks correctly, to make subjects and verbs agree, or to use the right form of a pronoun. See 2b for advice on keeping an editing log.

2a See revising as a social process.

To revise is to *re-see*, and the comments you receive from reviewers — instructors, peers, and writing center tutors — will help you re-see your draft from your readers' point of view. When you ask readers for their comments, revision becomes a social experience, connecting you with the suggestions and insights of readers who help you shape your work in progress.

Often the comments you'll receive from reviewers are written as shorthand commands ("Be specific!") or as questions ("What is your main point?"). Such comments don't immediately show you *how* to revise, but they do identify where revision might improve your draft. Ask reviewers to explain their comments if you don't understand them.

2b Use peer review: Revise with comments.

Peer review gives you the benefit of real readers and an opportunity to see your draft through their eyes. When peers read your work, they offer feedback, pointing out where they are intrigued or confused. They offer their suggestions, answer your questions, and help you strengthen your draft.

The following guidelines will help you learn from reviewers' comments and revise successfully.

- **Be active.** Help reviewers understand your purpose for writing and provide background about why you chose your topic, why it matters to you, and what you hope to accomplish in your draft. Ask reviewers specific questions so that they can focus their feedback.

- **Listen with an open mind.** After you've worked hard on a draft, you might be surprised to hear reviewers tell you it needs more development. Don't take criticism personally. Your readers are responding to your essay, not to you. If comments show that a reviewer doesn't understand what you're trying to do, don't be defensive. Instead, consider why your reader is confused, and figure out how to clarify your point. Responding to readers' objections instead of dismissing them may strengthen your ideas and make your essay more persuasive.

- **Weigh feedback carefully.** As you revise, you may find yourself sorting through suggestions from many people, including instructors, writing tutors, and peer reviewers. Sometimes these readers will agree, but often their advice will differ. You'll receive more suggestions than you can use, so be strategic. Sort through the comments with your original goals in mind, and focus on global concerns first (see 2e) — otherwise, you'll be facing the impossible task of trying to incorporate everyone's advice.

- **Keep a revision and editing log.** Make a clear and simple list of the global and sentence-level concerns that keep coming up in most of your reviewers' comments. That list can help you learn about your strengths and challenges as a writer.

2c Use peer review: Give constructive comments.

Peer review gives you and your classmates an opportunity to read each other's work and to learn from the peer review process. As you offer advice about how to strengthen a peer's thesis or how to use a visual to convey concise information, you are thinking about the purpose of a thesis and the role of visuals. When you propose a strategy for focusing an introduction or for anticipating a counterargument, you not only help your classmate but also benefit from the process of thinking strategically about revision.

HOW TO
Write helpful peer review comments

1 **View yourself as a coach, not a judge.** Think of yourself as asking questions and proposing possibilities, not dictating solutions. Help the writer identify the strengths and limitations of a draft. Try phrasing comments this way: "Have you thought about . . . ?" or "How can you help a reader understand this point?"

2 **Pay attention to global issues first.** Focus on the big picture — purpose, thesis, organization, and content — before sentence structure, word choice, and grammar.

3 **Restate the writer's main idea.** As a reader, you can help the writer see whether he or she is expressing points clearly. Can you follow the writer's train of thought? Restate the writer's thesis and main ideas to check your understanding.

4 **Be specific.** Point to specific places in a draft and show your classmate how, why, and where a draft is effective or confusing. Instead of saying "I like your draft," say exactly what you like: "You use a surprising statistic in your introduction, and it really hooks me as a reader." Or instead of offering a generality such as "Your draft doesn't have much support," give a specific suggestion: "Try putting the data from paragraph three into a graph."

As a peer reviewer, your work is to engage with a writer as a reader. It isn't your job to rewrite or correct the work of your peers. It is your job to offer thoughtful, encouraging comments to show peers what they're doing well and how they might build on their strengths.

The following excerpt from an online peer review session shows a peer reviewer offering constructive comments:

Excerpt from an online peer review session

Juan (peer reviewer): *Rachel, your essay makes a great point that credit card companies often hook students on a cycle of spending. But it sounds as if you're blaming students for their spending habits and credit card companies for their deceptive actions. Is this what you want to say?*

Peer reviewer restates writer's main point and asks a question to help her clarify her ideas.

Rachel (writer): No, I want to keep the focus on the credit card companies. I didn't realize I was blaming students. What could I change?

Writer takes comment seriously and asks for specific suggestion.

Juan: *In paragraphs three and four, you group all students together as if all students had the same bad spending habits. If students are your audience, you'll be insulting them. What reader is motivated to read something that's alienating? What is your purpose for writing this draft?*

Reviewer points to specific places in the draft and helps writer focus on audience and purpose.

Rachel: Well . . . It's true that students don't always have good spending habits, but I don't want to blame students. My purpose is to call students to action about the dangers of credit card debt. Any suggestions for narrowing the focus?

Writer is engaged with reviewer's comments and doesn't take criticism personally.

Juan: *Most students know about the dangers of credit card debt, but they might not know about specific deceptive practices companies use to lure them. Maybe ask yourself what would surprise your audience about these practices.*

Peer reviewer acts as a coach to suggest possible solutions.

Rachel: Thanks for the good idea. I'll try it.

Writer thanks reviewer for his help and leaves session with a specific revision strategy.

POST COMMENT

2d Highlights of one student's peer review process

Student writer Michelle Nguyen's assignment asked her to explore this question: *How have your experiences with writing shaped you as a writer?*

Here is Nguyen's draft, along with the questions she gave her peer reviewers before they read her draft.

QUESTIONS FROM NGUYEN TO PEER REVIEWERS

Alex, Brian, and Sameera: Thanks for reading my draft. Here are three questions I have about my draft: Is my focus clear? Is there anything that confuses you? What specifically should I cut or add to strengthen my draft?

Rough draft with peer comments

My family used to live in the heart of Hanoi, Vietnam. The neighborhood was small but swamped with crime. Drug addicts scoured the alleys and stole the most mundane things — old clothes, worn slippers, even license plates of motorbikes. Like anyone else in Vietnam in the '90s, we struggled with poverty. There was no entertainment device in our house aside from an 11" black-and-white television. Even then, electricity went off for hours on a weekly basis.

Alex F: You might want to add a title to focus readers.

Sameera K: I really like your introduction. It's so vivid. Think about adding a photo so readers can relate. What does Hanoi look like?

Brian S: You have great details here to set the scene in Hanoi, but why does it matter that you didn't have an "entertainment device"? Maybe choose the most interesting among all these details.

I was particularly close to a Vietnam War veteran. My parents were away a lot, so the old man became like a grandfather to me. He taught me how to ride a bicycle, how to read, how to take care of small pets. He worked sporadically from home, fixing bicycle tires and broken pedals. He was a wrinkly old man who didn't talk much. His vocal cords were damaged during the war, and it caused him pain to speak. In a neighborhood full of screaming babies and angry shop owners and slimy criminals, his home was my quiet haven. I could read and write and think and bond with someone whose worldliness came from his wordlessness.

The tiny house he lived in stood at the far end of our neighborhood. It always smelled of old clothes and forgotten memories. He was a slight man, but his piercing black eyes retained their intensity even after all these years. He must have made one fierce soldier.

Brian S: Worldliness came from wordlessness— great phrase! Is this part of your main idea? What is your main idea?

"I almost died once," he said, dusting a picture frame. It was one of those rare instances he ever mentioned his life during the war. As he talked, I perched myself on the side of an armchair, rested my head on my tiny hands, and listened intently. I didn't understand much. I just liked hearing his low, humming voice. The concept of war for me was strictly confined to the classroom, and even then, the details of combat were always murky. The teachers just needed us to know that the communist troops enjoyed a glorious victory.

Sameera K: You do a good job of showing us why this Vietnam veteran was important to you, but it seems like this draft is more a story about the man and not about you. What do you want readers to understand about you?

"I was the only survivor of my unit. 20 guys. All dead within a year. Then they let me go," he said. His voice cracked a little and his eyes misted over as he stared at pictures from his combatant past. "We didn't even live long enough to understand what we were fighting for."

He finished the sentence with a drawn-out sigh, a small set of wrinkles gathering at the end of his eyes. Years later, as I thought about his stories, I started to wonder why he referred to his deceased comrades by the collective pronoun "we." It was as if a little bit of him died on the battlefield with them too.

Three years after my family left the neighborhood, I learned that the old man became stricken with cancer. When I came home the next summer, I visited his house and sat by his sickbed. His shoulder-length mop of salt and pepper hair now dwarfed his rail-thin figure. We barely exchanged a word. He just held my hands tightly until my mother called for me to leave, his skeletal fingers leaving a mark on my pale palms. Perhaps he was trying to transmit to me some of his worldliness and his wisdom. Perhaps he was telling me to go out into the world and live the free life he never had.

Some people say that writers are selfish and vain. The truth is, I learned to write because it gave me peace in the much too noisy world of my Vietnamese childhood. In the quiet of the old man's house, I gazed out the window, listened to my thoughts, and wrote them down. It all started with a story about a wrinkly Vietnam War veteran who didn't talk much.

> **Sameera K:** I'm curious to hear more about you and why this man was so important to you. What did he teach you about writing? What did he see in you?

> **Alex F:** This sentence is confusing. Your draft doesn't seem to be about the selfishness or vanity of writers.

> **Brian S:** What does "it" refer to? I think you're trying to say something important about silence and noise and literacy, but I'm not sure what it is.

After rereading her draft and considering the feedback from her classmates, Nguyen realized that she had chosen a good direction but that she hadn't focused her draft to meet the expectations of the assignment. Her classmates offered valuable suggestions about adding a photograph of her Hanoi neighborhood and clarifying her main idea. With her classmates' specific questions and suggestions in mind, and their encouragement to see the undeveloped possibilities in her draft, Nguyen developed some goals for revising.

MICHELLE NGUYEN'S REVISION GOALS

- Add a title.
- Revise the introduction to set the scene more dramatically. Use Sameera's idea to include a photo of my neighborhood.
- Make the story my story, not the man's story. Answer Sameera's question: What did the man see in me and I in him? Delete extra material about the old man.
- What is my main idea? Figure out what I'm trying to say about learning to write in the presence of silence, not in the noisy exchange of voices in my neighborhood.
- Follow Brian's suggestion about the connection between wordlessness and worldliness.
- Make the contrasts sharper between the neighborhood and the man's house.

See 2i for Nguyen's revised draft.

2e Approach global revision in cycles.

Revision is more effective when you approach it in cycles, rather than attempting to change everything all at once. Four common cycles of global revision are discussed in this section:

- Engaging the audience
- Sharpening the focus
- Improving the organization
- Strengthening the content

Engaging the audience

Sometimes a draft needs an overhaul because it is directed at no particular audience. A good question to ask yourself and your reviewers is the toughest question a reader might ask: "So what?" or "Why does it matter?" If your draft can't pass the "So what?" test, you may need to rethink your approach.

Once you have made sure that your draft is directed at readers who have a stake in the topic, you may still need to refine your tone. The *tone* of a piece of writing expresses the writer's feelings toward the audience and the topic, so it is important to get it right. When you seek responses to your draft, ask your readers about your tone. If they respond that your tone seems self-centered, breezy, bossy, patronizing, or hostile, you'll want to modify it to show respect for your readers.

The following paragraph was drafted by a student who hoped to persuade his audience to buy organic produce.

A PARAGRAPH THAT ALIENATES READERS

If you choose to buy organic produce, you are supporting local farmers as well as demonstrating your opposition to chemical pesticides. As more and more supermarkets carry organic fruits and vegetables, consumers have fewer reasons not to buy organic. Some consumers do not buy organic produce because they are not willing to spend the extra money. But if you care at all about the environment or the small farmer, you should be willing to support organic farms in your area.

When the student asked a classmate to review his draft, his classmate recommended a more diplomatic tone so that readers wouldn't feel insulted or attacked. The classmate also questioned why the writer assumed his readers didn't care about the environment.

A PARAGRAPH THAT RESPECTS READERS

By choosing to buy organic produce, you have the opportunity to support local farmers, to oppose the use of chemical pesticides, and to taste some of the freshest produce available. Because more supermarkets carry organic produce than ever, you won't even have to miss out on any of your favorite fruits or vegetables. Although organic produce can be more expensive than conventional produce, the costs are not prohibitive. For example, a pound of organic bananas at my local grocery store is eighty-nine cents, while the conventional bananas are sixty-nine cents a pound. If you can afford this small price difference, you will have the opportunity to make a difference for the environment and for the small farmer.

— Leon Nage, student

Sharpening the focus

A clearly focused draft fixes readers' attention on one central idea and does not stray from that idea. You can sharpen the focus of a draft by clarifying the introduction (especially the thesis) and by deleting any text that is off point.

Clarifying the introduction   Reread your introduction to see if it clearly states the essay's main idea. To help you revise, ask your reviewers questions such as the following:

- Does the introduction let readers know what to expect as they read on?

- Does it make the significance of the subject clear so that readers will want to keep reading?
- Can readers tell where the introduction stops and the body of the essay begins? Is the introduction too broad or unfocused?
- Does the thesis accurately state the main idea of the essay?

Deleting text that is off the point Compare the introduction, especially the thesis statement, with the body of the essay. Does the body fulfill the promise of the introduction? If not, you will need to adjust one or the other. Either rebuild the introduction to fit the body or keep the introduction and delete body sentences or paragraphs that stray from its point.

Improving the organization

A draft is well organized when its major divisions are logical and easy to follow. To improve the organization of your draft, you may need to take one or more of the following actions: adding or sharpening topic sentences, moving blocks of text, and inserting headings.

Adding or sharpening topic sentences Topic sentences state the main ideas of the paragraphs in the body of an essay. (See 3a.) You can review the organization of a draft by reading only the topic sentences. Do the topic sentences clearly support the essay's main idea? Can you turn them into a reasonable sentence outline of the paper? (See 1d.) If your draft lacks topic sentences, add them unless you have a good reason for omitting them.

Moving blocks of text Improving the organization of a draft can be as simple as moving a few sentences from one paragraph to another or reordering paragraphs. You may also find that you can clarify the organization of a draft by combining choppy paragraphs or by dividing those that are too long for easy reading. (See 3e.) Often, however, the process is more complex. As you move blocks of text, you may need to write transitions to make the text fit smoothly in the new positions; you may also need to rework topic sentences to make your new organization clear.

Before moving text, consider sketching a revised outline. Divisions in the outline might become topic sentences in the restructured essay. (See 3e.)

Inserting headings In long documents, such as complex research papers or business reports, headings can help readers follow your organization. Typically, headings are presented as phrases (*The effects of sleep deprivation*), declarative or imperative sentences (*Understand the effects of sleep deprivation*), or questions (*What are the effects of sleep deprivation?*). To draw attention to headings, you can center them, put them in boldface, underline them, use all capital letters, or use some combination of these techniques. (See also 58b for use of headings in APA papers.)

Strengthening the content

In reviewing the content of a draft, first consider whether your argument is sound. Second, consider whether you should add or delete any text (sentences or paragraphs). If your purpose is to argue a point, consider how persuasively you have supported your point. If your purpose is to inform, be sure that you have presented your ideas clearly and with enough detail to meet your readers' expectations.

Rethinking your argument A first draft presents you with an opportunity to rethink your argument. You can often develop your ideas about a subject by asking yourself some questions:

- Is your claim more sweeping than the evidence supports?
- Have you left out an important step in the argument?
- Have you dealt fairly with opposing arguments?

Adding text If any paragraphs or sections of the essay are too skimpy to be clear and convincing (a common problem in rough drafts), add specific facts, details, and examples. You may need to go back to the beginning of the writing process: listing specifics, brainstorming ideas with friends or classmates, perhaps doing more research. As you revise paragraphs, it's helpful to ask questions such as *Why?* and *How?*

Deleting text Look for sentences and paragraphs that can be cut without serious loss of meaning. Ask your reviewers if they can show you sentences where you have repeated yourself or strayed from your point. Maybe you have given too much emphasis to minor ideas. Or you may have to cut if your assignment has a word limit.

Checklist for global revision

Purpose and audience

- Does the draft address a question, a problem, or an issue that readers care about?
- Is the draft appropriate for its audience? Does it account for the audience's knowledge of and possible attitudes toward the subject?

Focus

- Is the thesis clear? Is it prominently placed?
- Does the thesis answer a reader's "So what?" question? (See 1c.)
- If the draft has no thesis, is there a good reason for omitting one?

Organization and paragraphing

- Is each paragraph unified around a main point?
- Does each paragraph support and develop the thesis?
- Have you provided organizational cues for readers (such as topic sentences and headings)?
- Have you presented ideas in a logical order?

Content

- Is the supporting material relevant and persuasive?
- Which ideas need further development? Have you left readers with any unanswered questions?
- Are the parts proportioned sensibly? Do major ideas receive enough attention?
- Where might you delete redundant or irrelevant information?

Point of view

- Is the dominant point of view — first person (*I* or *we*), second person (*you*), or third person (*he*, *she*, *it*, *one*, or *they*) — appropriate for your purpose and audience?

2f Revise and edit sentences.

When you *revise* sentences, you focus on clarity and effectiveness; when you *edit*, you check for correctness. Sentences that are wordy, vague, or rambling may distract readers and make it hard for readers to focus on your purpose or grasp your ideas. Read each sentence slowly to determine if it is as specific and clear as possible. You might find it helpful to read your work aloud and trust your ears to detect awkwardness, wordiness, or repetition.

Below is an excerpt from a student draft that included both errors that needed editing (blue comments) and ineffective or unclear sentences that needed revising (black comment). References to relevant handbook sections appear in parentheses.

DRAFT PASSAGE

Long and wordy sentence (16c, 16d) — Unnecessary comma (33a) — Vague pronoun (23b)

Although some cities have found creative ways to improve access to public transportation for passengers with physical disabilities, and to fund other programs, there have been problems in our city due to the need to address budget constraints and competing problems. This has led citizens to question how funds are distributed. *Wrong punctuation for a statement (38a)*

REVISED AND EDITED PASSAGE

Although some cities have found creative ways to improve access to public transportation for passengers with physical disabilities, our city has struggled with budget constraints and competing priorities. The budget crunch has led citizens to question how funds are distributed.

The revised and edited passage is clearer, easier to read, and correct.

2g Proofread the final manuscript.

Proofreading is a special kind of reading: a slow and methodical search for misspellings, mistakes, and missing words or word endings. Such errors can be difficult to spot in your own work because you may read what you intended to write, not what is actually on the page. See the proofreading tips on page 35.

HOW TO

Improve your writing with an editing log

An important aspect of becoming a college writer is learning how to identify the grammar, punctuation, and spelling errors that you make frequently. You can use an editing log to keep a list of your common errors, anticipate error patterns, and learn the rules needed to correct the errors.

1 **When your instructor or tutor returns a draft, review any errors** he or she has identified.

2 **Note which errors you commonly make.** For example, have you seen "run-on sentence" or "need a transition" marked in other drafts?

3 **Identify the advice in the handbook** that will help you correct the errors.

4 **Make an entry in your editing log.** A suggested format appears below.

Sample editing log page

ORIGINAL SENTENCE

Athletes who use any type of biotechnology give themselves

an unfair advantage they should be banned from competition.

EDITED SENTENCE

Athletes who use any type of biotechnology give themselves

        , and
an unfair advantage they should be banned from competition.
      ^

RULE OR PATTERN APPLIED

To edit a run-on sentence, use a comma and a coordinating

conjunction (*and, but, or*). *Rules for Writers,* section 20a

---

A carefully proofread essay sends a positive message: It shows that you value your writing and respect your readers. Try one or more of the following tips.

Proofreading tips

- Remove distractions and allow yourself ten to fifteen minutes of pure concentration — without your cell phone.
- Proofread out loud, articulating each word as it is actually written.
- Proofread your sentences in reverse order.
- Proofread hard-copy pages; mistakes can be difficult to catch on screen.
- Don't rely too heavily on spell checkers and grammar checkers. Before automatically accepting their changes, consider accuracy and appropriateness.
- Ask a volunteer (a friend, roommate, or co-worker) to proofread after you. A second reader may catch something you didn't.

2h Format the final manuscript.

Use the manuscript format recommended by your instructor or for your academic discipline. For MLA, see "Formatting the paper" (p. 464) and examples of MLA formatting, 4e and 57b. For an example that shows APA formatting, see 62b.

2i Sample student revision

In section 2d, you'll find Michelle Nguyen's first draft, along with the highlights of her peer review process. Comments from reviewers helped Nguyen to see her draft through her readers' eyes and to develop a revision plan (see p. 28). One reviewer asked: "What is your main idea?" Another reviewer asked: "What do you want readers to understand about you?" As she revised, Nguyen made both global revisions and sentence-level revisions to clarify her main idea and to delete extra material that might distract readers from her story. Here is Nguyen's final draft, "A Place to Begin."

Nguyen 1

Michelle Nguyen

Professor Wilson

English 101

21 September 2018

Nguyen formats her final draft using MLA guidelines.

A Place to Begin

I grew up in the heart of Hanoi, Vietnam — Nhà Dầu — a small but busy neighborhood swamped with crime. Houses, wedged in among cafés and other local businesses (see fig. 1), measured uniformly about 200 square feet, and the walls were so thin that we could hear every heated debate and impassioned disagreement. Drug addicts scoured the vicinity and stole the most mundane things — old clothes, worn slippers, even license plates of motorbikes. It was a neighborhood where dogs howled and kids ran amok and where the earth was always moist and marked with stains. It was the 1990s Vietnam in miniature, with all the turmoil and growing pains of a newly reborn nation.

In a city perpetually inundated with screaming children and slimy criminals, I found my place in the home of a Vietnam War veteran. My parents were away a lot, so the old man became like a grandfather to me. He was a slight man who didn't talk much. His vocal cords had been damaged during the war, and it caused him pain to speak. In his quiet home, I could read and write in the presence of someone whose worldliness grew from his wordlessness.

His tiny house stood at the far end of our neighborhood and always smelled of old clothes and forgotten memories. His wall was plastered with pictures from his combatant past, pictures that told his life story when his own voice couldn't. "I almost died once," he said, dusting a picture frame. It was one of those rare instances he ever mentioned his life during the war.

Nguyen formats her final draft using MLA guidelines.

Nguyen revises her introduction to engage readers with vivid details.

Sentences are revised for clarity and specificity.

Nguyen focuses on one key story in response to reviewers' questions.

Nguyen's revisions clarify her main idea.

Marginal annotations indicate MLA-style formatting and effective writing.

Nguyen 2

As her peer reviewers suggested, Nguyen adds a photograph to help readers visualize Hanoi.

Fig. 1. Nhà Dầu neighborhood in Hanoi (personal photograph by author).

I perched myself on the side of the armchair, rested my head on my tiny hands, and listened intently. I didn't understand much. I just liked hearing his low, raspy voice.

"I was the only survivor of my unit. Twenty guys. All dead within a year. Then they let me go."

He finished the sentence with a drawn-out sigh, a small set of wrinkles gathering at the corner of his eye.

Nguyen develops her narrative with dialogue.

I wanted to hear the details of that story yet was too afraid to ask. But the bits and pieces I did hear, I wrote down in a notebook. I wanted to make sure that there were not only photos but also written words to bear witness to the old veteran's existence.

Once, I caught him looking at the jumbled mess of sentences I'd written. I ran to the table and snatched my notebook, my cheeks warmed with a bright tinge of pink. I was embarrassed. But mostly, I was terrified that he'd hate me for stealing his life story and turning it into a collection of words and characters and ambivalent feelings.

Nguyen revises to keep the focus on her story and not the old man's, as her peer reviewers suggested.

Nguyen 3

"I'm sorry," I muttered, my gaze drilling a hole into the tiled floor.

Quietly, he peeled the notebook from my fingers and placed it back on the table.

In his muted way, with his mouth barely twisted in a smile, he seemed to be granting me permission and encouraging me to keep writing. Maybe he saw a storyteller and a writer in me, a little girl with a pencil and too much free time.

Nguyen revises her final two paragraphs, circling back to the scene from the introduction, giving the narrative coherence.

The last time I visited Nhà Dầu was for the veteran's funeral two years ago. It was a cold November afternoon, but the weather didn't dampen the usual tumultuous spirit of the neighborhood. I could hear the jumble of shouting voices and howling dogs, yet it didn't bother me. For a minute I closed my eyes, remembering myself as a little girl with a big pencil, gazing out a window and scribbling words in my first notebook.

Nguyen revises the final paragraph to show readers the significance of her narrative.

Following a peer reviewer's advice, Nguyen chooses words from her final sentence for her title.

Many people think that words emerge from words and from the exchange of voices. Perhaps this is true. But the surprising paradox of writing for me is that I started to write in the presence of silence. It was only in the utter stillness of a Vietnam War veteran's house that I could hear my thoughts for the first time, appreciate language, and find the confidence to put words on a page. With one notebook and a pencil, and with the encouragement of a wordless man to tell his story, I began to write. Sometimes that's all a writer needs, a quiet place to begin.

2j Prepare a portfolio; reflect on your writing.

At the end of the semester, your instructor may ask you to submit a portfolio, or collection, of your writing. A writing portfolio often consists of drafts, revisions, and reflections that demonstrate a writer's thinking and learning processes or that showcase the writer's best work.

As early in the course as possible, be sure you know the answers to the following questions:

- Should the portfolio be a paper collection or an electronic one? Is it your choice?

- Will the portfolio be checked or assessed before the end of the term? If so, when or how often? By whom?

- Are you free to choose any or all of the pieces to include?

- Are you free to include a variety of items (not just rough and final drafts of papers), such as outlines and notes, journal entries, comments from reviewers, or visuals?

TIP: Save your notes, drafts, and reviewers' comments for possible use in your portfolio. The more you have assembled, the more you have to choose from to represent your best work.

Understand the benefits of reflection

Reflection — the process of stepping back periodically to examine your decisions, preferences, strengths, and challenges as a writer — helps you recognize your growth as a writer and is the backbone of portfolio keeping.

When you submit your portfolio for a final evaluation or reading, you may be asked to include a reflective opening statement in the form of a cover letter, an introduction, a preface, a memo, or an essay.

Reflective writing allows you to do the following:

- show that you can identify the strengths and weaknesses in your writing

- comment on the progress you've made in the course

- understand your own writing process

- demonstrate that you've made good writing decisions

- comment on how you might transfer skills developed in your writing course to other courses where writing is assigned

Check with your instructor about the guidelines for your reflective opening statement.

3 Building effective paragraphs

A paragraph is a group of sentences that focuses on one main point or example. Except for special-purpose paragraphs, such as introductions and conclusions (see 1e and 1g), paragraphs develop and support an essay's main point, or thesis. Aim for paragraphs that are well developed, organized, coherent, and neither too long nor too short for easy reading.

3a Focus on a main point.

A paragraph should be unified around a main point. The point should be clear to readers, and all sentences in the paragraph should relate to it.

Stating the main point in a topic sentence

As readers move into a paragraph, they need to know where they are in relation to the whole essay and what to expect in the sentences to come. A good topic sentence, a one-sentence summary of the paragraph's main point, acts as a signpost pointing in two directions: backward toward the thesis of the essay and forward toward the body of the paragraph.

Usually the topic sentence (highlighted in the following example) comes first in the paragraph.

> All living creatures manage some form of communication. The dance patterns of bees in their hive help to point the way to distant flower fields or announce successful foraging. Male stickleback fish regularly swim upside-down to indicate outrage in a courtship contest. Male deer and lemurs mark territorial ownership by rubbing their own body secretions on boundary stones or trees. Everyone has seen a frightened dog put his tail between his legs and run in panic. We, too, use gestures, expressions, postures, and movement to give our words point.
>
> — Olivia Vlahos, *Human Beginnings*

In college writing, topic sentences are often necessary for advancing or clarifying lines of an argument or reporting the research in a field. In the following paragraph on the effects of a 2010 oil spill in the Gulf of Mexico, the writer uses a topic sentence (highlighted) to state that the extent of the threat is unknown before quoting three sources that illustrate her point.

> To date, the full ramifications [of the oil spill] remain a question mark. An August report from the National Oceanic and Atmospheric Administration estimated that 75 percent of the oil had "either evaporated or been burned, skimmed, recovered from the wellhead, or dispersed." However, Woods Hole Oceanographic Institution researchers reported that a 1.2-mile-wide, 650-foot-high plume caused by the spill "had and will persist for some time." And University of Georgia scientists concluded that almost 80 percent of the released oil hadn't been recovered and "remains a threat to the ecosystem."
>
> — Michele Berger, "Volunteer Army"

Occasionally the topic sentence may be withheld until the end of the paragraph — but only if the earlier sentences hang together so well that readers perceive their direction, if not their exact point.

Sticking to the point

Sentences that do not support the topic sentence destroy the unity of a paragraph. If the paragraph is otherwise focused, such sentences can simply be deleted or perhaps moved elsewhere. In the following paragraph describing the inadequate facilities in a high school, the information about the chemistry teacher (highlighted) is off the point.

> As the result of tax cuts, the educational facilities of Lincoln High School have reached an all-time low. Some of the books date back to 1990 and have long since shed their covers. The few computers in working order must share one printer. The lack of lab equipment makes it necessary for four or five students to work at one table, with most watching rather than performing experiments. Also, the chemistry teacher left to have a baby at the beginning of the semester, and most of the students don't like the substitute. As for the furniture, many of the upright chairs have become recliners, and the desk legs are so unbalanced that they play seesaw on the floor.

Exercise 3–1 Underline the topic sentence in the following paragraph and cross out any material that does not clarify or develop the central idea.

Quilt making has served as an important means of social, political, and artistic expression for women. In the nineteenth century, quilting circles provided one of the few opportunities for women to forge social bonds outside of their families. Once a week or more, they came together to sew as well as trade small talk, advice, and news. They used dyed cotton fabrics much like the fabrics quilters use today; surprisingly, quilters' basic materials haven't changed that much over the years. Sometimes the women joined their efforts in support of a political cause, making quilts that would be raffled to raise money for temperance societies, hospitals for sick and wounded soldiers, and the fight against slavery. Quilt making also afforded women a means of artistic expression at a time when they had few other creative outlets. Within their socially acceptable roles as homemakers, many quilters subtly pushed back at the restrictions placed on them by experimenting with color, design, and technique.

3b Develop the main point.

Though an occasional short paragraph is fine, particularly if it functions as a transition or emphasizes a point, a series of brief paragraphs suggests inadequate development. How much development is enough? That varies, depending on the writer's purpose and audience.

For example, a writer who wants to convince readers of the psychological benefits of running might start out with the following draft paragraph. However, the draft is light on specific evidence about the benefits and may leave a reader with more questions than answers.

UNDERDEVELOPED PARAGRAPH

In addition to boosting physical health, running can also improve a person's mental health. Running can produce a "high" that can help people be less depressed. Those who have spent any time training for a race know that the psychological benefits of solitary time on the road outweigh the physical demands of the sport.

This three-sentence paragraph is too skimpy to be convincing. The writer could provide readers with a more robust look at specific conditions that might be improved with running. This writer chooses to incorporate evidence from a source to help develop the point.

WELL-DEVELOPED PARAGRAPH

In addition to boosting physical health, running can also improve a person's mental health. Running, and especially training for a race, can help those fighting addiction, for example. The addict can channel his or her addictive tendencies toward a healthy behavior that substitutes for a destructive behavior. Running also produces a "high" that can take the place of a chemically induced high. Running, for some people, can be used therapeutically to battle depression and anxiety. Duke University researcher Blumenthal concluded in 2007 that exercise can work as well as antidepressant medication for most people with major depressive disorder (Weir). Similarly, Boston University professor Michael Otto has argued that exercise can be a powerful "intervention" if not a cure for depression (Weir). Those who have spent any time running consistently and perhaps training for a race know that the psychological benefits of solitary time on the road outweigh the physical demands of the sport. A more positive outlook on life is an added benefit to physical fitness.

3c Choose a suitable pattern of organization.

Although paragraphs and essays may be patterned in any number of ways, certain patterns of organization occur frequently, either alone or in combination: examples and illustrations, narration, description, process, comparison and contrast, analogy, cause and effect, classification and division, and definition.

These patterns (sometimes called *methods of development*) have different uses, depending on the writer's subject and purpose.

Examples and illustrations

Examples, perhaps the most common pattern of development, are appropriate whenever the reader might be tempted to ask, "For example?" Though examples are just selected instances, not a complete catalog, they are enough to suggest the truth of many topic sentences, as in the following paragraph.

Normally my parents abided scrupulously by "The Budget," but several times a year Dad would dip into his battered black strongbox and splurge on some irrational, totally satisfying luxury. Once he bought over a hundred comic books at a flea market, doled out to us thereafter at the tantalizing rate of two a week. He always got a whole flat of pansies, Mom's favorite flower, for us to give her on Mother's Day. One day a boy stopped at our house selling fifty-cent raffle tickets on a sailboat, and Dad bought every ticket the boy had left — three books' worth.

— Connie Hailey, student

Illustrations are extended examples, frequently presented in story form. Because they require several sentences apiece, they are used more sparingly than examples. When well selected, they can be a vivid and effective means of developing a point.

Part of [Harriet Tubman's] strategy of conducting was, as in all battle-field operations, the knowledge of how and when to retreat. Numerous allusions have been made to her moves when she suspected that she was in danger. When she feared the party was closely pursued, she would take it for a time on a train southward bound. No one seeing Negroes going in this direction would for an instant suppose them to be fugitives. Once on her return she was at a railroad station. She saw some men reading a poster and she heard one of them reading it aloud. It was a description of her, offering a reward for her capture. She took a southbound train to avert suspicion. At another time when Harriet heard men talking about her, she pretended to read a book which she carried. One man remarked, "This can't be the woman. The one we want can't read or write." Harriet devoutly hoped the book was right side up.

— Earl Conrad, *Harriet Tubman*

Narration

A paragraph of narration tells a story or part of a story. Narrative paragraphs are usually arranged in chronological order, but they may also contain flashbacks, interruptions that take the story back to an earlier time. The following paragraph recounts one of the author's experiences in the African wild.

One evening when I was wading in the shallows of the lake to pass a rocky outcrop, I suddenly stopped dead as I saw the sinuous black body of a snake in the water. It was all of six feet long, and from the slight hood and the dark stripes at the back of the neck I knew it to be a Storm's water cobra — a deadly reptile for the bite of which there was, at that time, no serum. As I stared at it an incoming wave gently deposited part of its body on one of my feet. I remained motionless, not even breathing, until the wave rolled back into the lake, drawing the snake with it. Then I leaped out of the water as fast as I could, my heart hammering.

— Jane Goodall, *In the Shadow of Man*

Description

A descriptive paragraph sketches a portrait of a person, place, or thing by using concrete and specific details that appeal to one or more of our senses — sight, sound, smell, taste, and touch. Consider, for example, the following description of the grasshopper invasions that devastated the midwestern landscape in the United States in the late 1860s.

> They came like dive bombers out of the west. They came by the millions with the rustle of their wings roaring overhead. They came in waves, like the rolls of the sea, descending with a terrifying speed, breaking now and again like a mighty surf. They came with the force of a williwaw and they formed a huge, ominous, dark brown cloud that eclipsed the sun. They dipped and touched earth, hitting objects and people like hailstones. But they were not hail. These were *live* demons. They popped, snapped, crackled, and roared. They were dark brown, an inch or longer in length, plump in the middle and tapered at the ends. They had transparent wings, slender legs, and two black eyes that flashed with a fierce intelligence.
>
> — Eugene Boe, "Pioneers to Eternity"

Process

A process paragraph is structured in chronological order. A writer may choose this pattern either to describe how something is made or done or to explain to readers, step by step, how to do something. The following paragraph explains how to perform a "roll cast," a popular fly-fishing technique.

> Begin by taking up a suitable stance, with one foot slightly in front of the other and the rod pointing down the line. Then begin a smooth, steady draw, raising your rod hand to just above shoulder height and lifting the rod to the 10:30 or 11:00 position. This steady draw allows a loop of line to form between the rod top and the water. While the line is still moving, raise the rod slightly, then punch it rapidly forward and down. The rod is now flexed and under maximum compression, and the line follows its path, bellying out slightly behind you and coming off the water close to your feet. As you power the rod down through the 3:00 position, the belly of line will roll forward. Follow through smoothly so that the line unfolds and straightens above the water.
>
> — *The Dorling Kindersley Encyclopedia of Fishing*

Comparison and contrast

To compare two subjects is to draw attention to their similarities, although the word *compare* also has a broader meaning that includes a consideration of differences. To contrast is to focus only on differences.

Whether a paragraph stresses similarities or differences, it may be patterned in one of two ways. The two subjects may be presented one at a time, as in the following paragraph of contrast.

> So Grant and Lee were in complete contrast, representing two diametrically opposed elements in American life. Grant was the modern man emerging; beyond him, ready to come on the stage, was the great age of steel and machinery, of crowded cities and a restless, burgeoning vitality. Lee might have ridden down from the old age of chivalry, lance in hand, silken banner fluttering over his head. Each man was the perfect champion of his cause, drawing both his strengths and his weaknesses from the people he led.
>
> — Bruce Catton, "Grant and Lee: A Study in Contrasts"

Or a paragraph may proceed point by point, treating the two subjects together, one aspect at a time. The following paragraph uses the point-by-point method to contrast speeches given by Abraham Lincoln in 1860 and Barack Obama in 2008.

> Two men, two speeches. The men, both lawyers, both from Illinois, were seeking the presidency, despite what seemed their crippling connection with extremists. Each was young by modern standards for a president. Abraham Lincoln had turned fifty-one just five days before delivering his speech. Barack Obama was forty-six when he gave his. Their political experience was mainly provincial, in the Illinois legislature for both of them, and they had received little exposure at the national level — two years in the House of Representatives for Lincoln, four years in the Senate for Obama. Yet each was seeking his party's nomination against a New York senator of longer standing and greater prior reputation — Lincoln against Senator William Seward, Obama against Senator Hillary Clinton.
>
> — Garry Wills, "Two Speeches on Race"

Analogy

Analogies draw comparisons between items that appear to have little in common. Writers use analogies to make something abstract or unfamiliar easier to grasp or to provoke fresh thoughts about a common subject. In the following paragraph, physician

Lewis Thomas draws an analogy between the behavior of ants and that of humans.

> Ants are so much like human beings as to be an embarrassment. They farm fungi, raise aphids as livestock, launch armies into wars, use chemical sprays to alarm and confuse enemies, capture slaves. The families of weaver ants engage in child labor, holding their larvae like shuttles to spin out the thread that sews the leaves together for their fungus gardens. They exchange information ceaselessly. They do everything but watch television.
>
> — Lewis Thomas, "On Societies as Organisms"

Cause and effect

A paragraph may move from cause to effects or from an effect to its causes. The topic sentence in the following paragraph mentions an effect; the rest of the paragraph lists several causes.

> The fantastic water clarity of the Mount Gambier sinkholes results from several factors. The holes are fed from aquifers holding rainwater that fell decades — even centuries — ago, and that has been filtered through miles of limestone. The high level of calcium that limestone adds causes the silty detritus from dead plants and animals to cling together and settle quickly to the bottom. Abundant bottom vegetation in the shallow sinkholes also helps bind the silt. And the rapid turnover of water prohibits stagnation.
>
> — Hillary Hauser, "Exploring a Sunken Realm in Australia"

In the following paragraph, the topic sentence identifies a cause; the rest of the paragraph lists the effects.

> The rise of rail transport in the nineteenth century forever changed American farming — for better and for worse. Farmers who once raised crops and livestock to sustain just their own families could now make a profit by selling their goods in towns and cities miles away. These new markets improved the living standard of struggling farm families and encouraged them to seek out innovations that would increase their profits. On the downside, the competition fostered by the new markets sometimes created hostility among neighboring farm families where there had once been a spirit of cooperation. Those farmers who couldn't compete with their neighbors left farming forever, facing poverty worse than they had ever known.
>
> — Chris Mileski, student

Classification and division

Classification is the grouping of items into categories according to some consistent principle. The principle of classification that a writer chooses ultimately depends on the purpose of the classification. The following paragraph classifies species of electric fish.

> Scientists sort electric fishes into three categories. The first comprises the strongly electric species like the marine electric rays or the freshwater African electric catfish and South American electric eel. Known since the dawn of history, these deliver a punch strong enough to stun a human. In recent years, biologists have focused on a second category: weakly electric fish in the South American and African rivers that use tiny voltages for communication and navigation. The third group contains sharks, nonelectric rays, and catfish, which do not emit a field but possess sensors that enable them to detect the minute amounts of electricity that leak out of other organisms.
>
> — Anne and Jack Rudloe, "Electric Warfare: The Fish That Kill with Thunderbolts"

Division takes one item and divides it into parts. Like classification, division should be made according to some consistent principle. The following passage describes the components that make up a baseball.

> Like the game itself, a baseball is composed of many layers. One of the delicious joys of childhood is to take apart a baseball and examine the wonders within. You begin by removing the red cotton thread and peeling off the leather cover — which comes from the hide of a Holstein cow and has been tanned, cut, printed, and punched with holes. Beneath the cover is a thin layer of cotton string, followed by several hundred yards of woolen yarn, which makes up the bulk of the ball. Finally, in the middle is a rubber ball, or "pill," which is a little smaller than a golf ball. Slice into the rubber and you'll find the ball's heart — a cork core. The cork is from Portugal, the rubber from southeast Asia, the covers are American, and the balls are assembled in Costa Rica.
>
> — Dan Gutman, *The Way Baseball Works*

Definition

A definition puts a word or concept into a general class and then provides enough details to distinguish it from others in the same class. In the following paragraph, the writer defines *crowdsourcing* as a savvy business practice.

> Despite the jargony name, crowdsourcing is a very real and important business idea. Definitions and terms vary, but the basic idea is to tap into the collective intelligence of the public at large to complete business-related tasks that a company would normally either perform itself or outsource to a third-party provider. Yet free labor is only a narrow part of crowdsourcing's appeal. More importantly, it enables managers to expand the size of their talent pool while also gaining deeper insight into what customers really want.
>
> — Jennifer Alsever, "What Is Crowdsourcing?"

3d Make paragraphs coherent.

Coherent sentences and paragraphs flow from one to another without discernible bumps, gaps, or shifts. Coherence can be improved by strengthening the ties between old information and new. A number of techniques for strengthening those ties are detailed in this section.

Linking ideas clearly

Readers expect to learn a paragraph's main point in a topic sentence early in the paragraph. Then, as they move into the body of the paragraph, they expect to encounter specific details, facts, or examples that support the topic sentence — either directly or indirectly.

If a sentence does not support the topic sentence directly, readers expect it to support another sentence in the paragraph and therefore to support the topic sentence indirectly. The following paragraph begins with a topic sentence. The highlighted sentences are direct supports, and the rest of the sentences are indirect supports.

Topic sentence previews the paragraph	Though the open-space classroom works for many children, it is not practical for my son, David. First, David is hyperactive. When he was placed in an open-space
First support idea (answers the question *Why is the classroom not practical?*)	classroom, he became distracted and confused. He was tempted to watch the movement going on around him instead of concentrating on his own work. Second, David has a tendency to transpose letters and numbers, a tendency

Second support idea

that can be overcome only by individual attention from the instructor. In the open classroom he was moved from teacher to teacher, with each one responsible for a different subject. No single teacher worked with David long enough to diagnose the problem, let alone help him with it. Finally, David is not a highly motivated learner. In the open classroom, he was graded "at his own level," not by criteria for a certain grade. He could receive a B in reading and still be a grade level behind, because he was doing satisfactory work "at his own level."

Third support idea

— Margaret Smith, student

Repeating key words

Repetition of key words is an important technique for gaining coherence. To prevent repetitions from becoming dull, you can use variations of a key word (*hike, hiker, hiking*), pronouns referring to the word (*gamblers . . . they*), and synonyms (*run, spring, race, dash*). In the following paragraph describing plots among indentured servants in the seventeenth century, historian Richard Hofstadter binds sentences together by repeating the key word *plots* and echoing it with a variety of synonyms (highlighted).

> Plots hatched by several servants to run away together occurred mostly in the plantation colonies, and the few recorded servant uprisings were entirely limited to those colonies. Virginia had been forced from its very earliest years to take stringent steps against mutinous plots, and severe punishments for such behavior were recorded. Most servant plots occurred in the seventeenth century: a contemplated uprising was nipped in the bud in York County in 1661; apparently led by some left-wing offshoots of the Great Rebellion, servants plotted an insurrection in Gloucester County in 1663, and four leaders were condemned and executed; some discontented servants apparently joined Bacon's Rebellion in the 1670's.

— Richard Hofstadter, *America at 1750*

Using parallel structures

Parallel structures are frequently used within sentences to underscore the similarity of ideas (see 9). They may also be used to bind together a series of sentences expressing similar information. In the following passage describing folk beliefs, anthropologist Margaret Mead presents similar information (highlighted) in parallel grammatical form.

Actually, almost every day, even in the most sophisticated home, something is likely to happen that evokes the memory of some old folk belief. The salt spills. A knife falls to the floor. Your nose tickles. Then perhaps, with a slightly embarrassed smile, the person who spilled the salt tosses a pinch over his left shoulder. Or someone recites the old rhyme, "Knife falls, gentleman calls." Or as you rub your nose you think, That means a letter. I wonder who's writing?

— Margaret Mead, "New Superstitions for Old"

Maintaining consistency

Coherence suffers whenever a draft shifts confusingly from one point of view to another or from one verb tense to another. (See 13.) In addition, coherence can suffer when new information is introduced with the subject of each sentence. As a rule, a sentence's subject should echo a subject or an object in the previous sentence.

Providing transitions

Transitions are bridges between what has been read and what is about to be read. They help readers move from sentence to sentence; they also alert readers to more global connections of ideas — those between paragraphs or even larger blocks of text.

Sentence-level transitions Certain words and phrases signal connections between (or within) sentences. Frequently used transitions are included in the chart later in this section.

Skilled writers use transitional expressions with care, making sure, for example, not to use *consequently* when *also* would be more precise. They are also careful to select transitions with an appropriate tone, perhaps preferring *so* to *thus* in an informal piece, *in summary* to *in short* for a scholarly essay.

In the following paragraph, an excerpt taken from an article about how Amazon has changed our consumption habits, writer Joshua Rothman uses transitions (highlighted) to guide readers from one idea to the next.

It hasn't always been obvious that Amazon would transform the feeling of everyday life. At first, the company looked like a bookstore; next, it became a mass retailer; later, for somewhat obscure reasons, it transformed into a television and movie studio. It seemed to be growing horizontally, by learning to sell new kinds of products. But Amazon wasn't just getting wider; it was getting deeper, too. It wasn't just selling products but inventing a new method of selling; behind the scenes, it was using technology to vertically integrate nearly the entire process of consumption.

— Joshua Rothman, "What Amazon's Purchase of Whole Foods Really Means"

Academic English Choose transitions carefully and vary them appropriately. Each transition has a different meaning (see the chart later in this section). If you do not use a transition with an appropriate meaning, you might confuse your readers.

▶ Although taking eight o'clock classes may seem unappealing, coming to school early has its advantages. ~~Moreover,~~ *For example,* students who arrive early typically avoid the worst traffic and find the best parking spaces.

Paragraph-level transitions Paragraph-level transitions usually link the *first* sentence of a new paragraph with the *first* sentence of the previous paragraph. In other words, the topic sentences signal global connections.

Look for opportunities to echo the subject of a previous paragraph (as summed up in its topic sentence) in the topic sentence of the next one. In his essay "Little Green Lies," Jonathan H. Adler uses this paragraph-level transition strategy to link topic sentences.

Consider aseptic packaging, the synthetic packaging for the "juice boxes" so many children bring to school with their lunch. One criticism of aseptic packaging is that it is nearly impossible to recycle, yet on almost every other count, aseptic packaging is environmentally preferable to the packaging alternatives. Not only do aseptic containers not require refrigeration to keep their contents from spoiling, but their manufacture requires less than one-10th the energy of making glass bottles.

What is true for juice boxes is also true for other forms of synthetic packaging. The use of polystyrene, which is commonly (and mistakenly) referred to as "Styrofoam," can reduce food waste dramatically due to its insulating properties. (Thanks to these properties, polystyrene cups are much preferred over paper for that morning cup of coffee.) Polystyrene also requires significantly fewer resources to produce than its paper counterpart.

—Jonathan H. Adler, "Little Green Lies"

Common transitions

TO SHOW ADDITION and, also, besides, further, furthermore, in addition, moreover, next, too, first, second

TO GIVE EXAMPLES for example, for instance, to illustrate, in fact, specifically

TO COMPARE also, in the same manner, similarly, likewise

TO CONTRAST but, however, on the other hand, in contrast, nevertheless, still, even though, on the contrary, yet, although

TO SUMMARIZE OR CONCLUDE in short, in summary, in conclusion, to sum up, therefore

TO SHOW TIME after, as, before, next, during, later, finally, meanwhile, then, when, while, immediately

TO SHOW PLACE OR DIRECTION above, below, beyond, nearby, opposite, close, to the left

TO INDICATE LOGICAL RELATIONSHIP if, so, therefore, consequently, thus, as a result, for this reason, because, since

Transitions between blocks of text In long essays, you will need to alert readers to connections between blocks of text that are more than one paragraph long. You can do this by inserting transitional sentences or short paragraphs at key points in the essay. Here, for example, is a transitional paragraph from a student research paper. It announces that the first part of the paper has come to a close and the second part is about to begin.

Although the great apes have demonstrated significant language skills, one central question remains: Can they be taught to use that uniquely human language tool we call grammar, to learn the difference, for instance, between "ape bite human" and "human bite ape"? In other words, can an ape create a sentence?

Another strategy to help readers move from one block of text to another is to insert headings in your essay. Headings, which usually sit above blocks of text, allow you to announce a new topic without the need for subtle transitions.

3e If necessary, adjust paragraph length.

Most readers feel comfortable reading paragraphs that range between one hundred and two hundred words. There are exceptions to this guideline, however. Paragraphs longer than two hundred words frequently appear in scholarly writing, where scholars explore complex ideas. Paragraphs shorter than one hundred words occur in business writing and on websites, where readers routinely skim for main ideas; in newspapers because of narrow columns; and in informal essays to quicken the pace.

In an essay, the first and last paragraphs will ordinarily be the introduction and the conclusion. These special-purpose paragraphs are often shorter than other paragraphs in the essay. Typically, the body paragraphs will follow the essay's outline: one paragraph per point in short essays, several paragraphs per point in longer ones. Some ideas require more development than others, however, so it is best to be flexible. If an idea stretches to a length unreasonable for a paragraph, you should divide the paragraph, even if you have presented comparable points in the essay in single paragraphs.

Paragraph breaks are not always made for strictly logical reasons. Writers use them for the following reasons as well.

REASONS FOR BEGINNING A NEW PARAGRAPH

- to set off the introduction and the conclusion
- to signal a shift to a new idea
- to indicate an important shift in time or place
- to emphasize a point (by placing it at the beginning or the end, not in the middle, of a paragraph)
- to highlight a contrast
- to provide readers with a needed pause

Beware of using too many short, choppy paragraphs, however. Readers want to see how your ideas connect, and they become confused when you break their momentum by forcing them to pause every few sentences. Here are some reasons you might have for combining some of the paragraphs in a rough draft.

REASONS FOR COMBINING PARAGRAPHS

- to clarify the essay's organization
- to connect closely related ideas
- to bind together text that looks too choppy

ACADEMIC READING AND WRITING

4 Reading and writing critically

College writing requires you to become a critical reader, questioning and conversing with the texts you read. When you read critically, you read with an open, curious mind to understand both what is said and why. And when you write critically, you respond to a text with thoughtful questions and insights. One of the best ways to become a strong college writer is to become a strong reader. The more you take from your reading, the more you have to give as a writer.

4a Read actively.

Reading, like writing, is an active process that happens in steps. Most texts, such as the ones assigned in college, don't yield their meaning with one quick reading. Rather, they require you to read and reread to grasp their main points and to comprehend layers of meaning.

When you read actively, you pay attention to details you would miss if you just skimmed a text. First, you read to understand the main ideas. Then you make note of what interests, surprises, or puzzles you. Active readers preview a text, annotate it, and then converse with it.

Previewing a text

Previewing, or looking quickly through a text before you read, helps you understand its basic features and structure. A text's title, for example, may reveal an author's purpose; a text's format or design may reveal what kind of text it is. The more you know about a text before you read it, the easier it will be to dig deeper into it.

Annotating a text

Annotating helps you record your responses to a text. As you annotate, you write questions and reactions in the margins of the text or in digital comments. You might circle or underline

 LaunchPad Solo
macmillan learning

Activities for Chapter 4
6 Writing practice activities, 1 LearningCurve activity, 4 Video tutorials, 1 Sample student paper

the author's main points or place question marks or asterisks by the text's thesis or major pieces of evidence. Annotating a text will help you answer the question "What is this text about?"

The following example shows how one student, Emilia Sanchez, annotated an article from *CQ Researcher*, a newsletter about social and political issues.

Annotated article

Big Box Stores Are ⟨Bad⟩ for Main Street

BETSY TAYLOR

Title gives away Taylor's position.

There is plenty of reason to be concerned about the proliferation of Wal-Marts and other so-called "big box" stores. The question, however, is not whether or not these types of stores create jobs (although several studies claim they produce a net job loss in local communities) or whether they ultimately save consumers money. The real concern about having a 25-acre slab of concrete with a 100,000 square foot box of stuff land on a town is whether it's good for a community's soul.

Assumes readers are concerned.

Main point of article. But what does she mean by "community's soul"?

The worst thing about "big boxes" is that they have a tendency to produce Ross Perot's famous "big sucking sound" — sucking the life out of cities and small towns across the country. On the other hand, small businesses are great for a community. They offer more personal service; they won't threaten to pack up and leave town if they don't get tax breaks, free roads and other blandishments; and small-business owners are much more responsive to a customer's needs. (Ever try to complain about bad service or poor quality products to the president of Home Depot?)

Lumps all big boxes together.

"Either/or" argument — Main Street is good, big boxes are bad.

Assumes all small businesses are attentive.

Yet, if big boxes are so bad, why are they so successful? One glaring reason is that we've become a nation of hyper-consumers, and the big-box boys know this. Downtown shopping districts comprised of small businesses take some of the efficiency out of over-consumption. There's all that hassle of having to travel from store to store, and having to pull out your credit card so many times. Occasionally, we even find ourselves

True?

Word choice makes author seem sentimental.

chatting with the shopkeeper, wandering into a coffee shop to visit with a friend or otherwise wasting precious time that could be spent on acquiring more stuff.

Author's argument seems one-sided and makes assumptions about consumers.

But let's face it — bustling, thriving city centers are fun. They breathe life into a community. They allow cities and towns to stand out from each other. They provide an atmosphere for people to interact with each other that just cannot be found at Target, or Wal-Mart or Home Depot.

Shopping at Target to save money — is that bad?

Is it anti-American to be against having a retail giant set up shop in one's community? Some people would say so. On the other hand, if you board up Main Street, what's left of America?

Ends with emotional appeal. Seems too simplistic!

Conversing with a text

Conversing with a text, responding to a text and its author, helps you move beyond your initial notes to draw conclusions about what you've read. Perhaps you ask additional questions, point out something that doesn't make sense, or explain how the author's points suggest wider implications. As you talk back to a text, you look more closely at how the author works through a topic, analyzing the author's evidence and conclusions and posing counterpositions.

You might start conversing with a text by using sentence openers such as

- But what about _____?
- Have you considered _____?
- Couldn't we also see it this way: _____?
- What if we conclude _____ instead of _____?

Double-entry notebook

Many writers use a double-entry notebook to converse with a text and its author and to generate ideas. On the left side, record what the author says; include quotations, sentences, and key terms from the text. On the right side, record your observations and questions. A double-entry notebook allows you to visualize the conversation between you and the author as it develops.

Here is an excerpt from student writer Emilia Sanchez's double-entry notebook (with sentence openers highlighted).

IDEAS FROM THE TEXT	MY RESPONSES
"The question, however, is not whether or not these types of stores create jobs (although several studies claim they produce a net job loss in local communities) or whether they ultimately save consumers money" (1011).	*Why are big-box stores bad if they create jobs or save people money? Taylor dismisses these possibilities without acknowledging their importance. But what about my family — we need to save money and we need jobs more than "chatting with the shopkeeper" (1011).*
"The real concern . . . is whether [big-box stores are] good for a community's soul" (1011). "[S]mall businesses are great for a community" (1011).	*Taylor is missing something here. Are all big-box stores bad? Are all small businesses great? Has Taylor considered that getting rid of big-box stores won't necessarily save the "soul" of America (1011)? Taylor concludes that small businesses are always better for consumers. But couldn't we conclude that some big-box stores are better for consumers because they save them time and money?*

★ **Using sources responsibly** Put quotation marks around words you copy from the text, and keep an accurate record of page numbers for quotations.

Asking the "So what?" question

As you read and annotate a text, make sure you understand its thesis, or central idea. Ask yourself: "What is the author's thesis?" Then put the author's thesis to the "So what?" test: "Why does this thesis matter? Why does it need to be argued?" Perhaps you'll conclude that the thesis is too obvious and doesn't matter at all — or that it matters so much that you believe the author stopped short and overlooked key details. Or perhaps you'll think that a reasonable person might draw different conclusions about the issue.

Guidelines for active reading

Preview a written text.

- Who is the author? What are the author's credentials?
- What is the author's purpose: To inform? To persuade? To call to action?
- Who is the expected audience?
- When was the text written? Where was it published?
- What kind of text is it: A book? A report? A scholarly article?

Annotate a written text.

- What surprises, puzzles, or intrigues you about the text?
- What question does the text attempt to answer?
- What is the author's thesis, or central claim?
- What type of evidence does the author provide to support the thesis? How persuasive is this evidence?

Converse with a written text.

- What are the strengths and limitations of the text?
- Has the author drawn conclusions that you question? Do you have a different interpretation of the evidence?
- Does the text raise questions that it does not answer?
- Does the author consider opposing points of view and treat them fairly?

Ask the "So what?" question.

- Why does the author's thesis need to be argued or explained? What's at stake?
- What has the author overlooked in presenting this thesis?
- Could a reasonable person draw different conclusions?
- To put an author's thesis to the "So what?" test, use language like the following:

  The author overlooks this important point: _____.

  The author's argument is convincing because _____.

HOW TO

Read like a writer

Reading like a writer helps you identify the techniques writers use so that you can use them, too. To read like a writer is to pay attention to *how* a text is written and *how* it creates an effect on you.

1 **Review any notes you've made on a text.** What passages did you find effective? What words did you underline? If you think the text is powerful or well written, commit yourself to figuring out *why* and *how* the text works.

2 **Ask *what, why,* and *how* questions about the techniques writers use.** *What* introductory techniques, for instance, do writers use to hook readers? *Why* and *how* are these techniques effective? *How* do they keep readers reading? As a reader, identify the specific techniques you appreciate so that they may become part of your repertoire as a writer.

3 **Observe how writers use specific writing techniques you want to learn.** For instance, if you're interested in learning how writers vary their sentence structure, pay attention to these techniques when you read.

4 **Use your experiences as a reader to plan the effect you want to create for your readers.** Make deliberate choices to create this effect.

4b Outline a text to identify main ideas.

You may be familiar with using an outline as a planning tool to help organize your ideas. An outline is a useful tool for reading, too. Outlining a text by identifying its main idea and major parts can be an important step in your reading process.

As you outline, look closely for a text's thesis statement (main idea) and topic sentences, because they serve as important signposts for readers. A thesis statement often appears in the introduction, usually in the first or second paragraph. Topic sentences can be found at the beginning of most body paragraphs, where they announce a shift to a new idea. (See 1e and 3a.)

Put the author's thesis and key points in your own words. Here, for example, are the points Emilia Sanchez identified as she prepared to write her analysis of the text printed in 4a. Notice that Sanchez does not simply trace the author's ideas paragraph by paragraph; instead, she sums up the article's central points.

OUTLINE OF "BIG BOX STORES ARE BAD FOR MAIN STREET"

Thesis: Whether or not they take jobs away from a community or offer low prices to consumers, we should be worried about "big-box" stores like Wal-Mart, Target, and Home Depot because they harm communities by taking the life out of downtown shopping districts.

I. Small businesses are better for cities and towns than big-box stores are.

    A. Small businesses offer personal service; big-box stores do not.

    B. Small businesses don't make demands on community resources as big-box stores do.

    C. Small businesses respond to customer concerns; big-box stores do not.

II. Big-box stores are successful because they cater to consumption at the expense of benefits to the community.

    A. Buying everything in one place is convenient.

    B. Shopping at small businesses may be inefficient, but it provides opportunities for socializing.

    C. Downtown shopping districts give each city or town a special identity.

Conclusion: Although some people say that it's anti-American to oppose big-box stores, actually these stores threaten the communities that make up America by encouraging buying at the expense of the traditional interactions of Main Street.

NOTE: For many assignments, you will be asked to read online sources. It is tempting to skim online texts rather than read them carefully. When you skim a text, you are less likely to remember what you have read and less inclined to reread to grasp layers of meaning. Slow down the pace of your reading and avoid multitasking. Use software tools and commenting features to annotate the text and to record your thoughts as you read.

4c Summarize to deepen your understanding.

Your goal in summarizing a text is to state the work's main ideas and key points simply, objectively, and accurately in your own words. Writing a summary does not require you to judge the author's ideas; it requires you to *understand* the author's ideas. In summarizing, you condense information, put the author's ideas in your own words, and test your understanding of what a text says. If you have sketched a brief outline of the text (see 4b), refer to it as you draft your summary.

Following is Emilia Sanchez's summary of the article that is printed in 4a. Notice how Sanchez uses an objective, neutral tone and third-person point of view to keep the focus on the text — "Taylor argues"; "Taylor asserts"; "She concludes."

First sentence names author, title of text, and author's thesis.

States central idea of text in a neutral tone.

Quotes author's words and cites a page number.

Summary written in Sanchez's own words, with key phrase from text integrated into her sentence.

In her essay "Big Box Stores Are Bad for Main Street," Betsy Taylor argues that chain stores harm communities by taking the life out of downtown shopping districts. Explaining that a community's "soul" is more important than low prices or consumer convenience, she argues that small businesses are better than stores like Home Depot and Target because they emphasize personal interactions and don't place demands on a community's resources. Taylor asserts that big-box stores are successful because "we've become a nation of hyper-consumers" (1011), although the convenience of shopping in these stores comes at the expense of benefits to the community. She concludes by suggesting that it's not "anti-American" to oppose big-box stores because the damage they inflict on downtown shopping districts extends to America itself.

Guidelines for writing a summary

- In the first sentence, mention the title of the text, the name of the author, and the author's thesis.
- Maintain a neutral tone; be objective.
- As you present the author's ideas, use the third-person point of view and the present tense: *Taylor argues.* . . . (If you are writing in APA style, see 60c.)
- Keep your focus on the text. Don't state the author's ideas as if they were your own.
- Put all or most of your summary in your own words; if you borrow a phrase or a sentence from the text, put it in quotation marks and provide the page number in parentheses.
- Limit yourself to presenting the text's key points.

4d Analyze to demonstrate your critical reading.

Whereas a summary answers the question of *what* a text says, an analysis looks at *how* a text conveys its main idea. Begin with an analytical question — one that speaks to a genuine problem in the text and yields an answer that is not obvious. A good analytical question leads you to a thesis and establishes the reason others need to read your essay.

 Writing for an audience

A good strategy for academic writing is to keep your audience in mind as you develop an analysis. Remember that readers want to hear your questions and ideas about a text. Some readers won't necessarily interpret a text as you do, nor will they necessarily draw the same conclusions. Through your careful reading of a text, you show your audience something that they might not have seen or understood about it. When you analyze a text, you say to readers: "Here's my reading of this text. This is what the text means to me and why my viewpoint matters."

Balancing summary with analysis

Summary and analysis need each other in an analytical essay; you can't have one without the other. Your readers may not be familiar with the text you are analyzing, so you need to summarize the

text briefly to orient readers and help them understand the basis of your analysis. The following strategies will help you balance summary with analysis.

- Remember that readers are interested in your ideas about a text.

- Pose *why* and *how* analytical questions that lead to an interpretation or a judgment of the text rather than to a summary (*Why is the author's argument unconvincing?*).

- Formulate a strong position (thesis) to answer your questions about the text.

- Make sure your summary sentences serve a purpose and provide a context for analysis.

- Focus your analysis on the text's main ideas or some prominent feature of the reading.

- Pay attention to your topic sentences to make sure they signal analysis.

Here is an example of how student writer Emilia Sanchez balances summary with analysis in her essay about Betsy Taylor's article (see 4a). Before stating her thesis, Sanchez summarizes the article's purpose and central idea.

Summary: provides context for analysis

[In her essay "Big Box Stores Are Bad for Main Street," Betsy Taylor focuses not on the economic effects of large chain stores but on the effects these stores have on the "soul" of America. She argues that stores like Home Depot, Target, and Wal-Mart are bad for America because they draw people out of downtown shopping districts and cause them to focus on consumption. In contrast, she believes that small businesses are good for America because they provide personal attention, encourage community interaction, and make each city and town unique.]

Analysis: responds to the summary sentence

[But Taylor's argument is unconvincing because it is based on sentimentality — on idealized images of a quaint Main Street — rather than on the roles that businesses play in consumers' lives and communities.]

HOW TO

Draft an analytical thesis statement

Analysis begins with asking questions about a text. As you draft your thesis, your questions will help you form a judgment about the text. Let these steps guide you as you develop an analytical thesis statement.

1 **Review your notes** to remind yourself of the author's main idea, supporting evidence, and, if possible, his or her purpose (reason for writing) and audience (intended reader).

2 **Ask *what, why,* or *how* questions.** What has the author overlooked or failed to consider? Why might a reasonable person draw a conclusion different from the author's? How does the text complicate or clarify something you've been thinking about or reading about?

3 **Write your thesis as an answer to the questions** you have posed or as the resolution of a problem you have identified in the text. Remember that your thesis isn't the same as the text's thesis. Your thesis presents your judgment of the text.

4 **Test your thesis.** Is your position clear? Is your position debatable? The answer to both questions should be yes.

5 **Revise your thesis.** Why does your position matter? Put your working thesis to the "So what?" test, and consider adding a *because* clause to your thesis (see 1c).

Drafting an analytical thesis statement

An effective thesis statement for analytical writing responds to an analytical or interpretive question about a text or tries to resolve a problem in the text. Remember that your thesis isn't the same as the text's thesis or main idea. Your thesis presents your judgment of the text's argument and shows readers what to expect when they read your essay.

If Emilia Sanchez had started her analysis of "Big Box Stores Are Bad for Main Street" (4a) with this thesis statement, she merely would have repeated the main idea of the article.

INEFFECTIVE THESIS STATEMENT (SUMMARY OF THE TEXT)

Big-box stores such as Wal-Mart and Home Depot promote consumerism by offering endless goods at low prices, but they do nothing to promote community.

Instead, Sanchez wrote the following thesis statement, which offers her judgment of Taylor's argument.

EFFECTIVE THESIS STATEMENT (THE WRITER'S JUDGMENT OF THE TEXT)

By ignoring the complex economic relationship between large chain stores and their communities, Taylor incorrectly assumes that simply getting rid of big-box stores would have a positive effect on America's communities.

4e Sample student writing: Analysis of an article

Following is Emilia Sanchez's analysis of the article by Betsy Taylor (see 4a). Sanchez used MLA (Modern Language Association) style to format her paper and cite the source.

Sanchez 1

Emilia Sanchez

Professor Goodwin

English 10

20 October 2017

Rethinking Big-Box Stores

    In her essay "Big Box Stores Are Bad for Main Street," Betsy Taylor focuses not on the economic effects of large chain stores but on the effects these stores have on the "soul" of America. She argues that stores like Home Depot, Target, and Wal-Mart are bad for America because they draw people out of downtown shopping districts and cause them to focus on consumption. In contrast, she believes that small businesses are good for America because they provide personal attention, encourage community interaction, and make each city and town unique. But Taylor's argument is unconvincing because it is based on sentimentality — on

> Opening briefly summarizes the article's purpose and thesis.

> Sanchez begins to analyze Taylor's argument.

Marginal annotations indicate MLA-style formatting and effective writing.

Sanchez 2

idealized images of a quaint Main Street — rather than
on the roles that businesses play in consumers' lives and
communities. By ignoring the complex economic relationship
between large chain stores and their communities, Taylor
incorrectly assumes that simply getting rid of big-box stores
would have a positive effect on America's communities.

> Thesis expresses Sanchez's judgment of Taylor's article.

Taylor's use of colorful language reveals that she
has a sentimental view of American society and does not
understand economic realities. In her first paragraph, Taylor
refers to a big-box store as a "25-acre slab of concrete
with a 100,000 square foot box of stuff " that "land[s] on
a town," evoking images of a powerful monster crushing
the American way of life (1011). But she oversimplifies
a complex issue. Taylor does not consider that many
downtown business districts failed long before chain stores
moved in, when factories and mills closed and workers lost
their jobs. In cities with struggling economies, big-box
stores can actually provide much-needed jobs. Similarly,
while Taylor blames big-box stores for harming local
economies by asking for tax breaks, free roads, and other
perks, she doesn't acknowledge that these stores also
enter into economic partnerships with the surrounding
communities by offering financial benefits to schools and
hospitals.

> Signal phrase introduces quotations from the source; Sanchez uses an MLA in-text citation.

> Sanchez identifies and challenges Taylor's assumptions.

Taylor's assumption that shopping in small businesses
is always better for the customer also seems driven by
nostalgia for an old-fashioned Main Street rather than
by the facts. While she may be right that many small
businesses offer personal service and are responsive to
customer complaints, she does not consider that many
customers appreciate the service at big-box stores. Just as
customer service is better at some small businesses than

> Clear topic sentence announces a shift to a new topic.

> Sanchez refutes Taylor's claim.

Sanchez 3

at others, it is impossible to generalize about service at all big-box stores. For example, customers depend on the lenient return policies and the wide variety of products at stores like Target and Home Depot.

Taylor blames big-box stores for encouraging American "hyper-consumerism," but she oversimplifies by equating big-box stores with bad values and small businesses with good values. Like her other points, this claim ignores the economic and social realities of American society today. Big-box stores do not force Americans to buy more. By offering lower prices in a convenient setting, however, they allow consumers to save time and purchase goods they might not be able to afford from small businesses. The existence of more small businesses would not change what most Americans can afford, nor would it reduce their desire to buy affordable merchandise.

Taylor may be right that some big-box stores have a negative impact on communities and that small businesses offer certain advantages. But she ignores the economic conditions that support big-box stores as well as the fact that Main Street was in decline before the big-box store arrived. Getting rid of big-box stores will not bring back a simpler America populated by thriving, unique Main Streets; in reality, Main Street will not survive if consumers cannot afford to shop there.

> Sanchez treats the author fairly.

> Conclusion returns to the thesis and shows the wider significance of Sanchez's analysis.

Sanchez 4

Work Cited

Taylor, Betsy. "Big Box Stores Are Bad for Main Street." *CQ Researcher,* vol. 9, no. 44, 1999, p. 1011.

> Work cited page is in MLA style.

How to write an analytical essay

An **analysis** of a text allows you to examine the parts of a text to understand *what* it means and *how* it makes its meaning. Your goal is to offer your judgment of the text and to persuade readers to see it through your analytical perspective. A sample analytical essay begins on page 67.

Key features

- **A careful and critical reading** of a text reveals what the text says, how it works, and what it means. In an analytical essay, you pay attention to the details of the text, especially its thesis and evidence.

- **A thesis that offers a clear judgment** of a text anchors your analysis. Your thesis might be the answer to a question you have posed about the text or the resolution of a problem you have identified in the text.

- **Support for the thesis** comes from evidence in the text. You summarize, paraphrase, and quote passages that support the claims you make about the text.

- **A balance of summary and analysis** helps readers who may not be familiar with the text you are analyzing. Summary answers the question of *what* a text says; an analysis looks at *how* a text makes its point.

Thinking ahead: Presenting and publishing

You may have the opportunity to present or publish your analysis in the form of a multimodal text such as a slide show presentation. Consider how adding images or sound might strengthen your analysis or help you to better reach your audience. (See 5.)

Writing your analytical essay

1 Explore

Generate ideas for your analysis by brainstorming responses to questions such as the following:

- What is the text about?
- What do you find interesting, surprising, or puzzling about this text?
- What is the author's thesis or central idea? Put the author's thesis to the "So what?" test. (See 1c.)
- What do your annotations of the text reveal about your response to it?

2 Draft

- Draft a working thesis to focus your analysis. Remember that your thesis is not the same as the author's thesis. Your thesis presents *your* judgment of the text.
- Draft a plan to organize your paragraphs. Your introductory paragraph will briefly summarize the text and offer your thesis.

Your body paragraphs will support your thesis with evidence from the text. Your conclusion will pull together the major points and show the significance of your analysis. (See 1d.)

- Identify specific words, phrases, and sentences from the text as evidence to support your thesis.

3 Revise

Ask your reviewers to give you specific comments. You can use the following questions to guide reviewers' feedback and to guide your own revision plan.

- Is the introduction effective and engaging?
- Does the thesis offer a clear judgment of the text?
- What objections might other writers pose to your analysis?
- Is the analysis well organized? Are there clear topic sentences and transitions? Is summary balanced with analysis?
- Is there sufficient evidence? Have you analyzed the evidence?
- Have you cited language that is summarized or quoted?

5 Reading and writing about multimodal texts

In many of your college classes, you'll have the opportunity to read and write about multimodal texts, such as advertisements, videos, and websites. Multimodal texts combine two or more of the following modes: words, static images, moving images, and sound.

Writing about multimodal texts differs from writing about written texts, but there are also similarities. All texts can be approached in a critical way. The strategies and advice offered in Chapter 4 for critically reading and writing about texts also apply to multimodal texts.

5a Read actively.

Any multimodal text can be read — that is, examined to understand *what* it says and *how* it communicates its purpose and reaches its audience. Use the guidelines for active reading on page 60 to help you preview, annotate, and converse with a multimodal text.

The next page shows an annotated advertisement.

Annotated advertisement

empowering
FARMERS

When you choose Equal Exchange fairly traded coffee, tea or chocolate, you join a network that empowers farmers in Latin America, Africa, and Asia to:

- Stay on their land
- Care for the environment
- Farm organically
- Support their family
- Plan for the future

www.equalexchange.coop

Photo: Jesus Choqueheranca de Quevero,
Coffee farmer & CEPICAFE Cooperative member, Peru

What is being exchanged?

Why is "fairly traded" so hard to read?

"Empowering" — why in an elegant font? Who is empowering farmers?

"Farmers" in all capital letters — shows strength?

Straightforward design and not much text.

Outstretched hands. Is she giving a gift? Inviting partnership?

Hands: heart-shaped, foregrounded.

Raw coffee beans are red: earthy, natural, warm.

Positive verbs: consumers choose, join, empower; farmers stay, care, farm, support, plan.

How do consumers know their money helps farmers stay on their land?

5b Summarize to deepen your understanding.

Your goal in summarizing a multimodal text is to state the work's central idea and key points simply, objectively, and accurately, in your own words, and usually in paragraph form. Since a summary must be fairly short, you must make judgments about what is most important. See the *how-to* box below.

5c Analyze to demonstrate your critical reading.

Summary answers the question of *what* a text says; analysis looks at *how* a text conveys its main idea or message. Your readers may not be familiar with the text you are analyzing, so you need to

HOW TO

Write a summary of a multimodal text

1. **In the first two sentences, mention the title** of the text and the name of the composer (or the sponsoring organization or company) and provide some brief information about the context: where the text appeared and when, why, and for whom the text was composed.

2. **State the text's central idea or message.**

3. **Maintain a neutral tone;** be objective.

4. **Use the third-person point of view and the present tense** as you present the text's ideas: *The focus of the Uber advertisement is. . . . Devaney uses the infographic to argue. . . .* (If you are writing in APA style, see 60c.) Limit yourself to presenting the text's major points.

5. **Keep your focus on the text.** Don't state the text's or composer's ideas as if they were your own.

6. **Put your summary in your own words;** if you borrow a phrase or a sentence from the text, put it in quotation marks and cite the text (see 51c).

summarize the text briefly to help readers understand the basis of your analysis.

These strategies will help you balance summary with analysis.

- Remember that readers are interested in your ideas about a text.
- Pose questions that lead to an interpretation or a judgment of a text rather than to a summary. Go beyond describing what you see or hear to ask *why* and *how* questions.
- Focus on a few significant features rather than listing every detail.

Drafting an analytical thesis statement

An effective thesis statement for analytical writing about a multimodal text responds to a question about the text or tries to resolve a problem in the text. Remember that your thesis isn't the same as the text's main idea. Your thesis presents your judgment of the text's argument. If your draft thesis restates the text's message, return to the questions you asked earlier in the process as you revise.

INEFFECTIVE THESIS STATEMENT (SUMMARY OF THE TEXT)

Consumers who purchase coffee from farmers in the Equal Exchange network are helping farmers stay on their land.

The thesis is ineffective because it summarizes the ad; it doesn't present an analysis. Ren Yoshida focused the thesis by questioning a single detail in the work.

QUESTIONS

The ad promises an equal exchange, but is the exchange equal between consumers and farmers? Do the words *equal exchange* and *empowering farmers* appeal to consumers' emotions?

EFFECTIVE THESIS STATEMENT (THE WRITER'S JUDGMENT OF THE TEXT)

Although the ad works successfully on an emotional level, it is less successful on a logical level because of its promise for an equal exchange between consumers and farmers.

5d Sample student writing: Analysis of an advertisement

On the following pages is Ren Yoshida's analysis of the Equal Exchange advertisement that appears in 5a.

Yoshida 1

Ren Yoshida

Professor Marcotte

English 101

4 November 2015

Sometimes a Cup of Coffee Is Just a Cup of Coffee

A farmer, her hardworking hands full of coffee beans, reaches out from an Equal Exchange advertisement ("Empowering"). The hands, in the shape of a heart, offer to consumers the fruit of the farmer's labor. The ad's message is straightforward: in choosing Equal Exchange, consumers become global citizens, partnering with farmers to help save the planet. Suddenly, a cup of coffee is more than just a morning ritual; a cup of coffee is a moral choice that empowers both consumers and farmers. This simple exchange appeals to a consumer's desire to be a good person — to protect the environment and do the right thing. Yet the ad is more complicated than it first seems, and its design raises some logical questions about such an exchange. Although the ad works successfully on an emotional level, it is less successful on a logical level because of its promise for an equal exchange between consumers and farmers.

The focus of the ad is a farmer, Jesus Choqueheranca de Quevero, and, more specifically, her outstretched, cupped hands. Her hands are full of red, raw coffee, her life's work. The ad successfully appeals to consumers' emotions, assuming they will find the farmer's welcoming face and hands, caked with dirt, more appealing than startling statistics about the state of the environment or the number of farmers who lose their land each year. It seems almost rude not to accept the farmer's generous offering since we know her name and, as the ad implies, have the choice to

The source is cited in the text. No page number is available for the online source.

Yoshida summarizes the content of the ad.

Thesis expresses Yoshida's analysis of the ad.

Details show how the ad appeals to consumers' emotions.

Yoshida interprets details such as the farmer's hands.

Marginal annotations indicate MLA-style formatting and effective writing.

Yoshida 2

"empower" her. In fact, how can a consumer resist helping the farmer "[c]are for the environment" and "[p]lan for the future," when it is a simple matter of choosing the right coffee? The ad sends the message that our future is a global future in which producers and consumers are bound together.

First impressions play a major role in the success of an advertisement. Consumers are pulled toward a product, or pushed away, by an ad's initial visual and emotional appeal. Here, the intended audience is busy people, so the ad tries to catch viewers' attention and make a strong impression immediately. Yet with a second or third viewing, consumers might start to ask some Logical questions about Equal Exchange before buying their morning coffee.

Yoshida begins to challenge the logic of the ad.

Although the farmer extends her heart-shaped hands to consumers, they are not actually buying a cup of coffee or the raw coffee directly from her. In reality, consumers are buying from Equal Exchange, even if the ad substitutes the more positive word *choose* for *buy*. Furthermore, consumers aren't actually empowering the farmer; they are joining

Words from the ad serve as evidence.

"a network that empowers farmers." The idea of a network makes a simple transaction more complicated. How do consumers know their money helps farmers "[s]tay on their land" and "[p]lan for the future" as the ad promises? They don't.

Clear topic sentence announces a shift.

The ad's design elements raise questions about the use of the key terms *equal exchange* and *empowering farmers*. The Equal Exchange logo suggests symmetry and equality, with two red arrows facing each other, but the words of the logo appear almost like an eye exam poster, with each line decreasing in font size and clarity. The words *fairly traded* are tiny. Below the logo, the words *empowering farmers* are presented in contradictory fonts. *Empowering* is written in

Summary of the ad's key features serves Yoshida's analysis.

Yoshida 3

a flowing, cursive font, almost the opposite of what might be considered empowering, whereas *farmers* is written in a plain, sturdy font. The ad's varying fonts communicate differently and make it hard to know exactly what is being exchanged and who is becoming empowered.

What is being exchanged? The logic of the ad suggests that consumers will improve the future by choosing Equal Exchange. The first exchange is economic: consumers give one thing — dollars — and receive something in return — a cup of coffee — and the farmer stays on her land. The second exchange is more complicated because it involves a moral exchange. The ad suggests that if consumers don't choose "fairly traded" products, farmers will be forced off their land and the environment destroyed. This exchange, when put into motion by consumers choosing to purchase products not "fairly traded," has negative consequences for both consumers and farmers. The message of the ad is that the actual exchange taking place is not economic but moral; after all, nothing is being bought, only chosen. Yet the logic of this exchange quickly falls apart. Consumers aren't empowered to become global citizens simply by choosing Equal Exchange, and farmers aren't empowered to plan for the future by consumers' choices. And even if all this empowerment magically happened, there is nothing equal about such an exchange.

Advertisements are themselves about empowerment — encouraging viewers to believe they can become someone or do something by identifying, emotionally or logically, with a product. In the Equal Exchange ad, consumers are emotionally persuaded to identify with a farmer whose face is not easily forgotten and whose heart-shaped hands hold a collective future. On a logical level, though, the ad raises

Yoshida shows why his thesis matters.

Conclusion includes a detail from the introduction.

Yoshida 4

Conclusion returns to Yoshida's thesis.

questions because empowerment, although a good concept to choose, is not easily or equally exchanged. Sometimes a cup of coffee is just a cup of coffee.

Yoshida 5

Work Cited

"Empowering Farmers." Equal Exchange, equalexchange.coop/. Advertisement. Accessed 14 Oct. 2015.

6 Reading arguments

Many of your college assignments will ask you to read and write arguments about debatable issues. The questions being debated might be matters of public policy (*Should corporations be allowed to advertise on public school property?*) or they might be scholarly issues (*What role do genes play in determining behavior?*). On such questions, reasonable people may disagree.

As you read arguments across the disciplines and enter into academic or public policy debates, pay attention to the questions being asked, the evidence being presented, and the various positions being argued. You'll find the critical reading strategies introduced in Chapter 4 — previewing, annotating, and conversing with texts — to be useful as you ask questions about an argument's logic, evidence, and use of appeals.

6a Distinguish between reasonable and fallacious argumentative tactics.

When you evaluate an argument, look closely at the reasoning and evidence behind it. Some unreasonable argumentative tactics are known as *logical fallacies*, or errors in logic. Most of the fallacies — such as hasty generalizations and false analogies — are misguided or dishonest uses of legitimate argumentative strategies. The examples in this section suggest when such strategies are reasonable and when they are not.

Generalizing (inductive reasoning)

Writers and thinkers generalize all the time. We look at a sample of data and conclude that data we have not observed will most likely conform to what we have seen. From a spoonful of soup, we conclude just how salty the whole bowl will be.

When we draw a conclusion from an array of facts, we are engaged in inductive reasoning. Such reasoning deals in probability, not certainty. For a conclusion to be highly probable, it must be based on evidence that is sufficient, representative, and relevant. (See the chart on the next page.)

> **Academic English** Many hasty generalizations contain words such as *all*, *ever*, *always*, and *never*, when qualifiers such as *most*, *many*, *usually*, and *seldom* would be more accurate.

Hasty generalization involves coming to a conclusion based on insufficient or unrepresentative evidence.

HASTY GENERALIZATION

In a single year, scores on standardized tests in California's public schools rose by ten points. Therefore, more children than ever are succeeding in America's public school systems.

Data from one state do not justify a conclusion about the whole United States.

A *stereotype* is a hasty generalization about a group. Here are two examples.

STEREOTYPES

Women are bad bosses.

Politicians are corrupt.

Stereotyping is common because of our human tendency to perceive selectively. We tend to see what we want to see; we notice evidence confirming our already formed opinions and fail to notice evidence to the contrary.

Testing inductive reasoning

Though inductive reasoning leads to probable and not absolute truth, you can assess a conclusion's likely probability by asking three questions. Here those questions are applied to a sample conclusion based on a survey.

CONCLUSION   The majority of students on our campus would volunteer at least five hours a week in a community organization if the school provided a placement service for volunteers.

EVIDENCE   In a recent survey, 723 of 1,215 students questioned said they would volunteer at least five hours a week in a community organization if the school provided a placement service for volunteers.

1. *Is the evidence sufficient?* That depends. On a campus of 3,000 students, the pool of students surveyed would be sufficient for research, but on a campus of 30,000 students, 1,215 students would be only 4 percent of the population. If those 4 percent were known to be truly representative of the other 96 percent, however, even such a small sample would be sufficient (see question 2).

2. *Is the evidence representative?* The evidence is representative if those responding to the survey reflect the characteristics of the entire student population with respect to age, gender, race, field of study, number of extracurricular commitments, and so on. If most of those surveyed are majors in a field like social work, the researchers should question the survey's conclusion.

3. *Is the evidence relevant?* Yes. The survey results are directly linked to the conclusion. A survey about the number of hours students work for pay, by contrast, would not be relevant because it would not be about *choosing to volunteer.*

Drawing analogies

An analogy points out a similarity between two things that are otherwise different. Analogies can be an effective means of arguing a point. It is not always easy to draw the line between a reasonable analogy and an unreasonable one. At times, however, an analogy is clearly off base, in which case it is called a *false analogy.*

> **FALSE ANALOGY**
>
> If we can send a spacecraft to Pluto, we should be able to find a cure for the common cold.

The writer has falsely assumed that because two things are alike in one respect, they must be alike in others. Exploring the solar system and finding a cure for the common cold are both scientific challenges, but the problems confronting medical researchers are quite different from those solved by space scientists.

Tracing causes and effects

Demonstrating a connection between causes and effects is rarely simple. For example, to explain why a chemistry course has a high failure rate, you would begin by listing possible causes: inadequate preparation of students, poor teaching, lack of qualified tutors, and so on. Next you would investigate each possible cause. Only after investigating the possible causes would you be able to weigh the impact of each cause and suggest appropriate remedies.

Because cause-and-effect reasoning is so complex, it is not surprising that writers frequently oversimplify it. In particular, writers sometimes assume that because one event follows another, the first is the cause of the second. This common fallacy is known as *post hoc*, from the Latin *post hoc, ergo propter hoc*, meaning "after this, therefore because of this."

> ***POST HOC* FALLACY**
>
> Since Governor Cho took office, unemployment among minorities in the state has decreased by 7 percent. Governor Cho should be applauded for reducing unemployment among minorities.

Is the governor responsible for the decrease or are there other reasons? The writer must show that Governor Cho's policies are responsible for the decrease in unemployment; it is not enough to show that the decrease followed the governor's taking office.

Weighing options

Especially when reasoning about problems and solutions, writers must weigh options. To be fair, a writer should mention the full range of options, showing why one is superior to the others or might work well in combination with others.

It is unfair to suggest that only two alternatives exist when in fact there are more. Writers who set up a false choice between their preferred option and one that is unsatisfactory use faulty *either . . . or* logic.

> ***EITHER . . . OR* FALLACY**
>
> Our current war against drugs has not worked. Either we should legalize drugs or we should turn the drug war over to our armed forces and let them fight it.

Are these the *only* solutions — legalizing drugs or calling out the army? This is a false choice because other options, such as funding drug abuse prevention programs, are possible.

Making assumptions

An assumption is a claim that is taken to be true — without the need of proof. Most arguments are based to some extent on assumptions, since writers rarely have the time and space to prove all the conceivable claims on which their argument is based.

There is a danger, however, in failing to spell out and prove a claim that is clearly controversial. Consider the following short argument, in which a key claim is missing.

> **ARGUMENT WITH MISSING CLAIM**
>
> Violent crime is increasing. Therefore, we should vigorously enforce the death penalty.

The writer seems to be assuming both that the death penalty deters violent criminals and that it is a fair punishment — and that most audiences will agree. These are not reasonable assumptions; the writer will need to state and support both claims.

When a missing claim is an assertion that few would agree with, we say that a writer is guilty of a *non sequitur* (Latin for "does not follow").

> **NON SEQUITUR**
>
> Christopher gets plenty of sleep; therefore, he will be a successful student in the university's pre-med program.

Does it take more than sleep to be a successful college student? The missing claim — that people with good sleep habits always make successful students — would be hard to prove.

Deducing conclusions (deductive reasoning)

When we deduce a conclusion, we put things together. We establish that a general principle is true, that a specific case is an example of that principle, and that therefore a particular conclusion about that case is a certainty.

Deductive reasoning can often be structured in a three-step argument called a *syllogism*. The three steps are the major premise, the minor premise, and the conclusion.

1. Anything that increases radiation in the environment is dangerous to public health. (Major premise)

2. Nuclear reactors increase radiation in the environment. (Minor premise)

3. Therefore, nuclear reactors are dangerous to public health. (Conclusion)

The major premise is a generalization. The minor premise is a specific case. The conclusion follows from applying the generalization to the specific case.

Deductive arguments break down if one of the premises is not true or if the conclusion does not follow logically from the premises. In the following brief argument, the major premise is very likely untrue.

UNTRUE PREMISE

The police do not give speeding tickets to people driving less than five miles per hour over the limit. Dominic is driving fifty-nine miles per hour in a fifty-five-mile-per-hour zone. Therefore, the police will not give Dominic a speeding ticket.

The conclusion is true only if the premises are true. If the police sometimes give tickets for driving less than five miles per hour over the limit, Dominic cannot safely conclude that he will avoid a ticket.

In the following argument, both premises might be true, but the conclusion does not follow logically from them.

CONCLUSION DOES NOT FOLLOW

All members of our club ran in this year's Boston Marathon. Jay ran in this year's Boston Marathon. Therefore, Jay is a member of our club.

The fact that Jay ran the race is no guarantee that he is a member of the club. Presumably, many runners are nonmembers.

Assuming that both premises are true, the following argument holds up.

CONCLUSION FOLLOWS

All members of our club ran in this year's Boston Marathon. Jay is a member of our club. Therefore, Jay ran in this year's Boston Marathon.

6b Distinguish between legitimate and unfair emotional appeals.

There is nothing wrong with appealing to readers' emotions. After all, many issues worth arguing about have an emotional as well as a logical dimension. Even the Greek logician Aristotle lists *pathos* (emotional appeals) as a legitimate argumentative tactic. For example, in an essay criticizing big-box stores (see 4a), writer Betsy Taylor has a good reason for tugging at readers' emotions: Her subject is the decline of city and town life. In her conclusion, Taylor appeals to readers' emotions by invoking their national pride.

LEGITIMATE EMOTIONAL APPEAL

Is it anti-American to be against having a retail giant set up shop in one's community? Some people would say so. On the other hand, if you board up Main Street, what's left of America?

Emotional appeals, however, are frequently misused. Many of the arguments we see in the media, for instance, strive to win our sympathy rather than our intelligent agreement. A TV commercial suggesting that you will be thin and attractive if you drink a certain diet beverage is making a pitch to emotions. So is a political speech that recommends electing a candidate because he is a devoted husband and father who serves as a volunteer firefighter.

The following passage illustrates several types of unfair emotional appeals.

UNFAIR EMOTIONAL APPEALS

This progressive proposal to build a ski resort in the state park has been carefully researched by Western Trust, the largest bank in the state; furthermore, it is favored by a majority of the local merchants. The only opposition comes from activist types who care more about trees than they do about people. One of their leaders was actually arrested for disturbing the peace several years ago.

Evaluating ethical, logical, and emotional appeals as a reader

Ancient Greek rhetoricians distinguished among three kinds of appeals used to influence readers: ethical, logical, and emotional. As you evaluate arguments, identify these appeals and question their effectiveness. Are they appropriate for the audience and the argument? Are they balanced and legitimate or lopsided and misleading?

Ethical appeals (*ethos*)

Ethical arguments call upon a writer's character, knowledge, and authority. Ask questions such as the following when you evaluate the ethical appeal of an argument.

- Is the writer informed and trustworthy? How does the writer establish authority and credibility?
- Is the writer fair-minded and unbiased? How does the writer establish reasonableness?
- Does the writer use sources knowledgeably and responsibly?
- How does the writer describe the views of others and deal with opposing views?

Logical appeals (*logos*)

Reasonable arguments appeal to readers' sense of logic, rely on evidence, and use inductive and deductive reasoning. Ask questions such as the following to evaluate the logical appeal of an argument.

- Is the evidence sufficient, representative, and relevant?
- Is the reasoning sound?
- Does the argument contain any logical fallacies or unwarranted assumptions?
- Are there any missing or mistaken premises?

Emotional appeals (*pathos*)

Emotional arguments appeal to readers' beliefs and values. Ask questions such as the following to evaluate the emotional appeal of an argument.

- What values or beliefs does the writer address, either directly or indirectly?
- Are the emotional appeals legitimate and fair?
- Does the writer oversimplify or dramatize an issue?
- Do the emotional arguments highlight or shift attention away from the evidence?

Words with strong positive or negative connotations, such as *progressive* and *activist types*, are examples of *biased language*. An approach that relies on attacking the people who hold a belief (environmentalists) rather than refuting their argument is called *ad hominem*, a Latin term meaning "to the man." Associating a prestigious name (Western Trust) with the writer's side is called *transfer*. Claiming that an idea should be accepted because a large number of people (the majority of merchants) are in favor is called the *bandwagon appeal*. Bringing in irrelevant issues (the arrest) is the *red herring fallacy*, named after a trick allegedly used to train hunting dogs, in which a smelly fish was dragged across the trail to mislead them.

Advertisement that uses *ethos* (ethical appeal)

Advertising makes use of ethical, logical, and emotional appeals to persuade consumers to buy a product or embrace a brand. This Patagonia ad makes an ethical appeal with its copy that invites customers to rethink their purchasing practices.

Exercise 6–1 In the following paragraph, identify the type of appeal used in each sentence ending with the three choices *ethos* (ethical appeal), *logos* (logical appeal), *pathos* (emotional appeal).

Elderspeak, the use of pet names such as "dear" and "sweetie" directed toward older adults, is generally intended as an endearment. However, the use of such language suggests a view of seniors as childlike or cognitively impaired. It should be no surprise, then, that older adults find these pet names condescending and demeaning (*ethos / logos / pathos*). Unfortunately, the effects of elderspeak go far beyond insulting older adults. Health care professionals have found that residents in nursing facilities, even those with dementia, respond to patronizing language by becoming uncooperative, aggressive, or depressed. In a 2009 study published in the *American Journal of Alzheimer's Disease and Other Dementias,* Ruth Herman and Kristine L. Williams reported that older adults responded to elderspeak by resisting care, yelling, or crying ("Elderspeak's Influence") (*ethos / logos / pathos*). Surprisingly, despite widely published research on the negative effects of elderspeak, the worst offenders are health care workers, the very people we trust to treat our elderly family members with respect and dignity — and the very people who are old enough to know better (*ethos / logos / pathos*).

6c Judge how fairly a writer handles opposing views.

The way in which a writer deals with opposing views is telling. Some writers address the arguments of the opposition fairly, conceding points when necessary and countering others. Other writers will do almost anything to win an argument: either ignoring opposing views altogether or misrepresenting such views and attacking their proponents.

Writers build credibility (*ethos*) by addressing opposing arguments fairly. As you read arguments, assess the credibility of your sources by looking at how they deal with views not in agreement with their own.

Describing the views of others

Some writers and speakers deliberately misrepresent the views of others. One way they do this is by setting up a "straw man," a character so weak that he is easily knocked down. The *straw man fallacy* consists of oversimplification or outright distortion of opposing views. For example, during the District of Columbia's struggle for voting representation, some politicians set up a straw man, as shown in the following example.

STRAW MAN FALLACY

Washington, DC, residents are lobbying for statehood. Giving a city such as the District of Columbia the status of a state would be unfair.

The straw man wanted statehood. In fact, most DC citizens lobbied for voting representation in any form, not necessarily through statehood.

Quoting opposing views

Writers often quote the words of writers who hold opposing views. In general, this is a good idea, for it assures some level of fairness and accuracy. At times, though, both the fairness and the accuracy are an illusion.

A source may be misrepresented when it is quoted out of context. All quotations are to some extent taken out of context, but a fair writer will explain the context to readers. To select a provocative sentence from a source and ignore the more moderate sentences surrounding it is both unfair and misleading. Sometimes a writer deliberately distorts a source through the device of ellipsis dots, which tell readers that words have been omitted from the original source. When those words are crucial to an author's meaning, omitting them is unfair. (See also 39d.)

ORIGINAL SOURCE

Johnson's *History of the American West* is riddled with inaccuracies and astonishing in its blatantly racist description of the Indian wars.

— B. R., reviewer

MISLEADING QUOTATION

Johnson's *History of the American West* is "astonishing in its . . . description of the Indian wars."

Checklist for reading and evaluating arguments

- What is the writer's thesis, or central claim?
- Are there any gaps in reasoning? Does the argument contain any logical fallacies (see 6a)?
- What assumptions does the argument rest on? Are there any unstated assumptions?
- What ethical, logical, or emotional appeals does the writer make? Are these appeals effective?
- What evidence does the writer use? Could there be alternative interpretations of the evidence?
- How does the writer handle opposing views?
- If you are not persuaded by the writer's argument, what counterarguments could you make to the writer?

Exercise 6–2   Explain what is illogical in the following brief arguments. It may be helpful to identify the logical fallacy or fallacies by name. Answers appear in the back of the book.

a. My roommate, who is an engineering major, is taking a course called Structures of Tall Buildings. All engineers have to know how to design tall buildings.

b. If you're old enough to vote, you're old enough to drink. Therefore, the drinking age should be lowered to eighteen.

c. If you're not part of the solution, you're part of the problem.

d. American students could be outperforming students in schools around the globe if it weren't for the outdated, behind-the-times thinking of many statewide education departments.

e. Charging a fee for curbside trash pickup will encourage everyone to recycle more because no one in my town likes to spend extra money.

7 Writing arguments

Evaluating the arguments of other writers prepares you to construct your own. When you ask questions about the logic and evidence of the arguments you read, you become aware of such

 LaunchPad Solo
macmillan learning

Activities for Chapter 7
4 Writing practice activities, 2 LearningCurve activities, 4 Video tutorials, 1 Sample student paper

needs in your own writing. And when you pose objections to arguments, you more readily anticipate and counter objections to your own arguments.

7a When writing arguments, identify your purpose and context.

In constructing an argument, you take a stand on a debatable issue. Your purpose is to explain your understanding of the truth about a subject or to propose the best solution to a problem, reasonably and logically, without being combative. Your aim is to persuade your readers to reconsider their positions by offering new reasons to question existing viewpoints.

It's best to start by informing yourself about the debate or conversation around a subject — sometimes called its *context*. If you are planning to write about the subject of offshore drilling, for example, you might want to read sources that shed light on the social context (the concerns of consumers, lawmakers, and environmentalists) and sources that inform you about the intellectual context (scientific or theoretical opinions of geologists, oceanographers, or economists) in which the debate is played out. Because your readers may be aware of the social and intellectual contexts in which your issue is grounded, you will be at a disadvantage if you are not informed. Reading even a few sources can deepen your understanding of the conversation around the issue.

7b View your audience as a panel of jurors.

Do not assume that your audience already agrees with you. Instead, envision skeptical readers who, like a panel of jurors, will make up their minds after listening to all sides of the argument. If you are arguing a public policy issue, you may want to aim your paper at readers who represent a variety of positions. In the case of a debate over offshore drilling, for example, imagine a jury that represents those who have a stake in the matter: consumers, policymakers, and environmentalists.

At times, you can deliberately narrow your audience. If you are working within a word limit, for example, you might not have enough space to address the concerns of all interested parties. Or you might be primarily interested in reaching one segment of a general audience, such as consumers. Once you identify a specific audience, it's helpful to think about what kinds of arguments and evidence will appeal to that audience.

Using ethical, logical, and emotional appeals as a writer

To construct a convincing argument, you must establish your credibility (*ethos*) and appeal to your readers' sense of logic and reason (*logos*) as well as to their values and beliefs (*pathos*).

Ethical appeals (*ethos*)

To accept your argument, a reader must see you as trustworthy, fair, and reasonable. When you acknowledge alternative positions, you build common ground with readers and gain their trust by showing that you are knowledgeable. And when you use sources responsibly and respectfully, you inspire readers' confidence in your judgment.

Logical appeals (*logos*)

To persuade readers, you need to appeal to their sense of logic and reason. When you provide sufficient evidence, you offer readers logical support for your argument. And when you clarify the assumptions that underlie your arguments and avoid logical fallacies, you appeal to readers' desire for reason.

Emotional appeals (*pathos*)

To establish common ground with readers, you need to appeal to their beliefs and values as well as to their minds. When you offer vivid examples and illustrations, surprising statistics, or compelling visuals, you engage readers and deepen their interest in your argument. And when you balance emotional appeals with logical appeals, you highlight the human dimension of an issue to show readers why they should care about your argument.

Academic English Academic audiences in the United States will expect your writing to be assertive and confident — neither aggressive nor passive. You can create an assertive tone by acknowledging different positions and supporting your ideas with specific evidence.

TOO AGGRESSIVE	Of course only registered organ donors should be eligible for organ transplants. It's selfish and shortsighted to think otherwise.
TOO PASSIVE	I might be wrong, but I think that maybe people should have to register as organ donors if they want to be considered for a transplant.
ASSERTIVE TONE	If only registered organ donors are eligible for transplants, more people will register as donors.

If you are uncertain about the tone of your work, ask for help at your school's writing center.

7c In your introduction, establish credibility and state your position.

When constructing an argument, make sure your introduction includes a thesis statement that establishes your position on the issue you have chosen to debate. In the sentences leading up to the thesis, establish your credibility (*ethos*) with readers by showing that you are knowledgeable and fair-minded. If possible, build common ground with readers who may not at first agree with your views, and show them why they should consider your thesis.

In the following introduction, student writer Kevin Smith establishes his credibility by introducing both sides of the debate.

Smith shows that he is familiar with the legal issues surrounding school prayer.

Although the Supreme Court has ruled against prayer in public schools on First Amendment grounds, many people still feel that prayer should be allowed. Such people value prayer as a practice central to their faith and believe that prayer is a way for schools to reinforce moral principles. They also compellingly point out a paradox in the First Amendment itself: at what point does the separation of church and state restrict the freedom

Smith is fair-minded, presenting the views of both sides.

of those who wish to practice their religion? What

proponents of school prayer fail to realize, however,

is that the Supreme Court's decision, although it was

Thesis builds common ground.

made on legal grounds, makes sense on religious

grounds as well. Prayer is too important to be

trusted to our public schools.

TIP: A good way to test a thesis while drafting and revising is to imagine a counterargument to your argument (see 7f). If you can't think of an opposing point of view, revise your thesis as a debatable statement.

HOW TO

Draft a thesis statement for an argument

1 **Identify the various positions in the debate you're writing about.** At the heart of a good argument are debate and disagreement. An argumentative thesis takes a clear position on a debatable issue and is supported by evidence. Identify the points in the debate on which there is disagreement. Consider your own questions and thoughts about the topic.

2 **Review any notes you have taken** to clarify your own thoughts about the debate.

3 **Pose a question that has not yet been dealt with sufficiently.** Write this question either in your draft or in your notes to guide your thinking. An open-ended question will make a stronger thesis. If your question can be answered with yes or no, add *why* or *how* to it.

4 **Write your thesis as an answer to your question.** Include the topic, your position, and any language that might preview the organization of your argument or show why you are making the argument.

5 **Test your thesis.** Is your position clear? Is your position debatable? The answer to both questions should be yes.

6 **Revise your thesis.** Why does your position matter? Put your working thesis to the "So what?" test, and consider adding a *because* clause to your thesis (see 1c).

7d Back up your thesis with persuasive lines of argument.

Arguments of any complexity contain lines of argument that, when taken together, might reasonably convince readers that the thesis has merit. The following, for example, are the main lines of argument that student writer Sam Jacobs used in his paper about the shift from print to online news (see 7h).

THESIS: CENTRAL CLAIM

The shift from print to online news provides unprecedented opportunities for readers to become more engaged with the news, to hold journalists accountable, and to participate as producers, not simply as consumers.

SUPPORTING CLAIMS

- Print news has traditionally had a one-sided relationship with its readers, delivering information for passive consumption.
- Online news invites readers to participate in a collaborative process — to question and even contribute to the content.
- Links within news stories provide transparency, allowing readers to move easily from the main story to original sources, related articles, or background materials.
- Technology has made it possible for readers to become news producers — posting text, audio, images, and video of news events.
- Citizen journalists can provide valuable information, sometimes more quickly than traditional journalists can.

If you sum up your main lines of argument, as Jacobs did, you will have a rough outline of your essay. In your paper, you will provide evidence for each of these claims.

7e Support your claims with specific evidence.

You will need to support your central claim (thesis) and any subordinate claims with evidence: facts, statistics, examples and illustrations, visuals, expert opinion, and so on. Supporting your position in a debate requires that you consult sources to establish your *ethos* and to persuade your audience. As you read through or view the sources, you will learn more about the arguments and counterarguments at the center of your debate.

★ **Using sources responsibly**   Whether your sources provide facts or statistics, examples, visuals, or expert opinion, remember that you must cite them. Doing so gives credit to authors and shows readers how to locate a source in case they want to assess its credibility or explore the issue. See 56 (MLA) and 61 (APA) for more help.

Using facts and statistics

A fact is something that is known with certainty because it has been objectively verified: Carbon has an atomic weight of 12. John F. Kennedy was assassinated on November 22, 1963. Statistics are collections of numerical facts: Alcohol impairment is a factor in nearly 31 percent of traffic fatalities. More than four in ten businesses in the United States are owned by women.

Most arguments are supported, at least to some extent, by facts and statistics. For example, in the following passage the writer uses statistics to show that college students' credit card debt is declining.

> A recent study revealed that undergraduates are relying less on credit cards and are carrying lower debt than they did five years ago. The study credits the change to wider availability of grant and scholarship money. The average credit card debt per college undergraduate dropped more than 70% from $3,173 in 2008 to $925 in 2013 (Papadimitriou).

Writers often use statistics in selective ways to bolster their own positions. If you suspect that a writer's handling of statistics is not quite fair, track down the original sources for those statistics or read authors with opposing views, who may give you a fuller understanding of the numbers.

Using examples and illustrations

Examples and illustrations (extended examples, often in story form) rarely prove a point by themselves, but when used in combination with other forms of evidence, they add detail to an argument and bring it to life. Because examples are often concrete and sometimes vivid, they can reach readers in ways that statistics and abstractions cannot.

In a paper arguing that online news provides opportunities for readers that print does not, Sam Jacobs describes how regular citizens using only cell phones and laptops helped save lives during Hurricane Katrina by sending important updates to the rest of the world.

> Citizen reporting made a difference in the wake of Hurricane Katrina in 2005. Armed with cell phones and laptops, regular citizens relayed critical news updates in a rapidly developing crisis, often before traditional journalists were even on the scene.

Using visuals

Visuals can support your argument by providing vivid and detailed evidence and by capturing your readers' attention. Bar or line graphs, for instance, describe and organize complex statistical data; photographs can convey abstract ideas. (See 1f.)

As you consider using visual evidence, ask yourself the following questions:

- Is the visual accurate, credible, and relevant?

- How will the visual appeal to readers: Logically? Ethically? Emotionally?

- How will the visual evidence function? Will it provide background information? Present complex numerical information or convey an abstract idea? Lend authority? Refute counterarguments?

Citing expert opinion

Although they are no substitute for careful reasoning of your own, the views of an expert can contribute to the force of your argument. For example, to help make the case that print journalism has a one-sided relationship with its readers, student writer Sam Jacobs integrates an expert's key description.

> With the rise of the Internet, however, this model
> has been criticized by journalists such as Dan
> Gillmor, founder of the Center for Citizen Media,
> who argues that traditional print journalism treats
> "news as a lecture," whereas online news is "more
> of a conversation" (xxiv).

Quotes key phrases from source, integrating them into his sentence.

Lists the source's title in a signal phrase.

Cites source.

When you rely on expert opinion, make sure that your source is an expert in the field you are writing about. To help readers recognize the expert, provide credentials showing why your source is worth listening to; list the person's position or title alongside his or her name (*Dan Gillmor, founder of the Center for Citizen Media*). When including expert testimony in your paper, you can summarize or paraphrase the expert's opinion or you can quote the expert's exact words. You will need to document the source, as Jacobs did.

7f Anticipate objections; counter opposing arguments.

Readers who already agree with you need no convincing, but skeptical readers may resist your arguments. To be willing to give up a position that seems reasonable, readers need to see that another position is even more reasonable. In addition to presenting your own case, therefore, you should consider the opposing arguments and attempt to counter them.

Anticipating and countering objections

To anticipate a possible objection to your argument, consider the following questions.

- Could a reasonable person draw a different conclusion from your facts or examples?
- Might a reader question any of your assumptions or offer an alternative explanation?
- Is there any evidence that might weaken your position?

The following questions may help you respond to a reader's potential objection.

- Can you concede the point but challenge the point's importance or usefulness?
- Can you explain why readers should consider a new perspective or question a piece of evidence?
- Should you explain how your position responds to contradictory evidence?
- Can you suggest a different interpretation of the evidence?

When you write, use sentence openers to signal to readers that you're about to present an objection.

Critics of this view argue that _____.

Some readers might point out that _____.

Researchers challenge these claims by _____.

It might seem that drawing attention to an opposing point of view or contradictory evidence would weaken your argument. Actually, when you acknowledge counterpositions and give the positions credibility, you strengthen your argument and show yourself as a reasonable and well-informed writer who has a thorough understanding of the issue.

There is no best place in an essay to deal with opposing views. Often it is useful to summarize the opposing position early in your essay. After stating your thesis, but before developing your own arguments, you might have a paragraph that addresses the most important counterargument. Or you can anticipate objections paragraph by paragraph as you develop your case. Wherever you decide to address opposing arguments, take the opposing view seriously and show your willingness to consider all sides of the argument.

Writing for an audience

When you counterargue, you consider a possible argument against your thesis, your evidence, or your reasoning. If you don't acknowledge counterpositions, your audience will say "But how could that be the only answer . . ." or ask "Have you thought about this viewpoint?" In anticipating your readers' doubts or objections, you establish common ground with your audience and show your respect for them.

7g Build common ground.

As you counter opposing arguments, try to find one or two assumptions you might share with readers who do not initially agree with your views. If you can show that you share their concerns, your readers will be more likely to accept that your argument is valid. For example, to convince parents that school uniforms will have a positive effect on academic achievement, a school board would want to create common ground with parents by emphasizing the shared values around learning. Having established these values in common, the board might convince parents that school uniforms will reduce distractions, save money, and focus students' attention on learning rather than on clothes.

7h Sample student writing: Argument

In the essay in this section, student writer Sam Jacobs argues that the shift from print to online news benefits readers by providing them with opportunities to produce news and to think more critically as consumers of news. Notice how he appeals to his readers by presenting opposing views fairly before providing his own arguments.

When Jacobs quotes, summarizes, or paraphrases information from a source, he cites the source with an in-text citation formatted in MLA style. Citations in the paper refer readers to the list of works cited at the end of the paper. (For more details about citing sources, see 54.)

A guide to writing an argument essay appears on pages 105–06.

Jacobs 1

Sam Jacobs

Professor Alperini

English 101

11 October 2016

From Lecture to Conversation: Redefining What's "Fit to Print"

"All the news that's fit to print," the motto of *The New York Times* since 1896, plays with the word *fit*, asserting that a news story must be newsworthy and must not exceed the limits of the printed page. The increase in online news consumption, however, challenges both meanings of the word *fit*, allowing producers and consumers alike to rethink who decides which topics are worth covering and how extensive that coverage should be. Any cultural shift usually means that something is lost, but in this case there are clear gains. The shift from print to online news provides unprecedented opportunities for readers to become more engaged with the news, to hold journalists accountable, and to participate as producers, not simply as consumers.

Guided by journalism's code of ethics — accuracy, objectivity, and fairness — print news reporters have

> In his opening sentences, Jacobs provides background for his thesis.

> Thesis states the main point.

> Jacobs does not need a citation for common knowledge.

Marginal annotations indicate MLA-style formatting and effective writing.

Jacobs 2

gathered and delivered stories according to what editors decide is fit for their readers. Except for op-ed pages and letters to the editor, print news has traditionally had a one-sided relationship with its readers. The print news media's reputation for objective reporting has been held up as "a stop sign" for readers, sending a clear message that no further inquiry is necessary (Weinberger). With the rise of the Internet, however, this model has been criticized by journalists such as Dan Gillmor, founder of the Center for Citizen Media, who argues that traditional print journalism treats "news as a lecture," whereas online news is "more of a conversation" (xxiv). Print news arrives on the doorstep every morning as a fully formed lecture, a product created without participation from its readership. By contrast, online news invites readers to participate in a collaborative process — to question and even help produce the content.

> Source is cited in MLA style.

One of the most important advantages online news offers over print news is the presence of built-in hyperlinks, which carry readers from one electronic document to another. If readers are curious about the definition of a term, the roots of a story, or other perspectives on a topic, links provide a path. Links help readers become more critical consumers of information by engaging them in a totally new way. For instance, the link embedded in the story "Credit-Shy: Younger Generation Is More Likely to Stick to a Cash-Only Policy" (Sapin) allows readers to find out more about the financial trends of young adults and provides statistics that confirm the article's accuracy (see fig. 1). Other links in the article widen the conversation. These kinds of links give readers the opportunity to conduct their own evaluation of the evidence and verify the journalist's claims.

> Transition moves from Jacobs's main argument to specific examples.

> Jacobs clarifies key terms *(transparency* and *accountability).*

Links provide a kind of transparency impossible in print because they allow readers to see through online

Jacobs 3

news to the "sources, disagreements, and the personal assumptions and values" that may have influenced a news story (Weinberger). The International Center for Media and the Public Agenda underscores the importance of news organizations letting "consumers in on the often tightly held little secrets of journalism." To do so, they suggest, will lead to accountability, and "accountability leads to credibility" ("Openness"). These tools alone don't guarantee that news producers will be responsible and trustworthy, but they encourage an open and transparent environment that benefits news consumers.

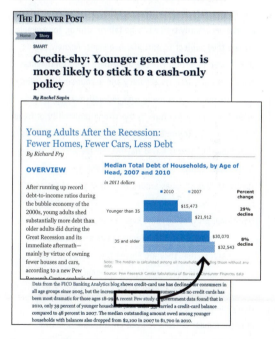

Fig. 1. Links embedded in online news articles allow readers to move from the main story to original sources, related articles, or background materials. The link in this online article (Sapin) points to a statistical report by the Pew Research Center, the original source of the author's data on young adults' spending practices.

Jacobs 4

Jacobs
develops the
thesis.

Not only has technology allowed readers to become more critical news consumers, but it also has helped some to become news producers. The Web gives ordinary people the power to report on the day's events. Anyone with an Internet connection can publish on blogs and Web sites, engage in online discussion forums, and contribute video and audio recordings. Citizen journalists with laptops, cell phones, and digital camcorders have become news producers alongside large news organizations.

Opposing views
are presented
fairly.

Not everyone embraces the spread of unregulated news reporting online. Critics point out that citizen journalists are not necessarily trained to be fair or ethical, for example, nor are they subject to editorial oversight. Acknowledging that citizen reporting is more immediate and experimental, critics also question its accuracy and accountability: "While it has its place . . . it really isn't journalism at all, and it opens up information flow to the strong probability of fraud and abuse. . . . Information without journalistic standards is called gossip," writes David Hazinski in *The Atlanta Journal-Constitution* (23A). In his book *Losing the News,* media specialist Alex S. Jones argues that what passes for news today is in fact "pseudo news" and is "far less reliable" than traditional print news (27). Even a supporter like Gillmor is willing to agree that citizen journalists are "nonexperts," but he argues that they are "using technology to make a profound contribution, and a real difference" (140).

Jacobs
counters
opposing
arguments.

A vivid example
helps Jacobs
make his point.

Citizen reporting made a difference in the wake of Hurricane Katrina in 2005. Armed with cell phones and laptops, regular citizens relayed critical news updates in a rapidly developing crisis, often before traditional journalists were even on the scene. In 2006, the enormous contributions of citizen journalists were recognized when the New Orleans *Times-Picayune* received the Pulitzer Prize in public service for its online coverage — largely

Jacobs 5

citizen-generated — of Hurricane Katrina. In recognizing the
paper's "meritorious public service," the Pulitzer Prize board
credited the newspaper's blog for "heroic, multi-faceted
coverage of [the storm] and its aftermath" ("2006").
Writing for the *Online Journalism Review,* Mark Glaser
emphasizes the role that blog updates played in saving
storm victims' lives. Further, he calls *The Times-Picayune's*
partnership with citizen journalists a "watershed for online
journalism."

> Jacobs uses specific evidence for support.

The Internet has enabled consumers to participate
in a new way in reading, questioning, interpreting, and
reporting the news. Decisions about appropriate content
and coverage are no longer exclusively in the hands of news
editors. Ordinary citizens now have a meaningful voice in
the conversation — a hand in deciding what's "fit to print."
Some skeptics worry about the apparent free-for-all and loss
of tradition. But the expanding definition of news provides
opportunities for consumers to be more engaged with events
in their communities, their nations, and the world.

> Conclusion echoes the thesis without merely repeating it.

Works Cited

Works cited page uses MLA style.

Gillmor, Dan. *We the Media: Grassroots Journalism by the People, for the People.* O'Reilly Media, 2006.

Glaser, Mark. "NOLA.com Blogs and Forums Help Save Lives after Katrina." *OJR: The Online Journalism Review,* Knight Digital Media Center, 13 Sept. 2005, www.ojr .org/050913glaser/.

List is alphabetized by authors' last names (or by title when a work has no author).

Hazinski, David. "Unfettered 'Citizen Journalism' Too Risky." *The Atlanta Journal-Constitution,* 13 Dec. 2007, p. 23A. General OneFile. go.galegroup.com/ps/.

Jones, Alex S. *Losing the News: The Future of the News That Feeds Democracy.* Oxford UP, 2009.

"Openness and Accountability: A Study of Transparency in Global Media Outlets." *ICMPA: International Center for Media and the Public Agenda,* 2006, www.icmpa.umd .edu/pages/studies/transparency/main.html/.

Sapin, Rachel. "Credit-Shy: Younger Generation Is More Likely to Stick to a Cash-Only Policy." *The Denver Post,* 26 Aug. 2013, www.denverpost.com/ci_23929523/ credit-shy-younger-generation-stick-cash-only -policy/.

Access date is used for a web source that has no update date.

"The 2006 Pulitzer Prize Winners: Public Service." *The Pulitzer Prizes.* Columbia U, www.pulitzer.org /prize-winners-by-year/2006/. Accessed 2 Oct. 2016.

Weinberger, David. "Transparency Is the New Objectivity." *Joho the Blog,* 19 July 2009, www.hyperorg .com/blogger/2009/07/19/transparency-is -the-new-objectivity/.

How to write an argument essay

Composing an **argument** gives you the opportunity to take a position on a debatable issue. You present your position, evidence to support your position, and your response to other views on the issue. A sample argument essay appears at the beginning of 7h.

Key features

- **A thesis, stated as a clear position on a debatable issue,** frames an argument essay. The issue is debatable because reasonable people disagree about it.

- **An examination of the issue's context** indicates why the issue is important, why readers should care about it, or how your position fits into the debates surrounding the topic.

- **Sufficient, representative, and relevant evidence** supports the argument's claims. Evidence needs to be specific and persuasive; quoted, summarized, or paraphrased fairly and accurately; and cited correctly.

- **Opposing positions are summarized and countered.** By anticipating and countering objections to your position, you establish common ground with readers and show yourself to be a reasonable and well-informed writer.

Writing your argument

1 Explore

Generate ideas by brainstorming responses to questions such as the following:

- What is the debate around your issue? What sources will help you learn more about your issue?

- What position will you take? Why does your position need to be argued?

- What evidence supports your position? What evidence makes you question your position?

- What types of appeals — *ethos*, *logos*, *pathos* — might you use to persuade readers? How will you build common ground with your readers?

2 Draft

Try to figure out the best way to structure your argument. A typical outline might include the following steps: Capture readers' attention; state your thesis; give background information; support your major claims with specific evidence; recognize and respond to opposing points of view; and end by reinforcing your thesis and reminding readers why it matters.

As you draft, think about the best order for your claims. You could organize by strength, building to your strongest argument (instead of starting with your strongest), or by concerns your audience might have.

3 Revise

Ask your reviewers for specific feedback. Here are some questions to guide their comments.

- Is the thesis clear? Is the issue debatable?

- Is the evidence persuasive? Is more needed?

- Is your argument organized logically?

- Are there any flaws in your reasoning or assumptions that weaken the argument?

- Have you presented yourself as a knowledgeable, trustworthy writer?

- Does the conclusion pull together your entire argument? How might the conclusion be more effective?

CLARITY

8 Prefer active verbs.

As a rule, choose an active verb and pair it with a subject that names the person or thing doing the action. Active verbs express meaning more emphatically than their weaker counterparts — verbs in the passive voice or forms of the verb *be*.

> PASSIVE   The pumps *were destroyed* by a surge of power.
>
> *BE* VERB   A surge of power *was* responsible for the
>   destruction of the pumps.
>
> ACTIVE   A surge of power *destroyed* the pumps.

Verbs in the passive voice lack strength because their subjects receive the action instead of doing it. Forms of the verb *be* (*be, am, is, are, was, were, being, been*) lack vigor because they convey no action.

Although passive verbs and the forms of *be* have legitimate uses, choose an active verb whenever possible. Even among active verbs, some are more vigorous and colorful than others. Carefully selected verbs can energize a piece of writing.

> ▶ The goalie crouched low, ~~reached~~ ^{swept} out his stick, and ~~sent~~ ^{hooked} the
>
>   rebound away from the mouth of the net.

> **Academic English** Although you may be tempted to avoid the passive voice completely, keep in mind that some writing situations call for it, including some scientific writing. For appropriate uses of the passive voice, see 8a; for advice about forming the passive voice, see 28b.

8a Choose the active voice or the passive voice, depending on your writing situation.

In the active voice, the subject does the action; in the passive voice, the subject receives the action. Although both voices are grammatically correct, the active voice is usually more effective because it is clearer and more direct.

| ACTIVE | Hernando *caught* the fly ball. |
| PASSIVE | The fly ball *was caught* by Hernando. |

Passive sentences often identify the actor in a *by* phrase, as in the preceding example. Sometimes, however, that phrase is omitted, and who or what is responsible for the action becomes unclear: *The fly ball was caught.*

Most of the time, you will want to emphasize the actor, so you should use the active voice. To replace a passive verb with an active one, make the actor the subject of the sentence.

▶ The settlers stripped the land of timber before realizing
~~The land was stripped of timber before the settlers realized~~ the
^
consequences of their actions.

The revision emphasizes the actors (*settlers*) by naming them in the subject.

Appropriate uses of the passive voice

The passive voice is appropriate if you want to emphasize the receiver of the action or to minimize the importance of the actor.

| APPROPRIATE PASSIVE | Many Hawaiians *were forced* to leave their homes after the earthquake. |
| APPROPRIATE PASSIVE | Near harvest time, the tobacco plants *are sprayed* with a chemical to slow the growth of suckers. |

The writer of the first sentence wished to emphasize the receiver of the action, *Hawaiians.* The writer of the second sentence wished to focus on the tobacco plants, not on the people spraying them.

In much scientific writing, the passive voice properly emphasizes the experiment or process being described, not the researcher. Check with your instructor for the preference in your discipline.

8b Replace *be* verbs that result in dull or wordy sentences.

Not every *be* verb needs replacing. The forms of *be* (*be, am, is, are, was, were, being, been*) work well when you want to link a subject to a noun that clearly renames it or to an adjective that describes it: *Orchard House was the home of Louisa May Alcott. The harvest will be bountiful after the summer rains.*

Be verbs also are essential as helping verbs before present participles (*is flying, are disappearing*) to express ongoing action: *Derrick was fighting the fire when his wife went into labor.* (See 27f.)

If using a *be* verb makes a sentence needlessly dull and wordy, however, consider replacing it.

> ► Burying nuclear waste in Antarctica would ~~be in violation of~~ *violate* an
>
> international treaty.

Violate is less wordy and more vigorous than *be in violation of.*

> ► When Rosa Parks ~~was resistant to~~ *resisted* giving up her seat on the bus,
>
> she became a civil rights hero.

Resisted is stronger than *was resistant to.*

8c As a rule, choose a subject that names the person or thing doing the action.

In weak, unemphatic prose, both the actor and the action may be buried in sentence elements other than the subject and the verb. In the following weak sentence, for example, both the actor and the action are de-emphasized in prepositional phrases.

> **WEAK** The institution of the New Deal had the effect of reversing some of the economic inequalities of the Great Depression.
>
> **EMPHATIC** The New Deal reversed some of the economic inequalities of the Great Depression.

Consider the subjects and verbs of the two versions — *institution had* versus *New Deal reversed*. The second version expresses the writer's point in a way that is clear and strong.

> ► ~~The use of~~ *P*ure oxygen can ~~cause~~ heal ~~ing in~~ wounds that are
>
> otherwise untreatable.

In the original sentence, the subject and verb — *use can cause* — express the point blandly. *Pure oxygen can heal* makes the point more emphatically and directly.

Exercise 8–1   Revise unemphatic sentences by replacing passive verbs or *be* verbs with active alternatives. You may need to name in the subject the person or thing doing the action. If a sentence is emphatic, do not change it. Possible revisions appear in the back of the book.

> The ranger doused the campfire before giving us
> ~~The campfire was doused by the ranger before we were given a~~
> ^
>
> ticket for unauthorized use of a campsite.

a. The Prussians were victorious over the Saxons in 1745.

b. The entire operation is managed by Ahmed, the producer.

c. The sea kayaks were expertly paddled by the tour guides.

d. At the crack of rocket and mortar blasts, I jumped from the top bunk and landed on my buddy below, who was crawling on the floor looking for his boots.

e. There were shouting protesters on the courthouse steps.

Exercise 8–2   For each writing situation below, decide whether it is more appropriate to use the active voice or the passive voice. Answers appear in the back of the book.

a. You are writing a research paper explaining the effects of a deadly bacterial outbreak in a remote Chilean village. (active / passive)

b. You are writing a letter to the editor, praising an emergency medical technician whose quick action saved an injured motorist. (active / passive)

c. You are writing a summary of the procedure you used in an experiment for your biology class. (active / passive)

d. To accompany your résumé, you must write a cover letter explaining your recent accomplishments as a manager. (active / passive)

e. You must fill out an incident report, explaining in detail how your actions led to a collision between the forklift you were operating and a wall of fully stocked shelves. (active / passive)

9 Balance parallel ideas.

If two or more ideas are parallel, they are easier to grasp when expressed in parallel grammatical form. Single words should be balanced with single words, phrases with phrases, clauses with clauses.

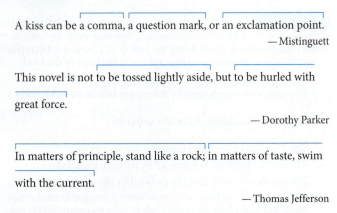

A kiss can be a comma, a question mark, or an exclamation point.

— Mistinguett

This novel is not to be tossed lightly aside, but to be hurled with great force.

— Dorothy Parker

In matters of principle, stand like a rock; in matters of taste, swim with the current.

— Thomas Jefferson

Writers often use parallelism to create emphasis. (See 14f.)

9a Balance parallel ideas in a series.

Readers expect items in a series to appear in parallel grammatical form. When one or more of the items violate readers' expectations, a sentence will be awkward.

▶ Children who study music also learn confidence, discipline, and ~~they are creative.~~ *creativity.*

The revision presents all the items in the series as nouns: *confidence*, *discipline*, and *creativity*.

▶ Impressionist painters believed in focusing on ordinary subjects, capturing the effects of light on those subjects, and ~~to use~~ *using* short brushstrokes.

The revision uses *-ing* forms for all the items in the series: *focusing*, *capturing*, and *using*.

9b Balance parallel ideas presented as pairs.

When pairing ideas, underscore their connection by expressing them in similar grammatical form. Paired ideas are usually connected in one of these ways:

• with a coordinating conjunction such as *and*, *but*, or *or*

- with a pair of correlative conjunctions such as *either . . . or* or *not only . . . but also*
- with a word introducing a comparison, usually *than* or *as*

Parallel ideas linked with coordinating conjunctions

Coordinating conjunctions (*and, but, or, nor, for, so,* and *yet*) link ideas of equal importance. When those ideas are closely parallel in content, they should be expressed in parallel grammatical form.

▶ Emily Dickinson's poetry features the use of dashes and ~~capitalizing~~ common words.
  the capitalization of

The revision balances the nouns *use* and *capitalization.*

▶ Many colleges are making SAT scores optional and ~~encourage~~ alternative application materials.
  encouraging

The revision balances the verb *making* with the verb *encouraging.*

Parallel ideas linked with correlative conjunctions

Correlative conjunctions come in pairs: *either . . . or, neither . . . nor, not only . . . but also, both . . . and, whether . . . or.* Make sure that the grammatical structure following the second half of the pair is the same as that following the first half.

▶ Thomas Edison was not only a prolific inventor but also ~~was~~ a successful entrepreneur.

The words *a prolific inventor* follow *not only,* so *a successful entrepreneur* should follow *but also.*

▶ The clerk told me either to change my flight or take the train.
  to

To change my flight, which follows *either,* should be balanced with *to take the train,* which follows *or.*

Comparisons linked with *than* or *as*

In comparisons linked with *than* or *as,* the elements being compared should be expressed in parallel grammatical structure.

▶ For some situations, it is easier to talk in person than ~~texting~~. *to text*

To talk is balanced with *to text*.

Comparisons should also be logical and complete. (See 10c.)

9c Repeat function words to clarify parallels.

Function words such as prepositions (*by, to*) and subordinating conjunctions (*that, because*) signal the grammatical nature of the word groups to follow. Although you can sometimes omit function words, be sure to include them whenever they signal parallel structures that readers might otherwise miss.

▶ Our study revealed that left-handed students were more likely
to have trouble with classroom desks and *that* rearranging desks for
exam periods was useful.

A second subordinating conjunction helps readers sort out the two parallel ideas: *that* left-handed students have trouble with classroom desks and *that* rearranging desks was useful.

Exercise 9–1 ▶ Edit the following sentences to correct faulty parallelism. Possible revisions appear in the back of the book.

Rowena began her workday by pouring a cup of coffee and
checking
~~checked~~ her email.

a. Police dogs are used for finding lost children, tracking criminals, and the detection of bombs and illegal drugs.

b. Hannah told her rock-climbing partner that she bought a new harness and of her desire to climb Otter Cliffs.

c. It is more difficult to sustain an exercise program than starting one.

d. During basic training, I was not only told what to do but also what to think.

e. Jan wanted to drive to the wine country or at least Sausalito.

Exercise 9–2 Revise the following paragraph to balance parallel ideas.

Community service can provide tremendous benefits not only for the organization receiving the help but the volunteer providing the help, too. This dual benefit idea is behind a recent move to make community service hours a graduation requirement in high schools across the country. For many nonprofit organizations, seeking volunteers is often smarter financially than to hire additional employees. For many young people, community service positions can help develop empathy, being committed, and leadership. Opponents of the trend argue that volunteerism should not be mandatory, but research shows that community service requirements are keeping students engaged in school and lower dropout rates dramatically. Parents, school administrators, and people who are leaders in the community all seem to favor the new initiatives.

10 Add needed words.

Sometimes writers leave out words intentionally, and the meaning of the sentence is not affected. But leaving out words can occasionally cause confusion for readers or make the sentence ungrammatical. Readers need to see at a glance how the parts of a sentence are connected.

> **Multilingual**
>
> Languages sometimes differ in the need for certain words. In particular, be alert for missing articles, verbs, subjects, or expletives. See 29, 30a, and 30b.

10a Add words needed to complete compound structures.

In compound structures, words are often left out for economy: *Tom is a man who means what he says and [who] says what he means.* Such omissions are acceptable as long as the omitted words are common to both parts of the compound structure.

If a sentence defies grammar or idiom because an omitted word is not common to both parts of the compound structure, the simplest solution is to put the word back in.

▶ Advertisers target customers whom they identify through

   who
   demographic research or have purchased their product in the past.
   ^

   The word *who* must be included because *whom . . . have purchased* is not grammatically correct.

   accepted
▶ Mayor Davis never has and never will accept a bribe.
   ^

   Has . . . accept is not grammatically correct.

   in
▶ Many South Pacific islanders still believe and live by ancient laws.
   ^

   Believe . . . by is not idiomatic in English. (For a list of common idioms, see 18d.)

10b Add the word *that* if there is any danger of misreading without it.

If there is no danger of misreading, the word *that* may be omitted when it introduces a subordinate clause. *The value of a principle is the number of things [that] it will explain.* When a sentence might be misread without *that*, however, include the word.

▶ In his famous obedience experiments, psychologist Stanley

   that
   Milgram discovered ordinary people were willing to inflict
   ^

   physical pain on strangers.

   Milgram didn't discover ordinary people; he discovered that ordinary people were willing to inflict pain on strangers. The word *that* tells readers to expect a clause, not just *ordinary people*, as the direct object of *discovered*.

10c Add words needed to make comparisons logical and complete.

Comparisons should be made between items that are alike. To compare unlike items is illogical and distracting.

▶ The forests of North America are much more extensive than
  those of
  Europe.
  ^

Forests must be compared with forests, not with all of Europe.

▶ Some say that Ella Fitzgerald's renditions of Cole Porter's songs
  singer's.
  are better than any other ~~singer.~~
  ^

Ella Fitzgerald's renditions cannot logically be compared with a singer.
The revision uses the possessive form *singer's*, with the word *renditions*
being implied.

Sometimes the word *other* must be inserted to make a comparison logical.

  other
▶ Jupiter is larger than any planet in our solar system.
  ^

Jupiter is a planet, and it cannot be larger than itself.

Sometimes the word *as* must be inserted to make a comparison grammatically complete.

  as
▶ The city of Lowell is as old, if not older than, the neighboring
  ^

city of Lawrence.

The construction *as old* is not complete without a second *as: as old as . . .
the neighboring city of Lawrence.*

Comparisons should be complete enough to ensure clarity.
The reader should understand what is being compared.

| INCOMPLETE | Brand X is less salty. |
| COMPLETE | Brand X is less salty than Brand Y. |

Finally, comparisons should leave no ambiguity for readers. If a sentence lends itself to more than one interpretation, revise the sentence to state clearly which interpretation you intend.

AMBIGUOUS	Ken helped me more than my roommate.
CLEAR	Ken helped me more than *he helped* my roommate.
CLEAR	Ken helped me more than my roommate *did*.

10d Add the articles *a*, *an*, and *the* where necessary for grammatical completeness.

It is not always necessary to repeat articles with paired items: *We bought a computer and printer.* However, if one of the items requires *a* and the other requires *an*, both articles must be included.

► We bought a computer and ^an^ antivirus program.

> **Multilingual**
>
> Choosing and using articles can be challenging for multilingual writers. See 29.

Exercise 10–1 ▶ Add any words needed for grammatical or logical completeness in the following sentences. Possible revisions appear in the back of the book.

The officer feared ^that^ the prisoner would escape.

a. A grapefruit or orange is a good source of vitamin C.

b. The women entering the military academy can expect haircuts as short as the male cadets.

c. Looking out the family room window, Sarah saw her favorite tree, which she had climbed as a child, was gone.

d. The graphic designers are interested and knowledgeable about producing posters for the balloon race.

e. The Great Barrier Reef is larger than any coral reef in the world.

11 Untangle mixed constructions.

A mixed construction contains sentence parts that do not sensibly fit together. The mismatch may be a matter of grammar or of logic. Untangling mixed constructions often requires rethinking the idea and then revising the sentence.

11a Untangle the grammatical structure.

Once you begin a sentence, your choices are limited by the range of grammatical patterns in English. (See 47 and 48.) You cannot begin with one grammatical plan and switch without warning to another. Often you must rethink the purpose of the sentence and revise.

> **MIXED**   For most drivers who have a blood alcohol content of .05 percent double their risk of causing an accident.

The writer begins the sentence with a long prepositional phrase and makes it the subject of the verb *double*. But a prepositional phrase can serve only as a modifier; it cannot be the subject of a sentence.

> **REVISED**   For most drivers who have a blood alcohol content of .05 percent, the risk of causing an accident is doubled.
>
> **REVISED**   Most drivers who have a blood alcohol content of .05 percent double their risk of causing an accident.

In the first revision, the writer begins with the prepositional phrase and finishes the sentence with a proper subject and verb (*risk . . . is doubled*). In the second revision, the writer stays with the original verb (*double*) and begins the sentence another way, making *drivers* the subject of *double*.

> Electing
> ▶ ~~When the country elects~~ a president is the most important
>   ^
>
> responsibility in a democracy.
>
> The adverb clause *When the country elects a president* cannot serve as the subject of the verb *is*. The revision replaces the adverb clause with a gerund phrase, a word group that can function as a subject. (See 48b and 48e.)

> ▶ Although the United States is a wealthy nation, ~~but~~ more than
>
> 20 percent of our children live in poverty.
>
> The coordinating conjunction *but* cannot link a subordinate clause (*Although the United States . . .*) with an independent clause (*more than 20 percent of our children live in poverty*).

Multilingual

English does not allow repeated subjects, objects, nouns, and adverbs in certain situations. See 30c and 30d.

▶ My father ~~he~~ moved to Peru before he met my mother.

　　　　　　　　　　　　　　　　　　the final exam
▶ ~~The final exam~~ I should really study for ~~it~~ to pass the course.
　　　　　　　　　　　　　　　　　　　　　^

11b Straighten out the logical connections.

The subject and the predicate (the verb and its modifiers) should make sense together; when they don't, the error is known as *faulty predication.*

　　　　　　　　　　　Tiffany
▶ The court decided that ~~Tiffany's welfare~~ would not be safe living
　　　　　　　　　　　　　　^

with her abusive parents.

Tiffany, not her welfare, may not be safe.

An appositive is a noun that renames a nearby noun. When an appositive and the noun it renames are not logically equivalent, the error is known as *faulty apposition.* (See 48c.)

　　Tax accounting,
▶ ~~The tax accountant,~~ a very lucrative profession, requires
　　^

intelligence, patience, and attention to mathematical detail.

The tax accountant is a person, not a profession.

11c Avoid *is when, is where,* and *reason . . . is because* constructions.

In formal English, many readers object to *is when, is where,* and *reason . . . is because* constructions when what follows does not make logical or grammatical sense.

The linking verb *is* (as well as *are, was,* and *were*) should generally be followed by a noun, an adjective, or a clause that renames or describes the subject, not by an adverb clause beginning with *when, where,* or *because,* which suggest relations of time, place, and cause.

▶ Anorexia nervosa is ~~where people~~ think they are overweight and
   ^{a disorder suffered by people who}
   ^

diet to the point of starvation.

Where refers to places. The linking verb *is* in such constructions requires a noun, an adjective, or a clause that can serve as a definition: Anorexia nervosa is a disorder, not a place.

▶ The reason the experiment failed is ~~because~~ conditions in the lab
   ^{that}
   ^

were not sterile.

▶ The ~~reason the~~ experiment failed ~~is~~ because conditions in the lab

were not sterile.

In the first revision, the noun clause beginning with *that* properly refers to the subject, *reason*. In the second revision, the adverb clause beginning with *because* properly modifies the verb *failed*. And that revision is also more concise.

Exercise 11–1 ▶ Edit the following sentences to untangle mixed constructions. Possible revisions appear in the back of the book.

   ^{Taking}
   ~~By taking~~ the oath of allegiance made Ling a US citizen.
   ^

a. Using surgical gloves is a precaution now worn by dentists to prevent contact with patients' blood and saliva.

b. A physician, the career my brother is pursuing, requires at least ten years of challenging work.

c. The reason the pharaohs had bad teeth was because tiny particles of sand found their way into Egyptian bread.

d. Recurring bouts of flu among team members set a record for number of games forfeited.

e. In this box contains the key to your future.

12 Repair misplaced and dangling modifiers.

Modifiers, whether they are single words, phrases, or clauses, should point clearly to the words they modify. As a rule, related words should be kept together.

12a Put limiting modifiers in front of the words they modify.

Limiting modifiers such as *only*, *even*, *almost*, *nearly*, and *just* should appear in front of a verb only if they modify the verb: *At first, I couldn't even touch my toes, much less grasp them.* If they limit the meaning of some other word in the sentence, they should be placed in front of that word.

▶ The literature reveals that students ~~only~~ learn new vocabulary
  only
words when they are encouraged to read.
  ^

Only limits the meaning of the *when* clause.

  just
▶ If you ~~just~~ interview seniors, your understanding of student
           ^

opinion will be incomplete.

The adverb *just* limits the meaning of *seniors*, not *interview*.

When the limiting modifier *not* is misplaced, the sentence usually suggests a meaning the writer did not intend.

     not
▶ In the United States in 1860, all black southerners were ~~not~~ slaves.
                                                           ^

The original sentence says that no black southerners were slaves. The revision is clearer: Some (but not all) black southerners were slaves.

12b Place phrases and clauses so that readers can see what they modify.

Although phrases and clauses can appear at some distance from the words they modify, make sure your meaning is clear. When phrases or clauses are oddly placed, absurd misreadings can result.

| MISPLACED | The soccer player returned to the clinic where he had undergone emergency surgery in 2014 in a limousine sent by Adidas. |
| REVISED | Traveling in a limousine sent by Adidas, the soccer player returned to the clinic where he had undergone emergency surgery in 2014. |

The revision corrects the false impression that the soccer player underwent emergency surgery in a limousine.

▶ ~~There~~ *On the walls* are many pictures of comedians who have performed at

Gavin's. ~~on the walls.~~

The comedians weren't performing on the walls; the pictures were on the walls.

Occasionally the placement of a modifier leads to an ambiguity — a squinting modifier. In such a case, two revisions will be possible, depending on the writer's intended meaning.

| AMBIGUOUS | The exchange students we met for coffee occasionally questioned us about our latest slang. |

It's not clear what happened occasionally, the meeting or the questioning.

| CLEAR | The exchange students we occasionally met for coffee questioned us about our latest slang. |
| CLEAR | The exchange students we met for coffee questioned us occasionally about our latest slang. |

12c Move awkwardly placed modifiers.

As a rule, a sentence should flow from subject to verb to object, without lengthy detours along the way. When a long adverbial word group separates a subject from its verb, a verb from its object, or a helping verb from its main verb, the result is often awkward.

▶ ~~Hong Kong,~~ *A* after more than 150 years of British rule, was *Hong Kong*

transferred back to Chinese control in 1997.

There is no reason to separate the subject, *Hong Kong*, from the verb, *was transferred*, with a long phrase.

Multilingual

English does not allow an adverb to appear between a verb and its object. See 30f.

easily
▶ Yolanda lifted ~~easily~~ the fifty-pound weight.
                ^

12d Avoid split infinitives when they are awkward.

An infinitive consists of *to* plus the base form of a verb: *to think, to breathe, to dance.* When a modifier appears between *to* and the verb, an infinitive is said to be "split": *to carefully balance, to completely understand.*

When a long word or a phrase appears between the parts of the infinitive, the result is usually awkward.

If possible, the
▶ ~~The~~ patient should try to ~~if possible~~ avoid going up and down
  ^

stairs.

Attempts to avoid split infinitives can result in equally awkward sentences. When alternative phrasing sounds unnatural, most experts encourage splitting the infinitive.

AWKWARD   We decided actually to enforce the law.

BETTER   We decided to actually enforce the law.

At times, neither the split infinitive nor its alternative sounds particularly awkward. In such situations, it is usually better not to split the infinitive.

▶ Nursing students learn to ~~accurately~~ record a patient's vital
                            accurately.
  signs/
       ^

Exercise 12–1 Edit the following sentences to correct misplaced or awkwardly placed modifiers. Possible revisions appear in the back of the book.

in a telephone survey
Answering questions can be annoying. ~~in a telephone survey.~~
                                    ^   ^

a. More research is needed to effectively evaluate the risks posed by volcanoes in the Pacific Northwest.

b. Many students graduate with debt from college totaling more than fifty thousand dollars.

c. It is a myth that humans only use 10 percent of their brains.

d. A coolhunter is a person who can find in the unnoticed corners of modern society the next wave of fashion.

e. All geese do not fly beyond Narragansett for the winter.

12e Repair dangling modifiers.

A dangling modifier fails to refer logically to any word in the sentence. Dangling modifiers are easy to repair, but they can be hard to recognize, especially in your own writing.

Recognizing dangling modifiers

Dangling modifiers are usually word groups (such as verbal phrases) that suggest but do not name an actor. When a sentence opens with such a modifier, readers expect the subject of the next clause to name the actor. If it doesn't, the modifier dangles.

▶ Understanding the need to create checks and balances on power,
the framers of
the Constitution divided the government into three branches.
^

The framers of the Constitution (not the document itself) understood the need for checks and balances.

users can easily view their
▶ After logging into the site, ~~users'~~ account balances. ~~can be easily~~
^   ^
~~viewed.~~

Users (not their account balances) log into the site.

The following sentences illustrate four common kinds of dangling modifiers.

DANGLING   *Deciding to join the navy*, the recruiter enthusiastically pumped Joe's hand. [Participial phrase]

DANGLING   *Upon entering the doctor's office*, a skeleton caught my attention. [Preposition followed by a gerund phrase]

DANGLING   *To satisfy her mother,* the piano had to be practiced every day. [Infinitive phrase]

DANGLING   *Though not eligible for the clinical trial,* the doctor prescribed the drug for Ethan on compassionate grounds. [Elliptical clause with an understood subject and verb]

These dangling modifiers falsely suggest that the recruiter decided to join the navy, that the skeleton entered the doctor's office, that the piano intended to satisfy the mother, and that the doctor was not eligible for the clinical trial.

Although most readers will understand the writer's intended meaning in such sentences, the unintended humor can be distracting.

Repairing dangling modifiers

To repair a dangling modifier, you can revise the sentence in one of two ways:

- Name the actor in the subject of the sentence.
- Name the actor in the modifier.

Depending on your sentence, one of these revision strategies may be more appropriate than the other.

ACTOR NAMED IN SUBJECT

▶ Upon entering the doctor's office, a skeleton. ~~caught my~~ I noticed
    ~~attention.~~

▶ To satisfy her mother, the piano ~~had to be practiced~~ every day. Jing-mei had to practice

ACTOR NAMED IN MODIFIER

▶ ~~Deciding~~ to join the navy, the recruiter enthusiastically When Joe decided
    pumped ~~Joe's~~ hand. his

▶ Though not eligible for the clinical trial, the doctor prescribed Ethan was
    the drug for ~~Ethan~~ on compassionate grounds. him

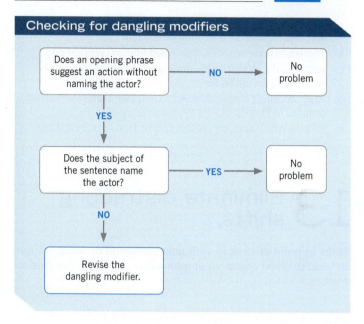

Checking for dangling modifiers

Does an opening phrase suggest an action without naming the actor? — **NO** → No problem

↓ **YES**

Does the subject of the sentence name the actor? — **YES** → No problem

↓ **NO**

Revise the dangling modifier.

NOTE: You cannot repair a dangling modifier just by moving it. Consider, for example, the sentence about the skeleton. If you put the modifier at the end of the sentence (*A skeleton caught my attention upon entering the doctor's office*), you are still suggesting that the skeleton entered the office. The only way to avoid the problem is to put the word *I* in the sentence, either as the subject or in the modifier.

                            I noticed
▶ Upon entering the doctor's office, a skeleton. ~~caught my attention.~~
                      ^   ^

   As I entered
▶ ~~Upon entering~~ the doctor's office, a skeleton caught my attention.
  ^

Exercise 12–2   Edit the following sentences to correct dangling modifiers. Most sentences can be revised in more than one way. Possible revisions appear in the back of the book.

         a student must complete
To graduate, two science courses. ~~must be completed.~~
  ^   ^

a. To complete an online purchase with a credit card, the expiration date and the security code must be entered.

b. Though only sixteen, UCLA accepted Martha's application.

c. Settled in the cockpit, the pounding of the engine was muffled only slightly by my helmet.

d. After studying polymer chemistry, computer games seemed less complex to Phuong.

e. When a young man, my mother enrolled me in ballet and tap dance classes.

13 Eliminate distracting shifts.

Shifts in point of view, in verb tense, in mood or voice, or from indirect to direct questions or quotations can distract or confuse readers.

13a Make the point of view consistent in person and number.

The point of view in a piece of writing is the perspective from which it is written: first person (*I* or *we*), second person (*you*), or third person (*he*, *she*, *it*, *one*, *they*, or any noun).

The *I* (or *we*) point of view, which emphasizes the writer, is a good choice for informal letters and writing based primarily on personal experience. The *you* point of view, which emphasizes the reader, works well for giving advice or explaining how to do something. The third-person point of view, which emphasizes the subject, is appropriate in formal academic and professional writing.

Writers who have trouble settling on an appropriate point of view sometimes shift confusingly from one to another and, in doing so, distract their readers. The solution is to choose a suitable perspective and stay with it.

▶ Our class practiced rescuing a victim trapped in a wrecked car.

We learned to dismantle the car with the essential tools.

We   *our*   *our*
~~You~~ were graded on ~~your~~ speed and ~~your~~ skill in freeing the
 ^   ^   ^

victim.

The writer should have stayed with the *we* point of view. *You* is inappropriate because the writer is not addressing readers directly. *You* should not be used in a vague sense meaning "anyone." (See 23d.)

You need
▶ ~~One needs~~ a password and a credit card number to access the
 ^

database. You will be billed at an hourly rate.

You is an appropriate choice for giving advice directly to readers.

Exercise 13–1 ▶   Edit the following paragraph to eliminate distracting shifts in point of view (person and number). Create two versions. First, imagine that this is an introductory paragraph designed to engage the reader with a personal story; write it in the first person (using *I* and *we*). Then write the paragraph in the third person (using *people* and *they*). In what contexts would each version be the best choice?

> When online dating first became available, many people thought that it would simplify romance. We believed that you could type in a list of criteria — sense of humor, college education, green eyes, good job — and a database would select the perfect mate. Thousands of people signed up for services and filled out their profiles, confident that true love was only a few mouse clicks away. As it turns out, however, virtual dating is no easier than traditional dating. I still have to contact the people I find, exchange emails and phone calls, and meet him in the real world. Although a database might produce a list of possibilities and screen out obviously undesirable people, you can't predict chemistry. More often than not, people who seem perfect online just don't click in person. Electronic services do help a single person expand their pool of potential dates, but it's no substitute for the hard work of romance.

13b Maintain consistent verb tenses.

Consistent verb tenses clearly establish the time of the actions being described. When a passage begins in one tense and then shifts without warning and for no reason to another, readers are distracted and confused.

▶ Our candidate lost in the debate. Just as we gave up hope, she

　soared
　~~soars~~ ahead in the polls.
　^

The writer thought that the present tense (*soars*) would convey
excitement. But having begun in the past tense (*lost, gave up*), the writer
should follow through in the past tense.

Writers often encounter difficulty with verb tenses when
writing about literature. Because fictional events occur outside
the time frames of real life, the past tense and the present tense
may seem equally appropriate. The literary convention is to describe fictional events consistently in the present tense. (See 27f.)

▶ The scarlet letter is a punishment sternly placed on Hester's

　　　　　　　　　　　　　　　　is
breast by the community, and yet it ~~was~~ a fanciful and
　　　　　　　　　　　　　　　　　　　^
imaginative product of Hester's own needlework.

Exercise 13-2　Edit the following paragraphs to eliminate distracting shifts in tense.

　The English colonists who settled in Massachusetts received
assistance at first from the local Indian tribes, but by 1675 there
had been friction between the English and the Indians for many
years. On June 20 of that year, Metacomet, whom the colonists
called Philip, leads the Wampanoag tribe in the first of a series
of attacks on the colonial settlements. The war, known today as
King Philip's War, rages on for more than a year and leaves three
thousand Indians and six hundred colonists dead. Metacomet's
attempt to retain power in his native land failed. Finally he too is
killed, and the victorious colonists sell his wife and children into
slavery.

　The Indians did not leave records of their encounters with the
English settlers, but the settlers recorded some of their experiences
at the hands of the Indians. One of the few accounts to survive was
written by a captured colonist, Mrs. Mary Rowlandson. She is a
minister's wife who is kidnapped by an Indian war party and held
captive for eleven weeks in 1676. Her history, *A Narrative of the
Captivity and Restoration of Mrs. Mary Rowlandson*, tells the story
of her experiences with the Wampanoags. Although it did not
paint a completely balanced picture of the Indians, Rowlandson's
narrative, which is considered a classic early American text,
showed its author to be a keen observer of life in an Indian camp.

13c Make verbs consistent in mood and voice.

Unnecessary shifts in the mood of a verb can be distracting and confusing to readers. There are three moods in English: the *indicative*, used for facts, opinions, and questions; the *imperative*, used for orders or advice; and the *subjunctive*, used to express wishes or conditions contrary to fact (see 27g).

The following passage shifts confusingly from the indicative to the imperative mood.

> ► The counselor advised us to spread out our core requirements over two or three semesters. ~~Also,~~ *She also suggested that we* pay attention to prerequisites for elective courses.

The writer began by reporting the counselor's advice in the indicative mood (*counselor advised*) and switched to the imperative mood (*pay attention*); the revision puts both sentences in the indicative.

A verb may be in either the active voice (with the subject doing the action) or the passive voice (with the subject receiving the action). (See 8a.) If a writer shifts without warning from one to the other, readers may be left wondering why.

> ► Each student completes a self-assessment~~,~~, *gives it* ~~The self-assessment is then given~~ to the teacher, and a copy ~~is exchanged~~ *exchanges* with a classmate.

Because the passage began in the active voice (*student completes*) and then switched to the passive (*self-assessment is given, copy is exchanged*), readers are left wondering who gives the self-assessment to the teacher and the classmate. The active voice, which is clearer and more direct, leaves no ambiguity.

13d Avoid sudden shifts from indirect to direct questions or quotations.

An indirect question reports a question without asking it: *We asked whether we could visit Miriam.* A direct question asks directly: *Can we visit Miriam?* Sudden shifts from indirect to direct questions are awkward. In addition, sentences containing such shifts are impossible to punctuate because indirect questions must end with a period and direct questions must end with a question mark. (See 38b.)

▶ LGBT business owners wonder whether their businesses are unfairly
    whether they can
targeted and ~~can they~~ reverse the trend~~?~~**.**

The revision poses both questions indirectly. The writer could also ask both questions directly: *Are LGBT-owned businesses being unfairly targeted? Can these business owners reverse the trend?*

An indirect quotation reports someone's words without quoting word for word. A direct quotation presents the exact words of a speaker or writer, set off with quotation marks. Unannounced shifts from indirect to direct quotations are distracting and confusing.

▶ The patient said she had been experiencing heart palpitations
    asked me to
and ~~please~~ run as many tests as possible to identify the problem.

The revision reports the patient's words indirectly. The writer also could quote the words directly: *The patient said, "I have been experiencing heart palpitations. Please run as many tests as possible to identify the problem."*

Exercise 13-3 ▶ Edit the following sentences to make the verbs consistent in mood and voice and to eliminate distracting shifts from indirect to direct questions or quotations. Possible revisions appear in the back of the book.

As a public relations intern, I wrote press releases, managed the
    fielded all phone calls.
website, and ~~all phone calls were fielded by me.~~

a. An incredibly talented musician, Ray Charles mastered R&B, soul, and gospel styles. Even country music was performed well by him.

b. Environmentalists point out that shrimp farming in Southeast Asia is polluting water and making farmlands useless. They warn that action must be taken by governments before it is too late.

c. The samples were observed for five days before we detected any growth.

d. In his famous soliloquy, Hamlet contemplates whether death would be preferable to his difficult life and, if so, is he capable of committing suicide?

e. The lawyer told the judge that Miranda Hale was innocent and allow her to prove the allegations false.

Exercise 13–4   Edit the following sentences to eliminate distracting shifts. Possible revisions appear in the back of the book.

For many first-year engineering students, adjusting to a rigorous

course load can be so challenging that ~~you~~ *they* sometimes feel

overwhelmed.

a. A courtroom lawyer has more than a touch of theater in their blood.

b. The interviewer asked if we had brought our proof of citizenship and did we bring our passports?

c. The experienced reconnaissance scout knows how to make fast decisions and use sophisticated equipment to keep their team from being detected.

d. After the animators finish their scenes, the production designer arranges the clips according to the storyboard. Synchronization notes must also be made for the sound editor and the composer.

e. Madame Defarge is a sinister figure in Dickens's *A Tale of Two Cities.* On a symbolic level, she represents fate; like the Greek Fates, she knitted the fabric of individual destiny.

14 Emphasize key ideas.

Within each sentence, emphasize your point by expressing it in the subject and verb of an independent clause, the words that receive the most attention from readers (see 14a–14e).

Within longer stretches of prose, you can draw attention to ideas deserving special emphasis by using a variety of techniques, often involving an unusual twist or some element of surprise (see 14f).

14a Coordinate equal ideas; subordinate minor ideas.

When combining two or more ideas in one sentence, you have two choices: coordination or subordination. Choose coordination to indicate that the ideas are equal or nearly equal in importance. Choose subordination to indicate that one idea is less important than another.

Coordination

Coordination draws attention equally to two or more ideas. To coordinate single words or phrases, join them with a coordinating conjunction (see the list on p. 135) or with a pair of correlative conjunctions: *bananas and strawberries; not only a lackluster plot but also inferior acting* (see 46g).

To coordinate independent clauses — word groups that express a complete thought and that can stand alone as a sentence — join them with a comma and a coordinating conjunction or with a semicolon. The semicolon is often accompanied by a conjunctive adverb such as *therefore* or *however* or by a transitional phrase such as *for example* or *in other words*. (For a longer list, see p. 135.)

Assume, for example, that your intention is to draw equal attention to the following two ideas.

> Social networking websites offer ways for people to connect in the virtual world. They do not replace face-to-face forms of social interaction.

To coordinate these ideas, you can join them with a comma and the coordinating conjunction *but* or with a semicolon and the conjunctive adverb *however*.

> Social networking websites offer ways for people to connect in the virtual world, but they do not replace face-to-face forms of social interaction.

> Social networking websites offer ways for people to connect in the virtual world; however, they do not replace face-to-face forms of social interaction.

It is important to choose a coordinating conjunction or conjunctive adverb appropriate to your meaning. In the preceding example, the two ideas contrast with each other, calling for *but* or *however*. (For specific coordination strategies, see the chart on p. 135.)

Using coordination to combine sentences of equal importance

1. Consider using a comma and a coordinating conjunction. (See 32a.)

, and	, but	, or	, nor
, for	, so	, yet	

   ▶ In Orthodox Jewish funeral ceremonies, the shroud is a simple linen
   and the
   vestment/, ~~The~~ coffin is plain wood.
   ^

2. Consider using a semicolon with a conjunctive adverb or transitional phrase. (See 34b.)

also	however	next
as a result	in addition	now
besides	in fact	of course
consequently	in other words	otherwise
finally	in the first place	still
for example	meanwhile	then
for instance	moreover	therefore
furthermore	nevertheless	thus

   in addition, she
   ▶ Alicia scored well on the SAT/; ~~She also~~ had excellent grades and a
   ^
   record of community service.

3. Consider using a semicolon alone. (See 34a.)

   in
   ▶ In youth we learn/; ~~In~~ age we understand.
   ^

Subordination

To give unequal emphasis to two or more ideas, express the major idea in an independent clause and place any minor ideas in subordinate clauses or phrases. (For specific subordination strategies, see the chart on p. 137.)

Let your intended meaning determine which idea you emphasize. Consider the two ideas about social networking websites.

> Social networking websites offer ways for people to connect in the virtual world. They do not replace face-to-face forms of social interaction.

If your purpose is to stress the ways that people can connect in the virtual world rather than the limitations of these connections, subordinate the idea about the limitations.

> Although they do not replace face-to-face forms of social interaction, social networking websites offer ways for people to connect in the virtual world.

To focus on the limitations of the virtual world, subordinate the idea about the ways people connect on these websites.

> Although they offer ways for people to connect in the virtual world, social networking websites do not replace face-to-face forms of social interaction.

Exercise 14–1   Use the coordination or subordination technique in brackets to combine each pair of independent clauses. Possible revisions appear in the back of the book.

> **Ted Williams was one of the best hitters in the history of**
> baseball, but he
> ~~baseball. He~~ **never won a World Series ring.** [*Use a comma*
> ^
> *and a coordinating conjunction.*]

a. Williams played for the Boston Red Sox from 1939 to 1960. He managed the Washington Senators and the Texas Rangers for several years after retiring as a player. [*Use a comma and a coordinating conjunction.*]

b. In 1941, Williams finished the season with a batting average of .406. No player has hit over .400 for a season since then. [*Use a semicolon.*]

c. Williams acknowledged that Joe DiMaggio was a better all-around player. Williams felt that he was a better hitter than DiMaggio. [*Use the subordinating conjunction* although.]

d. Williams was a stubborn man. He always refused to tip his cap to the crowd after a home run because he claimed that fans were fickle. [*Use a semicolon and the transitional phrase* for example.]

e. Williams's relationship with the media was unfriendly at best. He sarcastically called baseball writers the "knights of the keyboard" in his memoir. [*Use a semicolon.*]

Using subordination to combine sentences of unequal importance

1. Consider putting the less important idea in a subordinate clause beginning with one of the following words. (See 48e.)

after	before	that	which
although	even though	unless	while
as	if	until	who
as if	since	when	whom
because	so that	where	whose

▶ _When_
Elizabeth Cady Stanton proposed a convention to discuss the status ^

of women in America,/ Lucretia Mott agreed.
^

▶ _that she_
My sister owes much of her recovery to a yoga program/ She began

the program three years ago.

2. Consider putting the less important idea in an appositive phrase. (See 48c.)

▶ Karate, is a discipline based on the philosophy of nonviolence,/
^ ^

It teaches the art of self-defense.

3. Consider putting the less important idea in a participial phrase. (See 48b.)

▶ _E_
American essayist Cheryl Peck was encouraged by friends to write
^
, American essayist Cheryl Peck
about her life/ She began combining humor and irony in her essays
^

about being overweight.

14b Combine choppy sentences.

Short sentences demand attention, so you should use them primarily for emphasis. Too many short sentences, one after the other, make for a choppy style.

If an idea is not important enough to deserve its own sentence, try combining it with a sentence close by. Put any minor ideas in subordinate structures such as phrases or subordinate clauses. (See 48.)

▶ The Parks Department keeps the use of insecticides to a

    because the
minimum/ ~~The~~ city is concerned about the environment.

The writer wanted to emphasize that the Parks Department minimizes
its use of chemicals, so she put the reason in a subordinate clause
beginning with *because*.

▶ The Chesapeake and Ohio Canal, ~~is~~ a 184-mile waterway

constructed in the 1800s/, ~~It~~ was a major source of

transportation for goods during the Civil War.

A minor idea is now expressed in an appositive phrase (*a 184-mile
waterway constructed in the 1800s*).

Although subordination is ordinarily the most effective
technique for combining short, choppy sentences, coordination
is appropriate when the ideas are equal in importance.

                                                       and
▶ On January 1, lawmakers raised the minimum wage/ ~~Lawmakers~~

opened doors for thousands of poor families.

Combining two short sentences by joining their predicates (*raised . . .
opened*) is an effective coordination technique.

Multilingual

Unlike some other languages, English does not repeat objects or
adverbs in adjective clauses. See 30d.

▶ The apartment that we rented ~~it~~ needed repairs.

The pronoun *it* cannot repeat the relative pronoun *that*.

Exercise 14–2 ▶ Combine the following sentences by subordinating
minor ideas or by coordinating ideas of equal importance. You must decide which ideas are minor because the sentences are given out of context. Possible revisions appear in the back of the book.

Agnes, ~~was~~ another girl I worked with/, ~~She~~ was a hyperactive

child.

a. The X-Men comic books and Japanese woodcuts of kabuki dancers were part of Marlena's research project on popular culture. They covered the tabletop and the chairs.

b. Our waitress was costumed in a kimono. She had painted her face white. She had arranged her hair in a lacquered beehive.

c. Students can apply for a spot in the leadership program. The program teaches thinking and communication skills.

d. Shore houses were flooded up to the first floor. Beaches were washed away. Brant's Lighthouse was swallowed by the sea.

e. Laura Thackray is an engineer at Volvo Car Corporation. She addressed women's safety needs. She designed a pregnant crash-test dummy.

14c Avoid ineffective or excessive coordination.

Coordinate structures are appropriate only when you intend to draw readers' attention equally to two or more ideas: *Professor Sakellarios praises loudly, and she criticizes softly.* If one idea is more important than another, or if a coordinating conjunction does not clearly signal the relationship between the ideas, you should subordinate the less important idea.

INEFFECTIVE COORDINATION	Closets were taxed as rooms, and most colonists stored their clothes in chests or clothespresses.
IMPROVED WITH SUBORDINATION	Because closets were taxed as rooms, most colonists stored their clothes in chests or clothespresses.

The revision subordinates the less important idea (*closets were taxed as rooms*) by putting it in a subordinate clause. Notice that the subordinating conjunction *Because* signals the relation between the ideas more clearly than the coordinating conjunction *and*.

Because it is so easy to string ideas together with *and*, writers often rely too heavily on coordination in their rough drafts. The cure for excessive coordination is simple: Look for opportunities to tuck minor ideas into subordinate clauses or phrases.

▶ ~~Four hours went by, and~~ a rescue truck finally arrived, but

    After four hours,

  by that time we had been evacuated in a helicopter.

Having three independent clauses was excessive. The least important idea has become a prepositional phrase.

Exercise 14–3 The following sentences show coordinated ideas (ideas joined with a coordinating conjunction or a semicolon). Restructure the sentences by subordinating minor ideas. You must decide which ideas are minor because the sentences are given out of context. Possible revisions appear in the back of the book.

> ~~where they~~
> **The rowers returned to shore, ~~and~~ had a party on the beach**
>   ^
> *to celebrate*
> **~~and celebrated~~ the start of the season.**
>   ^

a. These particles are known as "stealth liposomes," and they can hide in the body for a long time without detection.

b. Irena is a competitive gymnast and majors in biology; her goal is to apply her athletic experience and her science degree to a career in sports medicine.

c. Students, textile workers, and labor unions have loudly protested sweatshop abuses, so apparel makers have been forced to examine their labor practices.

d. IRC (Internet relay chat) was developed in a European university; it was created as a way for a group of graduate students to talk about projects from their dorm rooms.

e. The cafeteria's new menu has an international flavor, and it includes everything from pizza to pad thai.

14d Do not subordinate major ideas.

If a sentence buries its major idea in a subordinate construction, readers may not give the idea enough attention. Make sure to express your major idea in an independent clause and to subordinate any minor ideas.

> *As*
> ▶ **I was driving home from my new job, heading down**
>   ^
> **Ranchitos Road, ~~when~~ my car suddenly overheated.**

The writer wanted to emphasize that the car overheated, not the fact of driving home. The revision expresses the major idea in an independent clause and places the less important idea in an adverb clause (*As I was driving home from my new job*).

14e Do not subordinate excessively.

In attempting to avoid short, choppy sentences, writers sometimes go to the opposite extreme, putting more subordinate ideas into a sentence than its structure can bear. If a sentence lacks focus because it contains too many ideas, occasionally it can be restructured. More often, however, such sentences must be divided.

▶ Some professional athletes argue that they should not be looked

on as role models, <u>and that they</u> believe that modeling behavior
^These athletes^

is a parent's responsibility.

By splitting the original sentence in two, the writer makes it easier for the reader to focus on the main claim, that modeling behavior is a parent's job.

Exercise 14-4 ▶ In each of the following sentences, the idea that the writer wished to emphasize is buried in a subordinate construction. Restructure each sentence so that the independent clause expresses the major idea, as indicated in brackets, and lesser ideas are subordinated. Possible revisions appear in the back of the book.

Although
Catherine has weathered many hardships, ~~although~~ she has
^

rarely become discouraged. [*Emphasize that Catherine has*

rarely become discouraged.]

a. Gina helped the relief effort, distributing food and medical supplies. [*Emphasize distributing food and medical supplies.*]
b. Janbir spent every Saturday learning tabla drumming, noticing that with each hour of practice his memory for complex patterns was growing stronger. [*Emphasize Janbir's memory.*]
c. The rotor hit, gouging a hole about an eighth of an inch deep in my helmet. [*Emphasize that the rotor gouged a hole in the helmet.*]
d. My grandfather, who raised his daughters the old-fashioned way, was born eighty years ago in Puerto Rico. [*Emphasize how the grandfather raised his daughters.*]
e. The Narcan reversed the depressive effect of the drug, saving the patient's life. [*Emphasize that the patient's life was saved.*]

14f Experiment with techniques for gaining special emphasis.

By experimenting with certain techniques, usually involving some element of surprise, you can draw attention to ideas that deserve special emphasis. Use such techniques sparingly, however, or they will lose their punch.

Using sentence endings for emphasis

You can highlight an idea simply by withholding it until the end of a sentence. The technique works something like a punch line.

> The only completely consistent people are the dead.
>
> — Aldous Huxley

Using parallel structure for emphasis

Parallel grammatical structure draws attention to paired ideas or to items in a series. (See 9.) When parallel ideas are paired, the emphasis falls on words that underscore comparisons or contrasts, especially when they occur at the end of a phrase or clause.

> We must *stop talking* about the *American dream* and *start listening* to the *dreams of Americans.*
>
> — Reubin Askew

In a parallel series, the emphasis falls at the end, so it is generally best to end with the most climactic item in the series.

> My uncle often talks about growing up in Sudan — playing soccer, eating goat stew, and dodging bullets.
>
> — Alec Hamza, student

15 Provide some variety.

When a rough draft is filled with too many sentences that begin the same way or have the same structure, try injecting some variety — as long as you can do so without sacrificing clarity or ease of reading.

15a Vary your sentence openings.

Most sentences in English begin with the subject, move to the verb, and continue to the object, with modifiers tucked in along

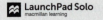

the way or put at the end. For the most part, such sentences are fine. Put too many of them in a row, however, and they become monotonous.

Adverbial modifiers are easily movable when they modify verbs; they can often be inserted ahead of the subject. Such modifiers might be single words, phrases, or clauses.

> Eventually a
> ▶ ~~A~~ few drops of sap ~~eventually~~ began to trickle into the bucket.
> ^

Like most adverbs, *eventually* does not need to appear close to the verb it modifies (*began*).

> Just as the sun was coming up, a
> ▶ ~~A~~ pair of black ducks flew over the pond~~.~~ ~~just as the sun was~~
> ^   ^
>
> ~~coming up.~~

The adverb clause, which modifies the verb *flew*, is as clear at the beginning of the sentence as it is at the end.

Adjectives and participial phrases can frequently be moved to the beginning of a sentence without loss of clarity.

> Dejected and down,
> ▶ Edward, ~~dejected and down,~~ nearly gave up his search for
> ^
>
> a job.

TIP: When beginning a sentence with an adjective or a participial phrase, make sure that the subject of the sentence names the person or thing described in the introductory phrase. If it doesn't, the phrase will dangle. (See 12e.)

15b Use a variety of sentence structures.

A writer should not rely too heavily on simple sentences and compound sentences, for the effect tends to be both monotonous and choppy. (See 14b and 14c.) Too many complex or compound-complex sentences, however, can be equally monotonous. If your style tends to one or the other extreme, try to achieve a better mix of sentence types.

The major sentence types are illustrated in the following sentences, all taken from Flannery O'Connor's "The King of the Birds."

SIMPLE	Frequently the cock combines the lifting of his tail with the raising of his voice.
COMPOUND	Any chicken's dusting hole is out of place in a flower bed, but the peafowl's hole, being the size of a small crater, is more so.
COMPLEX	The peacock does most of his serious strutting in the spring and summer when he has a full tail to do it with.
COMPOUND-COMPLEX	The cock's plumage requires two years to attain its pattern, and for the rest of his life, this chicken will act as though he designed it himself.

For a fuller discussion of sentence types, see 49a.

15c Try inverting sentences occasionally.

A sentence is inverted if it does not follow the normal subject-verb-object pattern. Many inversions sound artificial and should be avoided, except in the most formal contexts. But if an inversion sounds natural, it can provide a welcome touch of variety.

> *Set at the top two corners of the stage were huge*
> ► ~~Huge~~ lavender hearts outlined in bright white lights . ~~were set~~
>   ^   ^
>
> ~~at the top two corners of the stage.~~

In the revision, the subject, *hearts*, appears after the verb, *were set*. Notice that the two parts of the verb are also inverted — and separated from each other (*Set . . . were*) — without any awkwardness or loss of meaning.

Inverted sentences are used for emphasis as well as for variety (see 14f).

Exercise 15–1 Improve variety in each of the following sentences by using the technique suggested in brackets. Possible revisions appear in the back of the book.

> *To protect endangered marine turtles, fishing*
> ~~Fishing~~ crews place turtle excluder devices in fishing nets .
>   ^   ^
>
> ~~to protect endangered marine turtles.~~ [*Begin the sentence with*
>
> *the adverbial infinitive phrase.*]

a. The exhibits for insects and spiders are across the hall from the fossils exhibit. [*Invert the sentence.*]

b. Sayuri becomes a successful geisha after growing up desperately poor. [*Move the adverb clause to the beginning of the sentence.*]

c. Researchers have been studying Mount St. Helens for years. They believe that earthquakes may have caused the 1980 eruption. [*Combine the two sentences into a complex sentence.*]

d. Ice cream typically contains 10 percent milk fat. Premium ice cream may contain up to 16 percent milk fat and has less air in it. [*Combine the two sentences as a compound sentence.*]

e. The economy may recover quickly if home values climb. [*Move the adverb clause to the beginning of the sentence.*]

Exercise 15–2 Edit the following paragraph to increase sentence variety.

Making architectural models is a skill that requires patience and precision. It is an art that illuminates a design. Architects come up with a grand and intricate vision. Draftspersons convert that vision into blueprints. The model maker follows the blueprints. The model maker builds a miniature version of the structure. Modelers can work in traditional materials like wood and clay and paint. Modelers can work in newer materials like Styrofoam and liquid polymers. Some modelers still use cardboard, paper, and glue. Other modelers prefer glue guns, deformable plastic, and thin aluminum and brass wire. The modeler may seem to be making a small mess in the early stages of model building. In the end the modeler has completed a small-scale structure. Architect Rem Koolhaas has insisted that plans reveal the logic of a design. He has argued that models expose the architect's vision. The model maker's art makes this vision real.

16 Tighten wordy sentences.

Long sentences are not necessarily wordy, nor are short sentences always concise. A sentence is wordy if it can be tightened without loss of meaning.

16a Eliminate redundancies.

Writers often repeat themselves unnecessarily, thinking that expressions such as *cooperate together*, *yellow in color*, or *basic essentials* add emphasis to their writing. Such redundancies, though, do just the opposite. There is no need to say the same thing twice.

▶ Daniel ~~is now employed~~ at a private rehabilitation center ^{works}

~~working~~ as a registered physical therapist.

Though modifiers ordinarily add meaning to the words they modify, occasionally they are redundant.

▶ Gabriele Muccino's film *The Pursuit of Happyness* tells the story

of a single father determined ~~in his mind~~ to pull himself and his

son out of homelessness.

The word *determined* contains the idea that his resolution formed in his mind.

16b Avoid unnecessary repetition of words.

Though words may be repeated deliberately for effect, repetitions will seem awkward if they are clearly unnecessary. When a more concise version is possible, choose it.

▶ His third speech, delivered in Chicago, was ~~an~~ outstanding

~~speech.~~

▶ The best teachers help each student ~~become a better student~~ both ^{grow}

academically and emotionally.

16c Cut empty or inflated phrases.

An empty phrase can be cut with little or no loss of meaning. Common examples are introductory word groups that weaken the writer's authority by apologizing or hedging: *in my opinion, I think that, it seems that, one must admit that*, and so on.

▶ ~~In my opinion,~~ **Our current immigration policy is misguided.**

Readers understand without being told that they are hearing the writer's opinion.

Inflated phrases can be reduced to a word or two without loss of meaning.

INFLATED	CONCISE
along the lines of	like
as a matter of fact	in fact
at the present time	now (*or* currently)
at this point in time	now (*or* currently)
because of the fact that	because
by means of	by
due to the fact that	because
for the purpose of	for
have the ability to	be able to (*or* can)
in order to	to
in spite of the fact that	although (*or* though)
in the event that	if
in the final analysis	finally

16d Simplify the structure.

If the structure of a sentence is needlessly indirect, try simplifying it. Look for opportunities to strengthen the verb.

▶ **The analyst claimed that because of market volatility she could not ~~make an~~ estimate ~~of~~ the company's future profits.**

The verb *estimate* is more vigorous and concise than *make an estimate of*.

The colorless verbs *is*, *are*, *was*, and *were* often generate excess words.

► Investigators ~~were involved in studying~~ the effect of classical

music on unborn babies.

studied (insertion above *were involved in studying*)

> The revision is more direct and concise. The action (*studying*), originally appearing in a subordinate structure, has become a strong verb, *studied*.

The expletive constructions *there is* and *there are* (or *there was* and *there were*) can also lead to wordy sentences. The same is true of expletive constructions beginning with *it*.

► ~~There is~~ Another module ~~that~~ tells the story of Charles Darwin

and introduces the theory of evolution.

16e Reduce clauses to phrases, phrases to single words.

Word groups functioning as modifiers can often be made more compact. Look for opportunities to reduce clauses to phrases or phrases to single words.

► We took a side trip to Monticello, ~~which was~~ the home of

Thomas Jefferson.

► In ~~the~~ this essay, ~~that follows,~~ I argue against Kohn's claim that the

grading system discourages thinking, ~~which is a problematic~~

~~claim.~~ problematic

Exercise 16–1 ► Edit the following sentences to reduce wordiness. Possible revisions appear in the back of the book.

The Wilsons moved into the house ~~in spite of the fact that~~ the

back door was only ten yards from the train tracks.

even though

a. Martin Luther King Jr. was a man who set a high standard for future leaders to meet.

b. Alice has been deeply in love with cooking since she was little and could first peek over the edge of a big kitchen tabletop.

c. In my opinion, Bloom's race for the governorship is a futile exercise.

d. It is pretty important in being a successful graphic designer to have technical knowledge and at the same time an eye for color and balance.

e. Your task will be to set up digital mail communications capabilities for all employees in the company.

Exercise 16–2 Edit the following business memo to reduce wordiness.

To: District managers
From: Margaret Davenport, Vice President
Subject: Customer database

It has recently been brought to my attention that a percentage of our sales representatives have been failing to log reports of their client calls in our customer database each and every day. I have also learned that some representatives are not checking the database on a routine basis.

Our clients sometimes receive a multiple number of sales calls from us when a sales representative is not cognizant of the fact that the client has been contacted at a previous time. Repeated telephone calls from our representatives annoy our customers. These repeated telephone calls also portray our company as one that is lacking in organization.

Effective as of immediately, direct your representatives to do the following:

• Record each and every customer contact in the customer database at the end of each day, without fail.

• Check the database at the very beginning of each day to ensure that telephone communications will not be initiated with clients who have already been called.

Let me extend my appreciation to you for cooperating in this important matter.

17 Choose appropriate language.

Language is appropriate when it suits your subject, engages your audience, and reflects your natural way of speaking.

To some extent, your choice of language will be governed by the conventions of the genre in which you are writing. When in doubt about the conventions of a particular genre — lab reports, informal essays, business memos, and so on — consult your instructor or look at models written by experts in the field.

17a Avoid jargon, except in specialized writing situations.

Jargon is special language used among members of a trade, profession, or group. Use jargon only when readers will be familiar with it and only when plain English will not do as well.

JARGON	We outsourced the work to an outfit in Ohio because we didn't have the bandwidth to tackle it in-house.
REVISED	We hired a company in Ohio because we had too few employees to do the work.

Broadly defined, jargon includes puffed-up language designed more to impress readers than to inform them. The following are common examples from business, government, higher education, and the military, with plain English alternatives in parentheses.

ameliorate (improve)	optimal (best, most favorable)
commence (begin)	parameters (boundaries, limits)
components (parts)	peruse (read, look over)
endeavor (try)	prior to (before)
facilitate (help)	utilize (use)
indicator (sign)	viable (workable)

Sentences with jargon can be hard to read.

> The CEO should ~~dialogue~~ *talk* with investors about ~~partnering~~ *working* with
> clients to ~~purchase~~ *buy* land in ~~economically deprived zones.~~ *poor neighborhoods.*

17b Avoid pretentious language, most euphemisms, and "doublespeak."

Hoping to sound academic, some writers use large words and flowery phrases. Such pretentious language is so wordy that it obscures the writer's meaning.

> Taylor's ~~employment of multihued means of expression draws~~ *use of colorful language reveals that she has a* ~~back the curtains and lets slip the~~ nostalgic ~~vantage point~~ *view of* ~~from which she observes~~ American society.

Euphemisms, nice-sounding words or phrases substituted for words thought to sound harsh or ugly, are sometimes appropriate. Many cultures, for example, accept euphemisms when speaking or writing about excretion (*I have to go to the bathroom*), sexual intercourse (*They did not sleep together*), and the like. Most euphemisms, however, are needlessly evasive or even deceitful. Like pretentious language, they obscure the intended meaning.

EUPHEMISM	PLAIN ENGLISH
adult entertainment	pornography
chemical dependency	drug addiction
correctional facility	prison
economically deprived	poor
preowned automobile	used car
revenue enhancers	taxes

The term *doublespeak* applies to any deliberately evasive or deceptive language, including euphemisms. Doublespeak is especially common in politics and business. Torture is described as *enhanced interrogation*, for example, and *downsizing* really means "firing employees."

Exercise 17-1 ▶ Edit the following sentences to eliminate jargon, pretentious or flowery language, euphemisms, and doublespeak. You may need to make substantial changes in some sentences. Possible revisions appear in the back of the book.

> After two weeks in the legal department, Sue has ~~worked into~~ ^{mastered}
> the routine, ~~of the office,~~ and her ~~functional and self-~~ ^{office} ^{performance has^}
> ^ ^ ^
> ~~management skills have~~ exceeded all expectations.

a. In my youth, my family was under the constraints of difficult financial circumstances.

b. In order that I may increase my expertise in the area of delivery of services to clients, I feel that participation in this conference will be beneficial.

c. The prophetic meteorologist cautioned the general populace regarding the possible deleterious effects of the impending tempest.

d. Government-sanctioned investigations into the continued value of after-school programs indicate a perceived need in the public realm at large.

e. Passengers should endeavor to finalize the customs declaration form prior to exiting the aircraft.

Exercise 17-2 ▶ Edit the following email message to eliminate jargon.

Dear Ms. Jackson:

We members of the Nakamura Reyes team value our external partnering arrangements with Creative Software, and I look forward to seeing you next week at the trade show in Fresno. Per Mr. Reyes, please let me know when you'll have some downtime there so that he and I can conduct a strategizing session with you concerning our production schedule. It's crucial that we all be on the same page re our 2018–2019 product release dates.

Before we have some face time, however, I have some findings to share. Our customer-centric approach to the new products will necessitate that user testing periods trend upward. The enclosed data should help you effectuate any adjustments to your timeline; let me know ASAP if you require any additional information to facilitate the above.

Before we convene in Fresno, Mr. Reyes and I will agendize any further talking points. Thanks for your help.

Sincerely,

Sylvia Nakamura

17c In most contexts, avoid slang, regional expressions, and nonstandard English.

Slang is an informal and sometimes private vocabulary that expresses the unity of a group such as teenagers, rock musicians, or sports fans; it is subject to more rapid change than Standard English. For example, the slang teenagers use to express approval changes every few years; *cool, groovy, neat, awesome, sick,* and *dope* have replaced one another within the last several decades. Sometimes slang becomes so widespread that it is accepted as standard vocabulary. *Jazz,* for example, started out as slang but is now a standard term for a style of music.

Although slang has a certain vitality, it is an informal code that not everyone understands. Therefore, it is inappropriate in most academic writing.

▶ When the server crashed unexpectedly, *we lost* three hours of unsaved

data. ~~went down the tubes.~~

▶ The government's "filth" guidelines for food will ~~gross you out.~~ *disgust you.*

Regional expressions are common to a group in a geographic area. *Let's talk with the bark off* (for *Let's speak frankly*) is an expression in the southern United States, for example. Regional expressions have the same limitations as slang and are therefore inappropriate in most writing.

▶ John was four blocks from the house before he remembered to
turn off
~~cut~~ the headlights. ~~off.~~

Standard English is the language used in all academic, business, and professional fields. Nonstandard English is spoken by people with a common regional or social heritage. Although nonstandard English may be appropriate when spoken within a close group, it is out of place in academic writing.

▶ The governor said he ~~don't~~ *does not* know if he will approve the budget

without the clean air provision.

If you speak a nonstandard dialect, try to identify the ways in which your dialect differs from Standard English. Look especially for the following features of nonstandard English, which commonly cause problems in writing.

Misusing verb forms such as *began* and *begun* (See 27a.)

Leaving *-s* endings off verbs (See 27c.)

Leaving *-ed* endings off verbs (See 27d.)

Leaving out necessary verbs (See 27e.)

Using double negatives (See 26e.)

17d Choose an appropriate level of formality.

In deciding on a level of formality, consider both your subject and your audience. Does the subject demand a dignified treatment, or is a relaxed tone more suitable? Will readers be put off if you assume too close a relationship with them, or might you alienate them by seeming too distant?

For most college and professional writing, some degree of formality is appropriate. In a job application letter, for example, it is a mistake to sound too breezy and informal.

TOO INFORMAL	I'd like to get that sales job you've got on the website.
MORE FORMAL	I would like to apply for the position of sales manager posted on LinkedIn.

Informal writing is appropriate for private letters, personal email and text messages, and business correspondence between close associates. Like spoken conversation, informal writing allows contractions (*don't*, *I'll*) and colloquial words (*kids*, *kinda*). Vocabulary and sentence structure are rarely complex.

In choosing a level of formality, above all be consistent. When a writer's voice shifts from one level of formality to another, readers receive mixed messages.

▶ Jorge's pitching lesson ~~commenced~~ began with his famous curveball, ~~implemented~~ thrown by tucking the little finger behind the ball. Next he ~~elucidated~~ revealed the mysteries of the sucker pitch, a slow ball coming behind a fast windup.

Words such as *commenced* and *elucidated* are inappropriate for the subject matter, and they clash with informal terms such as *sucker pitch* and *fast windup*.

Exercise 17–3 Revise the following passage twice. First, use a level of formality appropriate for a newspaper editorial directed toward a general audience. Then use a level of formality appropriate for a blog post directed at young adults.

In pop culture, college grads who return home to live with the folks are seen as good-for-nothing losers who mooch off their families. And many older adults seem to feel that the trend of moving back home after school, which was rare in their day, is becoming too commonplace today. But society must realize that a cultural shift is taking place. Most young adults want to live on their own ASAP, but they graduate with heaps of debt and need some time to become financially stable. College tuition and the cost of housing have increased way more than salary increases in the past half century. Also, the job market is tighter and more jobs require advanced degrees than in the past. So before people go off on college graduates who move back into their parents' house for a spell, they must indeed consider all the facts.

17e Avoid sexist language.

Sexist and noninclusive language stereotypes or demeans women or men. Using nonsexist language is a matter of respect for and sensitivity to the feelings of others. As you write for different audiences, keep in mind that words matter, and always select words that show respect for your readers.

Recognizing sexist language

Some sexist language is easy to recognize because it reflects genuine contempt for women: referring to a woman as a "chick," for example, or calling a lawyer a "lady lawyer."

Other forms of sexist language are less blatant. The following practices, while they may not result from conscious sexism, reflect stereotypical thinking: referring to members of one profession as exclusively male or exclusively female (teachers as women or computer engineers as men, for instance) or using different conventions when naming or identifying women and men.

STEREOTYPICAL LANGUAGE

After a nursing student graduates, *she* must face a difficult state board examination. [Not all nursing students are women.]

Running for city council are Boris Stotsky, an attorney, and *Mrs. Cynthia Jones*, a professor of English and *mother of three*. [The title *Mrs.* and the phrase *mother of three* are irrelevant.]

Still other forms of sexist language result from outdated traditions. The pronouns *he*, *him*, and *his*, for instance, were traditionally used to refer generically to persons of either sex. To avoid sexist usage, some writers substitute the female pronouns (*she*, *her*, and *hers*) alternately with the male pronouns.

GENERIC PRONOUNS

A journalist is motivated by *his* deadline.

A good interior designer treats *her* clients' ideas respectfully.

But both forms are sexist — for excluding one sex entirely and for making assumptions about the members of particular professions.

Similarly, terms including *man* and *men* were once used to refer generically to persons of either sex. Current usage demands genderneutral terms for references to both men and women.

INAPPROPRIATE	APPROPRIATE
chairman	chairperson, moderator, chair, head
congressman	member of Congress, representative, legislator
fireman	firefighter
foreman	supervisor
mailman	mail carrier, postal worker, letter carrier
to man	to operate, to staff
mankind	people, humans
manpower	personnel, staff
policeman	police officer
weatherman	forecaster, meteorologist

Revising sexist language

When revising sexist language, you may be tempted to substitute *he or she* and *his or her*. This strategy is wordy and can become awkward when repeated throughout an essay. Also, some readers may think *he or she* or *his or her* excludes transgender individuals. A better revision strategy is to write in the plural; yet another strategy is to recast the sentence so that problems do not arise.

SEXIST

A journalist is motivated by *his* deadline.

A good interior designer treats *her* clients' ideas respectfully.

BETTER: USING THE PLURAL

Journalists are motivated by *their* deadlines.

Good interior designers treat *their* clients' ideas respectfully.

BETTER: REVISING THE SENTENCE

A journalist is motivated by *a* deadline.

A good interior designer treats clients' ideas respectfully.

For more examples of these revision strategies, see 22.

Exercise 17–4 Edit the following sentences to eliminate sexist language or sexist assumptions. Possible revisions appear in the back of the book.

Scholarship athletes   their
~~A scholarship athlete~~ must be as concerned about ~~his~~
                they are   their
academic performance as ~~he is~~ about ~~his~~ athletic performance.

a. Mrs. Geralyn Farmer, who is the mayor's wife, is the chief surgeon at University Hospital. Dr. Paul Green is her assistant.

b. Every applicant wants to know how much he will earn.

c. An elementary school teacher should understand the concept of nurturing if she intends to be effective.

d. An obstetrician needs to be available to his patients at all hours.

e. If man does not stop polluting his environment, mankind will perish.

Exercise 17–5 Eliminate sexist language or sexist assumptions in the following job posting for an elementary school teacher.

    We are looking for qualified women for the position of elementary school teacher. The ideal candidate should have a bachelor's degree, a state teaching certificate, and one year of student teaching. She should be knowledgeable in all elementary subject areas, including science and math. While we want our new teacher to have a commanding presence in the classroom, we are also looking for motherly characteristics such as patience and trustworthiness. She must be able to both motivate an entire classroom and work with each student one-on-one to assess his individual needs. She must also be comfortable communicating with the parents of her students. For salary and benefits information, including maternity leave policy, please contact the Martin County School Board. Any qualified applicant should submit her résumé by March 15.

17f Revise language that may offend groups of people.

Your writing should be respectful and free of stereotypical, biased, or other offensive language. Be especially careful when describing or labeling people. Labels can become dated, and it is important to recognize when their continued use is not acceptable. When naming groups of people, choose labels that the groups currently use themselves. For example, instead of *Eskimos*, use *Inuit*.

►   North Dakota takes its name from the ~~Indian~~ Lakota word meaning

"friend" or "ally."

►   Many ~~Oriental~~ Asian immigrants have recently settled in our town.

Negative stereotypes (such as "drives like a teenager") are of course offensive. But you should avoid stereotyping a person or a group even if you believe your generalization to be positive.

►   It was no surprise that Greer, ~~a Chinese American,~~ an excellent math and science student, was selected

for the honors chemistry program.

18 Find the exact words.

Two reference works (or their online equivalents) will help you find words to express your meaning exactly: a good dictionary, such as *The American Heritage Dictionary* or *Merriam-Webster* online, and a collection of synonyms and antonyms, such as *Roget's International Thesaurus*.

TIP: Do not turn to a thesaurus to find flowery or impressive words. Look for words that exactly express your meaning.

18a Select words with appropriate connotations.

In addition to their strict dictionary meanings (or *denotations*), words have *connotations*, emotional colorings that affect how readers respond to them. The word *steel* denotes "commercial iron that contains carbon," but it also calls up a cluster of images associated with steel. These associations give the word its connotations — cold, hard, smooth, unbending.

If the connotation of a word does not seem appropriate for your purpose, your audience, or your subject matter, you should change the word. When a more appropriate synonym does not come quickly to mind, consult a dictionary or a thesaurus.

▶ As I covered the boats with marsh grass, the ~~perspiration~~ *sweat* I had

worked up evaporated in the wind, and the cold morning air

seemed even colder.

The word *perspiration* is too dainty for the context, which suggests vigorous exercise.

Exercise 18–1   Use a dictionary and a thesaurus to find at least four synonyms for each of the following words. Be prepared to explain any slight differences in meaning.

1. decay (verb)
2. difficult (adjective)
3. hurry (verb)
4. pleasure (noun)
5. secret (adjective)
6. talent (noun)

18b Prefer specific, concrete nouns.

Unlike general nouns, which refer to broad classes of things, specific nouns point to particular items. *Film*, for example, names a general class, *fantasy film* names a narrower class, and *Alice through the Looking Glass* is more specific still. Other examples: *team, football team, Denver Broncos; music, symphony, Beethoven's Ninth.*

Unlike abstract nouns, which refer to qualities and ideas (*justice, beauty, realism*), concrete nouns point to immediate, often sensory experience and to physical objects (*steeple, lilac, stone*).

Specific, concrete nouns express meaning more vividly than general or abstract ones. Although general and abstract language is sometimes necessary to convey your meaning, use specific, concrete words when possible.

▶ The senator spoke about the challenges of the future:
   pollution, dwindling resources, and terrorism.
   ~~the environment and world peace.~~
   ^

Nouns such as *thing, area, aspect, factor,* and *individual* are especially dull and imprecise.

                                    motherhood, and memory.
▶ Toni Morrison's *Beloved* is about slavery, ~~among other things.~~
                                               ^

18c Do not misuse words.

If a word is not in your active vocabulary, you may find yourself misusing it, sometimes with embarrassing consequences. When in doubt, check the dictionary.

           climbing
▶ The fans were ~~migrating~~ up the bleachers in search of seats.
                ^

              permeated
▶ The Internet has so ~~diffused~~ our culture that it touches all
                      ^

segments of society.

Be especially alert for misused word forms — using a noun such as *absence* or *significance,* for example, when your meaning requires the adjective *absent* or *significant.*

             persistent
▶ Most dieters are not ~~persistence~~ enough to make a permanent
                       ^

change in their eating habits.

Exercise 18-2 ▶ Edit the following sentences to correct misused words. Possible revisions appear in the back of the book.

> These days the training required for a ballet dancer is
> all-absorbing.
> ~~all-absorbent.~~
> ^

a. We regret this delay; thank you for your patients.

b. Ada's plan is to require education and experience to prepare herself for a position as property manager.

c. Serena Williams, the penultimate competitor, has earned millions of dollars just in endorsements.

d. Many people take for granite that public libraries have up-to-date computer systems.

e. The affect of Gao Xinjian's novels on Chinese exiles is hard to gauge.

18d Use standard idioms.

Idioms are speech forms that follow no easily specified rules. The English say "Bernice went *to hospital*," an idiom strange to American ears, which are accustomed to hearing *the* in front of *hospital*. Native speakers of a language seldom have problems with idioms, but prepositions (such as *with*, *to*, *at*, and *of*) sometimes cause trouble, especially when they follow certain verbs and adjectives. When in doubt, consult a dictionary.

UNIDIOMATIC	IDIOMATIC
abide with (a decision)	abide by (a decision)
according with	according to
agree to (an idea)	agree with (an idea)
angry at (a person)	angry with (a person)
capable to	capable of
comply to	comply with
different than (a person or thing)	different from (a person or thing)
intend on doing	intend to do
off of	off
plan on doing	plan to do

UNIDIOMATIC	IDIOMATIC
preferable than	preferable to
similar than	similar to
sure and	sure to
think on	think of, about
try and	try to
type of a	type of

Multilingual

Because idioms follow no particular rules, you must learn them individually. You may find it helpful to keep a list of idioms that you frequently encounter in conversation and in reading.

Exercise 18–3 Edit the following sentences to eliminate errors in the use of idiomatic expressions. If a sentence is correct, write "correct" after it. Revisions appear in the back of the book.

> by
> **We agreed to abide with the decision of the judge.**
> ^

a. Queen Anne was so angry at Sarah Churchill that she refused to see her again.
b. Jean-Pierre's ambitious travel plans made it impossible for him to comply with the residency requirement for in-state tuition.
c. The parade moved off of the street and onto the beach.
d. The frightened refugees intend on making the dangerous trek across the mountains.
e. What type of a wedding are you planning?

18e Do not rely heavily on clichés.

The pioneer who first announced that he had "slept like a log" no doubt amused his companions with a fresh and unlikely comparison. Today, however, that comparison is a cliché, a saying that can no longer add emphasis or surprise.

To see just how predictable clichés are, put your hand over the right-hand column in the following list and then finish the phrases on the left.

avoid clichés like the	plague
beat around	the bush
busy as a	bee, beaver
cool as a	cucumber
crystal	clear
dead as a	doornail
light as a	feather
like a bull	in a china shop
out of the frying pan and	into the fire
playing with	fire
selling like	hotcakes
water under the	bridge

The solution for clichés is simple: Delete them or rewrite them.

▶ **When I received a full scholarship from my second-choice**
    felt pressured to settle for second best.
school, I ~~found myself between a rock and a hard place.~~
    ^

Sometimes you can write around a cliché by adding an element of surprise. One student, for example, who had written that she had butterflies in her stomach, revised her cliché like this:

If all of the action in my stomach is caused by butterflies, there must be a horde of them, with horseshoes on.

The image of butterflies wearing horseshoes is fresh and unlikely, not predictable like the original cliché.

18f Use figures of speech with care.

A figure of speech is an expression that uses words imaginatively (rather than literally) to make abstract ideas concrete. Most often, figures of speech compare two seemingly unlike things to reveal surprising similarities.

In a *simile*, the writer makes the comparison explicitly, usually by introducing it with *like* or *as*: *By the time cotton had to be picked, Grandfather's neck was as red as the clay he plowed.*

In a *metaphor*, the *like* or *as* is omitted, and the comparison is implied. For example, in the Old Testament Song of Solomon, a young woman compares the man she loves to a fruit tree: *With great delight I sat in his shadow, and his fruit was sweet to my taste*.

Although figures of speech are useful devices, writers sometimes use them without thinking through the images they evoke. The result is sometimes a *mixed metaphor*, the combination of two or more images that don't make sense together.

▶ **Our manager decided to put all controversial issues**

~~**in a holding pattern**~~ **on a back burner until after the**

annual meeting.

Here the writer is mixing airplanes and stoves. Simply deleting one of the images corrects the problem.

Exercise 18–4 Edit the following sentences to replace worn-out expressions and clarify mixed figures of speech. Possible revisions appear in the back of the book.

the color drained from his face.
When he heard about the accident, ~~he turned white as a sheet.~~
                                          ^

a. John stormed into the room like a bull in a china shop.

b. Some people insist that they'll always be there for you, even when they haven't been before.

c. The Cubs easily beat the Mets, who were in the soup early in the game today at Wrigley Field.

d. We ironed out the sticky spots in our relationship.

e. My mother accused me of beating around the bush when in fact I was just talking off the top of my head.

GRAMMAR

19 Repair sentence fragments.

A sentence fragment is a word group that pretends to be a sentence. Sentence fragments are easy to recognize when they appear out of context, like these:

> When the cat leaped onto the table.
>
> Running for the bus.

When fragments appear next to related sentences, however, they are harder to spot.

> We had just sat down to dinner. When the cat leaped onto the table.
>
> I tripped and twisted my ankle. Running for the bus.

Recognizing sentence fragments

To be a sentence, a word group must consist of at least one independent clause. An independent clause includes a subject and a verb, and it either stands alone or could stand alone.

To test whether a word group is a complete sentence or a fragment, use the flowchart in this section. By using the flowchart, you can see exactly why *When the cat leaped onto the table* is a fragment: It has a subject (*cat*) and a verb (*leaped*), but it begins with a subordinating word (*When*). *Running for the bus* is a fragment because it lacks a subject and a verb (*Running* is a verbal, not a verb). (See also 48b and 48e.)

Repairing sentence fragments

You can repair most fragments in one of two ways:

- Pull the fragment into a nearby sentence.
- Rewrite the fragment as a complete sentence.

> ► We had just sat down to dinner./~~When~~ ^{when} the cat leaped onto the table.

> ► I tripped and twisted my ankle. ^{Running for the bus,} ~~Running for the bus.~~

Test for fragments

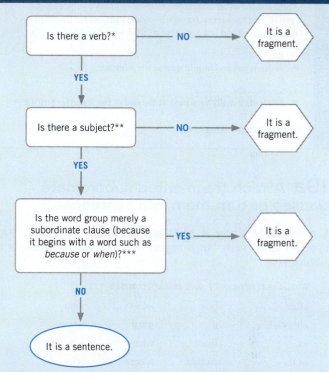

*Do not mistake verbals for verbs. A verbal is a verb form (such as *walking, to act*) that does not function as a verb of a clause. (See 48b.)

**The subject of a sentence may be *you*, understood but not present in the sentence. (See 47a.)

***A sentence may open with a subordinate clause, but the sentence must also include an independent clause. (See 19a and 49a.)

If you find any fragments, try one of these methods of revision (see 19a–19c):

1. Attach the fragment to a nearby sentence.
2. Rewrite the fragment as a complete sentence.

Unlike some other languages, English requires a subject and a verb in every sentence (except in commands, where the subject *you* is understood but not present: *Sit down*). See 30a and 30b.

It is
▶ ~~Is~~ often hot and humid during the summer.
   ^

                are
▶ Students usually very busy at the end of the semester writing
                ^

   papers and taking exams.

19a Attach fragmented subordinate clauses or turn them into sentences.

A subordinate clause is patterned like a sentence, with both a subject and a verb, but it begins with a word that marks it as subordinate.

WORDS THAT INTRODUCE SUBORDINATE CLAUSES

after	how	unless	who
although	if	until	whom
as	since	when	whose
as if	so that	where	why
because	than	whether	
before	that	which	
even though	though	while	

Subordinate clauses function within sentences as adjectives, as adverbs, or as nouns. They cannot stand alone. (See 48e.)

Most fragmented clauses can be pulled into a sentence nearby.

                                              because
▶ Americans have come to fear the West Nile virus/~~Because~~ it is
                                                       ^

   transmitted by the common mosquito.

Because introduces a subordinate clause, so it cannot stand alone. (For punctuation of subordinate clauses appearing at the end of a sentence, see 33f.)

▶ Although psychiatrist Peter Kramer expresses concerns

about Prozac/, ~~Many~~ other doctors believe that the
    many

benefits of antidepressants outweigh the risks.

Although introduces a subordinate clause, which cannot stand alone.
(For punctuation of subordinate clauses at the beginning of a sentence,
see 32b.)

If a fragmented clause cannot be attached to a nearby sentence or if attaching it would be awkward, try turning the clause
into a sentence. The simplest way to do this is to delete the opening word or words that mark the clause as subordinate.

▶ Uncontrolled development is taking a toll on the environment.
    Across
~~So that across~~ the globe, fragile ecosystems are collapsing.

19b Attach fragmented phrases or turn them into sentences.

Like subordinate clauses, phrases function within sentences as
adjectives, as adverbs, or as nouns. They cannot stand alone.
Fragmented phrases are often prepositional or verbal phrases;
sometimes they are appositives, words or word groups that rename nouns or pronouns. (See 48a, 48b, and 48c.)

Often a fragmented phrase may simply be pulled into a
nearby sentence.

▶ The archaeologists worked slowly/, ~~Examining~~ and labeling
    examining

every pottery shard they uncovered.

The word group beginning with *Examining* is a verbal phrase, so it
cannot stand alone.

▶ The patient displayed symptoms of ALS/, ~~A~~ neurodegenerative
    a

disease.

A neurodegenerative disease is an appositive renaming the noun *ALS*.
(For punctuation of appositives, see 32e.)

If a fragmented phrase cannot be pulled into a nearby sentence effectively, turn the phrase into a sentence. You may need to add a subject, a verb, or both.

▶ Jamie explained how to access our new database. ~~Also~~ how to *She also taught us*

submit expense reports and request vendor payments.

The revision turns the phrase into a sentence by adding a subject and a verb.

19c Attach other fragmented word groups or turn them into sentences.

Other word groups that are commonly fragmented include parts of compound predicates, lists, and examples introduced by *for example*, *in addition*, or similar expressions.

Parts of compound predicates

A predicate consists of a verb and its objects, complements, and modifiers (see 47b). A compound predicate includes two or more predicates joined with a coordinating conjunction such as *and*, *but*, or *or*. Because the parts of a compound predicate have the same subject, they should appear in the same sentence.

▶ The woodpecker finch carefully selects a twig of a certain size
and
and shape/ ~~And~~ then uses this tool to pry grubs from trees.

The subject is *finch*, and the compound predicate is *selects . . . and . . . uses*. (For punctuation of compound predicates, see 33a.)

Lists

To correct a fragmented list, often you can attach it to a nearby sentence with a colon or a dash. (See 35a and 39a.)

▶ It has been said that there are only three indigenous American art
musical
forms/: ~~Musical~~ comedy, jazz, and soap opera.

Sometimes terms like *especially*, *namely*, *like*, and *such as* introduce lists that are fragments. Such fragments can usually be attached to the preceding sentence.

▶ In the twentieth century, the South produced some great
American writers,/~~Such~~ **such** as Flannery O'Connor, William
Faulkner, Alice Walker, and Tennessee Williams.

Examples introduced by *for example, in addition,* or similar expressions

Other expressions that introduce examples or explanations can lead to unintentional fragments. Although you may begin a sentence with some of the following words or phrases, make sure that what follows has a subject and a verb.

also	for example	mainly
and	for instance	or
but	in addition	that is

Often the easiest solution is to turn the fragment into a sentence.

▶ In his memoir, Primo Levi describes the horrors of living in a
concentration camp. For example, **he worked** ~~working~~ without food and
suffered ~~suffering~~ emotional abuse.

The writer corrected this fragment by adding a subject — *he* — and substituting verbs for the verbals *working* and *suffering*.

19d Exception: A fragment may be used for effect.

Writers occasionally use sentence fragments for special purposes.

FOR EMPHASIS Following the dramatic Americanization of their children, even my parents grew more publicly confident. *Especially my mother.*

           — Richard Rodriguez

TO ANSWER A QUESTION	Are these new drug tests 100 percent reliable? *Not in the opinion of most experts.*
TRANSITIONS	*And now the opposing arguments.*
IN ADVERTISING	*Fewer carbs. Improved taste.*

Although fragments are sometimes appropriate, writers and readers do not always agree on when they are appropriate. That's why it is safer to write in complete sentences.

Exercise 19–1 Repair any fragment by attaching it to a nearby sentence or by rewriting it as a complete sentence. If a word group is correct, write "correct" after it. Possible revisions appear in the back of the book.

> One Greek island that should not be missed is Mykonos*/.* A vacation
>
> spot for Europeans and a playground for the rich and famous.

a. Listening to the CD her sister had sent, Mia was overcome with a mix of emotions. Happiness, homesickness, and nostalgia.

b. Cortés and his soldiers were astonished when they looked down from the mountains and saw Tenochtitlán. The magnificent capital of the Aztecs.

c. Although my spoken Spanish is not very good. I can read the language with ease.

d. There are several reasons for not eating meat. One reason being that dangerous chemicals are used throughout the various stages of meat production.

e. To learn how to sculpt beauty from everyday life. This is my intention in studying art and archaeology.

Exercise 19–2 Repair each fragment in the following passage by attaching it to a nearby sentence or by rewriting it as a complete sentence.

Digital technology has revolutionized information delivery. Forever blurring the lines between information and entertainment. Yesterday's readers of books and newspapers are today's readers of e-books and news blogs. Countless readers have moved on from print information entirely. Choosing instead to scroll their way through a text online or on an e-reader. Once a nation of people spoon-fed television commercials and the six o'clock evening news. We are now seemingly addicted to YouTube. Remember the family trip when Dad or Mom wrestled with a road map? On the way to St. Louis or Seattle? No wrestling is required with a GPS navigator by the driver's side. Unless it's Mom and Dad wrestling over who gets to program the address. Accessing information now seems to be America's favorite pastime. John Horrigan, associate director for research at the Pew Internet and American Life Project, reports that 31 percent of American adults are "elite" users of technology. Who are "highly engaged" with digital content. As a country, we embrace information and communication technologies. Which include iPads, smartphones, and tablets. Children rely on such devices and the Internet from an early age. For activities like socializing, gaming, and information gathering.

20 Revise run-on sentences.

Run-on sentences are independent clauses that have not been joined correctly. An independent clause is a word group that can stand alone as a sentence. (See 49a.) When two independent clauses appear in one sentence, they must be joined in one of these ways:

- with a comma and a coordinating conjunction (*and, but, or, nor, for, so, yet*)
- with a semicolon (or occasionally with a colon or a dash)

Recognizing run-on sentences

There are two types of run-on sentences. When a writer puts no mark of punctuation and no coordinating conjunction between independent clauses, the result is called a *fused sentence.*

|┌──────── INDEPENDENT CLAUSE ────────┐ ┌──── |
| FUSED   Air pollution poses risks to all humans it can be |
| ── INDEPENDENT CLAUSE ──┐ |
| deadly for asthma sufferers. |

A far more common type of run-on sentence is the *comma splice* — two or more independent clauses joined with a comma

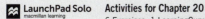

but without a coordinating conjunction. In some comma splices, the comma appears alone.

COMMA SPLICE Air pollution poses risks to all humans, it can be deadly for asthma sufferers.

In other comma splices, the comma is accompanied by a joining word that is *not* a coordinating conjunction. There are only seven coordinating conjunctions in English: *and, but, or, nor, for, so,* and *yet.*

COMMA SPLICE Air pollution poses risks to all humans, however, it can be deadly for asthma sufferers.

However is a transitional expression and cannot be used with only a comma to join two independent clauses (see 20b).

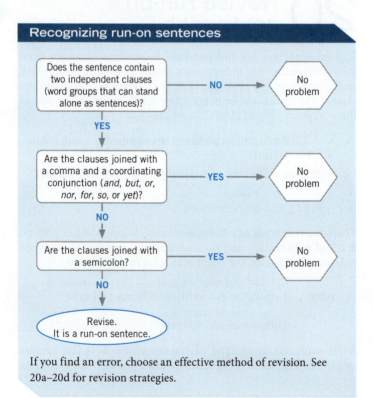

Recognizing run-on sentences

Does the sentence contain two independent clauses (word groups that can stand alone as sentences)? — **NO** → No problem

YES

Are the clauses joined with a comma and a coordinating conjunction (*and, but, or, nor, for, so,* or *yet*)? — **YES** → No problem

NO

Are the clauses joined with a semicolon? — **YES** → No problem

NO

Revise. It is a run-on sentence.

If you find an error, choose an effective method of revision. See 20a–20d for revision strategies.

Revising run-on sentences

To revise a run-on sentence, you have four choices.

1. Use a comma and a coordinating conjunction (*and*, *but*, *or*, *nor*, *for*, *so*, *yet*).

▶ Air pollution poses risks to all
   humans, ~~but~~ it can be deadly for
   people with asthma.

2. Use a semicolon (or, if appropriate, a colon or a dash). A semicolon may be used alone or with a transitional expression.

▶ Air pollution poses risks to all
   humans; it can be deadly for
   people with asthma.

▶ Air pollution poses risks to all
   humans; however, it can be deadly for
   people with asthma.

3. Make the clauses into separate sentences.

▶ Air pollution poses risks to all
   humans. It can be deadly for
   people with asthma.

4. Restructure the sentence, perhaps by subordinating one of the clauses.

▶ Although air pollution poses risks to all
   humans, it can be deadly for
   people with asthma.

One of these revision techniques usually works better than the others for a particular sentence. The fourth technique, the one requiring the most extensive revision, is often the most effective.

20a Consider separating the clauses with a comma and a coordinating conjunction.

There are seven coordinating conjunctions in English: *and*, *but*, *or*, *nor*, *for*, *so*, and *yet*. When a coordinating conjunction joins independent clauses, it is usually preceded by a comma. (See 32a.)

▶ Some lesson plans include exercises, ^but^ completing them should not

be the focus of all class periods.

▶ Many law enforcement officials admit that the polygraph is

unreliable, ^yet^ ~~however,~~ they still use it as an assessment tool.

However is a transitional expression, not a coordinating conjunction, so it cannot be used with only a comma to join independent clauses. (See also 20b.)

20b Consider separating the clauses with a semicolon, colon, or dash.

When the independent clauses are closely related and their relation is clear without a coordinating conjunction, a semicolon is an acceptable method of revision. (See 34a.)

▶ Tragedy depicts the individual confronted with the fact of

death^;^ comedy depicts the adaptability of human society.

A semicolon is required between independent clauses that have been linked with a transitional expression (such as *however, therefore, moreover, in fact,* or *for example*). For a longer list, see 34b.

▶ In his film adaptation, the director changed key details of the

plot^;^ in fact, he added whole scenes that do not appear in the story.

A colon or a dash may be more appropriate if the first independent clause introduces the second or if the second clause summarizes or explains the first. (See 35a and 39a.) In formal writing, the colon is usually preferred to the dash.

▶ Nuclear waste is hazardous^:^ this is an indisputable fact.

▶ The female black widow spider is often a widow of her own

making^—^ she has been known to eat her partner after mating.

A colon is an appropriate method of revision if the first independent clause introduces a quoted sentence.

▶ Nobel Peace Prize winner Al Gore had this to say about climate

change/: "The truth is that our circumstances are not only new;
　　　　^

they are completely different than they have ever been in all of

human history."

20c Consider making the clauses into separate sentences.

▶ Why should we spend money on expensive space
　　　　　　　　　　　We
exploration/? we have enough underfunded programs here
　　　　　　^

on Earth.

A question and a statement should be separate sentences.

NOTE: When two quoted independent clauses are divided by explanatory words, make each clause its own sentence.

▶ "It's always smart to learn from your mistakes," quipped my
　　　　　　　　　"It's
supervisor/. "it's even smarter to learn from the mistakes of
　　　　　　^

others."

20d Consider restructuring the sentence, perhaps by subordinating one of the clauses.

If one of the independent clauses is less important than the other, turn the less important clause into a subordinate clause or phrase. (For more about subordination, see the chart in 14a.)

▶ **One of the most famous advertising slogans is Wheaties cereal's**
which
"Breakfast of Champions," ~~it~~ associated the product with
‸

successful athletes.

▶ **Mary McLeod Bethune, ~~was~~ the seventeenth child of**
‸
former slaves, ~~she~~ founded the National Council of Negro

Women.

Minor ideas in these sentences are now expressed in subordinate clauses
or phrases.

Exercise 20–1 Revise the following run-on sentences using the
method of revision suggested in brackets. Possible revisions appear in
the back of the book.

Because
Daniel had been obsessed with his weight as a teenager, he
‸

rarely ate anything sweet. [*Restructure the sentence.*]

a. The city had one public swimming pool, it stayed packed with
children all summer long. [*Restructure the sentence.*]

b. The building is being renovated, therefore at times we have
no heat, water, or electricity. [*Use a comma and a coordinating
conjunction.*]

c. The view was not what the travel agent had described, where
were the rolling hills and the shimmering rivers? [*Make two
sentences.*]

d. Walker's coming-of-age novel is set against a gloomy scientific
backdrop, the earth's rotation has begun to slow down. [*Use a
semicolon.*]

e. City officials had good reason to fear a major earthquake, most of
the business district was built on landfill. [*Use a colon.*]

Exercise 20–2 Revise any run-on sentences using a technique
that you find effective. If a sentence is correct, write "correct" after it.
Possible revisions appear in the back of the book.

Crossing so many time zones on an eight-hour flight, I knew

but
I would be tired when I arrived, ~~however,~~ I was too excited to
^

sleep on the plane.

a. Wind power for the home is a supplementary source of energy, it can be combined with electricity, gas, or solar energy.

b. Aidan viewed Sofia Coppola's *Lost in Translation* three times and then wrote a paper describing the film as the work of a mysterious modern painter.

c. In the Middle Ages, the streets of London were dangerous places, it was safer to travel by boat along the Thames.

d. "He's not drunk," I said, "he's in a state of diabetic shock."

e. Are you able to endure extreme angle turns, high speeds, frequent jumps, and occasional crashes, then supermoto racing may be a sport for you.

Exercise 20-3 In the following rough draft, revise any run-on sentences.

Some parents and educators argue that requiring uniforms in public schools would improve student behavior and performance. They think that uniforms give students a more professional attitude toward school, moreover, they believe that uniforms help create a sense of community among students from diverse backgrounds. But parents and educators should consider the drawbacks to requiring uniforms in public schools.

Uniforms do create a sense of community, they do this, however, by stamping out individuality. Youth is a time to express originality, it is a time to develop a sense of self. One important way young people express their identities is through the clothes they wear. The self-patrolled dress code of high school students may be stricter than any school-imposed code, nevertheless, trying to control dress habits from above will only lead to resentment or to mindless conformity.

If children are going to act like adults, they need to be treated like adults, they need to be allowed to make their own choices. Telling young people what to wear to school merely prolongs their childhood. Requiring uniforms undermines the educational purpose of public schools, which is not just to teach facts and figures but to help young people grow into adults who are responsible for making their own choices.

21 Make subjects and verbs agree.

Verbs agree with their subjects in number (singular or plural) and in person (first, second, third): *I sing, you sing, he sings, she sings, we sing, they sing.* Even if your ear recognizes the standard subject-verb combinations presented in 21a, you will no doubt encounter tricky situations such as those described in 21b–21k.

21a Learn to recognize the standard subject-verb combinations.

This section describes the basic guidelines for making present-tense verbs agree with their subjects. The present-tense ending *-s* (or *-es*) is used on a verb if its subject is third-person singular (*he, she, it,* and singular nouns); otherwise, the verb takes no ending. Consider, for example, the present-tense forms of the verbs *love* and *try,* given at the beginning of the chart on page 182.

The verb *be* varies from this pattern; it has special forms in *both* the present and the past tense. These forms appear at the end of the chart.

If you aren't sure of the standard forms, use the charts on pages 182 and 183 as you proofread your work for subject-verb agreement. You may also want to look at 27c on *-s* endings of regular and irregular verbs.

21b Make the verb agree with its subject, not with a word that comes between.

Word groups often come between the subject and the verb. Such word groups, usually modifying the subject, may contain a noun that appears to be the subject. By mentally stripping away such modifiers, you can isolate the noun that is in fact the subject.

The *samples* on the tray in the lab *need* testing.

► High levels of air pollution cause$ damage to the respiratory

tract.

The subject is *levels*, not *pollution*. Strip away the phrase *of air pollution* to hear the correct verb: *levels cause*.

                                                    has
► The slaughter of pandas for their pelts ~~have~~ caused the panda
                                          ^

population to decline drastically.

The subject is *slaughter*, not *pandas* or *pelts*.

NOTE: Phrases beginning with the prepositions *as well as*, *in addition to*, *accompanied by*, and *along with* do not make a singular subject plural.

                                              was
► The governor as well as his press secretary ~~were~~ on the plane.
                                               ^

To emphasize that two people were on the plane, the writer could use *and* instead: *The governor and his press secretary were on the plane.*

21c Treat most subjects joined with *and* as plural.

A subject with two or more parts is said to be compound. If the parts are connected with *and*, the subject is almost always plural.

Leon and Jan often *jog* together.

► The Supreme Court's willingness to hear the case and its
                                                    have
affirmation of the original decision ~~has~~ set a new precedent.
                                     ^

EXCEPTION 1: When the parts of the subject form a single unit or when they refer to the same person or thing, treat the subject as singular.

Fish and chips was a last-minute addition to the menu.

Sue's friend and adviser was surprised by her decision.

Subject-verb agreement at a glance

Present-tense forms of *love* and *try* (typical verbs)

	SINGULAR		PLURAL	
FIRST PERSON	I	love	we	love
SECOND PERSON	you	love	you	love
THIRD PERSON	he/she/it*	loves	they**	love

	SINGULAR		PLURAL	
FIRST PERSON	I	try	we	try
SECOND PERSON	you	try	you	try
THIRD PERSON	he/she/it*	tries	they**	try

Present-tense forms of *have*

	SINGULAR		PLURAL	
FIRST PERSON	I	have	we	have
SECOND PERSON	you	have	you	have
THIRD PERSON	he/she/it*	has	they**	have

Present-tense forms of *do* (including negative forms)

	SINGULAR		PLURAL	
FIRST PERSON	I	do/don't	we	do/don't
SECOND PERSON	you	do/don't	you	do/don't
THIRD PERSON	he/she/it*	does/doesn't	they**	do/don't

Present-tense and past-tense forms of *be*

	SINGULAR		PLURAL	
FIRST PERSON	I	am/was	we	are/were
SECOND PERSON	you	are/were	you	are/were
THIRD PERSON	he/she/it*	is/was	they**	are/were

*And singular nouns (*child*, *Roger*)
**And plural nouns (*children*, *the Mannings*)

When to use the -s (or -es) form of a present-tense verb

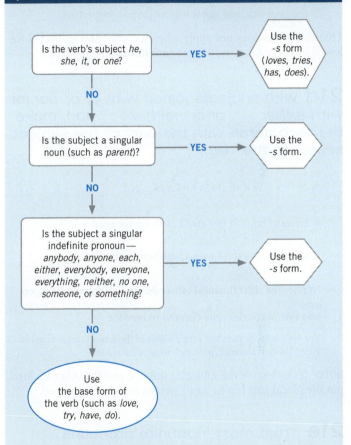

Is the verb's subject *he, she, it,* or *one*? — YES → Use the -s form (*loves, tries, has, does*).

NO ↓

Is the subject a singular noun (such as *parent*)? — YES → Use the -s form.

NO ↓

Is the subject a singular indefinite pronoun— *anybody, anyone, each, either, everybody, everyone, everything, neither, no one, someone,* or *something*? — YES → Use the -s form.

NO ↓

Use the base form of the verb (such as *love, try, have, do*).

EXCEPTION: Choosing the correct present-tense form of *be* (*am, is,* or *are*) is not quite so simple. See the chart on the previous page for both present- and past-tense forms of *be*.

TIP: Do not use the -s form of a verb if it follows a modal verb such as *can, must,* or *should* or another helping verb. (See 28c.)

EXCEPTION 2: When a compound subject is preceded by *each* or *every*, treat it as singular.

> Every car, truck, and van is required to pass inspection.

This exception does not apply when a compound subject is followed by *each*: *Alan and Marcia each have different ideas.*

21d With subjects joined with *or* or *nor* (or with *either . . . or* or *neither . . . nor*), make the verb agree with the part of the subject nearer to the verb.

> A driver's *license* or credit *card is* required.

> A driver's *license* or two credit *cards are* required.

> has
> ► If an infant or a child ~~have~~ a high fever, call a doctor.
>   ^

> ► Neither the chief financial officer nor the marketing managers
>   were
>   ~~was~~ able to convince the client to reconsider.
>   ^
> The verb must be matched with the part of the subject closer to it: *child has* in the first sentence, *managers were* in the second.

NOTE: If one part of the subject is singular and the other is plural, put the plural part last to avoid awkwardness.

21e Treat most indefinite pronouns as singular.

Indefinite pronouns, those that do not refer to specific persons or things, are singular.

COMMONLY USED INDEFINITE PRONOUNS

anybody	each	everyone	nobody	somebody
anyone	either	everything	no one	someone
anything	everybody	neither	nothing	something

Many of these words appear to have plural meanings, and they are often treated as plural in casual speech. In formal written English, however, they are nearly always treated as singular.

Everyone on the team *supports* the coach.

▶ Each of the essays ~~have~~ been graded.
     has

▶ Nobody who participated in the clinical trials ~~were~~ given a
     was

placebo.

The subjects of these sentences are *Each* and *Nobody.* These indefinite pronouns are third-person singular, so the verbs must be *has* and *was.*

A few indefinite pronouns (*all, any, none, some*) may be singular or plural depending on the noun or pronoun they refer to.

SINGULAR   *Some* of our *luggage was* lost.

               None of his *advice makes* sense.

PLURAL   *Some* of the *rocks are* slippery.

               None of the *eggs were* broken.

NOTE: When the meaning of *none* is emphatically "not one," *none* may be treated as singular: *None* [meaning "Not one"] *of the eggs was broken.* Using *not one* instead is sometimes clearer: *Not one of the eggs was broken.*

21f Treat collective nouns as singular unless the meaning is clearly plural.

Collective nouns such as *jury, committee, audience, crowd, troop, family,* and *couple* name a class or a group. In American English, collective nouns are nearly always treated as singular: They emphasize the group as a unit. Occasionally, when there is some reason to draw attention to the individual members of the group, a collective noun may be treated as plural. (See also 22b.)

SINGULAR   The *class respects* the teacher.

PLURAL   The *class are* debating among themselves.

To underscore the notion of individuality in the second sentence, many writers would add a clearly plural noun.

PLURAL   The class *members are* debating among themselves.

▶ The board of trustees ~~meet~~ *meets* in Denver twice a year.

The board as a whole meets; there is no reason to draw attention to its individual members.

▶ A young couple ~~was~~ *were* arguing about politics while holding hands.

The meaning is clearly plural. Only separate individuals can argue and hold hands.

NOTE: The phrase *the number* is treated as singular, *a number* as plural.

SINGULAR   *The number* of school-age children *is* declining.

PLURAL   *A number* of children *are* attending the wedding.

NOTE: In general, when fractions or units of measurement are used with a singular noun, treat them as singular; when they are used with a plural noun, treat them as plural.

SINGULAR   *Three-fourths* of the salad *has* been eaten.

Twenty *inches* of wallboard *was* covered with mud.

PLURAL   *One-fourth* of the drivers *were* texting.

Two *pounds* of blueberries *were* used to make the pie.

21g Make the verb agree with its subject even when the subject follows the verb.

Verbs ordinarily follow subjects. When this order is reversed, it is easy to become confused. Sentences beginning with *there is* or *there are* (or *there was* or *there were*) are inverted; the subject follows the verb.

> There *are* surprisingly few *honeybees* left in southern China.

> ▶ There ~~was~~ **were** a social worker and a journalist at the meeting.
>
> The subject, *worker and journalist*, is plural, so the verb must be *were*.

Occasionally, you may decide to invert a sentence for variety or effect. When you do so, check to make sure that your subject and verb agree.

> ▶ Of particular concern ~~is~~ **are** penicillin and tetracycline, antibiotics
>
> used to make animals more resistant to disease.
>
> The subject, *penicillin and tetracycline*, is plural, so the verb must be *are*.

21h Make the verb agree with its subject, not with a subject complement.

One basic sentence pattern in English consists of a subject, a linking verb, and a subject complement: *Jack is a lawyer.* Because the subject complement (*lawyer*) names or describes the subject (*Jack*), it is sometimes mistaken for the subject. (See 47b on subject complements.)

> These *exercises are* a way to test your ability to perform under pressure.

> ▶ A tent and a sleeping bag ~~is~~ **are** the required equipment.
>
> *Tent and bag* is the subject, not *equipment*.

▶ A major force in today's economy ~~are~~ ^{is} children — as consumers,

decision makers, and trend spotters.

> *Force* is the subject, not *children*. If the corrected version seems too
> awkward, make *children* the subject: *Children are a major force in today's
> economy — as consumers, decision makers, and trend spotters.*

21i *Who, which,* and *that* take verbs that agree with their antecedents.

Like most pronouns, the relative pronouns *who, which,* and
that have antecedents, nouns or pronouns to which they refer.
Relative pronouns used as subjects of subordinate clauses take
verbs that agree with their antecedents.

ANT   PN   V
Take a *course that prepares* you for classroom management.

One of the

Constructions such as *one of the students who* [or *one of the things
that*] cause problems for writers. Do not assume that the antecedent must be *one*. Instead, consider the logic of the sentence.

▶ Our ability to use language is one of the things that sets us

apart from animals.

> The antecedent of *that* is *things*, not *one*. Several things set us apart from
> animals.

Only one of the

When the phrase *the only* comes before *one*, you are safe in
assuming that *one* is the antecedent of the relative pronoun.

▶ Veronica was the only one of the first-year Spanish students

^{was}
who ~~were~~ fluent enough to apply for the exchange program.

> The antecedent of *who* is *one*, not *students*. Only one student was fluent
> enough.

21j Words such as *athletics*, *economics*, *mathematics*, and *news* are usually singular, despite their plural form.

> is
> ▶ Politics ~~are~~ among my mother's favorite pastimes.
>   ^

EXCEPTION: Occasionally some of these words, especially *economics, mathematics, politics,* and *statistics,* have plural meanings: *Office politics often sway decisions about hiring and promotion. The economics of the building plan are prohibitive.*

21k Titles of works, company names, words mentioned as words, and gerund phrases are singular.

> describes
> ▶ *Lost Cities* ~~describe~~ the discoveries of fifty ancient civilizations.
>   ^

> specializes
> ▶ Delmonico Brothers ~~specialize~~ in organic produce.
>   ^

> is
> ▶ *Controlled substances* ~~are~~ a legal term for illegal drugs.
>   ^

A gerund phrase consists of an *-ing* verb form followed by any objects, complements, or modifiers (see 48b). Treat gerund phrases as singular.

> makes
> ▶ Encountering long wait times ~~make~~ customers impatient.
>   ^

Exercise 21–1 ▶ Edit the following sentences to eliminate problems with subject-verb agreement. If a sentence is correct, write "correct" after it. Answers appear in the back of the book.

> were
> Jack's first days in the infantry ~~was~~ grueling.
>   ^

a. One of the main reasons for elephant poaching are the profits received from selling the ivory tusks.

b. Not until my interview with Dr. Hwang were other possibilities opened to me.

c. A number of students in the seminar was aware of the importance of joining the discussion.

d. Batik cloth from Bali, blue and white ceramics from Delft, and a bocce ball from Turin has made Angelie's room the talk of the dorm.

e. The board of directors, ignoring the wishes of the neighborhood, has voted to allow further development.

Exercise 21-2   For each sentence in the following passage, underline the subject (or compound subject) and then select the verb that agrees with it. (If you have trouble identifying the subject, consult 47a.)

Loggerhead sea turtles (migrate / migrates) thousands of miles before returning to their nesting location every two to three years. The nesting season for loggerhead turtles (span / spans) the hottest months of the summer. Although the habitat of Atlantic loggerheads (range / ranges) from Newfoundland to Argentina, nesting for these turtles (take / takes) place primarily along the southeastern coast of the United States. Female turtles that have reached sexual maturity (crawl / crawls) ashore at night to lay their eggs. The cavity that serves as a nest for the eggs (is / are) dug out with the female's strong flippers. Deposited into each nest (is / are) anywhere from fifty to two hundred spherical eggs, also known as a *clutch*. After a two-month incubation period, all eggs in the clutch (begin / begins) to hatch, and within a few days the young turtles attempt to make their way into the ocean. A major cause of the loggerhead's decreasing numbers (is / are) natural predators such as raccoons, birds, and crabs. Beach erosion and coastal development also (threaten / threatens) the turtles' survival. For example, a crowd of curious humans or lights from beachfront residences (is / are) enough to make the female abandon her nesting plans and return to the ocean. Since only one in one thousand loggerheads (survive / survives) to adulthood, special care should be taken to protect this threatened species.

22 Make pronouns and antecedents agree.

A pronoun is a word that substitutes for a noun. Many pronouns have antecedents, nouns or pronouns to which they refer. A pronoun and its antecedent agree when they are both singular or both plural.

| SINGULAR | Dr. Ava Berto finished *her* rounds. |
| PLURAL | The hospital *interns* finished *their* rounds. |

> **Multilingual**
>
> The pronouns *he, his, she, her, it,* and *its* must agree in gender (masculine, feminine, or neuter) with their antecedents, not with the words they modify.
>
> *Steve* visited *his* [not *her*] sister in Seattle.

22a In general, use singular pronouns to refer to singular antecedents.

Writers are frequently tempted to use plural pronouns to refer to two kinds of singular antecedents: indefinite pronouns and generic nouns.

Indefinite pronouns

Indefinite pronouns refer to nonspecific persons or things. Even though some of the following indefinite pronouns may seem to have plural meanings, treat them as singular in formal English.

anybody	each	everyone	nobody	somebody
anyone	either	everything	no one	someone
anything	everybody	neither	nothing	something

Traditionally, indefinite pronouns have been treated as singular in formal English. Using a singular pronoun to refer to an indefinite pronoun can result in a sentence that is sexist, and the traditional alternative (*he or she*) is now often considered noninclusive.

SEXIST	*Everyone* performs at *his* own fitness level.
SEXIST	*Everyone* performs at *her* own fitness level.
NONINCLUSIVE	*Everyone* performs at *his or her* own fitness level.

Using *he/his* or *she/her* to refer generically to any person is considered sexist. Using *he or she* or *his or her* is wordy, and it doesn't include people who prefer not to refer to themselves as *he* or *she*. It is therefore becoming increasingly acceptable in many contexts, including formal writing, to use the plural pronoun *they* to refer to an indefinite pronoun: *everyone performs at their own fitness level.* (Check with your instructor for any preferences.)

The following are usually your best options for revision.

1. Make the antecedent plural.
2. Rewrite the sentence so that no problem of agreement exists.
3. Use the plural pronoun *they* to refer to the singular antecedent.

► When ~~someone travels~~ people travel outside the United States for the first

time, ~~he needs~~ they need to apply for a passport.

► ~~When someone travels outside the United States for the first time,~~ Anyone who travels outside the United States for the first time

~~he~~ needs to apply for a passport.

► When someone travels outside the United States for the first time,

~~he needs~~ they need to apply for a passport.

If you change a pronoun from singular to plural (or vice versa), check to be sure that the verb agrees with the new pronoun (see 21e).

See 17e for more on avoiding sexist language.

NOTE: When using pronouns to refer to people, choose the pronouns that people would use to refer to themselves. Doing so shows respect and communicates your audience awareness. Some transgender and gender-fluid individuals refer to themselves by new pronouns (*ze/hir*, for example), but if you are unfamiliar with such preferences, *they* and *them* are acceptable gender-neutral options.

Generic nouns

A generic noun represents a typical member of a group, such as a typical student, or any member of a group, such as a lawyer. Although generic nouns may seem to have plural meanings, they traditionally have been considered singular. However, you should avoid using *he* to refer to generic nouns, as in *A runner must train if he wants to excel.* As with indefinite pronouns, the singular use of *they* is becoming increasingly acceptable with generic nouns.

When you have trouble with generic nouns, you will usually have the same revision options as mentioned in the previous section on indefinite pronouns.

> Medical students   they need
> ▶ ~~A medical student~~ must study hard if ~~he wants~~ to succeed.
>   ^   ^

> ▶ A medical student must study hard ~~if he wants~~ to succeed.

>   they want
> ▶ A medical student must study hard if ~~he wants~~ to succeed.
>   ^

22b Treat collective nouns as singular unless the meaning is clearly plural.

Collective nouns such as *jury, committee, audience, crowd, class, troop, family, team,* and *couple* name a group. Ordinarily the group functions as a unit, so the noun should be treated as singular; if the members of the group function as individuals, however, the noun should be treated as plural. (See also 21f.)

AS A UNIT   The *committee* granted *its* permission to build.

AS INDIVIDUALS   The *committee* put *their* signatures on the document.

When treating a collective noun as plural, many writers prefer to add a clearly plural antecedent such as *members* to the sentence: *The members of the committee put their signatures on the document.*

>   its
> ▶ After only an hour of deliberation, the jury returned ~~their~~
>   ^
>
> verdict.

There is no reason to draw attention to the individual members of the jury, so *jury* should be treated as singular.

22c Treat most compound antecedents joined with *and* as plural.

In 1987, *Reagan and Gorbachev* held a summit where *they* signed the Intermediate-Range Nuclear Forces Treaty.

22d With compound antecedents joined with *or* or *nor* (or with *either . . . or* or *neither . . . nor*), make the pronoun agree with the nearer antecedent.

Either *Bruce* or *Tom* should receive first prize for *his* poem.

Neither the *mouse* nor the *rats* could find *their* way through the maze.

NOTE: If one of the antecedents is singular and the other plural, as in the second example, put the plural antecedent last to avoid awkwardness.

EXCEPTION: If one antecedent is male and the other female, do not follow the traditional rule. The sentence *Either Bruce or Elizabeth should receive first prize for her short story* makes no sense. The best solution is to recast the sentence: *The prize for best short story should go to either Bruce or Elizabeth.*

Exercise 22–1 Edit the following sentences to eliminate problems with pronoun-antecedent agreement. Most of the sentences can be revised in more than one way, so experiment before choosing a solution. If a sentence is correct, write "correct" after it. Possible revisions appear in the back of the book.

> Recruiters
> ~~The recruiter~~ may tell the truth, but there is much that they
> ^
> choose not to tell.

a. Every presidential candidate must appeal to a wide variety of ethnic and social groups if they want to win the election.

b. Either Tom Hanks or Harrison Ford will win an award for their lifetime achievement in cinema.

c. The aerobics teacher motioned for everyone to move their arms in wide, slow circles.

d. The parade committee was unanimous in its decision to allow all groups and organizations to join the festivities.

e. The applicant should be bilingual if they want to qualify for this position.

Exercise 22-2 Edit the following paragraph to eliminate problems with pronoun-antecedent agreement or sexist language.

A common practice in businesses is to put each employee in their own cubicle. A typical cubicle resembles an office, but their walls don't reach the ceiling. Many office managers feel that a cubicle floor plan has its advantages. Cubicles make a large area feel spacious. In addition, they can be moved around so that each new employee can be accommodated in his own work area. Of course, the cubicle model also has problems. The typical employee is not as happy with a cubicle as they would be with a traditional office. Also, productivity can suffer. Neither a manager nor a frontline worker can ordinarily do their best work in a cubicle because of noise and lack of privacy. Each worker can hear his neighbors tapping on computer keyboards, making telephone calls, and muttering under their breath.

23 Make pronoun references clear.

Pronouns substitute for nouns; they are a kind of shorthand. In a sentence like *After Andrew intercepted the ball, he kicked it as hard as he could,* the pronouns *he* and *it* substitute for the nouns *Andrew* and *ball.* The word a pronoun refers to is called its *antecedent.*

23a Avoid ambiguous or remote pronoun reference.

Ambiguous pronoun reference occurs when a pronoun could refer to two possible antecedents.

▶ *The pitcher broke when Gloria set it*
~~When Gloria set the pitcher~~ on the glass-topped table~~/. it broke.~~
  ^   ^

▶ Tom told James, <del>that he had</del> won the lottery." *"You have*

What broke — the pitcher or the table? Who won the lottery — Tom or James? The revisions eliminate the ambiguity.

Remote pronoun reference occurs when a pronoun is too far away from its antecedent for easy reading.

▶ After the court ordered my ex-husband to pay child support,

he refused. Eight months later, the judge ordered him to make

payments directly to the court, which would in turn pay me.

After six months, payments stopped. Again <del>he</del> was summoned to *my ex-husband*

appear in court; he did not respond.

The pronoun *he* was too distant from its antecedent, *ex-husband*, which appeared several sentences earlier.

23b Generally, avoid making broad references with *this*, *that*, *which*, and *it*.

For clarity, the pronouns *this*, *that*, *which*, and *it* should ordinarily refer to specific antecedents rather than to whole ideas or sentences. When a pronoun's reference is needlessly broad, either replace the pronoun with a noun or supply an antecedent to which the pronoun clearly refers.

▶ With advertising, pharmaceutical companies gain exposure for

their prescription drugs. Patients respond to <del>this</del> by requesting *the ads*

drugs they might not need.

The writer substituted the noun *ads* for the pronoun *this*, which referred broadly to the idea expressed in the preceding sentence.

▶ Romeo and Juliet were both too young to have acquired much

wisdom, <del>and</del> that accounts for their rash actions. *a fact*

The writer added an antecedent (*fact*) that the pronoun *that* clearly refers to.

23c Do not use a pronoun to refer to an implied antecedent.

A pronoun should refer to a specific antecedent, not to a word that is implied but not present in the sentence.

the braids
▶ After braiding Ann's hair, Sue decorated ~~them~~ with ribbons.
                                              ^

The pronoun *them* referred to Ann's braids (implied by the term *braiding*), but the word *braids* did not appear in the sentence.

Modifiers, such as possessives, cannot serve as antecedents. A modifier may strongly imply the noun that a pronoun might logically refer to, but it is not itself that noun.

Jamaica Kincaid
▶ In ~~Jamaica Kincaid's~~ "Girl," ~~she~~ describes the advice a mother
                                    ^

gives her daughter, including the mysterious warning not

to be "the kind of woman who the baker won't let near the

bread" (454).

Using the possessive form of an author's name to introduce a source leads to a problem later in this sentence: The pronoun *she* cannot refer logically to a possessive modifier (*Jamaica Kincaid's*). The revision substitutes the noun *Jamaica Kincaid* for the pronoun *she,* thereby eliminating the problem. (For more on writing with sources in MLA style, see 55.)

23d Avoid the indefinite use of *they, it,* and *you*.

Do not use the pronoun *they* to refer indefinitely to persons who have not been specifically mentioned. *They* should always refer to a specific antecedent.

the school board
▶ In June, ~~they~~ voted to charge a fee for students to participate in
           ^

sports and music programs.

The word *it* should not be used indefinitely in constructions such as *In the article, it says that.* . . . In academic writing, be clear about who is doing the "saying": *In her article, Hood argues that.* . . .

The pronoun *you* is appropriate only when the writer is addressing the reader directly: *Once you have signed the form, return it to your adviser.* Except in informal contexts, however, *you* should not be used to mean "anyone in general." Use a noun instead.

▶ Etiquette experts advise that ~~you should~~ not arrive at a party too

               ^a guest

early or leave too late.

23e To refer to persons, use *who*, *whom*, or *whose*, not *which* or *that*.

In most contexts, use *who*, *whom*, or *whose* to refer to persons, *which* or *that* to refer to animals or things. It is impolite to use *which* or *that* to refer to people.

▶ During the two-day festival El Día de los Muertos (Day of the

                           who
Dead), Mexican families celebrate loved ones ~~that~~ have died.
                                     ^

Exercise 23–1 ▶ Edit the following sentences to correct errors in pronoun reference. In some cases, you will need to decide on an antecedent that the pronoun might logically refer to. Possible revisions appear in the back of the book.

    Although Apple makes the most widely recognized

    smartphone, other companies have gained a share of the

        The competition
    market. ~~This~~ has kept prices from skyrocketing.
         ^

a. They say that engineering students should have hands-on experience with dismantling and reassembling machines.

b. She had decorated her living room with posters from chamber music festivals. This led her date to believe that she was interested in classical music. Actually, she preferred rock.

c. In my high school, you didn't need to get all A's to be considered a success; you just needed to work to your ability.

d. Marianne told Jenny that she was worried about her mother's illness.

e. Though Lewis cried for several minutes after scraping his knee, eventually it subsided.

Exercise 23–2 Edit the following passage to correct errors in pronoun reference. In some cases, you will need to decide on an antecedent that the pronoun might logically refer to.

Since its launch in the 1980s, the Internet has grown to be one of the largest communications forums in the world. The Internet was created by a team of academics who were building on a platform that government scientists had started developing in the 1950s. They initially viewed it as a noncommercial enterprise that would serve only the needs of the academic and technical communities. But with the introduction of user-friendly browser technology in the 1990s, it expanded tremendously. By the late 1990s, many businesses were connecting to the Internet with high-speed broadband and fiber-optic connections, which is also true of many home users today. Accessing information, shopping, and communicating are easier than ever before. This, however, can lead to some possible drawbacks. You forfeit privacy when you search, shop, and communicate. They say that avoiding disclosure of personal information and routinely adjusting your privacy settings on social media sites are the best ways to protect yourself on the Internet.

24 Distinguish between pronouns such as *I* and *me*.

The personal pronouns in the following chart change what is known as *case form* according to their grammatical function in a sentence. Pronouns functioning as subjects or subject complements appear in the *subjective* case; those functioning as objects appear in the *objective* case; and those showing ownership appear in the *possessive* case.

	SUBJECTIVE CASE	OBJECTIVE CASE	POSSESSIVE CASE
SINGULAR	I	me	my
	you	you	your
	he/she/it	him/her/it	his/her/its
PLURAL	we	us	our
	you	you	your
	they	them	their

Pronouns in the subjective and objective cases are frequently confused. Most of the rules in this section specify when to use one or the other of these cases. Section 24f explains a special use of pronouns and nouns in the possessive case.

24a Use the subjective case (*I, you, he, she, it, we, they*) for subjects and subject complements.

When personal pronouns are used as subjects, ordinarily your ear will tell you the correct pronoun. Problems sometimes arise, however, with compound word groups containing a pronoun.

▶ Joel left because his stepfather and ~~him~~ *he* had argued.

> *His stepfather and he* is the subject of the verb *had argued.* If we strip away the words *his stepfather and,* the correct pronoun becomes clear: *he had argued* (not *him had argued*).

When a pronoun is used as a subject complement (a word following a linking verb), your ear may mislead you, since the incorrect form is frequently heard in casual speech. (See "Linking verbs and subject complements," 47b.)

▶ During the Lindbergh trial, Bruno Hauptmann repeatedly
denied that the kidnapper was ~~him.~~ *he.*

> If *kidnapper was he* seems too stilted, rewrite the sentence: . . . *Bruno Hauptmann repeatedly denied that he was the kidnapper.*

24b Use the objective case (*me, you, him, her, it, us, them*) for all objects.

When a personal pronoun is used as a direct object, an indirect object, or the object of a preposition, ordinarily your ear will lead you to the correct pronoun. When an object is compound, however, you may occasionally become confused.

▶ The most traumatic experience for her father and ~~I~~ *me* occurred
long after her operation.

> *Her father and me* is the object of the preposition *for.* Strip away the words *her father and* to test for the correct pronoun: *for me* (not *for I*).

When in doubt about the correct pronoun, some writers try to avoid making the choice by using a reflexive pronoun such as *myself.* Using a reflexive pronoun in such situations is nonstandard.

▶ Nidra gave my cousin and ~~myself~~ *me* some good tips on traveling in

New Delhi.

> *My cousin and me* is the indirect object of the verb *gave.* For correct uses of *myself,* see the glossary of usage in the appendixes.

24c Put an appositive and the word to which it refers in the same case.

Appositives are noun phrases that rename nouns or pronouns. A pronoun used as an appositive has the same function (usually subject or object) as the word(s) it renames.

▶ The managers, Dr. Bell and ~~me,~~ *I,* could not agree on a plan.

> The appositive *Dr. Bell and I* renames the subject, *managers.* Test: *I could not agree* (not *me could not agree*).

▶ The reporter interviewed only two witnesses, the bicyclist and ~~I.~~ *me.*

> The appositive *the bicyclist and me* renames the direct object, *witnesses.* Test: *interviewed me* (not *interviewed I*).

24d Following *than* or *as,* choose the pronoun that expresses your meaning.

When a comparison begins with *than* or *as,* your choice of a pronoun will depend on your intended meaning. To test for the correct pronoun, mentally complete the sentence: *My roommate likes football more than I [do].*

▶ In our report on nationalized health care in the United States,

we argued that Canadians are much better off than ~~us.~~ *we.*

> *We* is the subject of the verb *are,* which is understood: *Canadians are much better off than we [are].* If the correct English seems too formal, you can always add the verb.

> ► We respected no other candidate as much as ~~she.~~ *her.*

This sentence means that we respected no other candidate as much as *we respected her. Her* is the direct object of the understood verb *respected*.

24e Use the objective case for subjects and objects of infinitives.

An infinitive is the word *to* followed by the base form of a verb. (See 48b.) Subjects of infinitives are an exception to the rule that subjects must be in the subjective case. Whenever an infinitive has a subject, it must be in the objective case. Objects of infinitives also are in the objective case.

> ► Sue asked John and ~~I~~ *me* to drive the senator and ~~she~~ *her* to the airport.

John and me is the subject of the infinitive *to drive; senator and her* is the direct object of the infinitive.

24f Use the possessive case to modify a gerund.

A pronoun that modifies a gerund or a gerund phrase should be in the possessive case (*my, our, your, his, her, its, their*). A gerund is a verb form ending in *-ing* that functions as a noun. Gerunds frequently appear in phrases; when they do, the whole gerund phrase functions as a noun. (See 48b.)

> ► The chances of ~~you~~ *your* being hit by lightning are slim.

Your modifies the gerund phrase *being hit by lightning*.

Nouns as well as pronouns may modify gerunds. To form the possessive case of a noun, use an apostrophe and an *-s* (*victim's*) or just an apostrophe (*victims'*). (See 36a.)

> ► The old order in France paid a high price for the ~~aristocracy~~ *aristocracy's*
>
> exploiting the lower classes.

The possessive noun *aristocracy's* modifies the gerund phrase *exploiting the lower classes*.

Exercise 24–1 Edit the following sentences to eliminate errors in pronoun case. If a sentence is correct, write "correct" after it. Answers appear in the back of the book.

> *he.*
> **Papa chops wood for neighbors much younger than ~~him.~~**
> ^

a. Rick applied for the job even though he heard that other candidates were more experienced than he.

b. The volleyball team could not believe that the coach was she.

c. She appreciated him telling the truth in such a difficult situation.

d. The director has asked you and I to draft a proposal for a new recycling plan.

e. Five close friends and myself rented a station wagon, packed it with food, and drove two hundred miles to Mardi Gras.

Exercise 24–2 In the following paragraph, choose the correct pronoun in each set of parentheses.

We may blame television for the number of products based on characters in children's TV shows — from Big Bird to SpongeBob — but in fact merchandising that capitalizes on a character's popularity started long before television. Raggedy Ann began as a child's rag doll, and a few years later books about (she / her) and her brother, Raggedy Andy, were published. A cartoonist named Johnny Gruelle painted a cloth face on a family doll and applied for a patent in 1915. Later Gruelle began writing and illustrating stories about Raggedy Ann, and in 1918 (he / him) and a publisher teamed up to publish the books and sell the dolls. He was not the only one to try to sell products linked to children's stories. Beatrix Potter published the first of many Peter Rabbit picture books in 1902, and no one was better than (she / her) at making a living from spin-offs. After Peter Rabbit and Benjamin Bunny became popular, Potter began putting pictures of (they / them) and their little animal friends on merchandise. Potter had fans all over the world, and she understood (them / their) wanting to see Peter Rabbit not only in books but also on teapots and plates and lamps and other furnishings for the nursery. Potter and Gruelle, like countless others before and since, knew that entertaining children could be a profitable business.

25 Distinguish between *who* and *whom*.

The choice between *who* and *whom* (or *whoever* and *whomever*) occurs primarily in subordinate clauses and in questions. *Who* and *whoever*, subjective-case pronouns, are used for subjects and subject complements. *Whom* and *whomever*, objective-case pronouns, are used for objects. (See 25a and 25b.)

An exception to this general rule occurs when the pronoun functions as the subject of an infinitive (see 25c). See also 24e.

25a Use *who* and *whom* correctly in subordinate clauses.

When *who* and *whom* (or *whoever* and *whomever*) introduce subordinate clauses, their case is determined by their function *within the clause they introduce*.

In the following two examples, the pronouns *who* and *whoever* function as the subjects of the clauses they introduce.

▶ First prize goes to the runner ~~whom~~ ^{who} earns the most points.

The subordinate clause is *who earns the most points*. The verb of the clause is *earns*, and its subject is *who*.

▶ Maya Angelou's *I Know Why the Caged Bird Sings* should be read by ~~whomever~~ ^{whoever} is interested in the effects of racial prejudice on children.

The writer selected the pronoun *whomever*, thinking that it was the object of the preposition *by*. However, the object of the preposition is the entire subordinate clause *whoever is interested in the effects of racial prejudice on children*. The verb of the clause is *is*, and the subject of the verb is *whoever*.

When functioning as an object in a subordinate clause, *whom* (or *whomever*) also appears out of order, before the subject and verb. To choose the correct pronoun, you can mentally restructure the clause.

> *whom*
> You will work with our senior traders, ~~who~~ you will meet later.
>   ^

The subordinate clause is *whom you will meet later.* The subject of the clause is *you,* and the verb is *will meet. Whom* is the direct object of the verb. The correct choice becomes clear if you mentally restructure the clause: *you will meet whom.*

When functioning as the object of a preposition in a subordinate clause, *whom* is often separated from its preposition.

>   *whom*
> The tutor ~~who~~ I was assigned to was very supportive.
>   ^

Whom is the object of the preposition *to.* In this sentence, the writer might choose to drop *whom*: *The tutor I was assigned to was very supportive.*

25b Use *who* and *whom* correctly in questions.

When *who* and *whom* (or *whoever* and *whomever*) are used to open questions, their case is determined by their function within the question. In the following example, *who* functions as the subject of the question.

> *Who*
> ~~Whom~~ was responsible for creating that computer virus?
> ^

Who is the subject of the verb *was.*

When *whom* functions as the object of a verb or the object of a preposition in a question, it appears out of normal order. To choose the correct pronoun, you can mentally restructure the question.

> *Whom*
> ~~Who~~ did the Democratic Party nominate in 2008?
> ^

Whom is the direct object of the verb *did nominate.* This becomes clear if you restructure the question: *The Democratic Party did nominate whom in 2008?*

25c Use *whom* for subjects or objects of infinitives.

An infinitive is the word *to* followed by the base form of a verb. (See 48b.) Subjects of infinitives are an exception to the rule that subjects must be in the subjective case. The subject of an infinitive must be in the objective case. Objects of infinitives also are in the objective case.

> *whom*
> ► When it comes to money, I know ~~who~~ to believe.
>   ^
> The infinitive phrase *whom to believe* is the direct object of the verb *know*, and *whom* is the subject of the infinitive *to believe*.

Exercise 25–1 ▶ Edit the following sentences to eliminate errors in the use of *who* and *whom* (or *whoever* and *whomever*). If a sentence is correct, write "correct" after it. Answers appear in the back of the book.

whom
What is the address of the artist ~~who~~ Antonio hired?
                                     ^

a. Arriving late for rehearsal, we had no idea who was supposed to dance with whom.

b. The environmental policy conference featured scholars who I had never heard of.

c. Whom did you support in last month's election for student government president?

d. Daniel always gives a holiday donation to whomever needs it.

e. So many singers came to the audition that Natalia had trouble deciding who to select for the choir.

---

26 Choose adjectives and adverbs with care.

Adjectives modify nouns or pronouns. They usually come before the word they modify; occasionally they function as complements following the word they modify. Adverbs modify verbs, adjectives, or other adverbs. (See 46d and 46e.)

Many adverbs are formed by adding *-ly* to adjectives (*normal, normally; smooth, smoothly*). But don't assume that all words ending in *-ly* are adverbs or that all adverbs end in *-ly*. Some adjectives end in *-ly* (*lovely, friendly*), and some adverbs don't (*always, here, there*). When in doubt, consult a dictionary.

Multilingual

Placement of adjectives and adverbs can be a tricky matter for multilingual writers. See 30f and 30h.

26a Use adjectives to modify nouns.

Adjectives ordinarily precede the nouns they modify. But they can also function as subject complements or object complements, following the nouns they modify.

Multilingual

In English, adjectives are not pluralized to agree with the words they modify:

red
▶ The ~~reds~~ roses were a surprise.
 ∧

Subject complements

A subject complement follows a linking verb and completes the meaning of the subject. (See 47b.) When an adjective functions as a subject complement, it describes the subject.

Justice is *blind.*

Problems can arise with verbs such as *smell, taste, look,* and *feel,* which sometimes, but not always, function as linking verbs. If the word following one of these verbs describes the subject, use an adjective; if the word following the verb modifies the verb, use an adverb.

ADJECTIVE	The detective looked *cautious.*
ADVERB	The detective looked *cautiously* for fingerprints.

The adjective *cautious* describes the detective; the adverb *cautiously* modifies the verb *looked.*

Linking verbs suggest states of being, not actions. Notice, for example, the different meanings of *looked* in the preceding examples. To look cautious suggests the state of being cautious; to look cautiously is to perform an action in a cautious way.

▶ The lilacs in our backyard smell especially ~~sweetly~~ *sweet* this year.

The verb *smell* suggests a state of being, not an action. Therefore, it should be followed by an adjective, not an adverb.

▶ The drawings looked ~~well~~ *good* after the architect made a few changes.

The verb *looked* is a linking verb suggesting a state of being, not an action. The adjective *good* is appropriate following the linking verb to describe *drawings*. (See also 26c.)

Object complements

An object complement follows a direct object and completes its meaning. (See 47b.) When an adjective functions as an object complement, it describes the direct object.

Sorrow makes *us wise.*

Object complements occur with verbs such as *call, consider, create, find, keep,* and *make.* When a modifier follows the direct object of one of these verbs, use an adjective to describe the direct object; use an adverb to modify the verb.

| ADJECTIVE | The referee called the plays *perfect.* |
| ADVERB | The referee called the plays *perfectly.* |

The first sentence means that the referee considered the plays to be perfect; the second means that the referee did an excellent job of calling the plays.

26b Use adverbs to modify verbs, adjectives, and other adverbs.

When adverbs modify verbs (or verbals), they nearly always answer the question When? Where? How? Why? Under what conditions? How often? or To what degree? When adverbs modify adjectives or other adverbs, they usually qualify or intensify the meaning of the word they modify. (See 46e.)

Adjectives are often used incorrectly in place of adverbs in casual or nonstandard speech.

▶ The travel arrangement worked out ~~perfect~~ *perfectly* for everyone.

   The adverb *perfectly* modifies the verb *worked out.*

▶ The chance of recovering any lost property looks ~~real~~ *really* slim.

   Only adverbs can modify adjectives or other adverbs. *Really* intensifies the meaning of the adjective *slim.*

26c Distinguish between *good* and *well*, *bad* and *badly*.

Good is an adjective (*good performance*). *Well* is an adverb when it modifies a verb (*speak well*). The use of the adjective *good* in place of the adverb *well* to modify a verb is nonstandard, even though it is common in casual speech.

▶ We were glad that Sanya had done ~~good~~ *well* on the CPA exam.

   The adverb *well* modifies the verb *had done.*

Confusion can arise because *well* is an adjective when it modifies a noun or pronoun and means "healthy" or "satisfactory" (*The babies were well and warm*).

▶ Adrienne did not feel ~~good,~~ *well,* but she performed anyway.

   As an adjective following the linking verb *did feel*, *well* describes Adrienne's health.

Bad is always an adjective and should be used to modify a noun; *badly* is always an adverb and should be used to modify a verb. The adverb *badly* is often used inappropriately to describe a noun, especially following a linking verb.

▶ The sisters felt ~~badly~~ *bad* when they realized they had left their brother out of the planning.

   The adjective *bad* is used after the linking verb *felt* to describe the noun *sisters.*

26d Use comparatives and superlatives with care.

Most adjectives and adverbs have three forms: the positive, the comparative, and the superlative.

POSITIVE	COMPARATIVE	SUPERLATIVE
fast	faster	fastest
careful	more careful	most careful
bad	worse	worst
good	better	best

Comparative versus superlative

Use the comparative to compare two things, the superlative to compare three or more.

▶ Which of these two low-carb drinks is ~~best?~~ *better?*

▶ Though Shaw and Jackson are impressive, Zhao is the ~~more~~ *most*

qualified of the three candidates running for mayor.

Forming comparatives and superlatives

To form comparatives and superlatives of most one- and two-syllable adjectives, use the endings *-er* and *-est*: *smooth, smoother, smoothest; easy, easier, easiest*. With longer adjectives, use *more* and *most* (or *less* and *least* for downward comparisons): *exciting, more exciting, most exciting; helpful, less helpful, least helpful*.

Some one-syllable adverbs take the endings *-er* and *-est* (*fast, faster, fastest*), but longer adverbs and all of those ending in *-ly* form the comparative and superlative with *more* and *most* (or *less* and *least*).

The comparative and superlative forms of some adjectives and adverbs are irregular: *good, better, best; well, better, best; bad, worse, worst; badly, worse, worst*.

▶ The Kirov is the ~~talentedest~~ *most talented* ballet company we have seen.

▶ According to our projections, sales at local businesses will be *worse* ~~worser~~ than those at the chain stores this winter.

Double comparatives or superlatives

Do not use double comparatives or superlatives. When you have added *-er* or *-est* to an adjective or adverb, do not also use *more* or *most* (or *less* or *least*).

▶ Of all her family, Julia is the ~~most~~ happiest about the move.

▶ The polls indicated that Gore was more <u>likely</u> ~~likelier~~ to win than Bush.

Absolute concepts

Avoid expressions such as *more straight, less perfect, very round,* and *most unique.* Either something is unique or it isn't. It is illogical to suggest that absolute concepts come in degrees.

▶ That is the most <u>unusual</u> ~~unique~~ wedding gown I have ever seen.

▶ The painting is even more <u>valuable</u> ~~priceless~~ because it is signed.

26e Avoid double negatives.

Standard English allows two negatives only if a positive meaning is intended: *The orchestra was not unhappy with its performance* (meaning that the orchestra was happy). Using a double negative to emphasize a negative meaning is nonstandard.

Negative modifiers such as *never, no,* and *not* should not be paired with other negative modifiers or with negative words such as *neither, none, no one, nobody,* and *nothing.*

▶ The county is not doing <u>anything</u> ~~nothing~~ to see that the trash is collected.

The double negative *not . . . nothing* is nonstandard.

Exercise 26–1 Edit the following sentences to eliminate errors in the use of adjectives and adverbs. If a sentence is correct, write "correct" after it. Answers appear in the back of the book.

We weren't surprised by how <u>well</u> ~~good~~ the sidecar racing team

flowed through the tricky course.

a. Do you expect to perform good on the exam next week?
b. With the budget deadline approaching, our office hasn't hardly had time to handle routine correspondence.
c. Some flowers smell surprisingly bad.
d. The customer complained that he hadn't been treated nice by the agent on the phone.
e. Of all the smart people in my family, Aunt Ida is the most cleverest.

Exercise 26–2 Edit the following passage to eliminate errors in the use of adjectives and adverbs.

Doctors recommend that to give skin the most fullest protection from ultraviolet rays, people should use plenty of sunscreen, limit sun exposure, and wear protective clothing. The commonest sunscreens today are known as "broad spectrum" because they block out both UVA and UVB rays. These lotions don't feel any differently on the skin from the old UVA-only types, but they work best at preventing premature aging and skin cancer. Many sunscreens claim to be waterproof, but they won't hardly provide adequate coverage after extended periods of swimming or perspiring. To protect good, even waterproof sunscreens should be reapplied liberal and often. All areas of exposed skin, including ears, backs of hands, and tops of feet, need to be coated good to avoid burning or damage. Some people's skin reacts bad to PABA, or para-aminobenzoic acid, so PABA-free (hypoallergenic) sunscreens are widely available. In addition to recommending sunscreen, doctors almost unanimously agree that people should stay out of the sun when rays are the most strongest — between 10:00 a.m. and 3:00 p.m. — and should limit time in the sun. They also suggest that people wear long-sleeved shirts, broad-brimmed hats, and long pants whenever possible.

27 Choose appropriate verb forms, tenses, and moods in Standard English.

In speech, some people use verb forms and tenses that match a home dialect or variety of English. In writing, use Standard English verb forms unless you are quoting nonstandard speech or using alternative forms for literary effect. (See 17c.)

Except for the verb *be*, all verbs in English have five forms. The following list shows the five forms and provides a sample sentence in which each might appear.

BASE FORM	Usually I (*walk, ride*).
PAST TENSE	Yesterday I (*walked, rode*).
PAST PARTICIPLE	I have (*walked, ridden*) many times before.
PRESENT PARTICIPLE	I am (*walking, riding*) right now.
-*S* FORM	He/she/it (*walks, rides*) regularly.

The verb *be* has eight forms instead of the usual five: *be, am, is, are, was, were, being, been.*

27a Choose Standard English forms of irregular verbs.

For all regular verbs, the past-tense and past-participle forms are the same (ending in *-ed* or *-d*), so there is no danger of confusion. This is not true, however, for irregular verbs, such as the following.

BASE FORM	PAST TENSE	PAST PARTICIPLE
go	went	gone
break	broke	broken
fly	flew	flown
sing	sang	sung

The past-tense form always occurs alone, without a helping verb. It expresses action that occurred entirely in the past: *I rode to work yesterday. I walked to work last Tuesday.* The past participle is used with a helping verb. It forms the perfect tenses with *has, have,* or *had*; it forms the passive voice with *be, am, is, are, was, were, being,* or *been.* (See 46c for a complete list of helping verbs and 27f for a survey of tenses.)

PAST TENSE	Last July, we *went* to Tokyo.
HELPING VERB + PAST PARTICIPLE	We *have gone* to Tokyo twice.

The list of common irregular verbs below will help you distinguish between the past tense and the past participle. Choose the past-participle form if the verb in your sentence requires a helping verb; choose the past-tense form if the verb does not require a helping verb. (See verb tenses in 27f.)

▶ Yesterday we ~~seen~~ a documentary about Isabel Allende.
saw

The past-tense *saw* is required because there is no helping verb.

▶ The truck was apparently ~~stole~~ while the driver ate lunch.
stolen

▶ By Friday, the stock market had ~~fell~~ two hundred points.
fallen

Because of the helping verbs *was* and *had*, the past-participle forms are required: *was stolen*, *had fallen*.

Common irregular verbs

BASE FORM	PAST TENSE	PAST PARTICIPLE
arise	arose	arisen
awake	awoke, awaked	awaked, awoke, awoken
be	was, were	been
beat	beat	beaten, beat
become	became	become
begin	began	begun
bend	bent	bent
bite	bit	bitten, bit
blow	blew	blown
break	broke	broken
bring	brought	brought
build	built	built
burst	burst	burst
buy	bought	bought
catch	caught	caught
choose	chose	chosen
cling	clung	clung
come	came	come
cost	cost	cost
deal	dealt	dealt
dig	dug	dug

BASE FORM	PAST TENSE	PAST PARTICIPLE
dive	dived, dove	dived
do	did	done
drag	dragged	dragged
draw	drew	drawn
dream	dreamed, dreamt	dreamed, dreamt
drink	drank	drunk
drive	drove	driven
eat	ate	eaten
fall	fell	fallen
fight	fought	fought
find	found	found
fly	flew	flown
forget	forgot	forgotten, forgot
freeze	froze	frozen
get	got	gotten, got
give	gave	given
go	went	gone
grow	grew	grown
hang (execute)	hanged	hanged
hang (suspend)	hung	hung
have	had	had
hear	heard	heard
hide	hid	hidden
hurt	hurt	hurt
keep	kept	kept
know	knew	known
lay (put)	laid	laid
lead	led	led
lend	lent	lent
let (allow)	let	let
lie (recline)	lay	lain
lose	lost	lost
make	made	made
prove	proved	proved, proven

(continued)

BASE FORM	PAST TENSE	PAST PARTICIPLE
read	read	read
ride	rode	ridden
ring	rang	rung
rise (get up)	rose	risen
run	ran	run
say	said	said
see	saw	seen
send	sent	sent
set (place)	set	set
shake	shook	shaken
shoot	shot	shot
shrink	shrank	shrunk
sing	sang	sung
sink	sank	sunk
sit (be seated)	sat	sat
slay	slew	slain
sleep	slept	slept
speak	spoke	spoken
spin	spun	spun
spring	sprang	sprung
stand	stood	stood
steal	stole	stolen
sting	stung	stung
strike	struck	struck, stricken
swear	swore	sworn
swim	swam	swum
swing	swung	swung
take	took	taken
teach	taught	taught
throw	threw	thrown
wake	woke, waked	waked, woken
wear	wore	worn
wring	wrung	wrung
write	wrote	written

27b Distinguish among the forms of *lie* and *lay*.

Writers and speakers frequently confuse the various forms of *lie* (meaning "to recline or rest on a surface") and *lay* (meaning "to put or place something"). *Lie* is an intransitive verb; it does not take a direct object: *The forms lie on the table.* The verb *lay* is transitive; it takes a direct object: *Please lay the forms on the table.* (See 47b.)

In addition to confusing the meaning of *lie* and *lay*, writers and speakers are often unfamiliar with the Standard English forms of these verbs.

BASE FORM	PAST TENSE	PAST PARTICIPLE	PRESENT PARTICIPLE
lie (recline)	lay	lain	lying
lay (put)	laid	laid	laying

▶ Sue was so exhausted that she ~~laid~~ lay down for a nap.

The past-tense form of *lie* ("to recline") is *lay.*

▶ The patient had ~~laid~~ lain in an uncomfortable position all night.

The past-participle form of *lie* ("to recline") is *lain.* If the correct English seems too stilted, recast the sentence: *The patient had been lying in an uncomfortable position all night.*

▶ The prosecutor ~~lay~~ laid the pistol on a table close to the jurors.

The past-tense form of *lay* ("to place") is *laid.*

▶ Letters dating from 1915 were ~~laying~~ lying in a corner of the chest.

The present participle of *lie* ("to rest on a surface") is *lying.*

Exercise 27–1   Edit the following sentences to eliminate problems with irregular verbs. If a sentence is correct, write "correct" after it. Answers appear in the back of the book.

The ranger ~~seen~~ saw the forest fire ten miles away.

a. When I get the urge to exercise, I lay down until it passes.

b. Grandmother had drove our new hybrid to the sunrise church service, so we were left with the station wagon.

c. A pile of dirty rags was laying at the bottom of the stairs.

d. How did the game know that the player had went from the room with the blue ogre to the hall where the gold was heaped?

e. Abraham Lincoln took good care of his legal clients; the contracts he drew for the Illinois Central Railroad could never be broke.

27c Use -s or -es endings on present-tense verbs that have third-person singular subjects.

All singular nouns (*child, tree*) and the pronouns *he*, *she*, and *it* are third-person singular; indefinite pronouns such as *everyone* and *neither* are also third-person singular. When the subject of a sentence is third-person singular, its verb takes an *-s* or *-es* ending in the present tense. (See also 21.)

	SINGULAR		PLURAL	
FIRST PERSON	I	know	we	know
SECOND PERSON	you	know	you	know
THIRD PERSON	he/she/it	knows	they	know
	child	knows	parents	know
	everyone	knows		

>   *drives*
> My neighbor d̶r̶i̶v̶e̶ to Marco Island every weekend.
>   ^

>   *turns*   *dissolves*   *eats*
> Sulfur dioxide t̶u̶r̶n̶ leaves yellow, d̶i̶s̶s̶o̶l̶v̶e̶ marble, and e̶a̶t̶ away
>   ^   ^   ^
>
> iron and steel.

The subjects *neighbor* and *sulfur dioxide* are third-person singular, so the verbs must end in *-s*.

TIP: Do not add the *-s* ending to the verb if the subject is not third-person singular. The writers of the following sentences added *–s* endings where they don't belong.

> I prepare$̶s̶$ system specifications for every installation.

The writer mistakenly concluded that the *-s* ending belongs on present-tense verbs used with *all* singular subjects, not just *third-person* singular subjects. The pronoun *I* is first-person singular, so its verb does not require the *-s*.

▶ The tile floors requires continual sweeping.

> The writer mistakenly thought that the verb needed an -s ending
> because of the plural subject. But the -s ending is used only on present-
> tense verbs with third-person *singular* subjects.

Has versus *have*

In the present tense, use *has* with third-person singular subjects;
all other subjects require *have*.

	SINGULAR		PLURAL	
FIRST PERSON	I	have	we	have
SECOND PERSON	you	have	you	have
THIRD PERSON	he/she/it	has	they	have

▶ This respected musician almost always ~~have~~ *has* a message to convey

in his work.

> The subject *musician* is third-person singular, so the verb should be *has*.

▶ My law classes ~~has~~ *have* helped me understand contracts.

> The subject of this sentence — *classes* — is third-person plural, so
> Standard English requires *have*. *Has* is used only with third-person
> singular subjects.

Does versus *do* and *doesn't* versus *don't*

In the present tense, use *does* and *doesn't* with third-person
singular subjects; all other subjects require *do* and *don't*.

	SINGULAR		PLURAL	
FIRST PERSON	I	do/don't	we	do/don't
SECOND PERSON	you	do/don't	you	do/don't
THIRD PERSON	he/she/it	does/doesn't	they	do/don't

▶ Grandfather really ~~don't~~ *doesn't* have a place to call home.

> *Grandfather* is third-person singular, so the verb should be *doesn't*.

Am, *is*, and *are*; *was* and *were*

The verb *be* has three forms in the present tense (*am*, *is*, *are*) and two in the past tense (*was*, *were*).

	SINGULAR		PLURAL	
FIRST PERSON	I	am/was	we	are/were
SECOND PERSON	you	are/were	you	are/were
THIRD PERSON	he/she/it	is/was	they	are/were

were

▶ Did you think you ~~was~~ going to drown?
^

The subject *you* is second-person singular, so the verb should be *were*.

27d Do not omit *-ed* endings on verbs.

Speakers who do not fully pronounce *-ed* endings sometimes omit them unintentionally in writing. Failure to pronounce *-ed* endings is common in many dialects and in informal speech, even in Standard English. For example, in the sentence *I used to visit Georgia every summer,* some speakers will say *use to.*

When a verb is regular, both the past tense and the past participle are formed by adding *-ed* (or *-d*) to the base form of the verb.

Past tense

Use the ending *-ed* or *-d* to express the past tense of regular verbs. The past tense is used when the action occurred entirely in the past.

decided

▶ In 1998, journalist Barbara Ehrenreich ~~decide~~ to try to live on
^

minimum wage.

advised

▶ Last summer, my counselor ~~advise~~ me to ask my chemistry
^

instructor for help.

Past participles

Past participles are used in three ways: (1) following *have*, *has*, or *had* to form one of the perfect tenses; (2) following *be*, *am*, *is*, *are, was, were, being,* or *been* to form the passive voice; and (3) as adjectives modifying nouns or pronouns. The perfect tenses are listed in 27f, and the passive voice is discussed in 8a. For a discussion of participles as adjectives, see 48b.

▶ Robin has ~~ask~~ **asked** for more housing staff for next year.

Has asked is present perfect tense (*have* or *has* followed by a past participle).

▶ Though it is not a new phenomenon, domestic violence is now ~~publicize~~ **publicized** more than ever.

Is publicized is a verb in the passive voice (a form of *be* followed by a past participle).

▶ All kickboxing classes end in a cool-down period to stretch ~~tighten~~ **tightened** muscles.

The past participle *tightened* functions as an adjective modifying the noun *muscles.*

27e Do not omit needed verbs.

Although Standard English allows some linking verbs and helping verbs to be contracted in informal contexts, it does not allow them to be omitted.

Linking verbs, used to link subjects to subject complements, are frequently a form of *be*: *be, am, is, are, was, were, being, been.* (See 47b.) Some of these forms may be contracted (*I'm, she's, we're, you're, they're*), but they should not be omitted altogether.

▶ When we **are** quiet in the evening, we can hear the crickets.

Helping verbs, used with main verbs, include forms of *be, do,* and *have* and the modal verbs *can, will, shall, could, would, should, may, might,* and *must.* (See 46c.) Some helping verbs may be contracted (*he's leaving, we'll celebrate, they've been told*), but they should not be omitted altogether.

▶ We **have** been in Chicago since last Thursday.

Multilingual

Some languages do not require a linking verb between a subject and its complement. English, however, requires a verb in every sentence. See 30a.

▶ Every night, I read to my daughter. When I ^{am} too busy, my husband reads to her.

Exercise 27–2 Edit the following sentences to eliminate problems with -s and -ed verb forms and with omitted verbs. If a sentence is correct, write "correct" after it. Answers appear in the back of the book.

The Pell Grant sometimes _{covers} ~~cover~~ the student's full tuition.

a. The glass sculptures of the Swan Boats was prominent in the brightly lit lobby.
b. Visitors to the glass museum were not suppose to touch the exhibits.
c. Our church has all the latest technology, even a close circuit TV.
d. Christos didn't know about Marlo's promotion because he never listens. He always talking.
e. Most psychologists agree that no one performs well under stress.

27f Choose the appropriate verb tense.

Tenses indicate the time of an action in relation to the time of the speaking or writing about that action.

The most common problem with tenses, shifting confusingly from one tense to another, is discussed in chapter 13. Other problems with tenses are detailed in this section, after the following survey of tenses.

Survey of tenses

Tenses are classified as present, past, and future, with simple, perfect, and progressive forms for each.

Simple tenses The simple tenses indicate relatively simple time relations. The *simple present* tense is used primarily for actions occurring at the same time they are being discussed or for actions occurring regularly. The *simple past* tense is used for actions completed in the past. The *simple future* tense is used for actions that will occur in the future. In the following table, the simple tenses are given for the regular verb *walk*, the irregular verb *ride*, and the highly irregular verb *be*.

SIMPLE PRESENT

SINGULAR		PLURAL	
I	walk, ride, am	we	walk, ride, are
you	walk, ride, are	you	walk, ride, are
he/she/it	walks, rides, is	they	walk, ride, are

SIMPLE PAST

SINGULAR		PLURAL	
I	walked, rode, was	we	walked, rode, were
you	walked, rode, were	you	walked, rode, were
he/she/it	walked, rode, was	they	walked, rode, were

SIMPLE FUTURE

I, you, he/she/it, we, they	will walk, ride, be

Perfect tenses   More complex time relations are indicated by the perfect tenses. A verb in one of the perfect tenses (a form of *have* plus the past participle) expresses an action that was or will be completed before another time.

PRESENT PERFECT

I, you, we, they	have walked, ridden, been
he/she/it	has walked, ridden, been

PAST PERFECT

I, you, he/she/it, we, they	had walked, ridden, been

FUTURE PERFECT

I, you, he/she/it, we, they	will have walked, ridden, been

Progressive forms   The simple and perfect tenses have progressive forms that describe actions in progress. A progressive verb consists of a form of *be* followed by a present participle. The progressive forms are not normally used with certain verbs, such as *believe*, *know*, *hear*, *seem*, and *think*.

PRESENT PROGRESSIVE

I	am walking, riding, being
he/she/it	is walking, riding, being
you, we, they	are walking, riding, being

PAST PROGRESSIVE

I, he/she/it	was walking, riding, being
you, we, they	were walking, riding, being

FUTURE PROGRESSIVE

I, you, he/she/it, we, they	will be walking, riding, being

PRESENT PERFECT PROGRESSIVE

I, you, we, they	have been walking, riding, being
he/she/it	has been walking, riding, being

PAST PERFECT PROGRESSIVE

I, you, he/she/it, we, they	had been walking, riding, being

FUTURE PERFECT PROGRESSIVE

I, you, he/she/it, we, they	will have been walking, riding, being

Multilingual

See 28a for more specific examples of verb tenses that can be challenging for multilingual writers.

Special uses of the present tense

Use the present tense when expressing general truths, when writing about literature, and when quoting, summarizing, or paraphrasing an author's views.

General truths or scientific principles should appear in the present tense unless such principles have been disproved.

 revolves
▶ Galileo taught that the earth ~~revolved~~ around the sun.
                                    ^

Because Galileo's teaching has not been discredited, the verb should be in the present tense. The following sentence, however, is acceptable: *Ptolemy taught that the sun revolved around the earth.*

When writing about a work of literature, you may be tempted to use the past tense. The convention, however, is to describe fictional events in the present tense.

▶ In Masuji Ibuse's *Black Rain*, a child ~~reached~~ *reaches* for a pomegranate in his mother's garden, and a moment later he ~~was~~ *is* dead, killed by the blast of the atomic bomb.

When you are quoting, summarizing, or paraphrasing the author of a nonliterary work, use present-tense verbs such as *writes*, *reports*, *asserts*, and so on to introduce the source. This convention is usually followed even when the author is dead (unless a date or the context specifies the time of writing).

▶ Dr. Jerome Groopman ~~argued~~ *argues* that doctors are "susceptible to the subtle and not so subtle efforts of the pharmaceutical industry to sculpt our thinking" (9).

In MLA style, signal phrases are written in the present tense, not the past tense. (See also 55c.)

APA NOTE: When you are documenting a paper with the APA (American Psychological Association) style of in-text citations, use past tense verbs such as *reported* or present perfect verbs such as *has reported* to introduce the source. (See also 60c.)

The past perfect tense

The past perfect tense consists of a past participle preceded by *had* (*had worked*, *had gone*). This tense is used for an action already completed by the time of another past action or for an action already completed at some specific past time.

Everyone *had spoken* by the time I arrived.

I pleaded my case, but Paula *had made up* her mind.

Writers sometimes use the simple past tense when they should use the past perfect.

▶ By the time dinner was served, the guest of honor *had* left.

The past perfect tense is needed because the action of leaving was already completed at a specific past time (when dinner was served).

Some writers overuse the past perfect tense. Do not use the past perfect if two past actions occurred at the same time.

▶ When Ernest Hemingway lived in Cuba, he ~~had written~~ *wrote* *For Whom the Bell Tolls.*

Sequence of tenses with infinitives and participles

An infinitive is the base form of a verb preceded by *to.* (See 48b.) Use the present infinitive to show action at the same time as or later than the action of the verb in the sentence.

▶ Sonia had hoped to ~~have paid~~ *pay* the bill by May 1.

The action expressed in the infinitive (*to pay*) occurred later than the action of the sentence's verb (*had hoped*).

Use the perfect form of an infinitive (*to have* followed by the past participle) for an action occurring earlier than that of the verb in the sentence.

▶ Dan would like to ~~join~~ *have joined* the navy, but he could not swim.

The liking occurs in the present; the joining would have occurred in the past.

Like the tense of an infinitive, the tense of a participle is governed by the tense of the sentence's verb. Use the present participle (ending in *-ing*) for an action occurring at the same time as that of the sentence's verb.

Hiking the Appalachian Trail, we spotted many wildflowers.

Use the past participle (such as *given* or *helped*) or the present perfect participle (*having* plus the past participle) for an action occurring before that of the verb.

Discovered off the coast of Florida, the Spanish galleon yielded many treasures.

Having worked her way through college, Lee graduated debt-free.

27g Use the subjunctive mood in the few contexts that require it.

There are three moods in English: the *indicative,* used for facts, opinions, and questions; the *imperative,* used for orders or advice;

and the *subjunctive*, used in certain contexts to express wishes, requests, or conditions contrary to fact. For many writers, the subjunctive causes the most problems.

Forms of the subjunctive

In the subjunctive mood, present-tense verbs do not change form to indicate the number and person of the subject (see 21). Instead, the subjunctive uses the base form of the verb (*be, drive, employ*) with all subjects. Also, in the subjunctive mood, there is only one past-tense form of *be*: *were* (never *was*).

> It is important that you *be* [not *are*] prepared for the interview.

> We asked that she *drive* [not *drives*] more slowly.

> If I *were* [not *was*] you, I'd try a new strategy.

Uses of the subjunctive

The subjunctive mood appears only in a few contexts: in contrary-to-fact clauses beginning with *if* or expressing a wish; in *that* clauses following verbs such as *ask, insist, recommend, request*, and *suggest*; and in certain set expressions.

In contrary-to-fact clauses beginning with *if* When a subordinate clause beginning with *if* expresses a condition contrary to fact, use the subjunctive *were* in place of *was*.

> ▶ If I ~~was~~ _were_ a member of the management team, I would organize
>
> more social events for employees.

> ▶ The astronomers would be able to see the moons of Jupiter
>
> tonight if the weather ~~was~~ _were_ clearer.
>
> The verbs in these sentences express conditions that do not exist; the writer is not a manager, and the weather is not clear.

Do not use the subjunctive mood in *if* clauses expressing conditions that exist or may exist.

> If Dana *wins* the contest, she will leave for Barcelona in June.

In contrary-to-fact clauses expressing a wish In formal English, use the subjunctive *were* in clauses expressing a wish or desire.

| INFORMAL | I wish that Dr. Vaughn *was* my professor. |
| FORMAL | I wish that Dr. Vaughn *were* my professor. |

In *that* clauses following verbs such as *ask*, *insist*, *request*, and *suggest* Because requests have not yet become reality, they are expressed in the subjunctive mood.

                                                    be
▶ Professor Moore insists that her students ~~are~~ on time for every
                                                    ^
   class.

                                           file
▶ We recommend that Mrs. Lambert ~~files~~ form 1050 as soon as
                                           ^
   possible.

In certain set expressions The subjunctive mood, once more widely used, remains in certain set expressions, including *be that as it may*, *as it were*, and *far be it from me*.

Exercise 27–3 Edit the following sentences to eliminate errors in verb tense or mood. If a sentence is correct, write "correct" after it. Answers appear in the back of the book.

                   had been
After the path ~~was~~ plowed, we were able to walk in the park.
               ^

a. The palace of Knossos in Crete is believed to have been destroyed by fire around 1375 BCE.

b. Watson and Crick discovered the mechanism that controlled inheritance in all life: the workings of the DNA molecule.

c. When city planners proposed rezoning the waterfront, did they know that the mayor promised to curb development in that neighborhood?

d. Tonight's concert begins at 9:30. If it was earlier, I'd consider going.

e. The math position was filled by the woman who had been running the tutoring center.

MULTILINGUAL WRITERS AND ESL TOPICS

This section of *Rules for Writers* is primarily for multilingual writers. You may find this section helpful if you learned English as a second language (ESL) or if you speak a language other than English with your friends and family.

28 Verbs

Both native and nonnative speakers of English encounter challenges with verbs. This chapter focuses on specific challenges that multilingual writers sometimes face. You can find more help with verbs in other sections in the book:

> making subjects and verbs agree (21)
>
> using irregular verb forms (27a, 27b)
>
> using correct verb endings (27c, 27d)
>
> choosing the correct verb tense (27f)
>
> avoiding inappropriate uses of the passive voice (8a)

28a Use the appropriate verb form and tense.

This section offers a brief review of English verb forms and tenses. For additional help, see 27 and 46c.

Basic verb forms

Every main verb in English has five forms, which are used to create all of the verb tenses in standard English. The first chart in this section shows these forms for the regular verb *help* and the irregular verbs *give* and *be*. See 27a for the forms of other common irregular verbs.

Verb tenses

Section 27f describes all the verb tenses in English, showing the forms of a regular verb, an irregular verb, and the verb *be* in each

Basic verb forms

	REGULAR VERB *HELP*	IRREGULAR VERB *GIVE*	IRREGULAR VERB *BE**
BASE FORM	help	give	be
PAST TENSE	helped	gave	was, were
PAST PARTICIPLE	helped	given	been
PRESENT PARTICIPLE	helping	giving	being
***-S* FORM**	helps	gives	is

*Be also has the forms *am* and *are*, which are used in the present tense.

tense. The following chart provides more details about the tenses commonly used in the active voice in writing; the chart on page 234 gives details about tenses commonly used in the passive voice.

Verb tenses commonly used in the active voice

For descriptions and examples of all verb tenses, see 27f. For verb tenses commonly used in the passive voice, see the chart on page 234.

Simple tenses
For general facts, states of being, habitual actions

Simple present	**Base form or *-s* form**
• general facts	College students often *study* late at night.
• states of being	Water *becomes* steam at 100 degrees centigrade.
• habitual, repetitive actions	We *donate* to a different charity each year.
• scheduled future events	The train *arrives* tomorrow at 6:30 p.m.

NOTE: For uses of the present tense in writing about literature, see pages 224–25.

Simple past	**Base form + *-ed* or *-d* or irregular form**
• completed actions at a specific time in the past	The storm *destroyed* their property. She *drove* to Montana three years ago.
• facts or states of being in the past	When I *was* young, I usually *walked* to school with my sister.

Simple future	***will* + base form**
• future actions, promises, or predictions	I *will exercise* tomorrow. The snowfall *will begin* around midnight.

➡

Verb tenses commonly used in the active voice, continued

Simple progressive forms
For continuing actions

Present progressive

am, is, are + present participle

- actions in progress at the present time, not continuing indefinitely

  The students *are taking* an exam in Room 105.

  The valet *is parking* the car.

- future actions (with *leave, go, come, move,* etc.)

  I *am leaving* tomorrow morning.

Past progressive

was, were + present participle

- actions in progress at a specific time in the past

  They *were swimming* when the storm struck.

- *was going to, were going to* for past plans that did not happen

  We *were going to* drive to Florida for spring break, but the car broke down.

NOTE: Some verbs are not normally used in the progressive: *appear, believe, belong, contain, have, hear, know, like, need, see, seem, taste, understand,* and *want*.

    want
▶ I ~~am wanting~~ to see August Wilson's *Radio Golf.*
    ^

Perfect tenses
For actions that happened or will happen before another time

Present perfect

has, have + past participle

- repetitive or constant actions that began in the past and continue to the present

  I *have loved* cats since I was a child. Alicia *has worked* in Kenya for ten years.

- actions that happened at an unknown or unspecific past time

  Stephen *has visited* Wales three times.

Past perfect

had + past participle

- actions that began or occurred before another time in the past

  She *had* just *crossed* the street when the runaway car crashed into the building.

NOTE: For more discussion of uses of the past perfect, see 27f. For uses of the past perfect in conditional sentences, see 28e.

Perfect progressive forms
For continuous past actions before another time

Present perfect progressive	***has***, ***have*** + ***been*** + present participle
• continuous actions that began in the past and continue to the present	Yolanda *has been trying* to get a job in Boston for five years.

Past perfect progressive	***had*** + ***been*** + present participle
• actions that began and continued in the past until another past action	By the time I moved to Georgia, I *had been supporting* myself for five years.

28b To write a verb in the passive voice, use a form of *be* with the past participle.

When a sentence is written in the passive voice, the subject receives the action instead of doing it.

> The solution *was heated* to 80 degrees Celsius.

To form the passive voice, use a form of *be* — *am, is, are, was, were, being, be,* or *been* — followed by the past participle of the main verb: *was chosen, are remembered.* (Sometimes a form of *be* follows another helping verb: *will be considered, could have been broken.*)

> ► *Dreaming in Cuban* was ~~writing~~ ^{written} by Cristina García.

In the passive voice, the past participle *written*, not the present participle *writing*, must follow *was* (the past tense of *be*).

> ► The child is being ~~test.~~ ^{tested.}

The past participle *tested*, not the base form *test*, must be used with *is being* to form the passive voice.

For details on forming the passive in various tenses, consult the chart on page 234. (For appropriate uses of the passive voice, see 8a.)

Verb tenses commonly used in the passive voice

Simple tenses (passive voice)

Simple present   *am*, *is*, *are* + past participle

- general facts   Breakfast is *served* daily.
- habitual, repetitive actions   The receipts *are counted* every night.

Simple past   *was*, *were* + past participle

- completed past actions   He *was rewarded* for being on time.

Simple future   *will be* + past participle

- future actions, promises, or predictions   The decision *will be made* by the committee next week.

Simple progressive forms (passive voice)

Present progressive   *am*, *is*, *are* + *being* + past participle

- actions in progress at the present time   The new stadium *is being built* with private money.
- future actions   Jo *is being promoted* to a new job next month.

Past progressive   *was*, *were* + *being* + past participle

- actions in progress at a specific time in the past   We thought we *were being followed*.

Perfect tenses (passive voice)

Present perfect   *has*, *have* + *been* + past participle

- actions that began in the past and continue to the present   The flight *has been delayed* because of storms in the Midwest.
- actions that happened at an unknown or unspecific time in the past   Wars *have been fought* throughout history.

Past perfect   *had* + *been* + past participle

- actions that began or occurred before another time in the past   He *had been given* all the hints he needed to complete the puzzle.

NOTE: Future progressive, future perfect, and perfect progressive forms are not used in the passive voice.

NOTE: Only transitive verbs, those that take direct objects, may be used in the passive voice. Intransitive verbs such as *occur*, *happen*, *sleep*, *die*, *become*, and *fall* are not used in the passive. (See 47b.)

▶ The accident ~~was~~ happened suddenly.

Exercise 28–1   Revise the following sentences to correct errors in verb forms and tenses in the active and the passive voice. You may need to look at 27a for the correct form of some irregular verbs and at 27f for help with tenses. Answers appear in the back of the book.

> *begins*
> The meeting ~~begin~~ tonight at 7:30.
>   ^

a. In the past, tobacco companies deny any connection between smoking and health problems.
b. The volunteer's compassion has touch many lives.
c. I am wanting to register for a summer tutoring session.
d. By the end of the year, the state will have test 139 birds for avian flu.
e. The golfers were prepare for all weather conditions.

28c Use the base form of the verb after a modal.

The modal verbs are *can*, *could*, *may*, *might*, *must*, *should*, *will*, and *would*. (*Ought to* is also considered a modal verb.) The modals are used with the base form of a verb to show ability, certainty, necessity, permission, obligation, or possibility.

Modals and the verbs that follow them do not change form to indicate tense. For a summary of modals and their meanings, see the chart in this section. (See also 27e.)

> *launch*
▶ The art museum will ~~launches~~ its fundraising campaign
>   ^
next month.

The modal *will* must be followed by the base form *launch*, not the present tense *launches*.

Modals and their meanings

can

- general ability (present)

  Ants *can survive* anywhere, even in space. Jorge *can run* a marathon faster than his brother.

- informal requests or permission

  Can you *tell* me where the light is? Sandy *can borrow* my calculator.

could

- general ability (past)

  Lea *could read* when she was only three years old.

- polite, informal requests or permission

  Could you *give* me that pen?

may

- formal requests or permission

  May I *see* the report? Students *may park* only in the yellow zone.

- possibility

  I *may try* to finish my homework tonight, or I *may wake up* early and *finish* it tomorrow.

might

- possibility

  Funding for the language lab *might double* by 2019.

NOTE: *Might* usually expresses a stronger possibility than *may*.

must

- necessity (present or future)

  To be effective, welfare-to-work programs *must provide* access to job training.

- strong probability

  Amy *must be* nervous. [She is probably nervous.]

- near certainty (present or past)

  I *must have left* my wallet at home. [I almost certainly left my wallet at home.]

should

- suggestions or advice

  Diabetics *should drink* plenty of water every day.

- obligations or duties

  The government *should protect* citizens' rights.

- expectations

  The books *should arrive* soon. [We expect the books to arrive soon.]

will		
• certainty	If you don't leave now, you *will be* late for your rehearsal.	
• requests	*Will* you *help* me study for my psychology exam?	
• promises and offers	Jonah *will arrange* the carpool.	

would		
• polite requests	*Would* you *help* me carry these books? I *would like* some coffee. [*Would like* is more polite than *want*.]	
• habitual or repeated actions (past)	Whenever Elena needed help with sewing, she *would call* her aunt.	

                speak
▶ The translator could ~~spoke~~ many languages, so the
                    ^

  ambassador hired her for the European tour.

    The modal *could* must be followed by the base form *speak*, not the past tense *spoke*.

TIP: Do not use *to* in front of a main verb that follows a modal.

▶ Gina can ~~to~~ drive us home if we miss the last train.

For the use of modals in conditional sentences, see 28e.

Exercise 28–2   Edit the following sentences to correct errors in the use of verb forms with modals. You may find it helpful to consult the chart in section 28c. If a sentence is correct, write "correct" after it. Answers appear in the back of the book.

    We should ~~to~~ order pizza for dinner.

a. A major league pitcher can to throw a baseball more than ninety-five miles per hour.
b. The writing center tutor will helps you revise your essay.
c. A reptile must adjusted its body temperature to its environment.
d. In some states, individuals may renew a driver's license online.
e. My uncle, a cartoonist, could sketched a face in less than two minutes.

28d To make negative verb forms, add *not* in the appropriate place.

If the verb is the simple present or past tense of *be* (*am*, *is*, *are*, *was*, *were*), add *not* after the verb.

> Gianna *is not* a member of the club.

For simple present-tense verbs other than *be*, use *do* or *does* plus *not* before the base form of the verb. (For the correct forms of *do* and *does*, see the subject-verb agreement chart in 21c.)

> ▶ Mariko ~~no~~ want more dessert.
>   ^does not

> ▶ Mariko does not wants more dessert.

For simple past-tense verbs other than *be*, use *did* plus *not* before the base form of the verb.

> ▶ They did not ~~planted~~ corn this year.
>   ^plant

In a verb phrase consisting of one or more helping verbs and a present or past participle (*is watching*, *were living*, *has played*, *could have been driven*), use the word *not* after the first helping verb.

> ▶ Inna should have ~~not~~ gone dancing last night.
>   ^not

> ▶ Bonnie is ~~no~~ singing this weekend.
>   ^not

NOTE: English allows only one negative in an independent clause to express a negative idea; using more than one is an error known as a *double negative* (see 26e).

> ▶ We could not find ~~no~~ books about the history of our school.
>   ^any

28e In a conditional sentence, choose verb tenses according to the type of condition expressed in the sentence.

Conditional sentences contain two clauses: a subordinate clause (usually starting with *if*, *when*, or *unless*) and an independent clause. The subordinate clause (sometimes called the *if* or *unless* clause) states the condition or cause; the independent clause states the result or effect. In each example in this section, the subordinate clause (*if* clause) is marked SUB, and the independent clause is marked IND. (See 48e on subordinate clauses.)

Factual

Factual conditional sentences express relationships based on facts. If the relationship is a scientific truth, use the present tense in both clauses.

> ┌─────── SUB ───────┐ ┌─ IND ─┐
> If water *cools* to 32 degrees Fahrenheit, it *freezes*.

If the sentence describes a condition that is (or was) habitually true, use the same tense in both clauses.

> ┌─────── SUB ───────┐ ┌─────── IND ───────┐
> When Sue *jogs* along the canal, her dog *runs* ahead of her.

> ┌─────── SUB ───────┐ ┌─── IND ───┐
> Whenever the coach *asked* for help, I *volunteered*.

Predictive

Predictive conditional sentences are used to predict the future or to express future plans or possibilities. To form a predictive sentence, use a present-tense verb in the subordinate clause; in the independent clause, use the modal *will*, *can*, *may*, *should*, or *might* plus the base form of the verb.

> ┌─────── SUB ───────┐ ┌─────── IND ───────┐
> If you *practice* regularly, your tennis game *should improve*.

> ┌─────── IND ───────┐ ┌─── SUB ───┐
> We *will lose* our remaining wetlands unless we *act* now.

TIP: In all types of conditional sentences (factual, predictive, and speculative), *if* or *unless* clauses do not use the modal verb *will*.

> passes
> ▶ If Jenna ~~will pass~~ her history test, she will graduate this year.
>   ^

Speculative

Speculative conditional sentences express unlikely, contrary-to-fact, or impossible conditions. English uses the past or past perfect tense in the *if* clause, even for conditions in the present or the future.

Unlikely possibilities   If the condition is possible but unlikely in the present or the future, use the past tense in the subordinate clause; in the independent clause, use *would*, *could*, or *might* plus the base form of the verb.

> ┌───── SUB ─────┐┌───── IND ─────────┐
> If I *won* the lottery, I *would travel* to Egypt.

The writer does not expect to win the lottery. Because this is a possible but unlikely present or future situation, the past tense is used in the subordinate clause.

Conditions contrary to fact   To express conditions that are currently unreal or contrary to fact, use the past-tense verb *were* (not *was*) in the *if* clause for all subjects. (See also 27g on the subjunctive mood.)

> *were*
> ► If I ~~was~~ president, I would make children's issues a priority.
>   ^

The writer is not president, so *were* is correct in the *if* clause.

Events that did not happen   In a conditional sentence that speculates about an event that did not happen or was impossible in the past, use the past perfect tense in the *if* clause; in the independent clause, use *would have*, *could have*, or *might have* with the past participle. (See also past perfect tense, p. 232.)

> ┌────── SUB ──────┐┌────── IND ──────────┐
> If I *had saved* more money, I *would have visited* Laos last year.

The writer did not save more money and did not travel to Laos. This sentence shows a possibility that did not happen.

> ┌──────── SUB ────────────┐┌── IND ──┐
> If Aunt Grace *had been* alive for your graduation, she *would*
> ┌──────────────────┐
> *have been* very proud.

Aunt Grace was not alive at the time of the graduation. This sentence shows an impossible situation in the past.

Exercise 28-3 Edit the following sentences to correct problems with verbs. In some cases, more than one revision is possible. Possible revisions appear in the back of the book.

> had
> If I ~~have~~ time, I would study both French and Russian next
> ^
> semester.

a. The electrician might have discovered the broken circuit if she went through the modules one at a time.

b. If Verena wins a scholarship, she would go to graduate school.

c. Whenever a rainbow appears after a storm, everybody came out to see it.

d. Sarah did not understood the terms of her internship.

e. If I live in Budapest with my cousin Szusza, she would teach me Hungarian cooking.

28f Become familiar with verbs that may be followed by gerunds or infinitives.

A gerund is a verb form that ends in *-ing* and is used as a noun: *sleeping*, *dreaming*. (See 48b on verbal phrases.) An infinitive is the word *to* plus the base form of the verb: *to sleep*, *to dream*. The word *to* is an infinitive marker, not a preposition, in this use. (See 48b on infinitive phrases.)

A few verbs may be followed by either a gerund or an infinitive; others may be followed by a gerund but not by an infinitive; still others may be followed by an infinitive but not by a gerund.

Verb + gerund or infinitive (no change in meaning)

The following commonly used verbs may be followed by a gerund or an infinitive, with little or no difference in meaning:

begin	hate	love
continue	like	start

I love *skiing*. I love *to ski*.

Verb + gerund or infinitive (change in meaning)

With a few verbs, the choice of a gerund or an infinitive affects the meaning dramatically:

forget   remember   stop   try

She stopped *speaking* to Lucia. [She no longer spoke to Lucia.]
She stopped *to speak* to Lucia. [She paused so that she could speak to Lucia.]

Verb + gerund

These verbs may be followed by a gerund but not by an infinitive:

admit	discuss	imagine	put off	risk
appreciate	enjoy	miss	quit	suggest
avoid	escape	postpone	recall	tolerate
deny	finish	practice	resist	

Bill enjoys *playing* [not *to play*] the piano.
Jamie quit *smoking*.

Verb + infinitive

These verbs may be followed by an infinitive but not by a gerund:

agree	decide	manage	plan	wait
ask	expect	mean	pretend	want
beg	help	need	promise	wish
claim	hope	offer	refuse	would like

Jill has offered *to water* [not *watering*] the plants while we are away.
Joe finally managed *to find* a parking space.

A few of these verbs may be followed either by an infinitive directly or by a noun or pronoun plus an infinitive:

ask	help	promise	would like
expect	need	want	

We asked *to speak* to the congregation.
We asked *Rabbi Abrams to speak* to our congregation.

Verb + noun or pronoun + infinitive

With certain verbs in the active voice, a noun or pronoun must come between the verb and the infinitive that follows it. The noun or pronoun usually names a person who is affected by the action of the verb.

advise	convince	order	tell
allow	encourage	persuade	urge
cause	have (own)	remind	warn
command	instruct	require	

       V   **N** ┌ **INF** ┐
The class encouraged Luis to tell the story of his escape.

The counselor *advised Haley to take* four courses instead of five.

Verb + noun or pronoun + unmarked infinitive

An unmarked infinitive is an infinitive without *to*. A few verbs (often called *causative verbs*) may be followed by a noun or pronoun and an unmarked infinitive.

have (cause)	let (allow)
help	make (force)

Jorge *had the valet park* his car.

▶ **Frank made me ~~to~~ carry his book for him.**

NOTE: *Help* can be followed by a noun or pronoun and either an unmarked or a marked infinitive.

Emma *helped Brian wash* the dishes.
Emma *helped Brian to wash* the dishes.

NOTE: The infinitive is used in some typical constructions with *too* and *enough*.

TOO + ADJECTIVE + INFINITIVE	The gift is *too large to wrap*.
ENOUGH + NOUN + INFINITIVE	Our emergency pack has *enough bottled water to last* a week.
ADJECTIVE + *ENOUGH* + INFINITIVE	Some of the hikers felt *strong enough to climb* another thousand feet.

> **Exercise 28–4** Form sentences by adding gerund or infinitive constructions to the following sentence openings. In some cases, more than one kind of construction is possible. Possible answers appear in the back of the book.

Please remind your sister to call me.
                    ^

a. I enjoy
b. The tutor told Samantha
c. The team hopes
d. Ricardo and his brothers miss
e. Jon remembered

29 Articles (*a, an, the*)

Articles (*a, an, the*) are part of a category of words known as *noun markers* or *determiners*.

29a Be familiar with articles and other noun markers.

Standard English uses noun markers to help identify the nouns that follow. In addition to articles (*a, an,* and *the*), noun markers include the following:

- possessive nouns, such as *Elena's* (See 36a.)
- possessive pronoun/adjectives: *my, your, his, her, its, our, their* (See 46b.)
- demonstrative pronoun/adjectives: *this, that, these, those* (See 46b.)
- quantifiers: *all, any, each, either, every, few, many, more, most, much, neither, several, some,* and so on (See 29d.)
- numbers: *one, twenty-three,* and so on

Using articles and other noun markers

Articles and other noun markers always appear before nouns; sometimes other modifiers, such as adjectives, come between a noun marker and a noun.

ART N
Felix is reading a book about mythology.

ART ADJ N
We took an exciting trip to Alaska last summer.

NOUN
MARKER ADV ADJ N
That very delicious meal was expensive.

In most cases, do not use an article with another noun marker.

▶ ~~The~~ Natalie's older brother lives in Wisconsin.

Expressions like *a few*, *the most*, and *all the* are exceptions: *a few potatoes*, *all the rain*. See also 29d.

Types of articles and types of nouns

To choose an appropriate article for a noun, first determine whether the noun is *common* or *proper*, *count* or *noncount*, *singular* or *plural*, and *specific* or *general*. The chart in 29b describes the types of nouns.

Articles are classified as *indefinite* and *definite*. The indefinite articles, *a* and *an*, are used with general nouns. The definite article, *the*, is used with specific nouns. (The last section of the chart in 29b explains general and specific nouns.)

A and *an* both mean "one" or "one among many." Use *a* before a consonant sound: *a banana*, *a vacation*, *a picture*, *a happy child*, *a united family*. Use *an* before a vowel sound: *an eggplant*, *an occasion*, *an uncle*, *an honorable person*. (See also *a, an* in the glossary of usage.)

The shows that a noun is specific; use *the* with one or more than one specific thing: *the newspaper*, *the soldiers*.

29b Use *the* with most specific common nouns.

The definite article, *the*, is used with most nouns — both count and noncount — that the reader can identify specifically. Usually the identity will be clear to the reader for one of the six reasons that follow. (See the next page; see also the first chart in 29c.)

1. The noun has been previously mentioned.

the
▶ A truck cut in front of our van. When truck skidded a few
             ^

seconds later, we almost crashed into it.

The article *A* is used before *truck* when the noun is first mentioned. When the noun is mentioned again, it needs the article *the* because readers can now identify which truck skidded — the one that cut in front of the van.

2. A phrase or clause following the noun restricts its identity.

the
▶ Bryce warned me that GPS in his car was not working.
                       ^
The phrase *in his car* identifies the specific GPS.

NOTE: Descriptive adjectives do not necessarily make a noun specific. A specific noun is one that readers can identify within a group of nouns of the same type.

a
▶ If I win the lottery, I will buy ~~the~~ brand-new bright red
                                   ^

sports car.

The reader cannot identify which specific brand-new bright red sports car the writer will buy. Even though *car* has many adjectives in front of it, it is a general noun in this sentence.

3. A superlative adjective such as *best* or *most intelligent* makes the noun's identity specific. (See also 26d.)

the
▶ Our petite daughter dated tallest boy in her class.
                            ^
The superlative *tallest* makes the noun *boy* specific. Although there might be several tall boys, only one boy can be the tallest.

4. The noun describes a unique person, place, or thing.

the
▶ During an eclipse, one should not look directly at sun.
                                                     ^
There is only one sun in our solar system, so its identity is clear.

5. The context or situation makes the noun's identity clear.

the
▶ Please don't slam door when you leave.
                     ^
Both the speaker and the listener know which door is meant.

Types of nouns

Common or proper

Common nouns	**Examples**	
• name general persons, places, things, or ideas	religion	beauty
	knowledge	student
• begin with lowercase letters	rain	country

Proper nouns	**Examples**	
• name specific persons, places, things, or ideas	Hinduism	President Adams
	Philip	Blue Mosque
• begin with capital letters	Vietnam	Renaissance

Count or noncount (common nouns only)

Count nouns	**Examples**
• name persons, places, things, or ideas that can be counted	girl, girls
	city, cities
	goose, geese
• have plural forms	philosophy, philosophies

Noncount nouns	**Examples**	
• name things or abstract ideas that cannot be counted	water	patience
	silver	knowledge
	furniture	air
• cannot be made plural		

NOTE: See the second chart in 29c for commonly used noncount nouns.

Singular or plural (both common and proper)

Singular nouns (count and noncount)	**Examples**	
• represent one person, place, thing, or idea	backpack	rain
	country	beauty
	woman	Nile River
	achievement	Block Island

Plural nouns (count only)	**Examples**	
• represent more than one person, place, thing, or idea	backpacks	Ural Mountains
	countries	Falkland Islands
	women	achievements
• must be count nouns		

Types of nouns, continued

Specific (definite) or general (indefinite) (count and noncount)

Specific nouns	Examples
• name persons, places, things, or ideas that can be identified within a group of the same type	*The students* in Professor Martin's *class* should study. *The airplane* carrying *the senator* was late. *The furniture* in *the truck* was damaged.

General nouns	Examples
• name categories of persons, places, things, or ideas (often plural)	*Students* should study. *Books* bridge *gaps* between *cultures*. *The airplane* has made commuting between *cities* easy.

6. The noun is singular and refers to a scientific class or category of items (most often animals, musical instruments, and inventions).

   The tin
▶ ~~Tin~~ whistle is common in traditional Irish music.
      ^

   The writer is referring to the tin whistle as a class of musical instruments.

29c Use *a* (or *an*) with common singular count nouns that refer to "one" or "any."

If a count noun refers to one unspecific item (not a whole category), use the indefinite article, *a* or *an*. *A* and *an* usually mean "one among many" but can also mean "any one." (See the first chart in this section.)

                                                        a
▶ My English professor asked me to bring dictionary to class.
                                                        ^

The noun *dictionary* refers to "one unspecific dictionary" or "any dictionary."

▶ We want to rent apartment close to the lake.

The noun *apartment* refers to "any apartment close to the lake," not a specific apartment.

Choosing articles for common nouns

Use *the*

• if the reader has enough information to identify the noun specifically	**COUNT:** Please turn on *the lights*. We're going to *the lake* tomorrow. **NONCOUNT:** *The food* throughout Italy is excellent.

Use *a* or *an*

• if the noun refers to one item *and* • if the item is singular but not specific	**COUNT:** Bring *a pencil* to class. Charles wrote *an essay* about his first job.

NOTE: Do not use *a* or *an* with plural or noncount nouns.

Use a quantifier (*enough*, *many*, *some*, etc.)

• if the noun represents an unspecified amount of something • if the amount is more than one but not all items in a category	**COUNT (plural):** Amir showed us *some photos* of India. *Many turtles* return to the same nesting site each year. **NONCOUNT:** We didn't get *enough rain* this summer.

NOTE: Sometimes no article conveys an unspecified amount: *Amir showed us photos of India.*

Use no article

• if the noun represents all items in a category • if the noun represents a category in general	**COUNT (plural):** *Students* can attend the show for free. **NONCOUNT:** *Coal* is a natural resource.

NOTE: *The* is occasionally used when a singular count noun refers to all items in a class or a specific category: *The bald eagle is no longer endangered in the United States.*

Commonly used noncount nouns

Food and drink

beef, bread, butter, candy, cereal, cheese, cream, meat, milk, pasta, rice, salt, sugar, water, wine

Nonfood substances

air, cement, coal, dirt, gasoline, gold, paper, petroleum, plastic, rain, silver, snow, soap, steel, wood, wool

Abstract nouns

advice, anger, beauty, confidence, courage, employment, fun, happiness, health, honesty, information, intelligence, knowledge, love, poverty, satisfaction, wealth

Use no article

biology (and other areas of study), clothing, equipment, furniture, homework, jewelry, luggage, machinery, mail, money, news, poetry, pollution, research, scenery, traffic, transportation, violence, weather, work

NOTE: A few noncount nouns (such as *love*) can also be used as count nouns: *He had two loves: music and archery.* To refer to all items in a specific category, sometimes writers pair *the* with a noncount noun: *The violence depicted in video games is quite realistic.*

29d Use a quantifier such as *some* or *more*, not *a* or *an*, with a noncount noun to express an approximate amount.

Do not use *a* or *an* with noncount nouns. Also do not use numbers or words such as *several* or *many*; they must be used with plural nouns, and noncount nouns do not have plural forms. (See the chart above for a list of commonly used noncount nouns.)

▶ Dr. Snyder gave us ~~an~~ information about the Peace Corps.

▶ Do you have ~~many~~ money with you?

You can use quantifiers such as *enough*, *less*, and *some* to suggest approximate amounts or nonspecific quantities of noncount nouns: *a little salt, any homework, enough wood, less information, much pollution.*

> some
> ▶ Vincent's mother told him that she had ~~a~~ news that would
>   ^
> surprise him.

29e Do not use articles with nouns that refer to all of something or something in general.

When a noncount noun refers to all of its type or to a concept in general, it is not marked with an article.

> Kindness
> ▶ ~~The kindness~~ is a virtue.
>   ^
> The noun represents kindness in general; it does not represent a specific type of kindness, such as *the kindness he showed me after my mother's death.*

> ▶ In some parts of the world, ~~the~~ rice is preferred to all other grains.
>
> The noun *rice* represents rice in general. To refer to a specific type or serving of rice, the definite article is appropriate: *The rice my husband served last night is the best I've ever tasted.*

In most cases, when you use a count noun to represent a general category, make the noun plural. Do not use unmarked singular count nouns to represent whole categories.

> Fountains are
> ▶ ~~Fountain is~~ an expensive element of landscape design.
>   ^
> *Fountains* is a count noun that represents fountains in general.

EXCEPTION: In some cases, *the* can be used with singular count nouns to represent a class or specific category: *The Chinese alligator is smaller than the American alligator.* See also number 6 in 29b.

29f Do not use articles with most singular proper nouns. Use *the* with most plural proper nouns.

Since singular proper nouns are already specific, they typically do not need an article: *Prime Minister Cameron, Jamaica, Lake Huron, Mount Etna.*

There are, however, many exceptions. In most cases, if the proper noun consists of a common noun with modifiers (adjectives or an *of* phrase), use *the* with the proper noun.

▶ We visited *the* Great Wall of China last year.

▶ Rob wants to be a translator for *the* Central Intelligence Agency.

The is used with most plural proper nouns: *the McGregors, the Bahamas, the Finger Lakes, the United States.*

Geographic names create problems because there are so many exceptions to the rules. When in doubt, consult the chart below, check a dictionary, or ask a native speaker.

Using *the* with geographic nouns	
When to omit *the*	
streets, squares, parks	Ivy Street, Union Square, Denali National Park
cities, states, counties	Miami, New Mexico, Bee County
most countries, continents	Italy, Nigeria, China, South America, Africa
bays, single lakes	Tampa Bay, Lake Geneva
single mountains, islands	Mount Everest, Crete
When to use *the*	
country names with *of* phrase	the United States (of America), the People's Republic of China
large regions, deserts	the East Coast, the Sahara
peninsulas	the Baja Peninsula, the Sinai Peninsula
oceans, seas, gulfs	the Pacific Ocean, the Dead Sea, the Persian Gulf
canals and rivers	the Panama Canal, the Amazon
mountain ranges	the Rocky Mountains, the Alps
groups of islands	the Solomon Islands

Exercise 29–1 ▶ Edit the following sentences for proper use of articles and nouns. If a sentence is correct, write "correct" after it. Answers appear in the back of the book.

~~The~~ Josefina's dance routine was flawless.

a. Doing volunteer work often brings a satisfaction.
b. As I looked out the window of the plane, I could see the Cape Cod.
c. Melina likes to drink her coffees with lots of cream.
d. Recovering from abdominal surgery requires patience.
e. I completed the my homework assignment quickly.

Exercise 29–2 ▶ Articles have been omitted from the following description of winter weather. Insert the articles *a*, *an*, and *the* where English requires them and be prepared to explain your choices.

Many people confuse terms *hail*, *sleet*, and *freezing rain*. Hail normally occurs in thunderstorm and is caused by strong updrafts that lift growing chunks of ice into clouds. When chunks of ice, called hailstones, become too heavy to be carried by updrafts, they fall to ground. Hailstones can cause damage to crops, windshields, and people. Sleet occurs during winter storms and is caused by snowflakes falling from layer of cold air into warm layer, where they become raindrops, and then into another cold layer. As they fall through last layer of cold air, raindrops freeze and become small ice pellets, forming sleet. When it hits car windshield or windows of house, sleet can make annoying racket. Driving and walking can be hazardous when sleet accumulates on roads and sidewalks. Freezing rain is basically rain that falls onto ground and then freezes after it hits ground. It causes icy glaze on trees and any surface that is below freezing.

30 Sentence structure

Although their structure can vary, sentences in English generally flow from subject to verb to object or complement: *Bears eat fish*. This section focuses on the major challenges that multilingual students face when writing sentences in English. For more details on parts of speech and parts of sentences, see chapters 46–49.

 LaunchPad Solo macmillan learning   **Activities for Chapter 30**
8 Exercises, 1 LearningCurve activity, 2 Grammar Girl podcasts

30a Use a linking verb between a subject and its complement.

Some languages, such as Russian and Turkish, do not use linking verbs (*is*, *are*, *was*, *were*) between subjects and complements (nouns or adjectives that rename or describe the subject). Every English sentence, however, must include a verb. For more on linking verbs, see 27e.

▶ Jim $\overset{is}{\wedge}$ intelligent.

▶ Many streets in San Francisco $\overset{are}{\wedge}$ very steep.

30b Include a subject in every sentence.

Some languages, such as Spanish and Japanese, do not require a subject in every sentence. Every English sentence, however, needs a subject.

▶ Your aunt is very energetic. $\overset{\text{She seems}}{\underset{\wedge}{\text{Seems}}}$ young for her age.

Commands are an exception: The subject *you* is understood but not present in the sentence ([*You*] *Give me the book*).

The word *it* is used as the subject of a sentence describing the weather or temperature, stating the time, indicating distance, or suggesting an environmental fact.

▶ $\overset{\text{It is}}{\underset{\wedge}{\text{Is}}}$ raining in the valley and snowing in the mountains.

▶ $\overset{\text{It is}}{\underset{\wedge}{\text{Is}}}$ 9:15 a.m.

In most English sentences, the subject appears before the verb. Some sentences, however, are inverted: The subject comes after the verb. In these sentences, a placeholder called an *expletive* (*there* or *it*) often comes before the verb.

EXP V ⌐─── S ───⌐
There are many people here today. (⌐─── S ───⌐ Many people are here today.)

▶ $\overset{\text{There is}}{\underset{\wedge}{\text{Is}}}$ an apple pie in the refrigerator.

> ~there are~
> As you know, ^ many religious sects in India.

Notice that the verb agrees with the subject that follows it: *apple pie is, sects are.* (See 21g.)

Sometimes an inverted sentence has an infinitive (*to work*) or a noun clause (*that she is intelligent*) as the subject. In such sentences, the placeholder *it* is needed before the verb. (See also 48b and 48e.)

EXP V ⌐ S ⌐ ⌐ S ⌐ V
It is important to study daily. (To study daily is important.)

> it
> Because the road is flooded, ^ is necessary to change our route.

TIP: When the words *here* and *there* mean "in this place" (*here*) or "in that place" (*there*), they are adverbs, which are never subjects.

> It
> I just returned from a vacation in Japan. ~There~ is very
> there.
> beautiful./
> ^

> This school   that school
> ~Here~ offers a master's degree in physical therapy; ~there~ has
> ^   ^
>
> only a bachelor's program.

30c Do not use both a noun and a pronoun to play the same grammatical role in a sentence.

English does not allow a subject to be repeated in its own clause.

> The doctor ~she~ advised me to cut down on salt.

The pronoun *she* cannot repeat the subject, *doctor*.

Do not add a pronoun even when a word group comes between the subject and the verb.

> The watch that I lost on vacation ~it~ was in my backpack.

The pronoun *it* cannot repeat the subject, *watch*.

Some languages allow "topic fronting," placing a word or phrase (a "topic") at the beginning of a sentence and following it with an independent clause that explains something about the topic. This form is not allowed in English because the sentence seems to start with one subject but then introduces a new subject in an independent clause.

┌ TOPIC ┐ ┌──── IND CLAUSE ────┐
INCORRECT   The seeds I planted them last fall.

The sentence can be corrected by bringing the topic (*seeds*) into the independent clause.

the seeds
▶ ~~The seeds~~ I planted ~~them~~ last fall.
             ∧

30d Do not repeat a subject, an object, or an adverb in an adjective clause.

Adjective clauses begin with relative pronouns (*who, whom, whose, which, that*) or relative adverbs (*when, where*). Relative pronouns usually serve as subjects or objects in the clauses they introduce; another word in the clause cannot serve the same function. Relative adverbs should not be repeated by other adverbs later in the clause.

┌──────── ADJ CLAUSE ────────┐
The cat ran under the car that was parked on the street.

▶ **The cat ran under the car that ~~it~~ was parked on the street.**

The relative pronoun *that* is the subject of the adjective clause, so the pronoun *it* cannot be added as a subject.

▶ **Myrna enjoyed the investment seminars that she attended**

~~**them**~~ **last week.**

The relative pronoun *that* is the object of the verb *attended*. The pronoun *them* cannot also serve as an object.

Sometimes the relative pronoun is understood but not present in the sentence. In such cases, do not add another word with the same function as the omitted pronoun.

▶ Myrna enjoyed the seminars she attended ~~them~~ last week.

The relative pronoun *that* is understood after *seminars* even though it is not present in the sentence.

Exercise 30–1 ▶ In the following sentences, add needed subjects or expletives and delete any repeated subjects, objects, or adverbs. Answers appear in the back of the book.

The new geology professor is the one whom we saw ~~him~~ on TV

this morning.

a. Are some cartons of ice cream in the freezer.
b. I don't use the subway because am afraid.
c. The prime minister she is the most popular leader in my country.
d. We tried to get in touch with the same manager whom we spoke to him earlier.
e. Recently have been a number of earthquakes in Turkey.

30e Avoid mixed constructions beginning with *although* or *because*.

A word group that begins with *although* cannot be linked to a word group that begins with *but* or *however*. The result is an error called a *mixed construction* (see also 11a). Similarly, a word group that begins with *because* cannot be linked to a word group that begins with *so* or *therefore*.

If you want to keep *although* or *because*, drop the other linking word. See the following examples.

▶ Although Nikki Giovanni is best known for her poetry for

adults, ~~but~~ she has written several books for children.

▶ Because German and Dutch are related languages, ~~therefore~~

tourists from Berlin can usually read a few signs in Amsterdam.

If you want to keep the other linking word, omit *although* or *because*.

▶ ~~Although~~ Nikki Giovanni is best known for her poetry for

adults, but she has written several books for children.

▶ ~~Because~~ German and Dutch are related languages, ; therefore ,

tourists from Berlin can usually read a few signs in

Amsterdam.

For advice about using commas and semicolons with linking words, see 32a and 34b.

30f Do not place an adverb between a verb and its direct object.

Adverbs modifying verbs can appear in various positions: at the beginning or end of a sentence, before or after a verb, or between a helping verb and its main verb.

Slowly, we drove along the rain-slick road.

Mia handled the teapot very *carefully*.

Martin *always* wins our tennis matches.

Christina is *rarely* late for our lunch dates.

My daughter has *often* spoken of you.

The election results were being *closely* followed by analysts.

However, an adverb cannot appear between a verb and its direct object.

carefully
▶ Mother wrapped ~~carefully~~ the gift.

The adverb *carefully* cannot appear between the verb, *wrapped*, and its direct object, *the gift*.

Exercise 30–2 ▶ Edit the following sentences for proper sentence structure. If a sentence is correct, write "correct" after it. Answers appear in the back of the book.

slowly.
She peeled ~~slowly~~ the banana/

a. Although freshwater freezes at 32 degrees Fahrenheit, however ocean water freezes at 28 degrees Fahrenheit.

b. Because we switched cable packages, so our channel lineup has changed.

c. The competitor mounted confidently his skateboard.

d. My sister performs well the *legong*, a Balinese dance.

e. Because product development is behind schedule, we will have to launch the product next spring.

30g Distinguish between present participles and past participles used as adjectives.

Both present and past participles may be used as adjectives. The present participle always ends in *-ing*. Past participles usually end in *-ed*, *-d*, *-en*, *-n*, or *-t*. (See 27a.)

PRESENT PARTICIPLES	confusing, speaking, boring
PAST PARTICIPLES	confused, spoken, bored

Like all other adjectives, participles can come before nouns; they also can follow linking verbs, in which case they describe the subject of the sentence. (See 47b.)

Use a present participle to describe a person or thing *causing or stimulating an experience.*

The *boring lecture* put us to sleep. [The lecture caused boredom.]

Use a past participle to describe a person or thing *undergoing an experience.*

The *audience* was *bored* by the lecture. [The audience experienced boredom.]

Participles that describe emotions or mental states often cause the most confusion.

annoying/annoyed	exhausting/exhausted
boring/bored	fascinating/fascinated
confusing/confused	frightening/frightened
depressing/depressed	satisfying/satisfied
exciting/excited	surprising/surprised

Exercise 30-3 Edit the following sentences for proper use of present and past participles. If a sentence is correct, write "correct" after it. Answers appear in the back of the book.

> excited
> Danielle and Monica were very ~~exciting~~ to be going to a
>   ^
> Broadway show for the first time.

a. Listening to everyone's complaints all day was irritated.
b. The long flight to Singapore was exhausted.
c. His skill at chess is amazing.
d. After a great deal of research, the scientist made a fascinated discovery.
e. Surviving that tornado was one of the most frightened experiences I've ever had.

30h Place cumulative adjectives in an appropriate order.

Adjectives usually come before the nouns they modify; they may also come after linking verbs. (See 46d and 47b.)

>   ADJ   N   V ADJ
> Janine wore a new necklace. Janine's necklace was new.

Cumulative adjectives are adjectives that build on one another, cannot be joined by the word *and*, and are not separated by commas. These adjectives must be listed in a particular order. If you use cumulative adjectives before a noun, see the chart in this section.

>   stained red plastic
> ▶ My dorm room has only a desk and a ~~plastic red stained~~ chair.
>   ^

Order of cumulative adjectives

FIRST   **ARTICLE OR OTHER NOUN MARKER**   a, an, the, her, Joe's, two, many, some

         EVALUATIVE WORD   attractive, dedicated, delicious, ugly, disgusting

         SIZE   large, enormous, small, little

         LENGTH OR SHAPE   long, short, round, square

         AGE   new, old, young, antique

         COLOR   yellow, blue, crimson

         NATIONALITY   French, Peruvian, Vietnamese

         RELIGION   Catholic, Protestant, Jewish, Muslim

         MATERIAL   silver, walnut, wool, marble

LAST   **NOUN/ADJECTIVE**   tree (as in *tree* house), kitchen (as in *kitchen* table)

THE NOUN MODIFIED   house, coat, bicycle, bread, woman, coin

My large blue wool **coat** is in the attic.

Exercise 30–4   Using the chart in 30h as necessary, arrange the following modifiers and nouns in their proper order. Answers appear in the back of the book.

     two new French racing bicycles
     new, French, two, bicycles, racing

a.   sculptor, young, an, Vietnamese, intelligent
b.   dedicated, a, priest, Catholic
c.   old, her, sweater, blue, wool
d.   delicious, Joe's, Scandinavian, bread
e.   many, boxes, jewelry, antique, beautiful

31 Prepositions and idiomatic expressions

31a Become familiar with prepositions that show time and place.

The most frequently used prepositions in English are *at*, *by*, *for*, *from*, *in*, *of*, *on*, *to*, and *with*. Prepositions can be difficult to master because the differences among them are subtle and idiomatic. The chart in this section is limited to three troublesome prepositions that show time and place: *at*, *on*, and *in*.

At, *on*, and *in* to show time and place

Showing time

AT	*at* a specific time: *at* 7:20, *at* dawn, *at* dinner
ON	*on* a specific day or date: *on* Tuesday, *on* June 4
IN	*in* a part of a 24-hour period: *in* the afternoon, *in* the daytime [but *at* night]
	in a year or month: *in* 2008, *in* July
	in a period of time: finished *in* three hours

Showing place

AT	*at* a meeting place or location: *at* home, *at* the club
	at the edge of something: sitting *at* the desk
	at the corner of something: turning *at* the intersection
	at a target: throwing the snowball *at* Lucy
ON	*on* a surface: placed *on* the table, hanging *on* the wall
	on a street: the house *on* Spring Street
	on an electronic medium: *on* television, *on* the Internet
IN	*in* an enclosed space: *in* the garage, *in* an envelope
	in a geographic location: *in* San Diego, *in* Texas
	in a print medium: *in* a book, *in* a magazine

 LaunchPad Solo macmillan learning **Activities for Chapter 31**
2 Exercises, 1 LearningCurve activity, 2 Grammar Girl podcasts

Not every possible use is listed in the chart, so don't be surprised when you encounter exceptions and idiomatic uses that you must learn one at a time. For example, in English a person rides *in* a car but *on* a bus, plane, train, or subway.

▶ My first class starts ~~on~~ *at* 8:00 a.m.

▶ The farmers go to market ~~in~~ *on* Wednesday.

Exercise 31-1 In the following sentences, replace prepositions that are not used correctly. You may need to refer to the chart in 31a. If a sentence is correct, write "correct" after it. Answers appear in the back of the book.

The play begins ~~on~~ *at* 7:20 p.m.

a. Whenever we eat at the Centerville Café, we sit at a small table on the corner of the room.

b. In the 1990s, entrepreneurs created new online businesses in record numbers.

c. In Thursday, Nancy will attend her first home repair class at the community center.

d. Alex began looking for her lost mitten in another location.

e. We decided to go to a restaurant because there was no fresh food on the refrigerator.

31b Use nouns (including *-ing* forms) after prepositions.

In a prepositional phrase, use a noun (not a verb) after the preposition. Sometimes the noun will be a gerund, the *-ing* verb form that functions as a noun (see 48b).

▶ Our student government is good at ~~save~~ *saving* money.

Distinguish between the preposition *to* and the infinitive marker *to*. If *to* is a preposition, it should be followed by a noun or a gerund.

▶ We are dedicated to ~~help~~ *helping* the poor.

If *to* is an infinitive marker, it should be followed by the base form of the verb.

▶ We want to ~~helping~~ the poor.
       ^help

To test whether *to* is a preposition or an infinitive marker, insert a word that you know is a noun after the word *to*. If the noun makes sense in that position, *to* is a preposition. If the noun does not make sense after *to*, then *to* is an infinitive marker.

Zoe is addicted *to* _____.

They are planning *to* _____.

In the first sentence, a noun (such as *magazines*) makes sense after *to*, so *to* is a preposition and should be followed by a noun or a gerund: Zoe is addicted *to magazines*. Zoe is addicted *to running*.

In the second sentence, a noun (such as *magazines*) does not make sense after *to*, so *to* is an infinitive marker and must be followed by the base form of the verb: They are planning *to build* a new school.

31c Become familiar with common adjective + preposition combinations.

Some adjectives appear only with certain prepositions. These expressions are idiomatic and may be different from the combinations used in your native language.

▶ Paula is married ~~with~~ Jon.
                    ^to

31d Become familiar with common verb + preposition combinations.

Many verbs and prepositions appear together in idiomatic phrases. Pay special attention to the combinations that are different from the combinations used in your native language.

▶ Your success depends ~~of~~ your effort.
                       ^on

Adjective + preposition combinations

accustomed to	connected to	guilty of	preferable to
addicted to	covered with	interested in	proud of
afraid of	dedicated to	involved in	responsible
angry with	devoted to	involved with	for
ashamed of	different from	known as	satisfied with
aware of	engaged in	known for	scared of
committed to	engaged to	made of (*or*	similar to
concerned	excited about	made from)	tired of
about	familiar with	married to	worried
concerned with	full of	opposed to	about

NOTE: Check an ESL dictionary for other combinations.

Verb + preposition combinations

agree with	compare with	forget about	speak to (*or*
apply to	concentrate on	happen to	speak with)
approve of	consist of	hope for	stare at
arrive at	count on	insist on	succeed at
arrive in	decide on	listen to	succeed in
ask for	depend on	participate in	take advantage of
believe in	differ from	rely on	take care of
belong to	disagree with	reply to	think about
care about	dream about	respond to	think of
care for	dream of	result in	wait for
compare to	feel like	search for	wait on

NOTE: Check an ESL dictionary for other combinations.

PUNCTUATION

32 The comma

The comma was invented to help readers. Without it, sentence parts can collide into one another unexpectedly, causing misreadings.

CONFUSING	If you cook Elmer will do the dishes.
CONFUSING	While we were eating a rattlesnake approached our campsite.

Add commas in the logical places (after *cook* and *eating*), and suddenly all is clear. No longer is Elmer being cooked, the rattlesnake being eaten.

Various rules have evolved to prevent such misreadings and to speed readers along through complex grammatical structures. Those rules are detailed in this section. (Section 33 explains when not to use commas.)

32a Use a comma before a coordinating conjunction joining independent clauses.

When a coordinating conjunction connects two or more independent clauses — word groups that could stand alone as separate sentences — a comma must come before the conjunction. There are seven coordinating conjunctions in English: *and*, *but*, *or*, *nor*, *for*, *so*, and *yet*.

A comma tells readers that one independent clause has come to a close and that another is about to begin.

▶ **The department sponsored a seminar on college survival skills ,**
 and it also hosted a barbecue for new students.

EXCEPTION: If the two independent clauses are short and there is no danger of misreading, the comma may be omitted: *The plane took off and we were on our way.*

TIP: Do *not* use a comma with a coordinating conjunction that joins only two words, phrases, or subordinate clauses. (See 33a.)

LaunchPad Solo Activities for Chapter 32
macmillan learning   8 Exercises, 1 LearningCurve activity, 8 Grammar Girl podcasts

▶ A good money manager controls expenses / and invests surplus

dollars to meet future needs.

The word group following *and* is not an independent clause; it is the
second half of a compound predicate (*controls . . . and invests*).

32b Use a comma after an introductory clause or phrase.

The most common introductory word groups are clauses and
phrases functioning as adverbs. Such word groups usually tell
when, where, how, why, or under what conditions the main
action of the sentence occurred. (See 48a, 48b, and 48e.)

A comma tells readers that the introductory clause or phrase
has come to a close and that the main part of the sentence is
about to begin.

▶ When Irwin was ready to iron, his cat tripped on the cord.
                                 ∧

Without the comma, readers may have Irwin ironing his cat. The
comma signals that *his cat* is the subject of a new clause, not part of the
introductory one.

EXCEPTION: The comma may be omitted after a short adverb
clause or phrase if there is no danger of misreading: *In no time
we were at 2,800 feet.*

Sentences also frequently begin with participial phrases that
function as adjectives, describing the noun or pronoun immediately following them. The comma tells readers that they are about
to learn the identity of the person or thing described; therefore,
the comma is usually required even when the phrase is short.
(See 48b.)

▶ Buried under layers of younger rocks, the earth's oldest rocks
                                       ∧

contain no fossils.

NOTE: Other introductory word groups include transitional expressions and absolute phrases (see 32f).

Exercise 32-1 ▶   Add or delete commas where necessary in the following sentences. If a sentence is correct, write "correct" after it. Answers appear in the back of the book.

> **Because we had been saving molding for a few weeks, we had**
>
> **enough wood to frame all thirty paintings.**

a.   Alisa brought the injured bird home, and fashioned a splint out of Popsicle sticks for its wing.

b.   Considered a classic of early animation *The Adventures of Prince Achmed* used hand-cut silhouettes against colored backgrounds.

c.   If you complete the evaluation form and return it within two weeks you will receive a free breakfast during your next stay.

d.   After retiring from the New York City Ballet in 1965, legendary dancer Maria Tallchief went on to found the Chicago City Ballet.

e.   Roger had always wanted a handmade violin but he couldn't afford one.

Exercise 32-2 ▶   Add or delete commas where necessary in the following sentences. If a sentence is correct, write "correct" after it. Answers appear in the back of the book.

> **The car had been sitting idle for a month, so the battery was**
>
> **completely dead.**

a.   J. R. R. Tolkien finished writing his draft of *The Lord of the Rings* trilogy in 1949 but the first book in the series wasn't published until 1954.

b.   In the first two minutes of its ascent the space shuttle had broken the sound barrier and reached a height of over twenty-five miles.

c.   German shepherds can be gentle guide dogs or they can be fierce attack dogs.

d.   Some former professional cyclists claim that the use of performance-enhancing drugs is widespread in cycling and they argue that no rider can be competitive without doping.

e.   As an intern, I learned most aspects of the broadcasting industry but I never learned about fundraising.

32c Use commas to separate items in a series.

When three or more items are presented in a series, those items should be separated from one another with commas. Items in a series may be single words, phrases, or clauses.

▶ Langston Hughes's poetry is concerned with racial pride, social

justice, and the diversity of the African American experience.
         ^

Although some writers view the last comma in a series as optional, most experts advise using the comma because its omission can result in ambiguity or misreading.

▶ My uncle willed me all of his property, houses, and boats.
                                                 ^

Did the uncle will his property *and* houses *and* boats — or simply his property, consisting of houses and boats? If the former meaning is intended, a comma is necessary to prevent ambiguity.

32d Use a comma between coordinate adjectives not joined with *and*. Do not use a comma between cumulative adjectives.

When two or more adjectives each modify a noun separately, they are coordinate.

Roberto is a *warm, gentle, affectionate* father.

If the adjectives can be joined with *and*, the adjectives are coordinate, so you should use commas: *warm* and *gentle* and *affectionate* (*warm, gentle, affectionate*).

Adjectives that build on one another instead of modifying the noun separately are cumulative.

Three large gray shapes moved slowly toward us.

Beginning with the adjective closest to the noun *shapes*, these modifiers lean on one another, piggyback style, with each modifying a larger word group. *Gray* modifies *shapes*, *large* modifies *gray shapes*, and *three* modifies *large gray shapes*. Cumulative adjectives cannot be joined with *and* (not *three* and *large* and *gray shapes*).

COORDINATE ADJECTIVES

▶ Should patients with severe, irreversible brain damage be put
                                    ^

on life support systems?

Adjectives that can be connected with *and* are coordinate: *severe and irreversible.*

CUMULATIVE ADJECTIVES

▶ Ira ordered a rich / chocolate / layer cake.

Ira didn't order a cake that was rich and chocolate and layer: He ordered a *layer cake* that was *chocolate*, a *chocolate layer cake* that was *rich*.

Exercise 32–3 ▶ Add or delete commas where necessary in the following sentences. If a sentence is correct, write "correct" after it. Answers appear in the back of the book.

We gathered our essentials, took off for the great outdoors, and
                                                              ^

ignored the fact that it was Friday the 13th.

a. The cold impersonal atmosphere of the university was unbearable.
b. An ambulance cut through police cars, fire trucks and bystanders.
c. The *1812 Overture* is a stirring, magnificent piece of music.
d. After two broken arms, three cracked ribs and one concussion, Ken quit the varsity football team.
e. My cat's pupils had constricted to small black shining slits.

Exercise 32–4 ▶ Add or delete commas where necessary in the following sentences. If a sentence is correct, write "correct" after it. Answers appear in the back of the book.

Good social workers excel in patience, diplomacy, and
                                                  ^

positive thinking.

a. NASA's rovers on Mars are equipped with special cameras that can take close-up high-resolution pictures of the terrain.
b. A baseball player achieves the triple crown by having the highest batting average, the most home runs, and the most runs batted in during the regular season.
c. If it does not get enough sunlight, a healthy green lawn can turn into a shriveled brown mess within a matter of days.
d. Love, greed and betrayal are common themes in fiction.
e. Sharks often mistake surfboards for small, injured seals.

32e Use commas to set off nonrestrictive (nonessential) elements. Do not use commas to set off restrictive (essential) elements.

Certain word groups that modify nouns or pronouns can be restrictive or nonrestrictive — that is, essential or not essential to the meaning of a sentence. These word groups are usually adjective clauses, adjective phrases, or appositives.

Restrictive elements

A restrictive element defines or limits the meaning of the word it modifies; it is therefore essential to the meaning of the sentence and is not set off with commas. If you remove a restrictive modifier from a sentence, the meaning changes significantly, becoming more general than you intended.

> RESTRICTIVE (NO COMMAS)
>
> The campers need clothes *that are durable.*
>
> Scientists *who study the earth's structure* are called geologists.

The first sentence does not mean that the campers need clothes in general. The intended meaning is more limited: The campers need durable clothes. The second sentence does not mean that scientists in general are called geologists; only those scientists who specifically study the earth's structure are called geologists. The italicized word groups are essential and are therefore not set off with commas.

Nonrestrictive elements

A nonrestrictive modifier describes a noun or pronoun whose meaning has already been clearly defined or limited. Because the modifier contains nonessential or parenthetical information, it is set off with commas. If you remove a nonrestrictive element from a sentence, the meaning does not change dramatically. You can think about it this way: The punctuation helps you "lift" the modifier up and out of the sentence without affecting the meaning.

> NONRESTRICTIVE (WITH COMMAS)
>
> The campers need sturdy shoes, *which are expensive*.
>
> The scientists, *who represented eight different universities*, met to review applications for the Advancements in Science Award.

In the first sentence, the campers need sturdy shoes, and the shoes happen to be expensive. In the second sentence, the scientists met to review applications for the award; that they represented eight different universities is informative but not critical to the meaning of the sentence. The nonessential information in both sentences is set off with commas.

NOTE: Often it is difficult to tell whether a word group is restrictive or nonrestrictive without seeing it in context and considering the writer's meaning. Both of the following sentences are grammatically correct, but their meaning is slightly different.

> The dessert made with fresh raspberries was delicious.

> The dessert, made with fresh raspberries, was delicious.

In the first example, the phrase *made with fresh raspberries* tells readers which of two or more desserts the writer is referring to. In the example with commas, the phrase merely adds information about the dessert.

Adjective clauses

Adjective clauses are patterned like sentences, containing subjects and verbs, but they function within sentences as modifiers of nouns or pronouns. They always follow the word they modify, usually immediately. Adjective clauses begin with a relative pronoun (*who, whom, whose, which, that*) or with a relative adverb (*where, when*). (See also 48e.)

Nonrestrictive adjective clauses are set off with commas; restrictive adjective clauses are not.

NONRESTRICTIVE CLAUSE (WITH COMMAS)

▶ **Ed's house, which is located on thirteen acres, was completely**

furnished with bats in the rafters and mice in the kitchen.

The adjective clause *which is located on thirteen acres* does not restrict the meaning of *Ed's house*; the information is nonessential and is therefore set off with commas.

RESTRICTIVE CLAUSE (NO COMMAS)

▶ **The giant panda/that was born at the San Diego Zoo in 2003/**

was sent to China in 2007.

Because the adjective clause *that was born at the San Diego Zoo in 2003* identifies one particular panda out of many, the information is essential and is therefore not set off with commas.

NOTE: Use *that* only with restrictive (essential) clauses. Many writers prefer to use *which* only with nonrestrictive (nonessential) clauses, but usage varies.

Adjective phrases

Prepositional or verbal phrases functioning as adjectives may be restrictive or nonrestrictive. Nonrestrictive phrases are set off with commas; restrictive phrases are not.

NONRESTRICTIVE PHRASE (WITH COMMAS)

▶ The helicopter, with its million-candlepower spotlight

illuminating the area, circled above.

The *with* phrase is nonessential because its purpose is not to specify which of two or more helicopters is being discussed. The phrase is not required for readers to understand the meaning of the sentence.

RESTRICTIVE PHRASE (NO COMMAS)

▶ One corner of the attic was filled with newspapers/ dating from

the early 1900s.

Dating from the early 1900s restricts the meaning of *newspapers*, so the comma should be omitted.

Appositives

An appositive is a noun or noun phrase that renames a nearby noun. Nonrestrictive appositives are set off with commas; restrictive appositives are not.

NONRESTRICTIVE APPOSITIVE (WITH COMMAS)

▶ Darwin's most important book, *On the Origin of Species,* was the

result of many years of research.

Most important restricts the meaning to one book, so the appositive *On the Origin of Species* is nonrestrictive and should be set off with commas.

RESTRICTIVE APPOSITIVE (NO COMMAS)

▶ The song / "Viva la Vida/" was blasted out of huge amplifiers.

Once they've read *song*, readers still don't know precisely which song the writer means. The appositive following *song* restricts its meaning, so the appositive should not be set off with commas.

Exercise 32-5 ▶ Add or delete commas where necessary in the following sentences. If a sentence is correct, write "correct" after it. Answers appear in the back of the book.

My sister⌄ who plays center for the Sparks⌄ now lives at The Sands⌄

a beach house near Los Angeles.

a. Choreographer Alvin Ailey's best-known work *Revelations* is more than just a crowd-pleaser.

b. Twyla Tharp's contemporary ballet *Push Comes to Shove* was made famous by the Russian dancer Baryshnikov. [*Tharp has written more than one contemporary ballet.*]

c. The glass sculptor sifting through hot red sand explained her technique to the other glassmakers. [*There is more than one glass sculptor.*]

d. A member of an organization, that provides job training for teens, was also appointed to the education commission.

e. Brian Eno who began his career as a rock musician turned to meditative compositions in the late 1970s.

32f Use commas to set off transitional expressions and other word groups.

Transitional expressions

Transitional expressions serve as bridges between sentences or parts of sentences. They include conjunctive adverbs such as *however, therefore,* and *moreover* and transitional phrases such as *for example, as a matter of fact,* and *in other words.* (For complete lists of these expressions, see 34b.)

When a transitional expression appears between independent clauses in a compound sentence, it is preceded by a semicolon and is usually followed by a comma. (See 34b.)

▶ Minh did not understand our language; moreover, he was

unfamiliar with our customs.

When a transitional expression appears at the beginning of a sentence or in the middle of an independent clause, it is usually set off with commas.

▶ Natural foods are not always salt free; celery, for example,

contains more sodium than most people would imagine.

EXCEPTION: If a transitional expression blends smoothly with the rest of the sentence, calling for little or no pause in reading, it does not need to be set off with a comma. Expressions such as *also, at least, certainly, consequently, indeed, of course, no doubt, perhaps, then,* and *therefore* do not always call for a pause.

Alice's bicycle is broken; *therefore* you will need to borrow Sue's.

Parenthetical expressions

Expressions that are distinctly parenthetical, providing only supplemental information, should be set off with commas. They interrupt the flow of a sentence or appear at the end as afterthoughts.

▶ Evolution, as far as we know, doesn't work this way.

Absolute phrases

An absolute phrase, which modifies the whole sentence, usually consists of a noun followed by a participle or participial phrase. (See 48d.) Absolute phrases may appear at the beginning or at the end of a sentence and should be set off with commas.

```
┌──────── ABSOLUTE PHRASE ────────┐
  N  PARTICIPLE
The sun appearing for the first time in a week, we were at last able
```

to begin the archaeological dig.

▶ Elvis Presley made music industry history in the 1950s, his

records having sold more than ten million copies.

NOTE: Do not insert a comma between the noun and the participle in an absolute construction.

▶ The next contestant / being five years old, the host adjusted the

height of the microphone.

Word groups expressing contrast

Sharp contrasts beginning with words such as *not*, *never*, and *unlike* are set off with commas.

▶ Unlike Robert, Celia loves using Instagram.
             ^

32g Use commas to set off nouns of direct address, the words *yes* and *no*, interrogative tags, and mild interjections.

▶ Forgive me, Angela, for forgetting your birthday.
           ^   ^

▶ Yes, the loan will probably be approved.
      ^

▶ The film was faithful to the book, wasn't it?
                                   ^

32h Use commas with expressions such as *he said* to set off direct quotations.

▶ In his "Letter from Birmingham Jail," Martin Luther King Jr.

wrote, "We know through painful experience that freedom is
      ^

never voluntarily given by the oppressor; it must be demanded

by the oppressed" (225).

See 37 on the use of quotation marks and pages 428–29 on citing literary sources in MLA style.

32i Use commas with dates, addresses, titles, and numbers.

Dates

In dates, set off the year from the rest of the sentence with a pair of commas.

> ▶ On December 12, 1890, orders were sent out for the arrest of
>
> Sitting Bull.

EXCEPTIONS: Commas are not needed if the date is inverted or if only the month and year are given.

> The security alert system went into effect on 15 April 2009.
>
> February 2015 was an extremely snowy month.

Addresses

The elements of an address or a place name are separated with commas. A zip code, however, is not preceded by a comma.

> ▶ Please send the package to Greg Tarvin at 708 Spring Street,
>
> Washington, IL 61571.

Titles

If a title follows a name, set off the title from the rest of the sentence with a pair of commas.

> ▶ Ann Hall, MD, has been appointed to the board of trustees.

Numbers

In numbers more than four digits long, use commas to separate the numbers into groups of three, starting from the right. In numbers four digits long, a comma is optional.

> 3,500 [*or* 3500]
>
> 100,000
>
> 5,000,000

EXCEPTIONS: Do not use commas in street numbers, zip codes, telephone numbers, or years with four or fewer digits.

Exercise 32-6 This exercise covers the major uses of the comma described in 32a–32e. Add or delete commas where necessary. If a sentence is correct, write "correct" after it. Answers appear in the back of the book.

> **Even though our brains actually can't focus on two tasks at a**
>
> **time, many people believe they can multitask.**

a. Cricket which originated in England is also popular in Australia, South Africa and India.

b. At the sound of the starting pistol the horses surged forward toward the first obstacle, a sharp incline three feet high.

c. After seeing an exhibition of Western art Gerhard Richter escaped from East Berlin, and smuggled out many of his notebooks.

d. Corrie's new wet suit has an intricate, blue pattern.

e. We replaced the rickety, old, spiral staircase with a sturdy, new ladder.

Exercise 32-7 This exercise covers the major uses of the comma described in 32a–32e. Edit the following paragraph to correct any comma errors.

> Hope for Paws, a nonprofit rescue organization in Los Angeles tells many sad stories of animal abuse and neglect. Most of the stories, however have happy endings. One such story involves Woody, a dog left behind, after his master died. For a long lonely year, Woody took refuge under a neighbor's shed, waiting in vain, for his master's return. He survived on occasional scraps from his neighbors who eventually contacted Hope for Paws. When rescuers reached Woody, they found a malnourished, and frightened dog who had one blind eye and dirty, matted, fur. Gently, Woody was pulled from beneath the shed, and taken to the home of a volunteer, who fosters orphaned pets. There, Woody was fed, shaved, bathed and loved. Woody's story had the happiest of endings, when a family adopted him. Now Woody has a new forever home and he is once again a happy, well-loved dog.

Exercise 32-8 This exercise covers all uses of the comma. Add or delete commas where necessary in the following sentences. If a sentence is correct, write "correct" after it. Answers appear in the back of the book.

"Yes, neighbors, we must work together to save the community

center," urged Mr. Owusu.

a. On January 16, 2017 our office moved to 29 Commonwealth Avenue, Mechanicsville VA 23111.

b. The coach having bawled us out thoroughly, we left the locker room with his harsh words ringing in our ears.

c. Ms. Carlson you are a valued customer whose satisfaction is very important to us.

d. Mr. Mundy was born on July 22, 1939 in Arkansas, where his family had lived for four generations.

e. Her board poised at the edge of the half-pipe, Nina waited her turn to drop in.

33 Unnecessary commas

Many common misuses of the comma result from a misunderstanding of the major comma rules presented in 32.

33a Do not use a comma with a coordinating conjunction that joins only two words, phrases, or subordinate clauses.

Though a comma should be used before a coordinating conjunction joining independent clauses (see 32a) or with a series of three or more elements (see 32c), these rules should not be extended to other compound word groups.

▶ Ron discovered a leak, and came back to fix it.

The coordinating conjunction *and* links two verbs in a compound predicate: *discovered* and *came*.

▶ We knew that she had won, but that the election was close.

The coordinating conjunction *but* links two subordinate clauses, each beginning with *that*.

33b Do not use a comma to separate a verb from its subject or object.

A sentence should flow from subject to verb to object without unnecessary pauses. Commas may appear between these major sentence elements only when a specific rule calls for them.

▶ Zoos large enough to give the animals freedom to roam,/ are

becoming more popular.

> The comma should not separate the subject, *Zoos*, from the verb, *are becoming*.

33c Do not use a comma before the first or after the last item in a series.

Though commas are required between items in a series (32c), do not place them either before or after the whole series.

▶ Other causes of asthmatic attacks are,/ stress, change in

temperature, and cold air.

▶ Even novels that focus on horror, evil, and alienation,/ often have

themes of spiritual renewal and redemption as well.

33d Do not use a comma between cumulative adjectives, between an adjective and a noun, or between an adverb and an adjective.

Commas are required between coordinate adjectives (those that can be joined with *and*), but they do not belong between cumulative adjectives (those that cannot be joined with *and*). (For a full discussion, see 32d.)

▶ In the corner of the closet, we found an old,/ maroon hatbox.

A comma should never be used between an adjective and the noun that follows it.

▶ It was a senseless, dangerous/ mission.

Nor should a comma be used between an adverb and an adjective that follows it.

▶ Rehabilitation often helps severely/ injured patients.

33e Do not use commas to set off restrictive elements.

Restrictive elements are modifiers or appositives that restrict the meaning of the nouns they follow. Because they are essential to the meaning of the sentence, they are not set off with commas. (For a full discussion of restrictive and nonrestrictive elements, see 32e.)

▶ Drivers/ who think they own the road/ make cycling a

dangerous sport.

> The modifier *who think they own the road* restricts the meaning of *Drivers* and is essential to the meaning of the sentence. Putting commas around the *who* clause falsely suggests that all drivers think they own the road.

33f Do not use a comma to set off a concluding adverb clause that is essential for meaning.

When adverb clauses introduce a sentence, they are nearly always followed by a comma (see 32b). When they conclude a sentence, however, they are not set off by a comma if their content is essential to the meaning of the earlier part of the sentence. Adverb clauses beginning with *after, as soon as, because, before, if, since, unless, until,* and *when* are usually essential.

▶ Don't visit Paris at the height of the tourist season/ unless you

have booked hotel reservations.

> Without the *unless* clause, the meaning of the sentence might at first seem broader than the writer intended.

When a concluding adverb clause is nonessential, it should be preceded by a comma. Clauses beginning with *although, even though, though,* and *whereas* are usually nonessential.

▶ The lecture seemed to last only a short time, although the clock

said it had gone on for more than an hour.

33g Do not use a comma after a phrase that begins an inverted sentence.

Though a comma belongs after most introductory phrases (see 32b), it does not belong after phrases that begin an inverted sentence. In an inverted sentence, the subject follows the verb, and a phrase that ordinarily would follow the verb is moved to the beginning.

▶ At the bottom of the hill,/ sat the stubborn mule.

33h Avoid other common misuses of the comma.

Do not use a comma in the following situations.

AFTER A COORDINATING CONJUNCTION (*AND*, *BUT*, *OR*, *NOR*, *FOR*, *SO*, *YET*)

▶ Occasionally TV talk shows are performed live, but,/ more often

they are taped.

AFTER *SUCH AS* OR *LIKE*

▶ Shade-loving plants such as,/ begonias, impatiens, and coleus

can add color to a shady garden.

AFTER *ALTHOUGH*

▶ Although,/ the air was balmy, the water was cold.

BEFORE A PARENTHESIS

▶ Though Sylvia's ACT score was low,/ (only 22), her application

essay was superior.

TO SET OFF AN INDIRECT (REPORTED) QUOTATION

▶ Samuel Goldwyn once said/ that a verbal contract isn't worth the

paper it's written on.

WITH A QUESTION MARK OR AN EXCLAMATION POINT

▶ "Why don't you try it?/" she coaxed. "You can't do any worse

than the rest of us."

Exercise 33–1 Delete any unnecessary commas in the following sentences. If a sentence is correct, write "correct" after it. Answers appear in the back of the book.

In his Silk Road Project, Yo-Yo Ma incorporates work by

musicians such as/ Kayhan Kalhor and Richard Danielpour.

a. After the morning rains cease, the swimmers emerge from their cottages.
b. Tricia's first artwork was a bright, blue, clay dolphin.
c. Some modern musicians, (trumpeter John Hassell is an example) blend several cultural traditions into a unique sound.
d. Myra liked hot, spicy foods such as, chili, kung pao chicken, and buffalo wings.
e. On the display screen, was a soothing pattern of light and shadow.

Exercise 33–2 Delete unnecessary commas in the following passage.

Each spring since 1970, New Orleans has hosted the Jazz and Heritage Festival, an event that celebrates the music, food, and culture, of the region. Although, it is often referred to as "Jazz Fest," the festival typically includes a wide variety of musical styles such as, gospel, Cajun, blues, zydeco, and, rock and roll. Famous musicians who have appeared regularly at Jazz Fest, include Dr. John, B. B. King, and Aretha Franklin. Large stages are set up throughout the fairgrounds in a way, that allows up to ten bands to play simultaneously without any sound overlap. Food tents are located throughout the festival, and offer popular, local dishes like crawfish Monica, jambalaya, and fried, green tomatoes. Following Hurricane Katrina in 2005, Jazz Fest revived quickly, and attendance has steadily increased each year. Fans, who cannot attend the festival, still enjoy the music by downloading songs, and watching performances online.

34 The semicolon

The semicolon is used to connect major sentence elements of equal grammatical rank.

34a Use a semicolon between closely related independent clauses not joined with a coordinating conjunction.

When two independent clauses appear in one sentence, they are usually linked with a comma and a coordinating conjunction (*and, but, or, nor, for, so, yet*). If the clauses are closely related and the relation is clear without a conjunction, they may be linked with a semicolon instead.

> In film, a low-angle shot makes the subject look powerful; a high-angle shot does just the opposite.

A semicolon must be used whenever a coordinating conjunction has been omitted between independent clauses. To use merely a comma creates a type of run-on sentence known as a *comma splice*. (See 20.)

▶ In 1800, a traveler needed six weeks to get from New York City

to Chicago/; in 1860, the trip by railroad took only two days.
      ^

34b Use a semicolon between independent clauses linked with a transitional expression.

Transitional expressions include conjunctive adverbs and transitional phrases.

CONJUNCTIVE ADVERBS

accordingly	certainly	furthermore	indeed
also	consequently	hence	instead
anyway	conversely	however	likewise
besides	finally	incidentally	meanwhile

CONJUNCTIVE ADVERBS

moreover	now	still	therefore
nevertheless	otherwise	subsequently	thus
next	similarly	then	
nonetheless	specifically		

TRANSITIONAL PHRASES

after all	even so	in fact
as a matter of fact	for example	in other words
as a result	for instance	in the first place
at any rate	in addition	on the contrary
at the same time	in conclusion	on the other hand

When a transitional expression appears between independent clauses, it is preceded by a semicolon and usually followed by a comma.

▶ Many corals grow very gradually,/; in fact, the creation of a

coral reef can take centuries.

When a transitional expression appears in the middle or at the end of the second independent clause, the semicolon goes *between the clauses.*

▶ Biologists have observed laughter in primates other than

humans,/; chimpanzees, however, sound more like they are

panting than laughing.

Transitional expressions should not be confused with the co-ordinating conjunctions *and, but, or, nor, for, so,* and *yet,* which are preceded by a comma when they link independent clauses. (See 32a.)

34c Use a semicolon between items in a series containing internal punctuation.

▶ Researchers point to key benefits of positive thinking: It leads

to high self-esteem, especially in people who focus on their

achievements/; it helps make social interactions, such as those
with co-workers, more enjoyable/; and, most important, it
results in better sleep and overall health.

Without the semicolons, the reader would have to sort out the major groupings, distinguishing between important and less important pauses according to the logic of the sentence. By inserting semicolons at the major breaks, the writer does this work for the reader.

34d Avoid common misuses of the semicolon.

Do not use a semicolon in the following situations.

BETWEEN A SUBORDINATE CLAUSE AND THE REST OF THE SENTENCE

► Although children's literature was added to the National

Book Awards in 1969/, it has had its own award, the Newbery

Medal, since 1922.

BETWEEN AN APPOSITIVE AND THE WORD IT REFERS TO

► The scientists were fascinated by the species *Argyroneta*

aquatica/, a spider that lives underwater.

TO INTRODUCE A LIST

► Some of my favorite celebrities have their own blogs/: Katy

Perry, Beyoncé, and Zooey Deschanel.

BETWEEN INDEPENDENT CLAUSES JOINED BY *AND*, *BUT*, *OR*, *NOR*, *FOR*, *SO*, OR *YET*

► Five of the applicants had worked with spreadsheets/, but

only one was familiar with database management.

EXCEPTIONS: If one or both of the independent clauses contain a comma, you may use a semicolon with a coordinating conjunction between the clauses.

Exercise 34–1 ▶ Add commas or semicolons where needed in the following well-known quotations. If a sentence is correct, write "correct" after it. Answers appear in the back of the book.

> **If an animal does something, we call it instinct; if we do**
>
> **the same thing, we call it intelligence.** — **Will Cuppy**

a. Do not ask me to be kind just ask me to act as though I were.
   — Jules Renard

b. When men talk about defense they always claim to be protecting women and children but they never ask the women and children what they think. — Pat Schroeder

c. When I get a little money I buy books if any is left I buy food and clothes. — Desiderius Erasmus

d. America is a country that doesn't know where it is going but is determined to set a speed record getting there.
   — Laurence J. Peter

e. Wit has truth in it wisecracking is simply calisthenics with words.
   — Dorothy Parker

Exercise 34–2 ▶ Edit the following sentences to correct errors in the use of the comma and the semicolon. If a sentence is correct, write "correct" after it. Answers appear in the back of the book.

> **Love is blind; envy has its eyes wide open.**

a. Strong black coffee will not sober you up, the truth is that time is the only way to get alcohol out of your system.

b. Margaret was not surprised to see hail and vivid lightning, conditions had been right for violent weather all day.

c. There is often a fine line between right and wrong; good and bad; truth and deception.

d. My mother always says that you can't learn common sense; either you're born with it or you're not.

e. Severe, unremitting pain is a ravaging force; especially when the patient tries to hide it from others.

35 The colon

The colon is used primarily to call attention to the words that follow it. In addition, the colon has some conventional uses.

35a Use a colon after an independent clause to direct attention to a list, an appositive, a quotation, or a summary or an explanation.

A LIST

The daily routine should include at least the following: ten minutes of stretching, forty abdominal crunches, and a twenty-minute run.

AN APPOSITIVE

My roommate seems to live on two things: sushi and social media.

A QUOTATION

Consider the words of Benjamin Franklin: "There never was a good war or a bad peace."

A SUMMARY OR AN EXPLANATION

Faith is like love: it cannot be forced.

NOTE: For other ways of introducing quotations, see "Introducing quoted material" in 37e. When an independent clause follows a colon, beginning with a capital letter is optional. Some disciplines use a lowercase letter (*Faith is like love: it cannot be forced*). See also 57a (MLA) or 62a (APA).

35b Use a colon according to convention.

SALUTATION IN A LETTER   Dear Editor:

HOURS AND MINUTES   5:30 p.m.

PROPORTIONS   The ratio of women to men was 2:1.

TITLE AND SUBTITLE   *The Glory of Hera: Greek Mythology and the Greek Family*

BIBLIOGRAPHIC ENTRIES   Boston: Bedford/St. Martin's, 2018

CHAPTER AND VERSE IN SACRED TEXT   Luke 2:14, Qur'an 67:3

35c Avoid common misuses of the colon.

A colon must be preceded by a full independent clause. Therefore, avoid using it in the following situations.

BETWEEN A VERB AND ITS OBJECT OR COMPLEMENT

▶ Some important vitamins found in vegetables are:̷vitamin A,

thiamine, niacin, and vitamin C.

BETWEEN A PREPOSITION AND ITS OBJECT

▶ The heart's two pumps each consist of:̷an upper chamber,

or atrium, and a lower chamber, or ventricle.

AFTER *SUCH AS*, *INCLUDING*, OR *FOR EXAMPLE*

▶ The NCAA regulates college athletic teams, including:̷

basketball, baseball, softball, and football.

Exercise 35–1 ▶ Edit the following sentences to correct errors in the use of the comma, the semicolon, or the colon. If a sentence is correct, write "correct" after it. Answers appear in the back of the book.

Lifting the cover gently, Luca found the source of the odd

sound;̷: a marble in the gears.
   ^

a. We always looked forward to Thanksgiving in Vermont: It was our only chance to see our Grady cousins.

b. If we have come to fight, we are far too few, if we have come to die, we are far too many.

c. The travel package includes: a round-trip ticket to Athens, a cruise through the Cyclades, and all hotel accommodations.

d. The news article portrays the land use proposal as reckless; although 62 percent of the town's residents support it.

e. Psychologists Kindlon and Thompson (2000) offer parents a simple starting point for raising male children, "Teach boys that there are many ways to be a man" (p. 256).

36 The apostrophe

36a Use an apostrophe to indicate that a noun is possessive.

Possessive nouns usually indicate ownership, as in *Tim's hat*, *the lawyer's desk*. Frequently, however, ownership is only loosely implied: *the tree's roots*, *a day's work*. If you are not sure whether a noun is possessive, try turning it into an *of* phrase: *the roots of the tree*, *the work of a day*. (Pronouns also have possessive forms. See 36b and 36e.)

When to add -'s

1. If the noun does not end in -s, add -'s.

    Luck often propels a rock musician's career.

    The Children's Defense Fund is a nonprofit organization that supports programs for poor and minority children.

2. If the noun is singular and ends in -s or an s sound, add -'s to indicate possession.

    Lois's sister spent last year in India.

    Her article presents an overview of Marx's teachings.

NOTE: To avoid potentially awkward pronunciation, some writers use only the apostrophe with a singular noun ending in -s: *Sophocles'*.

When to add only an apostrophe

If the noun is plural and ends in -s, add only an apostrophe.

    Both diplomats' briefcases were searched by guards.

Joint possession

To show joint possession, use *-'s* or (*-s'*) with the last noun only; to show individual possession, make all nouns possessive.

> Have you seen Joyce and Greg's new camper?
>
> John's and Marie's expectations of marriage couldn't have been more different.

Joyce and Greg jointly own one camper. John and Marie individually have different expectations.

Compound nouns

If a noun is compound, use *-'s* (or *-s'*) with the last element.

> My father-in-law's memoir about his childhood in Sri Lanka was just published.

36b Use an apostrophe and -s to indicate that an indefinite pronoun is possessive.

Indefinite pronouns refer to no specific person or thing: *everyone, someone, no one, something.* (See 46b.)

> Someone's raincoat has been left behind.

36c Use an apostrophe to mark omissions in contractions and numbers.

In a contraction, the apostrophe takes the place of one or more missing letters. *It's* stands for *it is*, *can't* for *cannot*.

> It's a shame that Frank can't go on the tour.

The apostrophe is also used to mark the omission of the first two digits of a year (*the class of '08*) or years (*the '60s generation*).

36d Do not use an apostrophe in certain situations.

An apostrophe typically is not used to form the plural of numbers, letters, abbreviations, and words mentioned as words. Note the few exceptions and be consistent throughout your paper.

Plural of numbers

Do not use an apostrophe in the plural of any numbers.

> Oksana skated nearly perfect figure 8s.
>
> The 1920s are known as the Jazz Age.

Plural of letters

Italicize the letter and use roman (regular) font style for the *-s* ending. Do not italicize academic grades.

> Two large *P*s were painted on the door.
>
> He received two Ds for the first time in his life.

However, to avoid misreading, most writers use an apostrophe to form the plural of lowercase letters and the capital letters *A* and *I*.

> Beginning readers often confuse *b*'s and *d*'s.
>
> Students with straight A's earn high honors.

MLA NOTE: MLA recommends using an apostrophe for the plural of single capital and lowercase letters: *H*'s, *p*'s.

Plural of abbreviations

Do not use an apostrophe to form the plural of an abbreviation.

> Harry Kloor earned two PhDs simultaneously in 1994.

Plural of words mentioned as words

Generally, omit the apostrophe to form the plural of words mentioned as words. If the word is italicized, the *-s* ending appears in roman (regular) type.

> We've heard enough *maybe*s.

Words mentioned as words may also appear in quotation marks. When you choose this option, use the apostrophe.

> We've heard enough "maybe's."

36e Avoid common misuses of the apostrophe.

Do not use an apostrophe with nouns that are not possessive or with the possessive pronouns *its, whose, his, hers, ours, yours,* and *theirs.*

▶ Some ~~outpatient's~~ ^{outpatients} have special parking permits.

▶ Each area has ~~it's~~ ^{its} own conference room.

It's means "it is." The possessive pronoun *its* contains no apostrophe despite the fact that it is possessive.

▶ We attended a reading by Michael Chabon, ~~who's~~ ^{whose} work often

focuses on Jewish identity.

Who's means "who is." The possessive pronoun is *whose.*

Exercise 36–1   Edit the following sentences to correct errors in the use of the apostrophe. If a sentence is correct, write "correct" after it. Answers appear in the back of the book.

Our favorite barbecue restaurant is Poor ~~Richards~~ ^{Richard's} Ribs.

a. This diet will improve almost anyone's health.
b. The innovative shoe fastener was inspired by the designers young son.
c. Each days menu features a different European country's dish.
d. Sue worked overtime to increase her families earnings.
e. Ms. Jacobs is unwilling to listen to students complaints about computer failures.

Exercise 36–2   Edit the following passage to correct errors in the use of the apostrophe.

Its never too soon to start holiday shopping. In fact, some people choose to start shopping as early as January, when last seasons leftover's are priced at their lowest. Many stores try to lure customers in with promise's of savings up to 90 percent. Their main objective, of course, is to make way for next years inventory. The big problem with postholiday shopping, though, is that there isn't much left to choose from. Store's shelves have been picked over by last-minute shoppers desperately searching for gifts. The other problem is that its hard to know what to buy so far in advance. Next year's hot items are anyones guess. But proper timing, mixed with lot's of luck and determination, can lead to good purchases at great price's.

37 Quotation marks

Writers use quotation marks primarily to enclose direct quotations of another person's spoken or written words. You will also find quotation marks used in the following situations:

- for quotations within quotations (single quotation marks: 37b)
- for titles of short works (37c)
- for words used as words (37d)
- with other marks of punctuation (37e)
- with brackets and ellipsis marks (39c, 39d)

Quotation marks should not be used for indirect quotations, paraphrases, or summaries or for long quotations (37a).

37a Use quotation marks to enclose direct quotations.

Direct quotations of a person's words, whether spoken or written, must be in quotation marks.

> "Twitter," according to social media researcher Jameson Brown, "is the best social network for brand to customer engagement."

In dialogue, begin a new paragraph to mark a change in speaker.

> "Mom, his name is Willie, not William. A thousand times I've told you, it's *Willie*."
> "Willie is a derivative of William, Lester. Surely his birth certificate doesn't have Willie on it, and I like calling people by their proper names."
> "Yes, it does, ma'am. My mother named me Willie K. Mason."
> — Gloria Naylor

If a single speaker utters more than one paragraph, introduce each paragraph with a quotation mark, but do not use a closing quotation mark until the end of the speech.

Exception: Indirect quotations

Do not use quotation marks around indirect quotations. An indirect quotation reports someone's ideas without using that person's exact words. In academic writing, indirect quotation is called *paraphrase* or *summary*.

> Researcher Jameson Brown claims that Twitter is the best social media tool for companies that want to reach their consumers.

Exception: Long quotations

Long quotations of prose or poetry are generally set off from the text by indenting. Quotation marks are not used because the indented format tells readers that the quotation is taken word-for-word from the source.

> After making an exhaustive study of the historical record, James Horan evaluates Billy the Kid like this:
>
> > The portrait that emerges of [the Kid] from the thousands of pages of affidavits, reports, trial transcripts, his letters, and his testimony is neither the mythical Robin Hood nor the stereotyped adenoidal moron and pathological killer. Rather Billy appears as a disturbed, lonely young man, honest, loyal to his friends, dedicated to his beliefs, and betrayed by our institutions and the corrupt, ambitious, and compromising politicians in his time. (158)

The number in parentheses is a citation in MLA style. (See 56a.)

MLA and APA have specific guidelines for what constitutes a long quotation and how it should be indented (see 55b and 60b, respectively).

37b Use single quotation marks to enclose a quotation within a quotation.

> Megan Marshall notes that Elizabeth Peabody's school focused on "not merely 'teaching' but 'educating children morally and spiritually as well as intellectually from the first' " (107).

37c Use quotation marks around the titles of short works.

Short works include newspaper and magazine articles, poems, short stories, songs, episodes of television and radio programs, and chapters or subdivisions of books.

> James Baldwin's story "Sonny's Blues" tells the story of two brothers who come to understand each other's suffering.

NOTE: Titles of long works such as books, plays, television and radio programs, films, magazines, and newspapers appear in italics. (See 42a.)

37d Quotation marks may be used to set off words used as words.

Although words used as words are ordinarily italicized (see 42d), quotation marks are also acceptable. Be consistent throughout your paper.

> The terms "migrant" and "refugee" are sometimes confused.
>
> The terms *migrant* and *refugee* are sometimes confused.

37e Use punctuation with quotation marks according to convention.

This section describes the conventions American publishers follow in placing various marks of punctuation inside or outside quotation marks. It also explains how to punctuate when introducing quoted material. (For the use of quotation marks in MLA and APA styles, see 56a and 61a, respectively. The examples in this section show MLA style.)

Periods and commas

Place periods and commas inside quotation marks.

> "I'm here as part of my service-learning project," I told the classroom teacher. "I'm hoping to become a reading specialist."

This rule applies to single quotation marks as well as double quotation marks. (See 37b.) It also applies to all uses of quotation marks: for quoted material, for titles of works, and for words used as words.

NOTE: In MLA and APA styles of parenthetical in-text citations, the period follows the citation in parentheses.

> James M. McPherson comments, approvingly, that the Whigs "were not averse to extending the blessings of American liberty, even to Mexicans and Indians" (48).

Colons and semicolons

Put colons and semicolons outside quotation marks.

> Harold wrote, "I regret that I am unable to attend the fundraiser for diabetes research"; his letter, however, came with a donation.

Question marks and exclamation points

Put question marks and exclamation points inside quotation marks unless they apply to the whole sentence.

> Dr. Abram's first question was "What three goals do you have for the course?"
>
> Have you heard the proverb "Do not climb the hill until you reach it"?

In the first sentence, the question mark applies only to the quoted question. In the second sentence, the question mark applies to the whole sentence.

NOTE: In MLA and APA styles for a quotation that ends with a question mark or an exclamation point, the parenthetical citation and a period should follow the entire quotation.

> Rosie Thomas asks, "Is nothing in life ever straight and clear, the way children see it?" (77).

Introducing quoted material

After a word group introducing a quotation, choose a colon, a comma, or no punctuation at all, whichever is appropriate in context.

Formal introduction If a quotation is formally introduced, a colon is appropriate. A formal introduction is a full independent clause, not just an expression such as *he said.*

> Thomas Friedman provides a challenging yet optimistic view of the future: "We need to get back to work on our country and on our planet. The hour is late, the stakes couldn't be higher, the project couldn't be harder, the payoff couldn't be greater" (25).

Expression such as *she writes* If a quotation is introduced with an expression such as *she writes* — or if it is followed by such an expression — a comma is needed.

> "With regard to air travel," Stephen Ambrose notes, "Jefferson was a full century ahead of the curve" (53).
>
> "Unless another war is prevented it is likely to bring destruction on a scale never before held possible and even now hardly conceived," Albert Einstein wrote in the aftermath of the atomic bomb (29).

Blended quotation When a quotation is blended into the writer's own sentence, either a comma or no punctuation is appropriate, depending on how the quotation fits into the sentence structure.

> The future champion could, as he put it, "float like a butterfly and sting like a bee."
>
> Virginia Woolf wrote in 1928 that "a woman must have money and a room of her own if she is to write fiction" (4).

Beginning of sentence If a quotation appears at the beginning of a sentence, use a comma after it unless the quotation ends with a question mark or an exclamation point.

> "I've always thought of myself as a reporter," American poet Gwendolyn Brooks once stated (162).
>
> "What is it?" she asked, bracing herself.

Interrupted quotation If a quoted sentence is interrupted by explanatory words, use commas to set off the explanatory words. If two successive quoted sentences from the same source are interrupted by explanatory words, use a comma before the explanatory words and a period after them.

> "Everyone agrees journalists must tell the truth," Bill Kovach and Tom Rosenstiel write. "Yet people are befuddled about what 'the truth' means" (37).

37f Avoid common misuses of quotation marks.

Do not use quotation marks to draw attention to familiar slang, to disown trite expressions, or to justify an attempt at humor.

▶ The economist noted that his prediction for a 5 percent decline

was only a ̶"̶ballpark figure.̶"̶

Do not use quotation marks around the title of your own essay.

Exercise 37–1 Add or delete quotation marks as needed and make any other necessary changes in punctuation in the following sentences. If a sentence is correct, write "correct" after it. Answers appear in the back of the book.

Gandhi once said, "An eye for an eye only ends up making the
            ^

whole world blind."
                  ^

a. As for the advertisement "Sailors have more fun", if you consider chipping paint and swabbing decks fun, then you will have plenty of it.

b. Even after forty minutes of discussion, our class could not agree on an interpretation of Robert Frost's poem "The Road Not Taken."

c. After winning the lottery, Juanita said that "she would give half the money to charity."

d. After the movie, Vicki said, "The reviewer called this flick "trash of the first order." I guess you can't believe everything you read."

e. "Cleaning your house while your kids are still growing," said Phyllis Diller, "is like shoveling the walk before it stops snowing."

Exercise 37–2 Add or delete quotation marks as needed and make any other necessary changes in punctuation in the following passage. Citations should conform to MLA style (see 54b).

In his article The Moment of Truth, former vice president Al Gore argues that global warming is a genuine threat to life on Earth and that we must act now to avoid catastrophe. Gore calls our situation a "true *planetary emergency*" and cites scientific evidence of the greenhouse effect and its consequences (170-71). "What is at stake, Gore insists, is the survival of our civilization and the habitability of the Earth (197)." With such a grim predicament at hand, Gore questions why so many political and economic leaders are reluctant to act. "Is it simply more convenient to ignore the warnings," he asks (171)?

The crisis, of course, will not go away if we just pretend it isn't there. Gore points out that in Chinese two symbols form the character for the word crisis. The first of those symbols means "danger", and the second means "opportunity." The danger we face, he claims, is accompanied by "unprecedented opportunity." (172) Gore contends that throughout history we have won battles against seemingly unbeatable evils such as slavery and fascism and that we did so by facing the truth and choosing the moral high ground. Gore's final appeal is to our humanity:

> "Ultimately, [the fight to end global warming] is not about any scientific discussion or political dialogue; it is about who we are as human beings. It is about our capacity to transcend our limitations, to rise to this new occasion. To see with our hearts, as well as our heads, the response that is now called for." (244)

Gore feels that the fate of our world rests in our own hands, and his hope is that we will make the choice to save the planet.

Source of quotations: Gore, Al. "The Moment of Truth." *Vanity Fair*, May 2006, pp. 170+.

38 End punctuation

38a The period

Use a period to end all sentences except direct questions or genuine exclamations. Also use periods in abbreviations according to convention.

To end sentences

Most sentences should end with a period. A sentence that reports a question instead of asking it directly (an indirect question) should end with a period, not a question mark.

▶ The professor asked whether talk therapy was more beneficial

than antidepressants~~?~~.
   ^

If a sentence is not a genuine exclamation, it should end with a period, not an exclamation point. (See also 38c.)

▶ After years of research, Dr. Low finally solved the equation~~!~~.
                                                     ^

In abbreviations

A period is conventionally used in abbreviations of titles and Latin words or phrases, including the time designations for morning and afternoon if lowercase letters are used.

Mr.	i.e.	a.m. (or AM)
Ms.	e.g.	p.m. (or PM)
Dr.	etc.	

NOTE: If a sentence ends with a period marking an abbreviation, do not add a second period.

Do not use a period with US Postal Service abbreviations for states: MD, TX, CA.

Current usage is to omit the period in abbreviations of organization names, academic degrees, and designations for eras.

NATO	UNESCO	UCLA	BS	BC
IRS	AFL-CIO	NIH	PhD	BCE

38b The question mark

A direct question should be followed by a question mark.

What is the horsepower of a 777 engine?

TIP: Use a period after an indirect question, one that is reported rather than asked directly.

▶ He asked me who was teaching the math course this year~~?~~.
                                                      ^

38c The exclamation point

Use an exclamation point after a word group or sentence to express exceptional feeling or to provide emphasis. The exclamation point is rarely appropriate in academic writing.

When Gloria entered the room, I switched on the lights, and we all yelled, "Surprise!"

TIP: Do not overuse the exclamation point.

▶ **In the fisherman's memory, the fish lives on, increasing in**

length and weight with each passing year, until at last it is

big enough to shade a fishing boat!.
                                      ^

This sentence doesn't need to be pumped up with an exclamation point. It is emphatic enough without it.

Exercise 38–1 Add appropriate end punctuation in the following paragraph.

Although I am generally rational, I am superstitious I never walk under ladders or put shoes on the table If I spill the salt, I go into frenzied calisthenics picking up the grains and tossing them over my left shoulder As a result of these curious activities, I've always wondered whether knowing the roots of superstitions would quell my irrational responses Superstition has it, for example, that one should never place a hat on the bed This superstition arises from a time when head lice were common and placing a guest's hat on the bed stood a good chance of spreading lice through the host's bed Doesn't this make good sense And doesn't it stand to reason that, if I know that my guests don't have lice, I shouldn't care where their hats go Of course it does It is fair to ask, then, whether I have changed my ways and place hats on beds Are you kidding I wouldn't put a hat on a bed if my life depended on it

39 Other punctuation marks

39a The dash

When typing, use two hyphens to form a dash (--). Do not put a space before or after the dash. If your word processing program has what is known as an "em-dash" (—), you may use it instead, with no space before or after it.

Use a dash to set off parenthetical material that deserves emphasis.

> One of music's rising trends — lyrics that promote the use of synthetic drugs — is leading some artists to speak out against their peers.

Use a dash to set off appositives that contain commas. An appositive is a noun or noun phrase that renames a nearby noun. Ordinarily, most appositives are set off with commas (32e), but when the appositive itself contains commas, a pair of dashes helps readers see the relative importance of all the pauses.

> In my hometown, people's basic needs — food, clothing, and shelter — are less costly than in a big city like Los Angeles.

A dash can also introduce a list, a restatement or an amplification, or a dramatic shift in tone or thought.

> Along the wall are the bulk liquids — sesame seed oil, honey, safflower oil, and that half-liquid "peanuts only" peanut butter.

> In his last semester, Peter tried to pay more attention to his priorities — applying to graduate school and getting financial aid.

> Kiere took a few steps back, came running full speed, kicked a mighty kick — and missed the ball.

In the first two examples, the writer could instead use a colon. (See 35a.) The colon is more formal than the dash and not quite as dramatic.

39b Parentheses

Use parentheses to enclose supplemental material, minor digressions, and afterthoughts.

> Nurses record patients' vital signs (temperature, pulse, and blood pressure) several times a day.

Use parentheses to enclose letters or numbers labeling items in a series.

> Regulations stipulated that only the following equipment could be used on the survival mission: (1) a knife, (2) thirty feet of parachute line, (3) a book of matches, (4) two ponchos, (5) an E tool, and (6) a signal flare.

TIP: Rough drafts sometimes contain unnecessary parentheses. As writers write, they often think of additional details, using parentheses to work them in as best they can. Such sentences usually can be revised to read more smoothly.

▶ Researchers have said that seventeen million ~~(estimates run as~~ *from* ^

~~high as~~ twenty-three million)~~ Americans have diabetes. *to* ^

39c Brackets

Use brackets to enclose any words or phrases that you have inserted into an otherwise word-for-word quotation.

> *Audubon* reports that "if there are not enough young to balance deaths, the end of the species [California condor] is inevitable" (4).

The sentence quoted from the *Audubon* article did not contain the words *California condor* (since the context of the full article made clear what species was meant), so the writer needed to add the name in brackets.

The Latin word "sic" in brackets indicates that an error in a quoted sentence appears in the original source.

> According to the review, Nelly Furtado's performance was brilliant, "exceding [sic] the expectations of even her most loyal fans."

Do not overuse "sic," however, since calling attention to others' mistakes can appear snobbish. The preceding quotation, for example, might have been paraphrased instead: *According to the review, even Nelly Furtado's most loyal fans were surprised by the brilliance of her performance.*

39d The ellipsis mark

The ellipsis mark consists of three spaced periods. Use an ellipsis mark to indicate that you have deleted words from an otherwise word-for-word quotation.

> Shute (2010) acknowledges that treatment for autism can be expensive: "Sensory integration therapy . . . can cost up to $200 an hour" (82).

If you delete a full sentence or more in the middle of a quoted passage, use a period before the three ellipsis dots.

> "If we don't properly train, teach, or treat our growing prison population," says longtime reform advocate Luis Rodríguez, "somebody else will. . . . This may well be the safety issue of the new century" (16).

TIP: Ordinarily, do not use the ellipsis mark at the beginning or at the end of a quotation. Readers will understand that the quoted material is taken from a longer passage. If you have cut some words from the end of the final quoted sentence, however, MLA requires an ellipsis mark.

In quoted poetry, use a full line of ellipsis dots to indicate that you have dropped a line or more from the poem, as in this example from "To His Coy Mistress" by Andrew Marvell:

> Had we but world enough, and time,
> This coyness, lady, were no crime.
> . . . .
> But at my back I always hear
> Time's wingèd chariot hurrying near; (1–2, 21–22)

39e The slash

Use the slash to separate two or three lines of poetry that have been run into your text. Add a space both before and after the slash.

> In the opening lines of "Jordan," George Herbert pokes gentle fun at popular poems of his time: "Who says that fictions only and false hair / Become a verse? Is there in truth no beauty?" (1–2).

Four or more lines of poetry should be handled as an indented quotation. (See 37a.)

The slash may occasionally be used to separate paired terms such as *pass/fail* and *producer/director*. Be sparing in this use of the slash. In particular, avoid the use of *and/or*, *he/she*, and *his/her*. Instead of using *he/she* and *his/her* to solve sexist language problems, you can usually find more graceful alternatives. (See 17e and 22a.)

Exercise 39–1 Edit the following sentences to correct errors in punctuation, focusing especially on appropriate use of the dash, parentheses, brackets, the ellipsis mark, and the slash. If a sentence is correct, write "correct" after it. Answers appear in the back of the book.

Social insects,/ — bees, for example,/— are able to communicate

complicated messages to one another.

a. A client left his/her cell phone in our conference room after the meeting.

b. The films we made of Kilauea — on our trip to Hawaii Volcanoes National Park — illustrate a typical spatter cone eruption.

c. Although he was confident in his course selections, Greg chose the pass/fail option for Chemistry 101.

d. Of three engineering fields, chemical, mechanical, and materials, Keegan chose materials engineering for its application to toy manufacturing.

e. The writer Chitra Divakaruni explained her work with other Indian American immigrants: "Many women who came to Maitri [a women's support group in San Francisco] needed to know simple things like opening a bank account or getting citizenship. . . . Many women in Maitri spoke English, but their English was functional rather than emotional. They needed someone who understands their problems and speaks their language."

MECHANICS

40 Abbreviations

Use abbreviations only when they are clearly appropriate and universally understood (such as *Dr., a.m., PhD,* and so on). This section provides details about common abbreviations and about how to handle abbreviations that might not be familiar to your audience.

40a Use standard abbreviations for titles immediately before and after proper names.

TITLES BEFORE PROPER NAMES	TITLES AFTER PROPER NAMES
Mr. Rafael Zabala	William Albert Sr.
Ms. Nancy Linehan	Thomas Hines Jr.
Dr. Margaret Simmons	Robert Simkowski, MD
Rev. John Stone	Margaret Chin, LLD

Do not abbreviate a title if it is not used with a proper name.

　　　　　　　professor
▶ My history ~~prof.~~ is an expert on race relations in South Africa.
　　　　　　　^

Avoid redundant titles such as *Dr. Amy Day, MD.* Choose one title or the other: *Dr. Amy Day* or *Amy Day, MD.*

40b Use abbreviations only when you are sure your readers will understand them.

Familiar abbreviations for the names of organizations, companies, countries, academic degrees, and common terms, written without periods, are generally acceptable.

NBA	CEO	PhD	DVD
FBI	MD	NAACP	ESL

Talk show host Conan O'Brien is a Harvard graduate with a BA in history.

The YMCA has opened a new gym close to my office.

When using an unfamiliar abbreviation (such as *NASW* for National Association of Social Workers) or a potentially ambiguous abbreviation (such as *AMA*, which might refer to the American Medical Association or the American Management Association), write the full name followed by the abbreviation in parentheses at the first mention. Then use just the abbreviation throughout the rest of the paper.

40c Use *BC*, *AD*, *a.m.*, *p.m.*, *No.*, and *$* only with specific dates, times, numbers, and amounts.

The abbreviation *BC* (before Christ) follows a date, and *AD* (*anno Domini*) precedes a date. Acceptable alternatives are *BCE* (before the common era) and *CE* (common era), both of which follow a date.

40 BC (or 40 BCE)	4:00 a.m. (or AM)	No. 12 (or no. 12)
AD 44 (or 44 CE)	6:00 p.m. (or PM)	$150

Avoid using *a.m.*, *p.m.*, *No.*, or *$* unaccompanied by a specific numeral: *in the morning* (not *in the a.m.*).

40d Units of measurement

The following are typical abbreviations for units of measurement. Most sciences and related fields use metric units (*km*, *mg*), but in other fields and in everyday use, US standard units (*mi*, *lb*) are typical. As a general rule, use the abbreviations for units when they appear with numerals; spell out the units when they are used alone or when they are used with spelled-out numbers (see also 41a).

METRIC UNITS	US STANDARD UNITS
m, cm, mm	yd, ft, in.
km, kph	mi, mph
kg, g, mg	lb, oz

Results were measured in pounds.

Runners in the 5-km race had to contend with pouring rain.

Use no periods after abbreviations for units of measurement. Only the abbreviation for "inch" (*in.*) takes a period, to distinguish it from the preposition *in*.

40e Be sparing in your use of Latin abbreviations.

Latin abbreviations are acceptable in footnotes and bibliographies.

cf. (Latin *confer*, "compare")

e.g. (Latin *exempli gratia*, "for example")

et al. (Latin *et alia*, "and others")

etc. (Latin *et cetera*, "and so forth")

i.e. (Latin *id est*, "that is")

N.B. (Latin *nota bene*, "note well")

In most academic writing, use the appropriate English phrases.

40f Plural of abbreviations

To form the plural of most abbreviations, add -*s*, without an apostrophe: *PhDs*, *DVDs*. Do not add -*s* to indicate the plural of units of measurement: *mm* (not *mms*).

40g Avoid inappropriate abbreviations.

In academic writing, abbreviations for the following are not commonly accepted.

PERSONAL NAMES Charles (not Chas.)

DAYS OF THE WEEK Monday (not Mon.)

HOLIDAYS Christmas (not Xmas)

MONTHS January, February, March (not Jan., Feb., Mar.)

COURSES OF STUDY political science (not poli. sci.)

DIVISIONS OF WRITTEN WORKS chapter, page (not ch., p.)

STATES AND COUNTRIES Massachusetts (not MA or Mass.)

PARTS OF A BUSINESS NAME Adams Lighting Company (not Adams Lighting Co.); Kim and Brothers (not Kim and Bros.)

NOTE: Use abbreviations for units of measurement when they are preceded by numerals (*13 cm*). Do not abbreviate them when they are used alone. (See 40d.)

EXCEPTION: Abbreviate states and provinces in complete addresses, and always abbreviate *DC* when used with *Washington*.

Exercise 40–1 Edit the following sentences to correct errors in abbreviations. If a sentence is correct, write "correct" after it. Answers appear in the back of the book.

This year ~~Xmas~~ Christmas will fall on a ~~Tues.~~ Tuesday.

a. Since its inception, the BBC has maintained a consistently high standard of radio and television broadcasting.

b. Some combat soldiers are trained by govt. diplomats to be sensitive to issues of culture, history, and religion.

c. Mahatma Gandhi has inspired many modern leaders, including Martin Luther King Jr.

d. A gluten-free diet is not always the best strategy for shedding lbs.

e. The work of Dr. Khan, a psych. professor and researcher, has helped practitioners better understand post-traumatic stress.

41 Numbers

41a Follow the conventions in your discipline for spelling out or using numerals to express numbers.

In the humanities, which generally follow Modern Language Association (MLA) style, use numerals only for specific numbers larger than one hundred: *353, 1,020*. Spell out numbers one hundred and below and large round numbers: *eleven, thirty-five, sixty, fifteen million.*

The social sciences and other disciplines that follow American Psychological Association (APA) style use numerals for all but the numbers one through nine. In APA style, spell out numbers from one to nine even when they are used with related numerals in a passage: *The survey found that nine of the 157 respondents had not taken a course on alcohol use.* See the sample APA-style student paper in 62b.

If a sentence begins with a number, spell out the number or rewrite the sentence.

> One hundred fifty
> ▶ ~~150~~ children in our program need expensive dental treatment.
> ⌃

Rewriting the sentence may be less awkward if the number is long:
In our program, 150 children need expensive dental treatment.

41b Use numerals according to convention in dates, addresses, and so on.

DATES July 4, 1776; 56 BC; AD 30

ADDRESSES 77 Latches Lane, 519 West 42nd Street

PERCENTAGES 55 percent (or 55%)

FRACTIONS, DECIMALS ⅞, 0.047

SCORES 7 to 3, 21–18

STATISTICS average age 37, average weight 180

SURVEYS 4 out of 5

EXACT AMOUNTS OF MONEY $105.37, $106,000

DIVISIONS OF BOOKS volume 3, chapter 4, page 189

DIVISIONS OF PLAYS act 3, scene 3 (or act III, scene iii)

TIME OF DAY 4:00 p.m., 1:30 a.m.

NOTE: When not using *a.m.* or *p.m.*, write out the time in words (*two o'clock in the afternoon, twelve noon, seven in the morning*).

Exercise 41–1 ▶ Edit the following sentences to correct errors in the use of numbers. If a sentence is correct, write "correct" after it. Answers appear in the back of the book.

$3.06
By the end of the evening, Ashanti had only ~~three dollars~~
⌃
~~and six cents~~ left.

a. The carpenters located 3 maple timbers, 21 sheets of cherry, and 10 oblongs of polished ebony for the theater set.

b. The program's cost is well over one billion dollars.

c. The score was tied at 5–5 when the momentum shifted and carried the Standards to a decisive 12–5 win.

d. 8 students in the class had been labeled "learning disabled."

e. The Vietnam Veterans Memorial in Washington, DC, had fifty-eight thousand one hundred thirty-two names inscribed on it when it was dedicated in 1982.

42 Italics

This section describes conventional uses for italics. (If your instructor requires underlining, simply substitute underlining for italics in the examples in this section.)

Some computer and online applications do not allow for italics. To indicate words that should be italicized, you can use underscore marks or asterisks before and after the words.

I will write my senior thesis on _ The Book Thief _.

NOTE: Excessive use of italics to emphasize words or ideas, especially in academic writing, is distracting.

42a Italicize the titles of works according to convention.

Titles of the following types of works should be italicized.

TITLES OF BOOKS *The Color Purple, The Round House*

MAGAZINES *Time, Scientific American, Slate*

NEWSPAPERS the *Baltimore Sun*, the *Orlando Sentinel Online*

PAMPHLETS *Common Sense, Facts about Marijuana*

LONG POEMS *The Waste Land, Paradise Lost*

PLAYS *The Humans, Hamilton*

FILMS *Casablanca, Moonlight*

TELEVISION PROGRAMS *The Voice*, *Frontline*

RADIO PROGRAMS *All Things Considered*

MUSICAL COMPOSITIONS *Porgy and Bess*

CHOREOGRAPHIC WORKS *Brief Fling*

WORKS OF VISUAL ART *American Gothic*

DATABASES [MLA] *JSTOR*

WEBSITES *Salon*, *Google*

COMPUTER SOFTWARE OR APPS [MLA] *Photoshop*, *Instagram*

The titles of other works — including short stories, essays, episodes of radio and television programs, songs, and short poems — are enclosed in quotation marks. (See 37c.)

NOTE: Do not use italics when referring to the Bible, titles of books in the Bible (Genesis, not *Genesis*), or titles of legal documents (the Constitution, not the *Constitution*).

42b Italicize the names of specific ships, spacecraft, and aircraft.

Queen Mary 2, *Endeavour*, *Wright Flyer*

The success of the Soviets' *Sputnik* energized the US space program.

42c Italicize foreign words used in an English sentence.

Shakespeare's Falstaff is a comic character known for both his excessive drinking and his general *joie de vivre*.

EXCEPTION: Do not italicize foreign terms that have become part of the English language — "laissez-faire" and "per diem," for example.

42d Italicize words mentioned as words, letters mentioned as letters, and numbers mentioned as numbers.

Tomás assured us that the chemicals could probably be safely mixed, but his *probably* stuck in our minds.

Some toddlers have trouble pronouncing the letters *f* and *s*.

A big *3* was painted on the stage door.

NOTE: Quotation marks may be used instead of italics to set off words mentioned as words. (See 37d.)

Exercise 42–1 Edit the following sentences to correct errors in the use of italics. If a sentence is correct, write "correct" after it. Answers appear in the back of the book.

The lecture was about Gini Alhadeff's memoir *The Sun at*

Midday. Correct

a. Howard Hughes commissioned the Spruce Goose, a beautifully built but thoroughly impractical wooden aircraft.

b. The old man *screamed* his anger, *shouting* to all of us, "I will not leave my money to you worthless layabouts!"

c. I learned the Latin term ad infinitum from an old nursery rhyme about fleas: "Great fleas have little fleas upon their back to bite 'em, / Little fleas have lesser fleas and so on ad infinitum."

d. Cinema audiences once gasped at hearing the word *damn* in *Gone with the Wind*.

e. Neve Campbell's lifelong interest in ballet inspired her involvement in the film "The Company," which portrays a season with the Joffrey Ballet.

43 Spelling

You learned to spell from repeated experience with words in both reading and writing. As you proofread, you may be able to tell if a word doesn't look quite right. Online tools or software may also signal spelling problems.

43a Become familiar with the major spelling rules.

i before *e* except after *c*

In general, use *i* before *e* except after *c* and except when sounded like *ay*, as in *neighbor* and *weigh*.

I BEFORE *E*	relieve, believe, sieve, niece, fierce, frieze
E BEFORE *I*	receive, deceive, sleigh, freight, eight
EXCEPTIONS	seize, either, weird, height, foreign, leisure

Suffixes

Final silent -*e* Generally, drop a final silent -*e* when adding a suffix that begins with a vowel. Keep the final -*e* if the suffix begins with a consonant.

combine, combination	achieve, achievement
desire, desiring	care, careful
prude, prudish	entire, entirety
remove, removable	gentle, gentleness
EXCEPTIONS	changeable, judgment, argument, truly

Final -*y* When adding -*s* or -*d* to words ending in -*y*, ordinarily change -*y* to -*ie* when the -*y* is preceded by a consonant but not when it is preceded by a vowel.

| comedy, comedies | monkey, monkeys |
| dry, dried | play, played |

With proper names, do not change the -*y* to -*ie* even if it is preceded by a consonant: *the Bradys* (*the Brady family*).

Final consonants If a final consonant is preceded by a single vowel *and* the consonant ends a one-syllable word or a stressed syllable, double the consonant when adding a suffix beginning with a vowel.

| bet, betting | occur, occurrence |
| commit, committed | |

Plurals

-*s* or -*es* Add -*s* to form the plural of most nouns; add -*es* to singular nouns ending in -*s*, -*sh*, -*ch*, and -*x*.

| table, tables | church, churches |
| paper, papers | dish, dishes |

Ordinarily, add *-s* to nouns ending in *-o* when the *-o* is preceded by a vowel. Add *-es* when the *-o* is preceded by a consonant.

hero, heroes

radio, radios

tomato, tomatoes

video, videos

Other plurals To form the plural of a hyphenated compound word, add *-s* to the chief word even if it does not appear at the end.

mother-in-law, mothers-in-law

English words derived from other languages such as Latin, Greek, or French sometimes form the plural as they would in their original language.

chateau, chateaux

criterion, criteria

medium, media

Multilingual

Spelling varieties among English-speaking countries can cause confusion. Following is a list of some common words with different American and British spellings. Consult a dictionary for others.

AMERICAN	BRITISH
canceled, traveled	cancelled, travelled
color, humor	colour, humour
judgment	judgement
realize, apologize	realise, apologise
defense	defence
anemia, anesthetic	anaemia, anaesthetic
theater, center	theatre, centre
civilization	civilisation
connection, inflection	connexion, inflexion

43b Discriminate between words that sound alike but have different meanings.

Words that sound alike or nearly alike but have different meanings and spellings are called *homophones*. The following sets of words are commonly confused. (See also the glossary of usage in the appendixes.)

affect (verb: to exert an influence)
effect (verb: to accomplish; noun: result)

its (possessive pronoun: of or belonging to it)
it's (contraction of *it is* or *it has*)

loose (adjective: free, not securely attached)
lose (verb: to fail to keep, to be deprived of)

principal (adjective: most important; noun: head of a school)
principle (noun: a fundamental guideline or truth)

their (possessive pronoun: belonging to them)
they're (contraction of *they are*)
there (adverb: that place or position)

who's (contraction of *who is* or *who has*)
whose (possessive form of *who*)

your (possessive pronoun: belonging to you)
you're (contraction of *you are*)

43c Be alert to commonly misspelled words.

absence	argument	conscientious	especially
academic	ascend	conscious	exaggerated
accidentally	attendance	criticism	exercise
accommodate	basically	criticize	existence
achievement	beginning	decision	familiar
acknowledge	believe	definitely	fascinate
acquaintance	benefited	descendant	February
acquire	business	desperate	foreign
all right	cemetery	disastrous	forty
analyze	commitment	eighth	fourth
answer	committed	eligible	friend
apparently	committee	embarrass	government
appearance	conceivable	emphasize	grammar
arctic	conscience	environment	harass

height	noticeable	prevalent	sincerely
humorous	occasion	privilege	sophomore
incredible	occurred	proceed	succeed
independence	occurrence	professor	surprise
indispensable	parallel	publicly	thorough
inevitable	particularly	quiet	tomorrow
irrelevant	permanent	quite	tragedy
irresistible	perseverance	receive	transferred
knowledge	phenomenon	recognize	unnecessarily
library	physically	referred	usually
license	practically	restaurant	vacuum
lightning	precede	rhythm	villain
maneuver	preference	schedule	weird
marriage	preferred	separate	whether
mathematics	prejudice	siege	
necessary	presence	similar	

Exercise 43-1 The following memo has been run through a spell checker. Proofread it carefully, editing the errors that remain.

November 3, 2017
To: Patricia Wise
From: Constance Mayhew
Subject: Express Tours annual report

Thank you for agreeing to draft the annual report for Express Tours. Before you begin you're work, let me outline the initial steps.

First, its essential for you to include brief profiles of top management. Early next week, I'll provide profiles for all manages accept Samuel Heath, who's biographical information is being revised. You should edit these profiles carefully and than format them according to the enclosed instructions. We may ask you to include other employee's profiles at some point.

Second, you should arrange to get complete financial information for fiscal year 2017 from our comptroller, Richard Chang. (Helen Boyes, to, can provide the necessary figures.) When you get this information, precede according to the plans we discuss in yesterday's meeting. By the way, you will notice from the figures that the sale of our Charterhouse division did not significantly effect net profits.

Third, you should email a first draft of the report by December 13. Of coarse, you should proofread you writing.

I am quiet pleased that you can take on this project. If I can answers questions, don't hesitate to call.

44 The hyphen

In addition to the guidelines in this section, a dictionary will help you make decisions about hyphenation.

44a Consult the dictionary to determine how to treat a compound word.

The dictionary indicates whether to treat a compound word as a hyphenated compound (*water-repellent*), one word (*waterproof*), or two words (*water table*). If the compound word is not in the dictionary, treat it as two words.

▶ The prosecutor chose not to cross‿examine any witnesses.

▶ All students are expected to record their data in a small note book.

▶ Alice walked through the looking/glass into a backward world.

44b Hyphenate two or more words used together as an adjective before a noun.

▶ Many teachers use web‿delivered content in the classroom.

▶ Richa Gupta is not yet a well‿known candidate.

Web-delivered in the first example and *well-known* in the second example are adjectives used before the nouns *content* and *candidate*.

Generally, do not use a hyphen when such compounds follow the noun.

▶ After our television campaign, Richa Gupta will be well/known.

Do not use a hyphen to connect *-ly* adverbs to the words they modify.

▶ A slowly/moving truck tied up traffic.

44c Hyphenate fractions and certain numbers when they are spelled out.

For numbers written as words, use a hyphen in all fractions (*two-thirds*) and in all forms of compound numbers from twenty-one to ninety-nine (*thirty-five*, *sixty-seventh*).

▶ One-fourth of my income goes to pay my child-care expenses.

44d Use a hyphen with the prefixes *all-*, *ex-* (meaning "former"), and *self-* and with the suffix *-elect*.

▶ The private foundation is funneling more money into self-help

projects.

▶ The Student Senate bylaws require the president-elect to attend

all meetings following the election.

44e Use a hyphen in certain words to avoid ambiguity.

Without the hyphen, there would be no way to distinguish between words such as *re-creation* and *recreation*.

Bicycling in the city is my favorite form of recreation.
The film was praised for its astonishing re-creation of nineteenth-century London.

Hyphens are sometimes used to separate awkward double or triple letters in compound words (*anti-intellectual*, *cross-stitch*).

44f Check for correct word breaks when words must be divided at the end of a line.

In academic writing, it's best to set your computer applications not to hyphenate automatically. This setting will ensure that only words already containing a hyphen (such as *long-distance* or *pre-Roman*) will be hyphenated at the ends of lines.

Email addresses and URLs need special attention when they occur at the end of a line of text or in bibliographic citations. You must make a decision about hyphenation in each case.

Do not insert a hyphen to divide electronic addresses. Instead, break an email address after the @ symbol or before a period. It is common practice to break a URL before most marks of punctuation. (For specific guidelines, see 57a and 62a.)

Exercise 44–1 Edit the following sentences to correct errors in hyphenation. If a sentence is correct, write "correct" after it. Answers appear in the back of the book.

> Émile Zola's first readers were scandalized by his slice-of-life novels.

a. Gold is the seventy-ninth element in the periodic table.

b. The swiftly-moving tugboat pulled alongside the barge and directed it away from the oil spill in the harbor.

c. The Moche were a pre-Columbian people who established a sophisticated culture in ancient Peru.

d. Your dog is well-known in our neighborhood.

e. Road-blocks were set up along all the major highways leading out of the city.

45 Capitalization

In addition to the rules in this section, a good dictionary can tell you when to use capital letters.

45a Capitalize proper nouns and words derived from them; do not capitalize common nouns.

Proper nouns are the names of specific persons, places, and things. All other nouns are common nouns. The following types of words are usually capitalized: names of deities, religions, religious followers, sacred books; words of family relationship used as names; particular places; nationalities and their languages, races, tribes; departments, degrees, particular courses at educational institutions; government departments, organizations, political parties; historical movements, periods, events, documents; and trade names.

PROPER NOUNS	COMMON NOUNS
God (used as a name)	a god
Book of Common Prayer	a sacred book
Uncle Pedro	my uncle
Father (used as a name)	my father
Lake Superior	a picturesque lake
the South	a southern state
Geology 101	geology
Environmental Protection Agency	a federal agency
the Democratic Party	a political party
the Enlightenment	the eighteenth century
the Treaty of Versailles	a treaty
Advil	a painkiller

Months, holidays, and days of the week are treated as proper nouns; the seasons and numbers of the days of the month are not.

> Our academic year begins on a Tuesday in early September, right after Labor Day.

> Graduation is in late spring, on the second of June.

EXCEPTION: Capitalize Fourth of July (or July Fourth) when referring to the holiday.

Names of school subjects are capitalized only if they are names of languages. Names of particular courses are capitalized.

> This semester Lee is taking math, geology, French, and English.

> Professor Obembe offers Modern American Fiction 501 to undergraduate students.

The term *Internet* is typically capitalized, but other common nouns related to the Internet and computers are not: *home page, operating system*. Usage varies widely, however, so check with your instructor about whether you should follow the guidelines for MLA or APA style (57a or 62a, respectively).

NOTE: Do not capitalize common nouns to make them seem important.

45b Capitalize titles of persons when used as part of a proper name but usually not when used alone.

> Professor Margaret Barnes; Dr. Sinyee Sein; John Scott Williams Jr.
>
> District Attorney Marshall was reprimanded for badgering the witness.
>
> The district attorney was elected for a two-year term.

Usage varies when the title of an important public figure is used alone: *The president* [or *President*] *vetoed the bill.*

45c Capitalize titles according to convention.

In both titles and subtitles of works mentioned in the text of a paper, major words such as nouns, pronouns, verbs, adjectives, and adverbs should be capitalized. Minor words such as articles, prepositions, and coordinating conjunctions are not capitalized unless they are the first or last word of a title or subtitle. (In APA style, capitalize all words of four or more letters. See 62a.)

Capitalize the second part of a hyphenated term in a title if it is a major word but not if it is a minor word. For chapter titles and the titles of other major divisions of a work, follow the same guidelines used for titles of complete works.

> *Seizing the Enigma: The Race to Break the German U-Boat Codes*
>
> *A River Runs through It*
>
> "I Want to Hold Your Hand"

To see why some of the titles in the list are italicized and some are put in quotation marks, see 42a and 37c.

Titles of works are handled differently in the APA reference list. See "Preparing the list of references" in 62a.

45d Capitalize the first word of a sentence.

The first word of a sentence should be capitalized. When a sentence appears within parentheses, capitalize its first word unless the parentheses appear within another sentence.

> Early detection of cancer increases survival rates. (See table 2.)
>
> Early detection of cancer increases survival rates (see table 2).

45e Capitalize the first word of a quoted sentence but not a quoted word or phrase.

> Dyson writes, "The best of our athletes have understood their responsibility to represent their people" (120).
>
> Russell Baker has written that in this country, sports are "the opiate of the masses" (46).

If a quoted sentence is interrupted by explanatory words, do not capitalize the first word after the interruption. (See 37e.)

> "If you want to go out," he said, "tell me now."

When quoting poetry, copy the poet's capitalization exactly. Many poets capitalize the first word of every line of poetry; a few contemporary poets dismiss capitalization altogether.

> it was the week   that
> i felt the city's narrow breezes rush about
> me   — Don L. Lee

45f Know your options when the first word after a colon begins an independent clause.

When a group of words following a colon can stand on its own as a complete sentence, capitalizing the first word is optional.

> Clinical trials altered the safety profile of the drug: A high percentage of participants reported hypertension and kidney problems.

Clinical trials altered the safety profile of the drug: a high percentage of participants reported hypertension and kidney problems.

Preferences vary. See 57a (MLA) or 62a (APA).

Always use lowercase for a list or an appositive that follows a colon (see 35a).

Students were divided into two groups: residents and commuters.

Exercise 45-1 ▸ Edit the following sentences to correct errors in capitalization. If a sentence is correct, write "correct" after it. Answers appear in the back of the book.

> On our trip to the West, we visited the $\overset{G}{\underset{\wedge}{\text{grand}}}$ $\overset{C}{\underset{\wedge}{\text{canyon}}}$ and the
>
> $\overset{G}{\underset{\wedge}{\text{great}}}$ $\overset{S}{\underset{\wedge}{\text{salt}}}$ $\overset{D}{\underset{\wedge}{\text{desert.}}}$

a. Assistant dean Shirin Ahmadi recommended offering more world language courses.

b. We went to the Mark Taper Forum to see a production of *Angels in America*.

c. Kalindi has an ambitious semester, studying differential calculus, classical hebrew, brochure design, and greek literature.

d. Lydia's Aunt and Uncle make modular houses as beautiful as modernist works of art.

e. We amused ourselves on the long flight by discussing how Spring in Kyoto stacks up against Summer in London.

GRAMMAR
BASICS

46 Parts of speech

Traditional grammar recognizes eight parts of speech: noun, pronoun, verb, adjective, adverb, preposition, conjunction, and interjection. Many words can function as more than one part of speech. For example, the word *paint* can be a noun (*The paint is wet*) or a verb (*Please paint the ceiling*).

46a Nouns

A noun is the name of a person, place, thing, or concept.

> The *lion* in the *cage* growled at the *zookeeper*.
> N   N   N

Nouns sometimes function as adjectives modifying other nouns. Because of their dual roles, nouns used in this manner may be called *noun/adjectives*.

> The *leather* notebook was tucked in the *student's* backpack.
> N/ADJ   N/ADJ

Nouns are classified in a variety of ways, and writers use these classifications to help them select nouns and determine how the nouns should be written.

- *Proper* nouns are capitalized, but *common* nouns are not (see 45a).
- For clarity, writers choose between *concrete* and *abstract* nouns (see 18b).
- The distinction between *count* nouns and *noncount* nouns can be helpful to multilingual writers (see 29a).
- Most nouns have *singular* and *plural* forms; *collective* nouns may be either singular or plural, depending on how they are used (see 21f and 22b).
- *Possessive* nouns require an apostrophe (see 36a).

Exercise 46–1 Underline the nouns (and noun/adjectives) in the following sentences. Answers appear in the back of the book.

The best part of dinner was the chef's newest dessert.

a. The stage was set for a confrontation of biblical proportions.
b. The courage of the hiker was an inspiration to the rescuers.
c. The need to arrive before the guest of honor motivated us to navigate the thick fog.
d. The defense attorney made a final appeal to the jury.
e. A national museum dedicated to women artists opened in 1987.

46b Pronouns

A pronoun is a word used in place of a noun. Usually the pronoun substitutes for a specific noun, known as its *antecedent*.

ANT ⟶ PN
When the *battery* wears down, we recharge *it*.

Although most pronouns function as substitutes for nouns, some can function as adjectives modifying nouns. Such pronouns may be called *pronoun/adjectives*.

PN/ADJ
That bird was at the same window yesterday morning.

Personal pronouns Personal pronouns refer to specific persons or things. They always function as subsitutes for nouns.

Singular: I, me, you, she, her, he, him, it
Plural: we, us, you, they, them

Possessive pronouns Possessive pronouns indicate ownership.

Singular: my, mine, your, yours, her, hers, his, its
Plural: our, ours, your, yours, their, theirs

Some of these possessive pronouns function as adjectives modifying nouns: *my, your, his, her, its, our, their*.

Intensive and reflexive pronouns Intensive pronouns emphasize a noun or another pronoun (The senator *herself* met us at the door). Reflexive pronouns name a receiver of an action identical with the doer of the action (Paula cut *herself*).

Singular: myself, yourself, himself, herself, itself
Plural: ourselves, yourselves, themselves

Relative pronouns   Relative pronouns introduce subordinate clauses functioning as adjectives (The writer *who won the award* refused to accept it). The relative pronoun, in this case *who*, also points back to a noun or pronoun that the clause modifies (*writer*). (See 48e.)

>   who, whom, whose, which, that

The pronouns *whichever*, *whoever*, *whomever*, *what*, and *whatever* are sometimes considered relative pronouns, but they introduce noun clauses and do not point back to a noun or pronoun. (See "Noun clauses" in 48e.)

Interrogative pronouns   Interrogative pronouns introduce questions (*Who* is expected to win the election?).

>   who, whom, whose, which, what

Demonstrative pronouns   Demonstrative pronouns identify or point to nouns. Frequently they function as adjectives (*This* chair is my favorite), but they may also function as substitutes for nouns (*This* is my favorite chair).

>   this, that, these, those

Indefinite pronouns   Indefinite pronouns refer to nonspecific persons or things. Most are always singular (*everyone*, *each*); some are always plural (*both*, *many*); a few may be singular or plural (see 21e). Most indefinite pronouns function as substitutes for nouns (*Something* is burning), but some can also function as adjectives (*All* campers must check in at the lodge).

all	anything	everyone	nobody	several
another	both	everything	none	some
any	each	few	no one	somebody
anybody	either	many	nothing	someone
anyone	everybody	neither	one	something

Reciprocal pronouns   Reciprocal pronouns refer to individual parts of a plural antecedent (By turns, the penguins fed *one another*).

>   each other, one another

NOTE: See also pronoun-antecedent agreement (22), pronoun reference (23), distinguishing between pronouns such as *I* and *me* (24), and distinguishing between *who* and *whom* (25).

Exercise 46–2   Underline the pronouns (and pronoun/adjectives) in the following sentences. Answers appear in the back of the book.

> We enjoyed the video <u>that</u> the fifth graders produced
>
> as <u>their</u> final project.

a. The governor's loyalty was his most appealing trait.
b. In the fall, the geese that fly south for the winter pass through our town in huge numbers.
c. As Carl Sandburg once said, even he himself did not understand some of his poetry.
d. I appealed my parking ticket, but you did not get one.
e. Angela did not mind gossip as long as no one gossiped about her.

46c Verbs

The verb of a sentence usually expresses action (*jump*, *think*) or being (*is*, *become*). It is composed of a main verb possibly preceded by one or more helping verbs.

> MV
> The horses *exercise* every day.

>   HV   MV
> The task force report *was* not *completed* on schedule.

> HV   HV   MV
> No one *has been defended* with more passion than our mayor.

Notice that words, usually adverbs, can intervene between the helping verb and the main verb (was *not* completed). (See 46e.)

Helping verbs

There are twenty-three helping verbs in English: forms of *have*, *do*, and *be*, which may also function as main verbs; and nine modals, which function only as helping verbs. *Have*, *do*, and *be* change form to indicate tense; the nine modals do not.

> FORMS OF *HAVE*, *DO*, AND *BE*
> have, has, had
> do, does, did
> be, am, is, are, was, were, being, been

MODALS

can, could, may, might, must, shall, should, will, would

The verb phrase *ought to* is often classified as a modal as well.

Main verbs

The main verb of a sentence is always the kind of word that would change form if put into these test sentences:

BASE FORM	Usually I (*walk, ride*).
PAST TENSE	Yesterday I (*walked, rode*).
PAST PARTICIPLE	I have (*walked, ridden*) many times before.
PRESENT PARTICIPLE	I am (*walking, riding*) right now.
-S FORM	Usually he/she/it (*walks, rides*).

If a word doesn't change form when slipped into the test sentences, you can be certain that it is not a main verb. For example, the noun *revolution*, though it may seem to suggest an action, can never function as a main verb. Just try to make it behave like one (*Today I revolution . . . Yesterday I revolutioned . . .*) and you'll see why.

When both the past-tense and the past-participle forms of a verb end in *-ed*, the verb is regular (*walked, walked*). Otherwise, the verb is irregular (*rode, ridden*). (See 27a.)

The verb *be* is highly irregular, having eight forms instead of the usual five: the base form *be*; the present-tense forms *am, is,* and *are*; the past-tense forms *was* and *were*; the present participle *being*; and the past participle *been*. Helping verbs combine with main verbs to create tenses. For a survey of tenses, see 28a.

NOTE: Some verbs are followed by *particles*, words that look like prepositions but that are actually part of the verbs. Common verb-particle combinations include *bring up, call off, drop off, give in, look up, run into,* and *take off*.

> Sharon *packed up* her broken laptop and *sent* it *off* to the repair shop.

TIP: For more information about using verbs, see these sections: active verbs (8), subject-verb agreement (21), Standard English verb forms (27), verb tense and mood (27f and 27g), and multilingual/ESL challenges with verbs (28).

Exercise 46-3 Underline the verbs in the following sentences, including helping verbs and particles. If a verb is part of a contraction (such as *is* in *isn't* or *would* in *I'd*), underline only the letters that represent the verb. Answers appear in the back of the book.

The ground under the pine trees <u>was</u>n't wet from the rain.

a. My grandmother always told me a soothing story before bed.
b. There were fifty apples on the tree before the frost killed them.
c. Morton brought down the box of letters from the attic.
d. Stay on the main road and you'll arrive at the base camp.
e. The fish struggled vigorously but was trapped in the net.

46d Adjectives

An adjective is a word used to modify, or describe, a noun or pronoun. An adjective usually answers one of these questions: Which one? What kind of? How many?

ADJ
the *broken* window   Which window?

ADJ   ADJ
cracked old plates   What kind of plates?

ADJ
nine months   How many months?

Adjectives usually come before the words they modify. They may also follow linking verbs, in which case they describe the subject. (See 47b.)

ADJ
The decision was *unpopular.*

The definite article *the* and the indefinite articles *a* and *an* are also classified as adjectives.

ART   ART   ART
A defendant should be judged on *the* evidence provided to *the* jury, not on hearsay.

Some possessive, demonstrative, and indefinite pronouns can function as adjectives: *their, its, this, all* (see 46b). And nouns can function as adjectives when they modify other nouns: *apple pie* (the noun *apple* modifies the noun *pie*; see 46a).

TIP: You can find more details about using adjectives in 26. If you are a multilingual writer, see 29, 30g, and 30h.

46e Adverbs

An adverb is a word used to modify, or qualify, a verb (or verbal), an adjective, or another adverb. It usually answers one of these questions: When? Where? How? Why? Under what conditions? To what degree?

> Pull *firmly* on the emergency handle.   Pull how?
>
> Read the text *first* and *then* complete the exercises.   Read when?
>   Complete when?

Adverbs modifying adjectives or other adverbs usually intensify or limit the intensity of the word they modify.

> ADV
> Be *extremely* kind, and you will have many friends.

> ADV
> We proceeded *very* cautiously in the dark house.

The words *not* and *never* are classified as adverbs.

Exercise 46-4   Underline the adjectives and circle the adverbs in the following sentences. If a word is a noun or pronoun functioning as an adjective, underline it and mark it as a noun/adjective or pronoun/adjective. Also treat the articles *a*, *an*, and *the* as adjectives. Answers appear in the back of the book.

> **Finding an available room during the convention**
>
> was (not) easy.

a. Generalizations lead to weak, unfocused essays.

b. The Spanish language is wonderfully flexible.

c. The wildflowers smelled especially fragrant after the steady rain.

d. I'd rather be slightly hot than bitterly cold.

e. The cat slept soundly in its wicker basket.

46f Prepositions

A preposition is a word placed before a noun or pronoun to form a phrase that modifies another word in the sentence. The prepositional phrase nearly always functions as an adjective or as an adverb.

> P   P   P
> The road *to* the summit travels *past* craters *from* an extinct volcano.

To the summit functions as an adjective modifying the noun *road*; *past craters* functions as an adverb modifying the verb *travels*; *from an extinct volcano* functions as an adjective modifying the noun *craters*. (For more on prepositional phrases, see 48a.)

English has a limited number of prepositions. The most common are included in the following list.

COMMON PREPOSITIONS

about	beside	from	outside	toward
above	besides	in	over	under
across	between	inside	past	underneath
after	beyond	into	plus	unlike
against	but	like	regarding	until
along	by	near	respecting	unto
among	concerning	next	round	up
around	considering	of	since	upon
as	despite	off	than	with
at	down	on	through	within
before	during	onto	throughout	without
behind	except	opposite	till	
below	for	out	to	

Some prepositions are more than one word long: *along with*, *as well as*, *in addition to*, *next to*, *rather than*.

TIP: Prepositions are used in idioms such as *capable of* and *dig up* (see 18d). For specific issues for multilingual writers, see 31.

46g Conjunctions

Conjunctions join words, phrases, or clauses, and they indicate the relation between the elements joined.

Coordinating conjunctions A coordinating conjunction is used to connect grammatically equal elements. (See 9b and 14a.) The coordinating conjunctions are *and*, *but*, *or*, *nor*, *for*, *so*, and *yet*.

> The sociologist interviewed children *but* not their parents.
>
> Write clearly, *and* your readers will appreciate your efforts.

In the first sentence, *but* connects two noun phrases; in the second, *and* connects two independent clauses.

Correlative conjunctions Correlative conjunctions come in pairs; they connect grammatically equal elements.

either . . . or   whether . . . or

neither . . . nor   both . . . and

not only . . . but also

Either the painting was brilliant *or* it was a forgery.

Subordinating conjunctions A subordinating conjunction introduces a subordinate clause and indicates the relation of the clause to the rest of the sentence. (See 48e.) The most common subordinating conjunctions are *after, although, as, as if, because, before, even though, if, in order that, once, since, so that, than, that, though, unless, until, when, where, whether,* and *while.*

When the fundraiser ends, we expect to have raised a million dollars.

Conjunctive adverbs Conjunctive adverbs connect independent clauses and indicate the relation between the clauses. They can be used with a semicolon to join two independent clauses in one sentence, or they can be used alone with an independent clause. The most common conjunctive adverbs are *finally, furthermore, however, moreover, nevertheless, similarly, then, therefore,* and *thus.*

The photographer failed to take a light reading; *therefore,* all the pictures were underexposed.

During the day, the kitten sleeps peacefully. *However,* when night falls, the kitten is wide awake and ready to play.

Conjunctive adverbs can appear at the beginning or in the middle of a clause.

When night falls, *however,* the kitten is wide awake and ready to play.

TIP: Recognizing conjunctive adverbs and coordinating conjunctions will help you avoid run-on sentences and make punctuation decisions (see 20, 32a, and 32f). Recognizing subordinating conjunctions will help you avoid sentence fragments (see 19).

46h Interjections

An interjection is a word used to express surprise or emotion (*Oh! Hey! Wow!*).

47 Sentence patterns

The vast majority of sentences in English conform to one of these five patterns:

> subject/verb/subject complement
> subject/verb/direct object
> subject/verb/indirect object/direct object
> subject/verb/direct object/object complement
> subject/verb

Adverbial modifiers (single words, phrases, or clauses) may be added to any of these patterns, and they may appear nearly anywhere — at the beginning, in the middle, or at the end.

Predicate is the grammatical term given to the verb plus its objects, complements, and adverbial modifiers.

47a Subjects

The subject of a sentence names whom or what the sentence is about. The simple subject is always a noun or pronoun; the complete subject consists of the simple subject and any words or word groups modifying the simple subject.

The complete subject

To find the complete subject, ask Who? or What?, insert the verb, and finish the question. The answer is the complete subject.

┌─── COMPLETE SUBJECT ───┐
The devastating effects of famine can last for many years.

Who or what can last for many years? *The devastating effects of famine.*

┌─── COMPLETE SUBJECT ───┐
Adventure novels that contain multiple subplots are often made into successful movies.

Who or what are often made into movies? *Adventure novels that contain multiple subplots.*

COMPLETE
SUBJECT

In our program, student teachers work full-time for ten months.

Who or what works full-time for ten months? *Student teachers.* Notice that *In our program, student teachers* is not a sensible answer to the question. (It is not safe to assume that the subject must always appear first in a sentence.)

The simple subject

To find the simple subject, strip away all modifiers in the complete subject. This includes single-word modifiers such as *the* and *devastating*, phrases such as *of famine*, and subordinate clauses such as *that contain multiple subplots.*

ㄷ SS ㄱ
The devastating effects of famine can last for many years.

ㄷ SS ㄱ
Adventure novels that contain multiple subplots are often made into successful movies.

A sentence may have a compound subject containing two or more simple subjects joined with a coordinating conjunction such as *and*, *but*, or *or*.

ㄷ—— SS ——ㄱ   ㄷSSㄱ
Great commitment and a little luck make a successful actor.

Understood subjects

In imperative sentences, which give advice or issue commands, the subject is understood but not actually present in the sentence. The subject of an imperative sentence is understood to be *you*.

[*You*] Put your hands on the steering wheel.

Subject after the verb

Although the subject ordinarily comes before the verb (*The planes took off*), occasionally it does not. When a sentence begins with *There is* or *There are* (or *There was* or *There were*), the subject follows the verb. In such inverted constructions, the word *There* is an expletive, an empty word serving merely to get the sentence started.

> ┌ SS ┐
> There are *eight planes waiting to take off.*

Occasionally a writer will invert a sentence for effect.

> ┌SS┐
> Joyful is *the child whose school closes for snow.*

Joyful is an adjective, so it cannot be the subject. Turn this sentence around and its structure becomes obvious.

> The *child* whose school closes for snow is joyful.

In questions, the subject frequently appears between the helping verb and the main verb.

> HV ┌── SS ──┐ MV
> Do *Kenyan marathoners* train year-round?

TIP: Recognizing the subject of a sentence will help you edit for fragments (19), subject-verb agreement (21), pronouns such as *I* and *me* (24), missing subjects (30b), and repeated subjects (30c).

Exercise 47–1 In the following sentences, underline the complete subject and write *SS* above the simple subject(s). If the subject is an understood *you*, insert *you* in parentheses. Answers appear in the back of the book.

> ┌ SS ┐   ┌ SS ┐
> <u>Parents and their children</u> often look alike.

a. The hills and mountains seemed endless, and the snow atop them glistened.
b. In foil fencing, points are scored by hitting an electronic target.
c. Do not stand in the aisles or sit on the stairs.
d. There were hundreds of fireflies in the open field.
e. The evidence against the defendant was staggering.

47b Verbs, objects, and complements

Section 46c explains how to find the verb of a sentence. A sentence's verb is classified as linking, transitive, or intransitive, depending on the kinds of objects or complements the verb can (or cannot) take.

Linking verbs and subject complements

Linking verbs connect the subject to a subject complement, a word or word group that completes the meaning of the subject by renaming or describing it.

```
┌─────────────── S ───────────────┐┌─ V ─┐┌─ SC ─┐
An email requesting personal information may be a scam.
```

```
┌────────── S ──────────┐  V    SC
Last month's temperatures were mild.
```

Whenever they appear as main verbs (rather than helping verbs), the forms of *be* — *be, am, is, are, was, were, being, been* — usually function as linking verbs. In the preceding examples, for instance, the main verbs are *be* and *were*.

Verbs such as *appear, become, feel, grow, look, make, seem, smell, sound,* and *taste* are linking when they are followed by a word or word group that renames or describes the subject.

```
┌── S ──┐┌─ V ──┐        SC
As it thickens, the sauce will look unappealing.
```

Transitive verbs and direct objects

A transitive verb takes a direct object, a word or word group that names a receiver of the action.

```
┌───── S ─────┐   V   ┌────── DO ──────┐
The hungry cat clawed the bag of dry food.
```

The simple direct object is always a noun or pronoun, in this case *bag*. To find it, simply strip away all modifiers.

Transitive verbs usually appear in the active voice, with the subject doing the action and a direct object receiving the action. Active-voice sentences can be transformed into the passive voice, with the subject receiving the action instead.

Transitive verbs, indirect objects, and direct objects

The direct object of a transitive verb is sometimes preceded by an indirect object, a noun or pronoun telling to whom or for whom the action of the sentence is done.

```
S  V  IO ┌─ DO ──┐      S ┌─ V ─┐ IO ┌─ DO ─┐
You give her some yarn, and she will knit you a scarf.
```

The simple indirect object is always a noun or pronoun. To test for an indirect object, insert the word *to* or *for* before the word or word group in question. If the sentence makes sense, the word or word group is an indirect object.

> You give [to] *her* some yarn, and she will knit [for] *you* a scarf.

Transitive verbs, direct objects, and object complements

The direct object of a transitive verb is sometimes followed by an object complement, a word or word group that renames or describes the object.

S   V   DO OC
People often consider chivalry a thing of the past.

S V DO OC
The kiln makes clay firm and strong.

When the object complement renames the direct object, it is a noun or pronoun (such as *thing*). When it describes the direct object, it is an adjective (such as *firm* and *strong*).

Intransitive verbs

Intransitive verbs take no objects or complements.

S V
The audience laughed.

S V
The driver accelerated in the straightaway.

Nothing receives the actions of laughing and accelerating in these sentences, so the verbs are intransitive. Notice that such verbs may or may not be followed by adverbial modifiers. In the second sentence, *in the straightaway* is an adverbial prepositional phrase modifying *accelerated*.

NOTE: The dictionary will tell you whether a verb is transitive or intransitive. Some verbs have both functions.

> **TRANSITIVE**   Sandra *flew* her small plane over the canyon.
>
> **INTRANSITIVE**   A flock of migrating geese *flew* overhead.

In the first example, *flew* has a direct object that receives the action: *her small plane*. In the second example, the verb is followed by an adverb (*overhead*), not by a direct object.

Exercise 47–2 Label the subject complements and direct objects in the following sentences, using the labels *SC* and *DO*. If a subject complement or direct object consists of more than one word, bracket and label all of it. Answers appear in the back of the book.

> ┌──── DO ────┐
> The sharp right turn confused most drivers.

a. Mangoes are expensive.
b. Samurai warriors never fear death.
c. Successful coaches always praise their players' efforts.
d. St. Petersburg was the capital of the Russian Empire for two centuries.
e. The medicine tasted bitter.

Exercise 47–3 Each of the following sentences has either an indirect object followed by a direct object or a direct object followed by an object complement. Label the objects and complements, using the labels *IO*, *DO*, and *OC*. If an object or a complement consists of more than one word, bracket and label all of it. Answers appear in the back of the book.

> ┌──── DO ────┐ ┌─ OC ─┐
> Most people consider their own experience normal.

a. Stress can make adults and children weary.
b. The dining hall offered students healthy meal choices.
c. Consider the work finished.
d. We showed the agent our tickets, and she gave us boarding passes.
e. Zita has made community service her priority this year.

48 Subordinate word groups

Subordinate word groups include phrases and clauses. Phrases are subordinate because they lack a subject and a verb; they are classified as prepositional, verbal, appositive, and absolute (see 48a–48d). Subordinate clauses have a subject and a verb, but they begin with a word (such as *although*, *that*, or *when*) that marks them as subordinate (see 48e).

48a Prepositional phrases

A prepositional phrase begins with a preposition such as *at, by, for, from, in, of, on, to,* or *with* (see 46f) and usually ends with a noun or noun equivalent: *on the table, for him, by sleeping late.* The noun or noun equivalent is known as the *object of the preposition.*

Prepositional phrases function either as adjectives or as adverbs. As an adjective, a prepositional phrase nearly always appears immediately following the noun or pronoun it modifies.

The hut had *walls of mud.*

Adjective phrases usually answer one or both of the questions Which one? and What kind of? If we ask Which walls? or What kind of walls? we get a sensible answer: *walls of mud.*

Adverbial prepositional phrases usually modify the verb, but they can also modify adjectives or other adverbs. When a prepositional phrase modifies the verb, it can appear nearly anywhere in a sentence.

James *walked* his dog *on a leash.*

Sabrina *in time adjusted* to life in Ecuador.

During a mudslide, the terrain *can change* drastically.

If a prepositional phrase is movable, you can be certain that it is adverbial.

> *In the cave,* the explorers found well-preserved prehistoric drawings.

> The explorers found well-preserved prehistoric drawings *in the cave.*

Adverbial word groups usually answer one of these questions: When? Where? How? Why? Under what conditions? To what degree?

> James walked his dog *how? On a leash.*

> Sabrina adjusted to life in Ecuador *when? In time.*

> The terrain can change drastically *under what conditions? During a mudslide.*

In questions and subordinate clauses, a preposition may appear after its object.

> *What* are you afraid *of*?
>
> We avoided the bike trail *that* John had warned us *about*.

Exercise 48–1 Underline the prepositional phrases in the following sentences. Tell whether each one is an adjective phrase or an adverb phrase and what it modifies in the sentence. Answers appear in the back of the book.

> **Flecks of mica glittered in the new granite floor.** (Adjective phrase modifying "Flecks"; adverb phrase modifying "glittered")

a. In northern Italy, we met many people who speak German as their first language.

b. William completed the three-mile hike through the thick forest with ease.

c. To my boss's dismay, I was late for work again.

d. The traveling exhibit of Mayan artifacts gave viewers new insight into pre-Columbian culture.

e. In 2002, the euro became the official currency in twelve European countries.

48b Verbal phrases

A verbal is a verb form that does not function as the verb of a clause. Verbals include infinitives (the word *to* plus the base form of the verb), present participles (the *-ing* form of the verb), and past participles (the verb form usually ending in *-d*, *-ed*, *-n*, *-en*, or *-t*). (See 27a and 46c.)

INFINITIVE	PRESENT PARTICIPLE	PAST PARTICIPLE
to dream	dreaming	dreamed
to choose	choosing	chosen
to build	building	built
to grow	growing	grown

Instead of functioning as the verb of a clause, a verbal functions as an adjective, a noun, or an adverb.

ADJECTIVE	*Broken* promises cannot be fixed.
NOUN	Constant *complaining* becomes wearisome.
ADVERB	Can you wait *to celebrate*?

Verbals with objects, complements, or modifiers form verbal phrases.

In my family, *singing loudly* is more appreciated than *singing well*.

Like verbals, verbal phrases function as adjectives, nouns, or adverbs. Verbal phrases are ordinarily classified as participial, gerund, and infinitive.

Participial phrases

Participial phrases always function as adjectives. Their verbals are either present participles (such as *dreaming, asking*) or past participles (such as *stolen, reached*).

Participial phrases frequently appear immediately following the noun or pronoun they modify.

Congress shall make no *law abridging the freedom of speech*

or of the press.

Participial phrases are often movable. They can precede the word they modify.

Being a weight-bearing joint, the *knee* is among the most frequently injured.

They may also appear at some distance from the word they modify.

Last night we saw a *play* that affected us deeply, *written with*

profound insight into the lives of immigrants.

Gerund phrases

Gerund phrases are built around present participles (verb forms that end in *-ing*), and they always function as nouns: usually as subjects, subject complements, direct objects, or objects of a preposition.

> ┌────── S ──────┐
> Rationalizing a fear can eliminate it.

> ┌────────── SC ──────────┐
> The key to a good sauce is browning the mushrooms.

> ┌────── DO ──────┐
> Lizards usually enjoy sunning themselves.

> The American Heart Association has documented the benefits of
> ┌────── OBJ OF PREP ──────┐
> diet and exercise in reducing the risk of heart attack.

Infinitive phrases

Infinitive phrases, usually constructed around *to* plus the base form of the verb (*to call*, *to drink*), can function as nouns, as adjectives, or as adverbs. When functioning as a noun, an infinitive phrase may appear in almost any noun slot in a sentence, usually as a subject, subject complement, or direct object.

> ┌────── S ──────┐
> To live without health insurance is risky.

Infinitive phrases functioning as adjectives usually appear immediately following the noun or pronoun they modify.

> The Nineteenth Amendment gave women the *right to vote.*

The infinitive phrase modifies the noun *right*. Which right? *The right to vote.*

Adverbial infinitive phrases usually qualify the meaning of the verb, telling when, where, how, why, under what conditions, or to what degree an action occurred.

> Volunteers *rolled up* their pants *to wade through the floodwaters.*

Why did they roll up their pants? *To wade through the floodwaters.*

Exercise 48–2   Underline the verbal phrases in the following sentences. Tell whether each phrase is participial, gerund, or infinitive and how each is used in the sentence. Answers appear in the back of the book.

> **Do you want <u>to watch that documentary</u>?** *(Infinitive phrase used as direct object of "Do want")*

a. Updating your software will fix the computer glitch.
b. The challenge in decreasing the town budget is identifying nonessential services.
c. Cathleen tried to help her mother by raking the lawn.
d. Understanding little, I had no hope of passing my biology final.
e. Working with animals gave Steve a sense of satisfaction.

48c Appositive phrases

Appositive phrases describe nouns or pronouns. Instead of modifying nouns or pronouns, however, appositive phrases rename them. In form they are nouns or noun equivalents.

> Bloggers, *conversationalists at heart*, are the online equivalent of radio talk show hosts.

48d Absolute phrases

An absolute phrase modifies a whole clause or sentence, not just one word. It consists of a noun or noun equivalent usually followed by a participial phrase.

> *Her words reverberating in the hushed arena*, the senator urged the crowd to support her former opponent.

48e Subordinate clauses

Subordinate clauses are patterned like sentences, having subjects and verbs and sometimes objects or complements. But they function within sentences as adjectives, adverbs, or nouns. They cannot stand alone as complete sentences.

A subordinate clause usually begins with a subordinating conjunction or a relative pronoun. The chart in this section classifies these words according to the kinds of clauses (adjective, adverb, or noun) they introduce.

Adjective clauses

Adjective clauses modify nouns or pronouns, usually answering the question Which one? or What kind of? Most adjective clauses begin with a relative pronoun (*who, whom, whose, which,* or *that*). In addition to introducing the clause, the relative pronoun points back to the noun that the clause modifies.

The coach chose *players who would benefit from intense drills.*

A *book that goes unread* is a writer's worst nightmare.

Relative pronouns are sometimes "understood."

The things [*that*] *we cherish most* are the things [*that*] *we might lose.*

Occasionally an adjective clause is introduced by a relative adverb, usually *when, where,* or *why.*

The aging actor returned to the *stage where he had made his debut as Hamlet half a century earlier.*

The parts of an adjective clause are often arranged as in sentences (subject/verb/object or complement).

Sometimes it is our closest friends who disappoint us.
[S   V   DO marked above "who disappoint us"]

Frequently, however, the object or complement appears first, out of the normal order of subject/verb/object.

They can be the very friends whom we disappoint.
[DO   S   V marked above "whom we disappoint"]

TIP: For punctuation of adjective clauses, see 32e and 33e. For advice about avoiding repeated words in adjective clauses, see 30d.

basic

Words that introduce subordinate clauses

Words introducing adjective clauses

RELATIVE PRONOUNS: that, which, who, whom, whose
RELATIVE ADVERBS: when, where, why

Words introducing adverb clauses

SUBORDINATING CONJUNCTIONS: after, although, as, as if, because, before, even though, if, in order that, once, since, so that, than, that, though, unless, until, when, where, whether, while

Words introducing noun clauses

RELATIVE PRONOUNS: that, which, who, whom, whose
OTHER PRONOUNS: what, whatever, whichever, whoever, whomever
OTHER SUBORDINATING WORDS: how, if, when, whenever, where, wherever, whether, why

Adverb clauses

Adverb clauses modify verbs, adjectives, or other adverbs, usually answering one of these questions: When? Where? Why? How? Under what conditions? To what degree? They always begin with a subordinating conjunction (such as *after*, *although*, *because*, *that*, *though*, *unless*, or *when*). (For a complete list, see the chart on this page.)

When the sun went down, the hikers *prepared* their camp.

Kate *would have made* the team *if she hadn't broken her ankle.*

Noun clauses

A noun clause functions just like a single-word noun, usually as a subject, a subject complement, a direct object, or an object of a preposition. It usually begins with one of the following words: *how*, *if*, *that*, *what*, *whatever*, *when*, *whenever*, *where*, *whether*, *which*, *whichever*, *who*, *whoever*, *whom*, *whomever*, *whose*, *why*.

S
Whoever leaves the house last must double-lock the door.

DO
Copernicus argued that the sun is the center of the universe.

The subordinating word introducing the clause may or may not play a significant role in the clause. In the preceding example sentences, *Whoever* is the subject of its clause, but *that* does not perform a function in its clause.

As with adjective clauses, the parts of a noun clause may appear in normal order (subject/verb/object or complement) or out of their normal order.

        S   V   ┌── DO ──┐ OC
Loyalty is what keeps a friendship strong.

        DO   S   V
New Mexico is where we live.

Exercise 48–3 ▶ Underline the subordinate clauses in the following sentences. Tell whether each clause is an adjective, adverb, or noun clause and how it is used in the sentence. Answers appear in the back of the book.

Show the committee the latest draft <u>before you print the</u>

<u>final report.</u> *(Adverb clause modifying "Show")*

a. The city's electoral commission adjusted the voting process so that every vote would count.

b. A marketing campaign that targets baby boomers may not appeal to young professionals.

c. After the Tambora volcano erupted in the southern Pacific in 1815, no one realized that it would contribute to the "year without a summer" in Europe and North America.

d. The concept of peak oil implies that at a certain point there will be no more oil to extract from the earth.

e. Details are easily overlooked when you are rushing.

49 Sentence types

Sentences are classified in two ways: according to their structure (simple, compound, complex, and compound-complex) and according to their purpose (declarative, imperative, interrogative, and exclamatory).

49a Sentence structures

Depending on the number and the types of clauses they contain, sentences are classified as simple, compound, complex, or compound-complex.

Clauses come in two varieties: independent and subordinate. An independent clause contains a subject and a predicate, and it either stands alone or could stand alone as a sentence. A subordinate clause also contains a subject and a predicate, but it functions within a sentence as an adjective, an adverb, or a noun; it cannot stand alone. (See 48e.)

Simple sentences

A simple sentence is one independent clause with no subordinate clauses.

INDEPENDENT CLAUSE
Without a passport, Eva could not visit her grandparents in

Hungary.

A simple sentence may contain compound elements—a compound subject, verb, or object, for example—but it does not contain more than one full sentence pattern. The following sentence is simple because its two verbs (*comes in* and *goes out*) share a subject (*Spring*).

INDEPENDENT CLAUSE
Spring comes in like a lion and goes out like a lamb.

Compound sentences

A compound sentence is composed of two or more independent clauses with no subordinate clauses. The independent clauses are usually joined with a comma and a coordinating conjunction (*and*, *but*, *or*, *nor*, *for*, *so*, *yet*) or with a semicolon. (See 14a.)

INDEPENDENT
CLAUSE
INDEPENDENT
CLAUSE
The car broke down, but a rescue van arrived within minutes.

INDEPENDENT CLAUSE
INDEPENDENT CLAUSE
A shark was spotted near shore; people left immediately.

Complex sentences

A complex sentence is composed of one independent clause with one or more subordinate clauses. (See 48e.)

ADJECTIVE	The pitcher <u>who won the game</u> is a rookie.
	— SUBORDINATE CLAUSE —
ADVERB	<u>If you leave late,</u> take a cab home.
	— SUBORDINATE CLAUSE —
NOUN	<u>What matters most to us</u> is a quick commute.
	— SUBORDINATE CLAUSE —

Compound-complex sentences

A compound-complex sentence contains at least two independent clauses and at least one subordinate clause. The following sentence contains two independent clauses, each of which contains a subordinate clause.

— INDEPENDENT CLAUSE — *— INDEPENDENT CLAUSE —*
— SUB CL —

Tell the doctor how you feel, and she will decide whether

— SUB CL —

you can go home.

49b Sentence purposes

Writers use declarative sentences to make statements, imperative sentences to issue requests or commands, interrogative sentences to ask questions, and exclamatory sentences to make exclamations.

DECLARATIVE	The echo sounded in our ears.
IMPERATIVE	Love your neighbor.
INTERROGATIVE	Did the better team win tonight?
EXCLAMATORY	We're here to save you!

Exercise 49–1 Identify the following sentences as simple, compound, complex, or compound-complex. Identify the subordinate clauses and classify them according to their function: adjective, adverb, or noun. (See 48e.) Answers appear in the back of the book.

> The deli in Courthouse Square was crowded with lawyers
>
> at lunchtime. (Simple)

a. Fires that are ignited in dry areas spread especially quickly.
b. The early Incas were advanced; they used a calendar and developed a decimal system.
c. Elaine's jacket was too thin to block the wintry air.
d. Before we leave for the station, we always check the Amtrak website.
e. Decide when you want to leave, and I will be there to pick you up.

RESEARCH

50 Thinking like a researcher; gathering sources

A college research assignment asks you to pose questions worth exploring, read widely in search of possible answers, interpret what you read, draw reasoned conclusions, and support those conclusions with evidence. In short, it asks you to enter a research conversation by being *in* conversation with other writers and thinkers who have explored and studied your topic. As you listen to and learn from the voices already in the conversation, you'll find entry points where you can add your own insights and ideas.

Keep an open mind throughout the research process, and enjoy the detective work of finding answers to questions that matter to you. Take time to find out what has been written about your topic and what's missing from the research conversation. You can stay organized by planning the search with a solid research question in mind and maintaining accurate records of the sources you consult.

50a Manage the project.

When you begin a research project, you will need to understand the assignment, choose a direction, and ask questions about your topic. The following tips will help you manage the beginning stage of research.

Managing time

When you receive your assignment, set a realistic schedule of deadlines. Think about how much time you might need for each step of your project. One student created a calendar to map out her tasks for a research paper assigned on October 3 and due October 31, keeping in mind that some tasks might overlap or need to be repeated.

Getting the big picture

As you consider a possible research topic, set aside time to learn what people are saying about it by reading sources on the web or in library databases. Ask yourself questions such as these:

LaunchPad Solo macmillan learning
Activities for Chapter 50
4 Writing practice activities, 1 Exercise

- What aspects of the topic are generating the most debate?
- Why and on what points are people disagreeing?
- Which arguments and approaches seem worth exploring?

Once you have an aerial view of the topic and are familiar with some of the existing research, you can zoom in closer to examine subtopics and debates that look interesting.

Keeping a research log

Research is a process. As your topic evolves, you may find yourself asking new questions that require you to create a new search strategy, find additional sources, and revise your initial assumptions. A research log will help you maintain orderly records of the sources you read and your ideas about those sources. Keeping an accurate source trail and working bibliography, as well as separating your own insights and ideas from those of your sources, will help you become a more efficient researcher.

Sample calendar for a research assignment

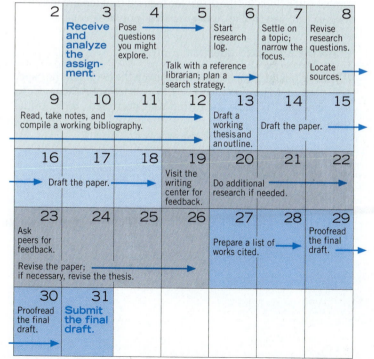

2	3	4	5	6	7	8
	Receive and analyze the assignment.	Pose questions you might explore. →	Start research log. Talk with a reference librarian; plan a search strategy.	Settle on a topic; narrow the focus.	Revise research questions. Locate sources. →
9	10	11	12	13	14	15
Read, take notes, and compile a working bibliography. →				Draft a working thesis and an outline.	Draft the paper. →	
16	17	18	19	20	21	22
→ Draft the paper. →			Visit the writing center for feedback.	Do additional research if needed. →		
23	24	25	26	27	28	29
Ask peers for feedback. Revise the paper; if necessary, revise the thesis. →				Prepare a list of works cited. →		Proofread the final draft. →
30	31					
Proofread the final draft.	Submit the final draft.					

50b Pose questions worth exploring.

Every research project starts with questions. Working within the guidelines of your assignment, come up with a few preliminary questions that seem worth researching — questions that you are interested in exploring, that you feel would engage your audience, and about which there is substantial debate. You might try using the journalist's questions — *Who? What? When? Where? Why?* and *How?* — to help you answer a research question.

Here, for example, are a few students' preliminary questions.

- How can nutritional food labels be redesigned so that they inform rather than confuse consumers?

- Why are boys diagnosed with attention deficit disorder more often than girls are?

- Under what circumstances should juvenile offenders be tried as adults?

As you evaluate possible questions as entry points into a conversation, look for those that are focused (not too broad), challenging (not just factual), and grounded (not too speculative).

Choosing a focused question

If your initial question is too broad, given the length of the paper you plan to write, look for ways to restrict your focus. Here, for example, is how two students narrowed their initial questions.

TOO BROAD	FOCUSED
What are the benefits of stricter auto emissions standards?	How will stricter auto emissions standards create new auto industry jobs and make US carmakers more competitive in the world market?
What causes depression?	How has the widespread use of antidepressant drugs affected teenage suicide rates?

HOW TO

Enter a research conversation

A college research project asks you to be in conversation with writers and researchers who have studied your topic — responding to their ideas and arguments and contributing your own insights to move the conversation forward. As you ask preliminary research questions, you may wonder where and how to step into a research conversation.

1 **Identify the experts and ideas in the conversation.** Ask: Who are the major writers and most influential people researching your topic? What are their credentials? What positions have they taken? How and why do the experts disagree?

2 **Identify any gaps in the conversation.** What is missing? Where are the gaps in the existing research? What questions haven't been asked yet? What positions need to be challenged?

3 **Try using a sentence guide,** which acts as a fill-in sentence starter to help you find a point of entry:

- *On one side of the debate is position X, on the other side is Y, but there is a middle position, Z.*

- *The conventional view about the problem needs to be challenged because _____ .*

- *Key details in this debate that have been overlooked are _____ .*

- *Researchers have drawn conclusion X from the evidence, but one could also draw conclusion Y.*

Choosing a challenging question

Your research paper will be more interesting to both you and your audience if you base it on an intellectually challenging line of inquiry. Avoid factual questions that fail to provoke thought or debate; such questions lead to reports or lists of facts, not to researched arguments.

TOO FACTUAL	CHALLENGING
Is autism on the rise?	Why is autism so difficult to treat?
Where is wind energy being used?	What makes wind farms economically viable?

You will probably need to address factual questions in the course of answering a more challenging question. For example, if you were writing about promising treatments for autism, you would answer the question "What is autism?" at some point in your paper and might even analyze competing definitions of autism to support your arguments about the challenges of treating the condition. A factual question, though, is too limited to be the focus for the entire paper.

 Writing for an audience

In developing your research question, follow your curiosity, but keep in mind how you'll engage readers, too. A good strategy is to ask a debatable question that puts you in the middle of a research conversation that both you and your audience care about. You can test how debatable your question is by trying to articulate possible ways you might answer it. If you can think of only one answer, chances are that your audience's engagement level will be low. Show your readers why the question needs to be asked and why the answer matters to them.

Choosing a grounded question

Make sure that your research question is grounded, not too speculative. Although speculative questions, such as those that address morality or beliefs, are worth asking in a research paper, they are not suitable central questions. For most college courses, the central argument of a research paper should be grounded in evidence and should not be based entirely on beliefs.

TOO SPECULATIVE	GROUNDED
Is it wrong to share pornographic personal photos by cell phone?	What role should the US government play in regulating mobile content?
Do medical scientists have the right to experiment on animals?	How have technical breakthroughs made medical experiments on animals increasingly unnecessary?

res

Testing a research question

- Does the question allow you to enter into a research conversation that you care about?
- Is the question flexible enough to allow for many possible answers?
- Is the question focused, challenging, and grounded?
- Can you show your audience why the question needs to be asked and why the answer matters?

50c Map out a search strategy.

Before you search for sources, think about what kinds of sources might be appropriate for your project. Considering the kinds of sources you need will help you develop a search strategy — a systematic plan for locating sources. To create an effective search strategy for your research question, consult a reference librarian and study your library's website for an overview of available resources.

No single search strategy works for every topic. For some topics, it may be useful to search for information in newspapers, government publications, and websites. For others, the best sources might be scholarly journals, books, research reports from think tanks, and specialized reference works. Still other topics might be enhanced by field research — interviews, surveys, or observation.

With the help of a librarian, each of the students whose research essays can be found in this handbook constructed a search strategy appropriate for his or her research question.

Researcher: Sophie Harba (Full paper: 57b)

Question: Should the government enact laws to regulate healthy eating choices?

Caiaimage/Sam Edwards/Getty Images

Strategy:

- search the *web* to locate current news, government publications, and information from organizations that focus on government regulation

- check a *library database* for current peer-reviewed research articles
- use the *library catalog* to search for a recently published book that was cited in another source

Researcher: April Wang
(Full paper: 62b)

Question: How can technology facilitate the shift to student-centered learning?

Courtesy April Bo Wang

Strategy:

- search *Google Scholar and CQ Researcher* to see which aspects of the question are generating debate
- view a *TED talk* to improve understanding of education technology
- use *specialized databases* related to education and technology to search for studies and articles

★ **Using sources responsibly** Use your research log to record information for every source you read or view. If you gather complete publication information from the start of your project, you'll find it easy to document your sources.

50d Search efficiently; master a few shortcuts to finding good sources.

Most students use a combination of library databases and the web in their research. You can save yourself a lot of time by becoming an efficient searcher.

Using the library

The website hosted by your college library links to databases and other references containing articles, studies, and reports written by key researchers. Use your library's resources, designed for academic researchers, to find the most authoritative sources for your project.

Go beyond a Google search

You might start with Google to gain an overview of your topic, but relying on the popular search engine to choose your sources isn't a research strategy. Good research involves going beyond the information available from a quick Google search. To locate reliable, authoritative sources, be strategic about *how* and *where* to search.

1 **Familiarize yourself with the research conversation.** Identify the current debate about the topic you have chosen and the most influential writers and experts in the debate. Where is the research conversation happening? In scholarly sources? Government agencies? The popular media?

2 **Generate keywords to focus your search.** Use specific words and combinations to search. Add words such as *debate, disagreements, proponents*, or *opponents* to track down the various positions in the research conversation. Use a journalist's questions— *Who? What? When? Where? Why? How?*—to refine a search.

3 **Search discipline-specific databases available through your school library** to locate carefully chosen scholarly (peer-reviewed) content that doesn't appear in search results on the open web. Use databases such as JSTOR and Academic Search Premier, designed for academic researchers, to locate sources in the most influential publications.

4 **If your topic has been in the news, try** *CQ Researcher*, available through most college libraries. Its brief articles provide pro/con arguments on current controversies in criminal justice, law, environment, technology, health, and education.

5 **Explore the Pew Research Center** (pewresearch.org), which sponsors original research and nonpartisan discussions of findings and trends in a wide range of academic fields.

Using the web

When conducting searches, use terms that are as specific as possible. The keywords you use will determine the quality of the results you see. You can refine your search by date or domain. Use clues in what you find (such as websites of organizations or government agencies that seem particularly informative) to refine your search.

This search phrase will lead to information about <u>autism</u>

autism site:.gov

on government (<u>.gov</u>) websites.

As you examine sites, look for "about" links to learn about the site's author or sponsoring agency. Examine URLs for clues. Those that contain .k12 may be intended for young audiences; URLs ending in .gov lead to official information from US government entities. URLs may also offer clues about the country of origin of a website: .au for Australia, .in for India, and so on. If you aren't sure

Check URLs for clues about sponsorship

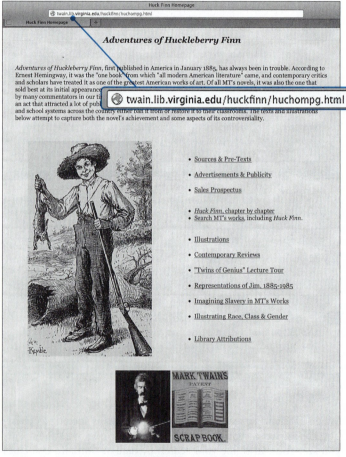

This source, from an internal page of a website, provides no indication of an author or a sponsor. Shortening the URL to http://twain.**lib.virginia.edu/** leads to a main page that lists a university literature professor as the author and the **University of Virginia Library** as the sponsor.

where a page originated, go to your address bar and erase everything in the URL after the first slash; the result should be the root page of the site, which may offer useful information about the site's purpose and audience. Avoid sites that provide information but no explanation of who the authors are or why the site was created. For more on evaluating websites, see 52c.

Using bibliographies and citations

Scholarly books and articles list the works the author has cited, usually at the end. These lists are useful shortcuts to additional reliable sources on your topic. For example, most of the scholarly articles that student writer Sophie Harba consulted contained citations to related research studies and helped her identify the most influential authors contributing to her research conversation. Through these citations, she located other sources and a network of relevant research related to her topic. Even popular sources such as news articles and TED talks may refer to additional relevant sources worth tracking down.

Tips for smart searching

FOR CURRENCY If you need current information, news outlets such as the *New York Times* and the BBC, think tanks, and government agencies may provide appropriate sources for your research. When using Google, limit a search to the most recent year, month, week, or day.

FOR AUTHORITY Keep an eye out for experts being cited in sources you examine. Following the trail of citations may lead you to helpful sources by those experts or the organizations they represent. You can limit a Google search by type of website and type of source. Add *site:.gov* to focus on government sources or *filetype:pdf* to zero in on reports and research provided as PDF files.

FOR SCHOLARSHIP Use a library database to look for reports of original scholarly research written by the people who conducted it. Read the abstract of a long article or the article's introductory paragraphs and conclusion to see if the source is worth further investigation.

FOR CONTEXT Books provide context that articles cannot. You may find a single chapter or even a few pages that are just what you need to gain a deeper perspective.

FOR FIRSTHAND AUTHENTICITY In some fields, primary sources may be required. In historical research, for example, a primary source is one that originated in the historical period under discussion or is a firsthand account from a witness. In the sciences, a primary source (sometimes called a *primary article*) is a published report of research written by the scientist who conducted it.

50e Conduct field research, if appropriate.

Your own field research can enhance or be the focus of a writing project. For a composition class, for example, you might want to interview a local politician about a current issue, such as the initiation of a city bike-share program. For a sociology class, you might decide to conduct a survey about campus trends in community service.

RESEARCH NOTE: Colleges and universities often require researchers to submit projects to an institutional review board (IRB) if the research involves human subjects outside a classroom setting. Before administering a survey or conducting other fieldwork, check with your instructor to see if IRB approval is required.

Interviewing

Interviews often shed new light on a topic. Look for an expert who has firsthand knowledge of the subject, or seek out a key participant whose personal experience provides a valuable perspective.

When asking for an interview, be clear about who you are, what the purpose of the interview is, and how you would prefer to conduct it: by email, over the phone, or in person. Ask questions that lead to facts, anecdotes, and opinions that will add a meaningful dimension to your paper.

INEFFECTIVE INTERVIEW QUESTIONS

How many years have you spent studying childhood obesity?

Is your work interesting?

EFFECTIVE INTERVIEW QUESTIONS

What are some current interpretations of the causes of childhood obesity?

What treatments have you found to be most effective? Why do you think they work?

★ **Using sources responsibly** When quoting your source (the interviewee), be accurate and fair. Do not change the meaning of your interviewee's words or take them out of context. To ensure accuracy, you might ask permission to record the interview or conduct it by email.

Surveying opinion

For some topics, you may find it useful to survey opinions through a written questionnaire, a phone or email poll, or questions posted on a social media site. Many people resist long questionnaires, so for a good response rate, limit your questions with your purpose in mind.

Surveys with yes/no questions or multiple-choice options can be completed quickly, and the results are easy to tally. You may also want to ask a few open-ended questions to elicit more individual responses, some of which may be worth quoting in your paper.

SAMPLE YES/NO QUESTION

Do you favor stricter return-to-play guidelines for student-athletes with concussions?

SAMPLE OPEN-ENDED QUESTION

How should the school community make decisions about return-to-play guidelines for student-athletes with concussions?

Using other field methods

Your firsthand visits to and observations of significant places, people, or events can enhance papers in a variety of disciplines. If you aren't able to visit an organization, a company, or a historic site, an official website may provide useful information or an email address you can use to contact a representative.

50f Write a research proposal.

One effective way to manage your research project and focus your thinking is to write a research proposal. A proposal gives you an opportunity to look back — to remind yourself why you chose your topic — and to look forward — to predict any difficulties or obstacles that might arise during your project. As you take stock of your project, you also have the opportunity to seek feedback about your research question and search strategy.

Organizing a research proposal

In a research proposal, you identify the question you plan to explore, the sources you plan to use, and the feasibility of the project, given the time and resources available.

The following questions will help you organize your proposal.

- **Research question.** What question will you be exploring? Why does this question need to be asked? What do you hope to learn from the project?

- **Research conversation.** What have you learned so far about the debate or specific research conversation you will enter? What entry point have you found to offer your own insights and ideas?

- **Search strategy.** What kinds of sources will you use to explore your question? What sources will be most useful, and why? How will you locate a variety of sources (primary/secondary, textual/visual)?

- **Research challenges.** What challenges, if any, do you anticipate (locating sufficient sources, managing the project, finding a position to take)? What resources are available to help you meet these challenges?

51 Managing information; taking notes responsibly

An effective researcher is a good record keeper. Whether you decide to keep records on paper or on a computer or mobile device, you will need methods for managing information: maintaining a working bibliography (see 51a), keeping track of source materials (see 51b), and taking notes without plagiarizing your sources (see 51c).

51a Maintain a working bibliography.

Keep a record of sources you read or view. This record, called a *working bibliography*, will help you keep track of publication information for the sources you might use so that you can easily refer to them as you write. You can also start to compile the list of sources that will appear at the end of your paper. The format of this list will depend on the documentation style you are

Information to collect for a working bibliography

For an article

- All authors of the article
- Title and subtitle of the article
- Title of the journal, magazine, or newspaper
- Date; volume, issue, and page numbers
- Date you accessed the source (for an online source that lists no publication date)

For an article retrieved from a database (in addition to preceding information)

- Name of the database
- Accession number or other number assigned by the database
- Digital object identifier (DOI), if there is one
- URL of the database home page or of the journal's home page if there is no DOI

For a web source (including visual, audio, and multimedia sources)

- All authors, editors, or composers of the source
- Title and subtitle of the source
- Title of the longer work, if the source is contained in a longer work
- Title of the website
- Print publication information for the source, if available
- Online page or paragraph numbers, if the source provides them
- Date of online publication (or of latest update)
- Sponsor or publisher of the site
- Date you accessed the source (for an undated source)
- URL or permalink of the page on which the source appears

For an entire book

- All authors; any editors or translators
- Title and subtitle
- Edition (if not the first)
- Publication information: city, publisher, and date
- Date you accessed the source (for an undated online book)

NOTE: For more details, see 56b (MLA) or 61b (APA).

using (for MLA style, see 56b; for APA style, see 61b). See 52d for advice on using your working bibliography as the basis for an annotated bibliography.

Most researchers save bibliographic information from the library's catalog and databases and from the web. The information you need to collect is given in the chart in this section. If you download a visual, gather the same information about it as you would for a print source.

For web sources, some bibliographic information may not be available, but spend some time looking for it before assuming that it doesn't exist. When information isn't available on the home page, you may have to drill into the site, following links to interior pages.

51b Keep track of source materials.

Save a copy of each potential source as you conduct your research. Many database services will allow you to email, text, save, or print citations or full texts, and you can easily download, copy, or take screen shots of information from the web.

Working with photocopies, printouts, and electronic files is better than relying on memory or hastily written notes and lets you annotate the source as you read. You can highlight key passages, perhaps even color-coding them to reflect topics in your outline. You also reduce the chances of unintentional plagiarism since you will be able to compare your use of a source in your paper with the actual source, not just with your notes.

51c As you take notes, avoid unintentional plagiarism.

Plagiarism, using someone's words or ideas without giving credit, is often accidental. After spending so much time thinking through your topic and reading sources, it's easy to forget where a helpful idea came from or to remember that the idea wasn't yours to begin with. Even if you half-copy an author's sentences — either by mixing the author's phrases with your own without using quotation marks or by plugging your synonyms into an author's sentence structure — you are committing plagiarism, a serious academic offense.

HOW TO

Take notes responsibly

1 **Understand the ideas in the source.** Ask: What is the argument? What is the evidence?

2 **Keep the source close by to check for accuracy,** but resist the temptation to look at the source as you take notes — except when you are quoting.

3 **Use quotation marks** around any borrowed words or phrases. Copy the words exactly and keep complete bibliographic information for each source.

4 **Use labels** to indicate a *summary* of the text or its data or a *paraphrase* of the author's words.

5 **Develop a system** to distinguish your insights and ideas from those of the source. Some researchers use a color-coding system.

The following strategies will help you take notes responsibly and avoid unintentionally plagiarizing a source.

Three kinds of note taking are covered in this section: summarizing, paraphrasing, and quoting.

Summarizing without plagiarizing

A summary condenses information and captures main ideas, perhaps reducing a chapter to a short paragraph or a paragraph to a single sentence. A summary should be written in your own words; if you use phrases from the source, put them in quotation marks.

The next page shows a passage about marine pollution from a National Oceanic and Atmospheric Administration (NOAA) website. Following the passage are the student's annotations — notes and questions that help him figure out the meaning — and then his summary of the passage. (The bibliographic information is recorded in MLA style.)

ORIGINAL SOURCE

A question that is often posed to the NOAA Marine Debris Program (MDP) is "How much debris is actually out there?" The MDP has recognized the need for this answer as well as the growing interest and value of citizen science. To that end, the MDP is developing and testing two types of monitoring and assessment protocols: 1) rigorous scientific survey and 2) volunteer at-sea visual survey. These types of monitoring programs are necessary in order to compare marine debris, composition, abundance, distribution, movement, and impact data on national and global scales.

> — NOAA Marine Debris Program, "Efforts and Activities Related to the 'Garbage Patches,'" *Marine Debris*, 2012, pm22100.net/docs/pdf/enercoop/pollutions/noaa-plastiques.pdf

ORIGINAL SOURCE WITH STUDENT ANNOTATIONS

by whom? *ocean* *trash*

A question that is often posed to the NOAA Marine Debris

Program (MDP) is "How much debris is actually out there?" The

MDP has recognized the need for this answer as well as the

aha

growing interest and value of (citizen) science. To that end, the MDP

is developing and testing two types of monitoring and assessment

ways of gathering information

protocols: 1) rigorous scientific survey and 2) volunteer at-sea visual

survey. These types of monitoring programs are necessary in order

kinds of materials *how much?*

to compare marine debris, composition, abundance, distribution,

why it matters

movement, and impact data on national and global scales.

SUMMARY

Source: NOAA Marine Debris Program. "Efforts and Activities Related to the 'Garbage Patches.'" *Marine Debris,* 2012, pm22100.net/ docs/pdf/enercoop/pollutions/noaa-plastiques.pdf.

Having to field citizens' questions about the size of debris fields in Earth's oceans, the Marine Debris Program, an arm of the US National Oceanic and Atmospheric Administration, is currently implementing methods to monitor and draw conclusions about our oceans' patches of pollution (NOAA Marine Debris Program).

> **Academic English** When you are summarizing or paraphrasing ideas from a source, keep these guidelines in mind: (1) Avoid replacing a source's words with synonyms. (2) Determine the meaning of the source. (3) Present your understanding of the author's meaning.

Paraphrasing without plagiarizing

Like a summary, a paraphrase is written in your own words; but whereas a summary reports significant information in fewer words than the source, a paraphrase restates the information in roughly the same number of words. A successful paraphrase also uses sentence structure that's different from the original. If you retain occasional choice phrases from the source, use quotation marks so that later you will know which phrases are not your own. If you paraphrase a source, you must still cite the source.

As you read the following paraphrase of the original source (see the previous page), notice that the language is significantly different from that in the original. It is the writer's own presentation of the author's idea.

PARAPHRASE

Source: NOAA Marine Debris Program. "Efforts and Activities Related to the 'Garbage Patches.'" *Marine Debris*, 2012, pm22100.net/docs/pdf/enercoop/pollutions/noaa-plastiques.pdf.

Citizens concerned and curious about the amount, makeup, and locations of debris patches in our oceans have been pressing NOAA's Marine Debris Program for answers. In response, the organization is preparing to implement plans and standards for expert study and nonexpert observation, both of which will yield results that will be helpful in determining the significance of the pollution problem (NOAA Marine Debris Program).

For additional advice on how to paraphrase, see 55c.

Using quotation marks to avoid plagiarizing

A quotation consists of exact words from a source. In your notes, put all quoted material in quotation marks; do not assume that you will remember later which words and phrases you have quoted and which are your own. When you quote, be sure to copy the source exactly, including punctuation and capitalization.

QUOTATION

Source: NOAA Marine Debris Program. "Efforts and Activities Related to the 'Garbage Patches.'" *Marine Debris*, 2012, pm22100.net/docs/pdf/enercoop/pollutions/noaa-plastiques.pdf.

The NOAA Marine Debris Program has noted that, as our oceans become increasingly polluted, surveillance is "necessary in order to compare marine debris, composition, abundance, distribution, movement, and impact data on national and global scales."

Note that because the source is from a website without page numbers, the in-text citation includes only the author's name.

HOW TO

Avoid plagiarizing from the web

1 **Understand what plagiarism is.** When you use another author's intellectual property (language, visuals, or ideas) in your own writing without giving proper credit, you commit a kind of academic theft called *plagiarism*.

2 **Treat online sources the same way you treat print sources.** Language, data, or images that you find on the web must be cited, even if the material is in the public domain (which includes older works no longer protected by copyright law), is publicly accessible on free sites or social media, or is on a government website.

3 **Keep track of words and ideas borrowed from sources.** When you copy and paste passages from online sources, put quotation marks around any text that you have copied. Develop a system for distinguishing your words and ideas from anything you've summarized, paraphrased, or quoted.

4 **Create a complete bibliographic entry for each source** to keep track of publication information. From the start of your research project, maintain accurate records for all online sources you read or view.

For details on avoiding plagiarism while working with sources, see 54b (MLA) and 59b (APA).

52 Evaluating sources

You can often locate far more potential sources for your topic than you will have time to read. Your challenge then is to determine what kinds of sources you need and what you need these sources to do and to select a reasonable number of trustworthy sources. This kind of decision making is referred to as *evaluating sources*. When you evaluate a source, you make a judgment about how useful the source is to your project.

Evaluating sources isn't something you do in one sitting, and it doesn't follow a formula (find sources > evaluate sources > write the paper). After you do some planning, searching, and reading, for example, you may reflect on the information you have collected and conclude that you need to rethink your research question — and so you return to assessing the kinds of sources you need. Or you may be midway through drafting your paper when you begin to question a particular source's credibility, at which point you return to searching and reading.

52a Think about how sources might contribute to your writing.

How you plan to use sources in your paper will affect how you evaluate them. Not every source must directly support your thesis; sources can have a range of functions in a paper. They can do any of the following:

- provide background information or context for your topic
- explain terms or concepts that your readers might not understand
- provide evidence for your argument
- lend authority to your argument
- identify a gap or contradiction in the conversation
- offer counterarguments to and alternative interpretations of your argument

Viewing evaluation as a process

When you use sources in your writing, make a habit of evaluating, or judging the value of, those sources at each stage of your project. The following questions may help.

Evaluate as you PLAN

- What kinds of sources do I need?

- What do I need these sources to help me do: Define? Persuade? Inform?

Evaluate as you READ

- What positions do these sources take in the debate on my topic? What are their biases?

- How do these sources inform my understanding of the topic and the position I will take?

Evaluate as you SEARCH

- How can I find the most reliable sources?

- Which sources will help me build my credibility as a researcher?

Evaluate as you WRITE

- How do the sources I've chosen help me support my thesis?

- How do my own ideas fit into the conversation on my research topic?

52b Select sources worth your time and attention.

As you search for sources in databases, the library catalog, and search engines, you're likely to find many more results than you can read or use. You will need to scan through the results for the most promising sources and preview those sources with your purpose in mind.

Scanning search results

As you scan through a list of search results, look for clues indicating whether a source might be useful for your purposes or not worth pursuing. You will need to use somewhat different strategies when scanning results from a database, a library catalog, and a web search engine.

Databases   Most databases list at least the following information, which can help you decide if a source is relevant, current, and scholarly (see the chart on p. 380).

- The title and a brief description (How relevant?)
- A date (How current?)
- The name of the periodical or other publication (How scholarly?)
- The length (How extensive in coverage?)

Many databases allow you to sort your list of results by relevance or date; sorting may help you scan the information more efficiently.

Catalogs   A library's catalog usually lists basic information about books, periodicals, DVDs, and other material — enough to give you a first impression. As in database search results, the title and date of publication of books and other sources listed in the catalog will often be your first clues as to whether the source is worth consulting. If the subject matter, currency, and authority of a potential source seem appropriate, it is probably worth taking a look at the source itself.

Web search engines   Reliable and unreliable sources live side by side online. As you scan through search results, look at the following aspects of a website for clues about its probable relevance, currency, and reliability:

- The title, keywords, headings, and lead-in text (How relevant?)
- The date (How current?)
- Any indication of the site's sponsor or purpose (How reliable?)
- The URL, especially URL endings such as .com, .edu, .gov, or .org (How relevant? How reliable?)

Previewing sources

Once you have decided that a source looks promising, preview it quickly to see whether it lives up to its promise.

PREVIEWING AN ARTICLE

- Consider the publication in which the article is printed. Is it a scholarly journal (see the chart on p. 380)? A popular magazine? A newspaper with a national reputation?

- For a journal or magazine article, look for an abstract or a statement of purpose at the beginning or a summary at the end. For a newspaper article, focus on the headline and the opening paragraphs to assess the article's relevance.

- Scan any headings and look at any visuals (graphs, diagrams, or illustrations) that might indicate the article's focus and scope.

PREVIEWING A WEBSITE

- Check to see if the sponsor is a reputable organization, a government agency, or a university. Is the group likely to look at only one side of a debatable issue?

- If you have landed on an internal page of a site and no author or sponsor is evident, try viewing the home page, either by clicking on a link or by shortening the URL (see the tip in 50d).

- Try to determine the purpose of the website. Is the site trying to sell a product? Promote an idea? Inform the public? Is the purpose consistent with your research?

- If the site includes statistical data, can you tell how and by whom the statistics were compiled? Is research cited?

- Find out when the site was created or last updated. Is it current enough for your purposes?

PREVIEWING A BOOK

- Glance through the table of contents, keeping your research question in mind. Even if the entire book is not relevant, parts of it may prove useful.

Determining if a source is scholarly

For many assignments, you will be asked to use scholarly sources. These are written by experts for a knowledgeable audience and go into more depth than books and articles written for a general audience. (Scholarly sources are often called *refereed* or *peer-reviewed* because the work is evaluated by experts in the field before publication.) To determine whether a source is scholarly, look for the following:

- Formal language and presentation
- Authors who are academics or scientists
- Footnotes or a bibliography documenting the works cited by the author in the source
- Original research and interpretation, rather than a summary of other people's work
- Quotations from and analysis of primary sources (in humanities disciplines such as literature, history, and philosophy)
- A description of research methods or a review of related research (in the sciences and social sciences)

NOTE: In some databases, searches can be limited to refereed or peer-reviewed journals.

- Scan the preface in search of a statement of the author's purposes.
- Use the index to look up a few words related to your topic.
- If a chapter looks useful, read its opening and closing paragraphs and skim any headings.

52c Read with an open mind and a critical eye.

As you begin reading the sources you have chosen, keep an open mind. Do not let your personal beliefs prevent you from being receptive to new ideas and opposing viewpoints. Be curious about the wide range of positions in the research conversation you are entering. Your research question should guide you as you read your sources.

Reading like a researcher

To read like a researcher is to read with an open, curious mind, to find out not only what has been written about a topic but also what is missing from the research conversation.

- **Read carefully.** Read to understand and summarize the main ideas of a source and an author's point of view. Ask questions: What does the source say? What is the author's central claim or thesis? What evidence does the author use to support the thesis?
- **Read skeptically.** Read to examine an author's assumptions, evidence, and conclusions and to pose counterarguments. Ask questions: Are any of the author's arguments or conclusions problematic? Is the author's evidence persuasive and sufficient?
- **Read evaluatively.** Read to judge the usefulness of a source for your research project. You may disagree with an author's argument or use of evidence, but refuting the author's ideas will help you clarify your position. Ask questions: Is the author an expert on the topic? Will the source provide background information, lend authority, explain a concept, or offer counterevidence for your claims?
- **Read responsibly.** Take time to read the entire source and to understand its author's arguments, assumptions, and conclusions. Avoid taking quotations from the first few pages of a source before you understand whether the ideas are representative of the work as a whole.

HOW TO

Detect fake news and misleading sources

Fake news and fabricated sources distort information or spread misinformation by taking information out of context or by promoting opinions as facts. As you evaluate sources, determine the authenticity of information and its source: Can the information be verified? Is the source reliable? If you are researching a controversial issue, verify facts and quotations by reading multiple sources and gathering a variety of perspectives. Because information and misinformation live side by side on the web, you need to read critically to determine the truth.

1 **Consider the source.**

Ask: Is more than one source covering the topic? Is the author anonymous or named? What can you learn about the author's credentials and the mission of the source from checking the "About Us" tab? Does the site present only one side of an issue? Be skeptical if the source is the only source reporting the story.

2 **Examine the source's language and visual clues.**

Does the headline use sensational (shocking or emotional) language? Is the language of the source offensive? Is the screen cluttered with ALL CAPS and unprofessional web design?

3 **Question the seriousness of the source.**

Is it possible that the source is satirical and humorous and is not intended to be read as factual?

4 **Fact-check the information.**

Can the facts be objectively verified? If the conclusions of a research study are cited, find the study to verify; if an authority is quoted, research the original source of the quotation, if possible, to see whether the quotation was taken out of context. Also, be skeptical if a source reports a research study but doesn't quote the study's principal investigator or other respected researchers. Check the facts before you report them in your research.

5 **Pay attention to the URL.**

Established news organizations have standard domain names. Fake sites often use web addresses that imitate the addresses of real sites, such as "Newslo" or "com.co," and package information with misinformation to make the site look authentic.

6 **Note your biases.**

If an article makes you angry or challenges your beliefs, or if it confirms your beliefs by ignoring evidence to the contrary, take notice, and try to be as objective as possible. Learn about an issue from a variety of reliable sources and from multiple perspectives.

Distinguishing between primary and secondary sources

As you begin assessing evidence in a source, determine whether you are reading a primary source or a secondary source. Primary sources include original documents such as letters, diaries, legislative bills, laboratory studies, field research reports, and eyewitness accounts. Secondary sources are commentaries on primary sources — another writer's opinions about or interpretation of a primary source.

Although a primary source is not necessarily more reliable than a secondary source, it has the advantage of being a firsthand account. You can better evaluate what a secondary source says if you have read any primary sources it discusses.

Being alert for signs of bias

Bias is a way of thinking, a tendency to be partial, that prevents people and publications from viewing a topic objectively. Both in print and online, some sources are more objective than others. If you are exploring the right of organizations like WikiLeaks to distribute sensitive government documents over the Internet, for example, you may not find objective, unbiased information in a US State Department report. If you are researching timber harvesting practices, you are likely to encounter bias in publications sponsored by environmental groups. As a researcher, you will need to consider any suspected bias as you assess each source.

res

Like publishers, some authors are more objective than others. If you have reason to believe that a writer is particularly biased, you will want to assess his or her arguments with special care.

Assessing the author's argument

In nearly all subjects worth writing about, there is some element of argument, so expect to encounter debates and disagreements among authors. In fact, areas of disagreement give you entry points into a research conversation.

Evaluating all sources

Checking for signs of bias

- Does the author or publisher endorse political or religious views that could affect objectivity?
- Is the author or publisher associated with a special-interest group, such as PETA or the National Rifle Association, that might emphasize one side of an issue?
- Does the author's language show signs of bias?

Assessing an argument

- What is the author's central claim or thesis?
- How does the author support this claim — with relevant and sufficient evidence or with just a few anecdotes or emotional examples?
- Are statistics consistent with those you encounter in other sources? Does the author explain where the statistics come from?
- Are any of the author's assumptions questionable?
- Does the author consider opposing arguments and refute them persuasively? (See 6c.)
- Does the author use flawed logic? (See 6a.)

Assessing web sources with care

Before using a web source in your paper, make sure you know who created the material and for what purpose. Sources with reliable information can stand up to scrutiny.

Evaluating a website: Checking reliability

1   This page on Internet monitoring and workplace privacy appears on a website sponsored by the National Conference of State Legislatures. The NCSL is a bipartisan group that functions as a clearinghouse of ideas and research of interest to state lawmakers. It is also a lobby for state issues before the US government. The URL ending .org marks this sponsor as a nonprofit organization.

2   A clear date of publication shows currency.

3   An "About Us" page confirms that this is a credible organization whose credentials can be verified.

Evaluating a website: Checking purpose

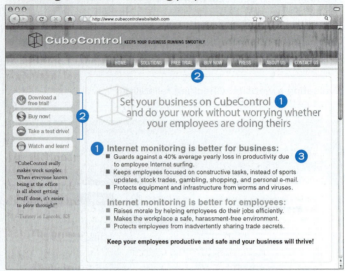

1 The site is sponsored by a company that specializes in employee-monitoring software.

2 Repeated links for trial downloads and purchase suggest the site's intended audience: consumers seeking to purchase software (probably not researchers seeking detailed information about employees' use of the Internet in the workplace).

3 The site appears to provide information and even shows statistics from studies, but ultimately the purpose of the site is to sell a product.

52d Construct an annotated bibliography.

Section 51a describes how to write a working bibliography, a document that helps you keep track of publication information for all the sources you may be considering for your project. At some point during your research process or as a separate assignment, your instructor may assign you to write an annotated bibliography.

Writing an annotated bibliography allows you to summarize, evaluate, and record publication information for your sources before drafting your research paper. You summarize each source to understand its main ideas; you evaluate each source to assess how it contributes to your research project; and you record bibliographic information to keep track of publication details for each source.

Constructing an annotated bibliography focuses your attention on the most promising sources you located, providing you with an opportunity to reflect on *how* and *why* these sources will help you answer your research question.

Take the following steps for *each* source in your annotated bibliography:

RECORD   Using MLA or APA style (or whatever style your assignment requires), record the publication information for your source.

SUMMARIZE   The summary is where you demonstrate your understanding of something you've read or viewed. Start by asking what you learned from a source. Did the source provide an important quotation or persuasive data, a definition of a concept, or a counterargument to your position? Use the author's or organization's name, and use verbs such as *claims, explains,* and *reports.* Avoid writing "The article says . . ."

EVALUATE   Then judge the strength of the ideas and ask yourself what role a source might play and how it will contribute to your research — providing background information, lending authority, supporting a claim, or anticipating and countering objections. Evaluating your sources' ideas will help you separate them from your own ideas and from one another, and it will help you move toward a draft in which you synthesize sources and present your own thesis.

In the following example, see how three steps — recording, summarizing, and evaluating — work together to create an effective annotated bibliography entry.

SAMPLE ANNOTATED BIBLIOGRAPHY ENTRY (MLA STYLE)

Resnik, David. "Trans Fat Bans and Human Freedom." *The American Journal of Bioethics*, vol. 10, no. 3, Mar. 2010, pp. 27–32.

Student indicates the type of source (scholarly article) and gives the author's name and credentials (bioethicist David Resnik).

In this scholarly article, bioethicist David Resnik argues that bans on unhealthy foods threaten our personal freedom. He claims that researchers don't have enough evidence to know whether banning trans fats will save lives or money; all we know is that such bans restrict dietary choices. Resnik explains why most Americans oppose food restrictions, noting our multiethnic and regional food traditions as well as our resistance to government limitations on personal freedoms. He acknowledges that few people would miss eating trans fats, but he fears that bans on such substances could lead to widespread restrictions on red meat, sugary sodas, and other foods known to have harmful effects. Resnik offers a well-reasoned argument, but he goes too far by insisting that all proposed food restrictions will do more harm than good. This article contributes important perspectives on American resistance to government intervention in food choice and counters arguments in other sources that support the idea of food legislation to advance public health.

Student presents the author's argument.

Additional summary sentences show the student's understanding of the author's points.

Student identifies the strengths of the source and establishes it as reliable. Additional evaluation comments show how the student might use the source in his essay.

How to write an annotated bibliography

An **annotated bibliography** gives you an opportunity to summarize, evaluate, and record publication information for your sources before drafting your research paper. You summarize each source to understand its main ideas; you evaluate each source for accuracy, quality, and relevance. Finally, you reflect, asking yourself how the source will contribute to your research project. A sample annotated bibliography entry appears on the previous page.

Key features

- **A list of sources arranged in alphabetical order by author** includes complete bibliographic information for each source.

- **A brief annotation or note for each source**, typically one hundred to two hundred words, is written in paragraph form.

- **A summary** of each source states the work's main ideas and key points briefly and accurately. The summary is written in the present tense, third person, directly and concisely. Summarizing helps you test your understanding of a source and restate its meaning responsibly.

- **An evaluation** of the source's role and usefulness in your project includes an assessment of the source's strengths and limitations, the author's qualifications and expertise, and the function of the source in your project. Evaluating a source helps you analyze how the source fits into your project and separate the source's ideas from your own.

→

Writing your annotated bibliography

1 Explore

For each source, begin by brainstorming responses to questions such as the following:

- What is the purpose of the source? Who is the author's intended audience?

- What is the author's thesis? What evidence supports the thesis?

- What qualifications and expertise does the author bring? Does the author have any biases or make any questionable assumptions?

- Why do you think this source is useful for your project?

- How does this source relate to the other sources in your bibliography?

2 Draft

The following tips can help you draft one or more entries in your annotated bibliography.

- Arrange the sources in alphabetical order by author (or by title for works with no author).

- Provide consistent bibliographic information for each source. For the exact bibliographic format, see 56b (MLA) or 61b (APA).

- Start your summary by identifying the thesis and purpose of the source as well as the credentials of the source's author.

- Keep your research question in mind. How does this source contribute to your project? How does it help you take your place in the conversation?

3 Revise

Ask reviewers for specific feedback. Here are some questions to guide their comments.

- Is each source summarized clearly? Have you identified the author's main idea?

- For each source, have you made a clear judgment about how and why the source is useful for your project?

- Have you used quotation marks around exact words from a source?

WRITING PAPERS IN MLA STYLE

Note: An in-text citation is a reference to a source that you place within your paper. A works cited entry is a reference to a source that you include at the end of your paper.

MLA-style papers in this book: See pages 36, 67, 99, and 467.

In English and other humanities courses, you may be asked to document your sources using the Modern Language Association (MLA) style of citations described in chapter 56. When writing an MLA-style paper that draws on sources, you face three main challenges: (1) supporting a thesis, (2) citing your sources accurately and avoiding plagiarism, and (3) integrating source material effectively.

Examples in chapters 53–55 are drawn from one student's research. Sophie Harba's research paper, in which she argues that state governments have the responsibility to advance health policies and to regulate healthy eating choices, appears in 57b.

53 Supporting a thesis

Most research assignments ask you to form a thesis, or main idea, and to support that thesis with well-organized evidence.

53a Form a working thesis.

Once you have read a variety of sources, considered your subject from different perspectives, and chosen an entry point in the research conversation (see 50b), you are ready to form a working thesis: a one-sentence (or occasionally two-sentence) statement of your central idea. (See also 1c and 53d.)

The working thesis expresses more than your opinion; it expresses your informed, reasoned answer to your research question — a question about which people might disagree. Here, for example, are student writer Sophie Harba's research question and working thesis.

RESEARCH QUESTION

Should the government enact laws to regulate healthy eating choices?

WORKING THESIS

State governments have the responsibility to regulate healthy eating choices because of the rise of chronic diseases.

 LaunchPad Solo   **Activities for Chapter 53**
macmillan learning
1 Writing practice activity, 2 Exercises

After you have written a rough draft and perhaps done more reading, you may decide to revise your thesis, as Harba did, to give it a sharper focus and to offer readers a "So what?" to show why the thesis matters.

REVISED THESIS

Additional language suggests why readers should care about the writer's thesis.

In the name of public health and safety, state governments have the responsibility to shape health policies and to regulate healthy eating choices, especially since doing so offers a potentially large social benefit for a relatively small cost.

The thesis usually appears at the end of the introductory paragraph. To read Sophie Harba's thesis in the context of her introduction, see 53c.

Testing your thesis

Keep the following guidelines in mind to develop an effective thesis statement.

- A thesis should be your answer to a question and should take a position that needs to be argued and supported. It should not be a fact or description.

- A thesis should match the scope of the research project. If your thesis is too broad, explore a subtopic of your original topic. If your thesis is too narrow, pose a research question that has more than one answer.

- A thesis should be focused. Avoid vague words such as *interesting* or *good*. Use concrete language and make sure your thesis lets readers know your position.

- A thesis should stand up to the "So what?" question (see 1c). Ask yourself why readers should be interested in your essay and care about your thesis.

53b Organize ideas with an informal plan.

The body of your paper will consist of evidence in support of your thesis. It is useful to sketch an informal plan that helps you begin to organize your ideas. Sophie Harba, for example, used this simple plan to outline the structure of her argument:

- Debates about the government's role in regulating food have a long history in the United States.

- Some experts argue that we should focus on the dangers of unhealthy eating habits and on preventing chronic diseases linked to diet.

- But food regulations are not a popular solution because many Americans object to government restrictions on personal choice.

- Food regulations designed to prevent chronic disease don't ask Americans to give up their freedom; they ask Americans to see health as a matter of public good.

After you have written a rough draft, a formal outline can help you test the organization of your argument. See 1d to read Harba's formal outline.

53c Draft an introduction for your thesis.

In a research paper, readers are accustomed to seeing the thesis statement, or the writer's main point, at the end of the first or second paragraph. The advantage of putting it in the first paragraph is that readers can easily recognize your position. The advantage of delaying the thesis until the second paragraph is that you can provide a fuller context for your main idea.

As you draft your introduction, you may revise your working thesis, either because you have refined your thinking or because new wording fits more smoothly into the context you have created for it.

In addition to stating your thesis, an introduction should hook readers by capturing their attention (see 1e). For example, in your first sentence or two you might introduce readers to the research conversation by connecting your topic to a recent news item or by pointing to emerging trends in an academic discipline. Other strategies are to pose a puzzling problem or to cite a surprising statistic. Student writer Sophie Harba begins her paper by engaging readers with her research question and offers her answer in her thesis.

SAMPLE INTRODUCTION FOR A RESEARCH PAPER

Should the government enact laws to regulate healthy eating choices? Many Americans would answer an emphatic "No," arguing that what and how much we eat should be left to individual choice rather than unreasonable laws.

Others might argue that it would be unreasonable for the government not to enact legislation, given the rise of

Writer uses an authoritative voice.

chronic diseases that result from harmful diets. In this debate, both the definition of reasonable regulations and the role of government to legislate food choices are

Writer presents her argument and offers readers a "So what?" to show why thesis matters.

at stake. In the name of public health and safety, state governments have the responsibility to shape health policies and to regulate healthy eating choices, especially since doing so offers a potentially large social benefit for a relatively small cost.

53d Use sources to inform and support your argument.

The source materials you have gathered can play many different roles and will help you support your thesis and develop your argument.

Providing background information or context

Readers need some background information and context to anchor their understanding of your topic. Describing a research study or offering statistics can help readers grasp your topic's significance. Student writer Sophie Harba uses a source to give context for her topic, the benefits of laws designed to prevent chronic disease.

> To give just one example, Marion Nestle, New York University professor of nutrition and public health, notes that "a 1% reduction in intake of saturated fat across the population would prevent more than 30,000 cases of coronary heart disease annually and save more than a billion dollars in health care costs" (7).

Explaining terms or concepts

If readers are unfamiliar with a term or a concept, you will want to define or explain it; or if your argument depends on a term with multiple meanings, you will want to explain your use of the term. Quoting or paraphrasing a source can help you define terms and concepts in accessible language. Harba defines the term *refined grains* as part of her claim that the typical American diet is getting less healthy over time.

> A diet that is low in nutritional value and high in sugars, fats, and refined grains—grains that have been processed to increase shelf life but that contain little fiber, iron, and B vitamins—can be damaging over time (United States, Dept. of Agriculture and Dept. of Health and Human Services 36).

Supporting your claims

As you develop your argument, back up your assertions with facts, examples, and other evidence from your research. (See also 7e.) Harba, for example, uses factual evidence to make the point that the typical American diet is damaging.

> Michael Pollan, who has written extensively about Americans' unhealthy eating habits, notes that "[t]he Centers for Disease Control estimates that fully three quarters of US health care spending goes to treat chronic diseases, most of which are preventable and linked to diet: heart disease, stroke, type 2 diabetes, and at least a third of all cancers."

Lending authority to your argument

Expert opinion can add weight and credibility to your argument. (See also 7e.) But don't rely on experts to make your points for you. State your ideas in your own words and, when appropriate, cite the judgment of an authority in the field to support your position.

> Debates surrounding the government's role in regulating food have a long history in the United States. According to Lorine Goodwin, a food historian, nineteenth-century reformers who sought to purify the food supply were called "fanatics" and "radicals" by critics who argued that consumers should be free to buy and eat what they want (77).

Anticipating and countering objections

Do not ignore sources that seem contrary to your position. Instead, use them to give voice to opposing points of view and to state potential objections to your argument before you counter them (see 7f). By anticipating her readers' argument that many Americans oppose laws to limit what they eat, Sophie Harba creates an opportunity to counter that objection and build common ground with her readers.

> Why is the public largely resistant to laws that would limit unhealthy choices or penalize those choices with so-called fat taxes? Many consumers and civil rights advocates find such laws to be an unreasonable restriction on individual freedom of choice. As health policy experts Mello and others point out, opposition to food and beverage regulation is similar to the opposition to early tobacco legislation: the public views the issue as one of personal responsibility rather than one requiring government intervention (2602). In other words, if a person eats unhealthy food and becomes ill as a result, that is his or her choice. But those who favor legislation claim that freedom of choice is a myth because of the strong influence of food and beverage industry marketing on consumers' dietary habits.

54 Citing sources; avoiding plagiarism

In a research paper, you will draw on the work of other writers, and you must document their contributions by citing your sources. Sources are cited for two reasons:

(1) to tell readers where your information comes from — so that they can assess its reliability and, if interested, find and read the original source

(2) to give credit to the writers from whom you have borrowed words and ideas

You must include a citation when you quote from a source, when you summarize or paraphrase, and when you borrow facts that are not common knowledge. Borrowing another writer's language, sentence structure, or ideas without proper acknowledgment is plagiarism.

The only exception is common knowledge — information that your readers may know or could easily locate in any number of general sources. As a rule, when you have seen information repeatedly in your reading, you don't need to cite it.

54a Understand how the MLA system works.

In the MLA citation style, you acknowledge your sources in a system organized by in-text citation and a works cited list. Here, briefly, is how the MLA citation system usually works. (See 56 for more details and model citations.)

IN-TEXT CITATION

A signal phrase names the author and often gives credentials.

Bioethicist David Resnik emphasizes that such policies "open the door to excessive government control over food, which could restrict dietary choices, interfere with cultural, ethnic, and religious traditions, and exacerbate socioeconomic inequalities" (31).

The material being cited is followed by a page number in parentheses (unless the source is an unpaginated web source) and then a period.

The in-text citation points readers to the Works Cited page.

ENTRY IN THE LIST OF WORKS CITED

Resnik, David. "Trans Fat Bans and Human Freedom." *The American Journal of Bioethics*, vol. 10, no. 3, Mar. 2010, pp. 27–32.

At the end of the paper, a list of works cited gives complete publication information for the source.

NOTE: This basic MLA format varies for different types of sources. For a detailed discussion and other models, see 56.

Writing for an audience

When you cite sources, you show readers where information comes from so that they can judge if it is reliable and so that they can find the source on their own. You show respect for your audience when your citations guide them quickly to the source of a quoted, paraphrased, or summarized idea. Ask yourself two questions: How can I make my documentation useful to my readers? What would readers need to know to find the source themselves?

54b Understand what plagiarism is.

In a research paper, you draw on the work of other writers. To be fair and responsible, you must document their contributions by citing your sources. When you acknowledge and document your sources, you avoid plagiarism, a form of academic dishonesty. (See also 51c.)

In general, these three acts are considered plagiarism:

(1) failing to cite quotations and borrowed ideas

(2) failing to enclose borrowed language in quotation marks

(3) failing to put summaries and paraphrases in your own words

Definitions of plagiarism vary; it's a good idea to find out how your school defines academic dishonesty.

54c Use quotation marks around borrowed language.

To indicate that you are using a source's exact phrases or sentences, you must enclose them in quotation marks unless they have been set off from the text by indenting (see 55b). To omit the quotation marks is to claim, falsely, that the language is your own, as in the example below. Such an omission is plagiarism even if you have cited the source.

ORIGINAL SOURCE

Although these policies may have a positive impact on human health, they open the door to excessive government control over food, which could restrict dietary choices, interfere with cultural, ethnic, and religious traditions, and exacerbate socioeconomic inequalities.

— David Resnik, "Trans Fat Bans and Human Freedom," p. 31

PLAGIARISM

Bioethicist David Resnik points out that policies to ban

The highlighted words are directly from the original.

trans fats may protect human health, but they open the door to excessive government control over food, which could restrict dietary choices and interfere with cultural, ethnic, and religious traditions (31).

BORROWED LANGUAGE IN QUOTATION MARKS

Bioethicist David Resnik points out that policies to ban

Borrowed language is in quotation marks.

trans fats may protect human health, but they "open the door to excessive government control over food, which could restrict dietary choices, interfere with cultural, ethnic, and religious traditions, and exacerbate socioeconomic inequalities" (31).

54d Put summaries and paraphrases in your own words.

A summary condenses information from a source; a paraphrase conveys the information using roughly the same number of words as the original source. When you summarize or paraphrase, it is not enough to name the source; you must restate the source's meaning using your own words and sentence structure. (See also 51c and 55a.) Half-copying the author's sentences either by using the author's phrases in your own sentences without quotation marks or by plugging synonyms into the author's sentence structure (sometimes called *patchwriting*) is a form of plagiarism.

The first paraphrase of the following source is plagiarism, even though the source is cited, because the paraphrase borrows too much of its language from the original. The highlighted strings of words have been copied exactly (without quotation marks).

In addition, the writer has closely echoed the sentence structure of the source, merely substituting some synonyms (*interfere with lifestyle choices* for *paternalistic intervention into lifestyle choices* and *decrease the feeling of personal responsibility* for *enfeeble the notion of personal responsibility*).

ORIGINAL SOURCE

[A]ntiobesity laws encounter strong opposition from some quarters on the grounds that they constitute paternalistic intervention into lifestyle choices and enfeeble the notion of personal responsibility. Such arguments echo those made in the early days of tobacco regulation.

— Michelle M. Mello et al.,
"Obesity—the New Frontier of Public Health Law," p. 2602

PLAGIARISM

The paraphrase borrows too much language from the original and follows the sentence structure of the original too closely.

Health policy experts Mello and others argue that antiobesity laws encounter strong opposition from some quarters because they interfere with lifestyle choices and decrease the feeling of personal responsibility. These arguments mirror those made in the early days of tobacco regulation (2602).

To avoid plagiarizing an author's language, resist the temptation to look at the source while you are summarizing or paraphrasing. After you have read the passage you want to paraphrase, set the source aside. Ask yourself, "What is the author's meaning?" In your own words, state your understanding of the author's ideas.

Then return to the source and check that you haven't used the author's language or sentence structure or misrepresented the author's ideas. When you fully understand another writer's meaning, you can more easily and accurately present those ideas in your own words.

ACCEPTABLE PARAPHRASE

The writer understands the ideas in the text and uses original language and structure to present them.

As health policy experts Mello and others point out, opposition to food and beverage regulation is similar to the opposition to early tobacco legislation: the public views the issue as one of personal responsibility rather than one requiring government intervention (2602).

HOW TO

Be a responsible research writer

Using good citation habits is the best way to avoid plagiarizing sources and to demonstrate your responsibility as a researcher.

1 **Cite your sources as you write drafts.** Don't wait until your final draft is complete to add citations. Include a citation when you quote from a source, when you summarize or paraphrase, and when you borrow facts that are not common knowledge.

2 **Place quotation marks around direct quotations,** both in your notes and in your drafts.

3 **Check each quotation, summary, and paraphrase against the source** to make certain you aren't misrepresenting the source. For paraphrases, be sure that your language and sentence structure differ from those in the original passage.

4 **Provide a full citation in your list of works cited.** It is not sufficient to cite a source only in the body of your paper; you must also provide complete publication information for each source in a list of works cited.

Exercise 54–1 ▶ Summarize the following passage from a research source. Then paraphrase the same source. Use MLA-style in-text citation.

> Until recently, school-readiness skills weren't high on anyone's agenda, nor was the idea that the youngest learners might be disqualified from moving on to a subsequent stage. But now that kindergarten serves as a gatekeeper, not a welcome mat, to elementary school, concerns about school preparedness kick in earlier and earlier. A child who's supposed to read by the end of kindergarten had better be getting ready in preschool.
>
> — Erika Christakis, "How the New Preschool Is Crushing Kids,"
> *The Atlantic*, Jan./Feb. 2016, p. 18

55 Integrating sources

Quotations, summaries, and paraphrases will help you develop your argument, but they cannot speak for you. You need to find a balance between the words of your sources and your own voice, so that readers always know who is speaking in your paper — you or your source. You can use several strategies to integrate sources into your paper while maintaining your own voice.

- Use sources as concisely as possible so that your own thinking and voice aren't lost (55a and 55b).
- Use signal phrases to avoid dropping quotations into your paper without indicating the boundary between your words and the source's words (55c).
- Use language that shows readers how each source supports your argument and how the sources relate to one another (55d).

55a Summarize and paraphrase effectively.

In your academic writing, keep the emphasis on your ideas and your language; use your own words to summarize and to paraphrase your sources and to explain your points. Whether you choose to summarize or paraphrase a source depends on your purpose.

Summarizing

When you summarize a source, you express another writer's ideas in your own words, condensing the author's key points and using fewer words than the author.

WHEN TO USE A SUMMARY

- When a passage is lengthy and you want to condense a chapter to a paragraph or a paragraph to a sentence
- When you want to state the source's main ideas simply and briefly in your own words

- When you want to compare arguments or ideas from various sources
- When you want to provide readers with an understanding of the source's argument before you respond to it or launch your own argument

Paraphrasing

When you paraphrase, you express an author's ideas in your own words and sentence structure, using approximately the same number of words and details as in the source.

WHEN TO USE A PARAPHRASE

- When the ideas and information are important but the author's exact words are not needed
- When you want to restate the source's ideas in your own words
- When you need to simplify and explain a technical or complicated source
- When you need to reorder a source's ideas

★ **Using sources responsibly** When you use your own words to summarize or paraphrase, the original idea remains the intellectual property of the author, so you must include a citation. (See 54d.)

55b Use quotations effectively.

When you quote a source, you borrow the author's exact words and enclose them in quotation marks. Quotation marks show your readers that both the idea and the words belong to the author.

WHEN TO USE QUOTATIONS

- When language is especially vivid or expressive
- When exact wording is needed for technical accuracy
- When it is important to let the debaters of an issue explain their positions in their own words
- When the words of an authority lend weight to an argument
- When the language of a source is the topic of your discussion

HOW TO

Paraphrase effectively

A paraphrase shows your readers that you understand a source and can explain it to them. When you choose to paraphrase a passage, you use the information and ideas of a source for your own purpose — to provide background information, explain a concept, or advance your argument — and yet maintain your voice. It is challenging to write a paraphrase that isn't a word-for-word translation of the original source and doesn't imitate the source's sentence structure. These strategies will help you paraphrase effectively.

1 Understand the source. Identify the source's key points and argument. Test your understanding by asking questions: *What* is being said? *Why* and *how* is it being said? Look up words you don't know to help you understand whole ideas, not just the words.

ORIGINAL

People's vision of the world has broadened with the advent of global media such as television and the Internet. Those thinking about going elsewhere can see what the alternatives are and appear to have fewer inhibitions about resettling.

— Darrell M. West, *Brain Gain: Rethinking U.S. Immigration Policy,* Brookings Institution Press, 2011, p. 5

STUDENT'S NOTES

– TV and Internet have opened our eyes, our minds
– We can imagine making big moves (country to country) as we never could before; the web offers a preview
– "resettling" = moving to a new location, out of the familiar region
– Lessens the anxiety about starting over in a new place

2 Use your own vocabulary and sentence structure to convey the source's information. Check to make sure there is no overlap in vocabulary or sentence structure with the original.

Since TV and the web can offer a preview of life in other places, people feel less uncertainty and anxiety about making moves from one area of the world to another.

→

3 **Use a signal phrase to identify the source** (*According to X, _____,* or *X argues that _____*).

> West argues that since TV and the web can offer a
> preview of life in other places, people feel less uncertainty
> and anxiety about making moves from one area of the world
> to another.

4 **Include a citation to give credit to the source.** Even though the words are yours, you need to give credit for the idea. Here, the author's name and the page number on which the original passage appeared are listed.

> West argues that since TV and the web can offer a
> preview of life in other places, people feel less uncertainty
> and anxiety about making moves from one area of the world
> to another (5).

NOTE: If you choose to use exact language from the source in a paraphrase, be sure to put quotation marks around any borrowed words or phrases.

> West argues that since TV and the web can offer a preview of
> life in other places, people "have fewer inhibitions" about making
> moves from one area of the world to another (5).

Limiting your use of quotations

Keep the emphasis on your own ideas. It is not always necessary to quote full sentences from a source. Often you can integrate words and phrases from a source into your own sentence structure. (For the use of signal phrases in integrating quotations, see 55c.)

> Resnik acknowledges that his argument relies on the "slippery slope"
> fallacy, but he insists that "social and political pressures" regarding
> food regulations make his concerns valid (31).

Using the ellipsis mark

To condense a quoted passage, you can use the ellipsis mark (three periods, with spaces between) to indicate that you have left words out. What remains must be grammatically complete.

> In Mississippi, legislators passed "a ban on bans — a law that
> forbids . . . local restrictions on food or drink" (Conly A23).

The writer has omitted from the source the words *municipalities to place* before *local restrictions* to condense the quoted material.

If you want to leave out one or more full sentences, use a period before the three ellipsis dots.

> Legal scholars Gostin and Gostin argue that "individuals have
> limited willpower to defer immediate gratification for longer-term
> health benefits. . . . A person understands that high-fat foods
> or a sedentary lifestyle will cause adverse health effects, or that
> excessive spending or gambling will cause financial hardship, but it
> is not always easy to refrain" (217).

Ordinarily, do not use an ellipsis mark at the beginning or at the end of a quotation. Your readers will understand that you have taken the quoted material from a longer passage, so such marks are not necessary. The only exception occurs when you have dropped words at the end of the final quoted sentence. In such cases, put three ellipsis dots before the closing quotation mark and parenthetical reference.

★ **Using sources responsibly**   Make sure that omissions and ellipsis marks do not distort the meaning of your source.

Using brackets

Brackets allow you to insert your own words into quoted material to clarify a confusing reference or to keep a sentence grammatical in the context of your own writing. You also use brackets to indicate that you are changing a letter from capital to lowercase (or vice versa) to fit into your sentence. In the following example, the writer inserted words in brackets to clarify the meaning of *help*.

> Neergaard and Agiesta argue that "a new poll finds people are split
> on how much the government should do to help [find solutions to

the national health crisis] — and most draw the line at attempts to force healthier eating."

To indicate an error such as a misspelling in a quotation, insert the word "sic" in brackets right after the error.

"While Americans of every race, gender and ethnicity are affected by this disease, diabetes disproportionately effects [sic] minority populations."

Setting off long quotations

When you quote more than four typed lines of prose or more than three lines of poetry, set off the quotation by indenting it one-half inch from the left margin.

Long quotations should be introduced by an informative sentence, usually followed by a colon. Quotation marks are unnecessary because the indented format tells readers that the passage is taken word for word from the source.

> In response to critics who claim that laws aimed at stopping us from eating whatever we want are an assault on our freedom of choice, Conly offers a persuasive counterargument:
>
>> [L]aws aren't designed for each one of us individually. Some of us can drive safely at 90 miles per hour, but we're bound by the same laws as the people who can't, because individual speeding laws aren't practical. Giving up a little liberty is something we agree to when we agree to live in a democratic society that is governed by laws. (A23)

At the end of an indented quotation, the parenthetical citation goes outside the final mark of punctuation. (When a quotation is run into your text, the opposite is true. See the sample citations in the ellipsis mark section earlier in 55b.)

55c Use signal phrases to integrate sources.

Whenever you include a paraphrase, summary, or direct quotation of another writer's work in your paper, prepare your readers for it with introductory words called a *signal phrase*. A signal phrase usually names the author of the source, provides some context for the source material — such as the author's credentials — and helps readers distinguish your ideas from those of the source.

Using signal phrases in MLA papers

To avoid monotony, try to vary both the language and the placement of your signal phrases.

Model signal phrases

Michael Pollan, who has written extensively about Americans' unhealthy eating habits, argues that ". . ."

As health policy experts Mello and others point out, ". . ."

Marion Nestle, New York University professor of nutrition and public health, notes, ". . ."

Bioethicist David Resnik acknowledges that his argument . . .

In response to critics, Conly offers a persuasive counterargument: ". . ."

Verbs in signal phrases

acknowledges	comments	endorses	reasons
adds	compares	grants	refutes
admits	confirms	illustrates	rejects
agrees	contends	implies	reports
argues	declares	insists	responds
asserts	denies	notes	suggests
believes	disputes	observes	thinks
claims	emphasizes	points out	writes

When you write a signal phrase, choose a verb that fits with the way you are using the source (see 53d). Are you providing background, explaining a concept, supporting a claim, lending authority, or refuting a belief?

> ▸ Lorine Goodwin, a food historian, ~~says~~: ". . ."
>   *rejects the claim*

NOTE: MLA style calls for verbs in the present tense or present perfect tense (*argues, has argued*) to introduce source material unless you include a date that specifies the time of the original author's writing.

Marking boundaries

Readers need to move from your words to the words of a source without feeling a jolt. Avoid dropping quotations into the text without warning. Instead, provide clear signal phrases, including at least the author's name, to indicate the boundary between your words and the source's words. (The signal phrase is highlighted in the second example.)

DROPPED QUOTATION

Laws designed to prevent chronic disease by promoting healthier food and beverage consumption also have potentially enormous economic benefits. "[A] 1% reduction in intake of saturated fat across the population would prevent more than 30,000 cases of coronary heart disease annually and would save more than a billion dollars in health care costs" (Nestle 7).

QUOTATION WITH SIGNAL PHRASE

Laws designed to prevent chronic disease by promoting healthier food and beverage consumption also have potentially enormous economic benefits. Marion Nestle, New York University professor of nutrition and public health, notes that "a 1% reduction in intake of saturated fat across the population would prevent more than 30,000 cases of coronary heart disease annually and would save more than a billion dollars in health care costs" (7).

Establishing authority

The first time you mention a source, include in the signal phrase the author's title, credentials, or experience to help your readers recognize the source's authority and your own credibility (*ethos*) as a responsible researcher who has located reliable sources.

SOURCE WITH NO CREDENTIALS

Readers aren't given any clues about the author.

Michael Pollan notes that "[t]he Centers for Disease Control estimates that fully three quarters of US health care spending goes to treat chronic diseases, most of which are preventable and linked to diet: heart disease, stroke, type 2 diabetes, and at least a third of all cancers."

SOURCE WITH CREDENTIALS

A brief note about the author in the signal phrase highlights his credibility.

> Michael Pollan, who has written extensively about Americans' unhealthy eating habits, notes that "[t]he Centers for Disease Control estimates that fully three quarters of US health care spending goes to treat chronic diseases, most of which are preventable and linked to diet: heart disease, stroke, type 2 diabetes, and at least a third of all cancers."

Introducing summaries and paraphrases

Introduce most summaries and paraphrases with a signal phrase that names the author and places the material in the context of your argument. Readers will then understand that everything between the signal phrase and the parenthetical citation summarizes or paraphrases the cited source.

Without the signal phrase, readers might think that only the quotation at the end is being cited, when in fact the whole paragraph is based on the source.

> To improve public health, advocates such as Bowdoin College philosophy professor Sarah Conly contend that it is the government's duty to prevent people from making harmful choices whenever feasible and whenever public benefits outweigh the costs. In response to critics who claim that laws aimed at stopping us from eating whatever we want are an assault on our freedom of choice, Conly asserts that "laws aren't designed for each one of us individually" (A23).

There are times when a summary or a paraphrase does not require a signal phrase naming the author. When the context makes clear where the cited material begins, you may omit the signal phrase and include the author's last name in parentheses.

Using signal phrases with statistics and other facts

When you are citing a statistic or another specific fact, a signal phrase is often not necessary. Readers usually will understand that the citation refers to the statistic or fact (not the whole paragraph).

> Seventy-five percent of Americans are opposed to laws that restrict or put limitations on access to unhealthy foods (Neergaard and Agiesta).

There is nothing wrong, however, with using signal phrases to introduce statistics or other facts.

Using sentence guides to integrate sources

You build your credibility (*ethos*) by accurately representing the views of others and by integrating these views into your paper. An important way to present the views of others before agreeing or disagreeing with them is to use sentence guides. These guides act as academic sentence starters; they show you how to use signal phrases in sentences to make clear to your reader whose ideas you're presenting — your own or those you have encountered in a source.

Presenting others' views. As an academic writer, you will be expected to demonstrate your understanding of a source by summarizing the views or arguments of its author. The following language will help you to do so:

X argues that _____.

X and Y emphasize the need for _____.

_____, according to X, is the most critical cause of _____.

Presenting direct quotations. To introduce the exact words of a source because their accuracy and authority are important for your argument, you might try phrases like these:

X describes the problem this way: ". . ."

X argues strongly in favor of the policy, pointing out that ". . ."

According to X, _____ is defined as ". . ."

Presenting alternative views. At times you will have to synthesize the views of multiple sources before you introduce your own.

While X and Y have supported these findings, new research by Z suggests that _____.

On the one hand, X reports that _____, but on the other hand, Y emphasizes that _____.

X, however, isn't convinced and instead argues _____.

Presenting your own views by agreeing or extending. You may agree with the author of a source but want to add your own voice to extend the point or go deeper. The following phrases could be useful:

X's argument is convincing because _____.

X makes the claim that _____. By extension, isn't it also true, then, that _____?

X's proposal is worth considering. Going one step further, _____.

Presenting your own views by disagreeing and questioning. College writing assignments encourage you to show your understanding of a subject but also to question or challenge ideas and conclusions about the subject. This language can help:

Couldn't it also be argued that _____?

X's claims about _____ are misguided.

Although X reports that _____, recent studies indicate that is not the case.

While X insists that _____ is so, she is perhaps asking the wrong question to begin with.

Presenting and countering objections to your argument. To anticipate objections that readers might make, try the following sentence guides:

Not everyone will embrace this argument; some may argue instead that _____.

Some will object to this proposal on the grounds that _____.

X and Y might argue with this position; however, _____ _____.

Putting source material in context

Readers should not have to guess why source material appears in your paper. A signal phrase can help you connect your own ideas with those of another writer by clarifying how the source will contribute to your paper (see 52a).

If you use another writer's words, you must explain how they relate to your argument. Quotations don't speak for themselves; you must create a context for readers. Sandwich each quotation between sentences of your own, introducing the quotation with a signal phrase and following it with interpretive comments that link the quotation to your paper's argument (see also 55d).

QUOTATION WITH EFFECTIVE CONTEXT (QUOTATION SANDWICH)

Long quotation is introduced with a signal phrase naming the author.

In response to critics who claim that laws aimed at stopping us from eating whatever we want are an assault on our freedom of choice, Conly offers a persuasive counterargument:

[L]aws aren't designed for each one of us individually. Some of us can drive safely at 90 miles per hour, but we're bound by the same laws as the people who can't, because individual speeding laws aren't practical. Giving up a little liberty is something we agree to when we agree to live in a democratic society that is governed by laws. (A23)

> Long quotation is set off from the text. Quotation marks are omitted.

As Conly suggests, we need to change our either/or thinking (either we have complete freedom of choice *or* we have government regulations and lose our freedom) and instead need to see health as a matter of public good, not individual liberty.

> Quotation is followed by analytical comments that connect the source to the student's argument.

55d Synthesize sources.

When you synthesize multiple sources in a research paper, you create a conversation about your research topic. You show readers that your argument is based on your analysis and integration of ideas and is not just a series of quotations and paraphrases strung together. Your synthesis will show how your sources relate to one another; one source may support, extend, or counter the ideas of another. Not every source has to "speak" to another in a research paper, but readers should understand how each source functions in your argument (see 52a).

Considering how sources relate to your argument

Before you integrate sources and show readers how they relate to one another, consider how each source might contribute to your own argument. As student writer Sophie Harba became more informed about her research topic, she asked herself these questions: *What have I learned from my sources? Which sources might support my ideas or illustrate the points I want to make? What counterarguments do I need to address to strengthen my position?* She annotated a passage from one of her sources — a nonprofit group's assertion that our choices about food are skewed by marketing messages.

STUDENT NOTES ON THE ORIGINAL SOURCE

useful factual information
The food and beverage industry spends approximately $2 billion per year marketing to children.

could use this to counter the point about personal choice in Mello.

— "Facts on Junk Food"

Placing sources in conversation

You can show readers how the ideas of one source relate to those of another by connecting and analyzing the ideas in your own voice. After all, you've done the research and thought through the issues, so you should control the conversation. Keep the emphasis on your own writing. The thread of your argument should be easy to identify and to understand, with or without your sources.

SAMPLE SYNTHESIS

Student writer Sophie Harba sets up her synthesis with a question.

Why is the public largely resistant to laws that would limit unhealthy choices or penalize those choices with so-called fat taxes? Many consumers and civil rights advocates find such laws to be an unreasonable restriction on individual freedom of choice. As health

Student writer

A signal phrase indicates how the source contributes to Harba's argument and shows that the idea that follows is not her own.

policy experts Mello and others point out, opposition to food and beverage regulation is similar to the opposition to early tobacco legislation: the public views the issue as one of personal responsibility rather than one requiring government intervention (2602).

Source 1

Harba interprets a paraphrased source.

In other words, if a person eats unhealthy food and becomes ill as a result, that is his or her choice. But those who favor legislation claim that freedom of choice is a myth because of the strong influence of food and beverage industry marketing on consumers' dietary habits. According

Student writer

Harba uses a source to support her counterargument.

to one nonprofit health advocacy group, food and beverage companies spend roughly two billion dollars per year marketing directly to children.

Source 2

As a result, kids see nearly four thousand ads per year encouraging them to eat unhealthy food and drinks ("Facts"). As was the case with antismoking laws passed in recent decades, taxes and legal restrictions on junk food sales could help to counter the strong marketing messages that promote unhealthy products.

> Student writer

The United States has a history of state and local public health laws that have successfully promoted a particular behavior by punishing an undesirable behavior. The decline in tobacco use as a result of antismoking taxes and laws is perhaps the most obvious example. Another example is legislation requiring the use of seat belts, which have significantly reduced fatalities in car crashes. One government agency reports that seat belt use saved an average of more than fourteen thousand lives per year in the United States between 2000 and 2010 (United States, Dept. of Transportation, Natl. Highway Traffic Safety Administration 231). Perhaps seat belt laws have public support because the cost of wearing a seat belt is small, especially when compared with the benefit of saving fourteen thousand lives per year.

> Harba extends the argument and follows it with an interpretive comment.

> Source 3

> Student writer

In this synthesis, Harba uses her own analysis to shape the conversation among her sources. She does not simply string quotations together or allow them to overwhelm her writing. She guides her readers through a conversation about a variety of laws that could promote and have promoted public health. She finds points of intersection among her sources, acknowledges the contributions of others to the conversation, and shows readers, in her own voice, how the various sources support her argument.

When synthesizing sources, ask yourself the following questions:

- How do your sources address your research question?
- How do your sources speak to one another?
- Have you varied the functions of sources — to provide background, explain concepts, lend authority, and anticipate counterarguments?
- Do you connect and analyze sources in your own voice?
- Is your own argument easy to identify and to understand, with or without your sources?

Reviewing an MLA paper: Use of sources

Use of quotations

- Have you used quotation marks around quoted material (unless it has been set off from the text)? (See 54c.)

- Have you checked that quoted language is word-for-word accurate? If it is not, do ellipsis marks or brackets indicate the omissions or changes? (See 55b.)

- Does a clear signal phrase (usually naming the author) prepare readers for each quotation and for the purpose the quotation serves? (See 55c.)

- Does a parenthetical citation follow each quotation? (See 56a.)

- Is each quotation put in context? (See 55c.)

Use of summaries and paraphrases

- Are summaries and paraphrases free of plagiarized wording — not copied or half-copied from the source? (See 54d.)

- Are summaries and paraphrases documented with parenthetical citations? (See 56a.)

- Will readers know where the cited material begins? In other words, does a signal phrase mark the boundary between your words and the summary or paraphrase? (See 55c.)

- Does a signal phrase prepare readers for the purpose of the summary or paraphrase in your argument?

Use of statistics and other facts

- Are statistics and facts (other than common knowledge) documented with parenthetical citations? (See 55c and 56a.)

- If there is no signal phrase, will readers understand exactly which facts are being cited? (See 55c.)

56 Documenting sources in MLA style

In English and other humanities classes, you may be asked to use the MLA (Modern Language Association) system for documenting sources, which is set forth in the *MLA Handbook*, 8th edition (MLA, 2016).

MLA recommends in-text citations that refer readers to a list of works cited. A typical in-text citation names the author of the source, often in a signal phrase, and gives a page number in parentheses. At the end of the paper, the list of works cited provides publication information about the source; the list is alphabetized by authors' last names (or by titles for works without authors). There is a direct connection between the in-text citation and the alphabetical listing. In the following example, that connection is highlighted in blue.

IN-TEXT CITATION

Bioethicist David Resnik emphasizes that such policies, despite their potential to make our society healthier, "open the door to excessive government control over food, which could restrict dietary choices, interfere with cultural, ethnic, and religious traditions, and exacerbate socioeconomic inequalities" (31).

ENTRY IN THE LIST OF WORKS CITED

Resnik, David. "Trans Fat Bans and Human Freedom." *The American Journal of Bioethics*, vol. 10, no. 3, Mar. 2010, pp. 27-32.

For a list of works cited that includes this entry, see 57b.

List of MLA in-text citation models

List of MLA works cited models

➡

List of MLA works cited models, continued

56a MLA in-text citations

MLA in-text citations are made with a combination of signal phrases and parenthetical references. A signal phrase introduces information taken from a source (a quotation, summary, paraphrase, or fact); usually the signal phrase includes the author's name. The parenthetical reference comes after the cited material, often at the end of the sentence. It includes at least a page number (except for unpaginated sources, such as those found on the web). In the models in this section, the elements of the in-text citation are highlighted in blue.

IN-TEXT CITATION

Resnik acknowledges that his argument relies on "slippery slope" thinking, but he insists that "social and political pressures" regarding food regulation make his concerns valid (31).

Readers can look up the author's last name in the alphabetized list of works cited, where they will learn the work's title and other publication information. If readers decide to consult the source, the page number will take them straight to the passage that has been cited.

General guidelines for signal phrases and page numbers

Items 1–5 explain how the MLA system usually works for all sources — in print, on the web, in other media, and with or without authors and page numbers. Items 6–25 give variations on the basic guidelines.

■ **1. Author named in a signal phrase**   Ordinarily, introduce the material being cited with a signal phrase that includes the author's name. In addition to preparing readers for the source, the signal phrase allows you to keep the parenthetical citation brief.

According to Lorine Goodwin, a food historian, nineteenth-century reformers who sought to purify the food supply were called "fanatics" and "radicals" by critics who argued that consumers should be free to buy and eat what they want (77).

The signal phrase *According to Lorine Goodwin* names the author; the parenthetical citation gives the number of the page on which the quoted words may be found.

Notice that the period follows the parenthetical citation. When a quotation ends with a question mark or an exclamation point, leave the end punctuation inside the quotation mark and add a period at the end of your sentence, after the parenthetical citation.

Burgess asks a critical question: "How can we think differently about food labeling?" (51).

■ **2. Author named in parentheses** If you do not give the author's name in a signal phrase, put the last name in parentheses along with the page number (if the source has one). Use no punctuation between the name and the page number: (Moran 351).

> According to a nationwide poll, 75% of Americans are opposed to
> laws that restrict or put limitations on access to unhealthy foods
> (Neergaard and Agiesta).

■ **3. Author unknown** If a source has no author, the works cited entry will begin with the title. In your in-text citation, either use the complete title in a signal phrase or use a short form of the title in parentheses. Titles of books and other long works are italicized; titles of articles and other short works are put in quotation marks.

> As a result, kids see nearly four thousand ads per year encouraging
> them to eat unhealthy food and drinks ("Facts").

NOTE: If the author is a corporation or a government agency, see items 8 and 16.

■ **4. Page number unknown** Do not include the page number if a work lacks page numbers, as is the case with many web sources. Do not use page numbers from a printout from a website. (When the pages of a web source are stable, as in PDF files, supply a page number in your in-text citation.)

> Michael Pollan points out that "cheap food" actually has "significant
> costs—to the environment, to public health, to the public purse,
> even to the culture."

If a source has numbered paragraphs or sections, use "par." (or "pars.") or "sec." (or "secs.") in the parentheses: (Smith, par. 4). Notice that a comma follows the author's name.

■ **5. One-page source** If the source is one page long, it is a good idea to include the page number; without it readers may not know where your citation ends or, worse, may not realize that you have provided a citation at all.

> **NO PAGE NUMBER IN CITATION**
>
> Sarah Conly uses John Stuart Mill's "harm principle" to argue
> that citizens need their government to intervene to prevent them
> from taking harmful actions—such as driving too fast or buying

unhealthy foods—out of ignorance of the harm they can do. But
government intervention may overstep in the case of food choices.

PAGE NUMBER IN CITATION

Sarah Conly uses John Stuart Mill's "harm principle" to argue that
citizens need their government to intervene to prevent them from
taking harmful actions—such as driving too fast or buying unhealthy
foods—out of ignorance of the harm they can do (A23). But
government intervention may overstep in the case of food choices.

Variations on the general guidelines

This section describes the MLA guidelines for handling a variety
of situations not covered in items 1–5.

■ **6. Two authors**   Name the authors in a signal phrase, as in the
following example, or include their last names in the parenthetical
reference: (Gostin and Gostin 214).

As legal scholars Gostin and Gostin explain, "[I]nterventions that
do not pose a truly significant burden on individual liberty" are
justified if they "go a long way towards safeguarding the health and
well-being of the populace" (214).

■ **7. Three or more authors**   In a parenthetical citation, give the
first author's name followed by "et al." (Latin for "and others"). In a
signal phrase, give the first author's name followed by "and others."

The clinical trials were extended for two years, and only after results
were reviewed by an independent panel did the researchers publish
their findings (Blaine et al. 35).

Researchers Blaine and others note that clinical trial results were
reviewed by an independent panel (35).

■ **8. Organization as author**   When the author is a corporation
or an organization, name that author either in the signal phrase
or in the parenthetical citation. (For a government agency as
author, see item 16.)

The American Diabetes Association estimates that the cost of
diagnosed diabetes in the United States in 2012 was $245 billion.

In the list of works cited, the American Diabetes Association is treated as the author and alphabetized under *A*. When you give the organization name in the text, spell out the name; when you use it in parentheses, abbreviate common words in the name: "Assn.," "Dept.," "Natl.," "Soc.," and so on.

> The cost of diagnosed diabetes in the United States in 2012 was estimated at $245 billion (Amer. Diabetes Assn.).

■ **9. Authors with the same last name** If your list of works cited includes works by two or more authors with the same last name, include the author's first name in the signal phrase or first initial in the parentheses.

> One approach to the problem is to introduce nutrition literacy at the K-5 level in public schools (E. Chen 15).

■ **10. Two or more works by the same author** Mention the title of the work in the signal phrase or include a short version of the title in the parentheses.

> The American Diabetes Association tracks trends in diabetes across age groups. In 2012, more than 200,000 children and adolescents had diabetes ("Fast"). Because of an expected dramatic increase in diabetes in young people over the next forty years, the association encourages "strategies for implementing childhood obesity prevention programs and primary prevention programs for youth at risk of developing type 2 diabetes" ("Number").

Titles of articles and other short works are placed in quotation marks; titles of books and other long works are italicized.

In the rare case when both the author's name and a short title must be given in parentheses, separate them with a comma.

> Researchers have estimated that "the number of youth with type 2 [diabetes] could quadruple and the number with type 1 could triple" by 2050, "with an increasing proportion of youth with diabetes from minority populations" (Amer. Diabetes Assn., "Number").

■ **11. Two or more works in one citation** To cite more than one source in the parentheses, list the authors (or titles) in alphabetical order and separate them with semicolons.

> The prevalence of early-onset type 2 diabetes has been well documented (Finn 68; Sharma 2037; Whitaker 118).

■ **12. Repeated citations from the same source** When you are writing about a single work, you do not need to include the author's name each time you quote from or paraphrase the work. After you mention the author's name at the beginning of your paper, you may include just the page number in your parenthetical citations.

> In Susan Glaspell's short story "A Jury of Her Peers," two women accompany their husbands and a county attorney to an isolated house where a farmer named John Wright has been choked to death in his bed with a rope. The chief suspect is Wright's wife, Minnie, who is in jail awaiting trial. The sheriff's wife, Mrs. Peters, has come along to gather some personal items for Minnie, and Mrs. Hale has joined her. Early in the story, Mrs. Hale sympathizes with Minnie and objects to the way the male investigators are "snoopin' round and criticizin'" her kitchen (249). In contrast, Mrs. Peters shows respect for the law, saying that the men are doing "no more than their duty" (249).

In a paper with multiple sources, if you are citing a source more than once in a paragraph, you may omit the author's name after the first mention in the paragraph as long as it is clear that you are still referring to the same source.

■ **13. Encyclopedia or dictionary entry** When an encyclopedia or a dictionary entry does not have an author, it will be alphabetized in the list of works cited under the word or entry that you consulted (see item 23 on p. 444). Either in your text or in your parenthetical citation, mention the word or entry and give the number of the page on which the entry may be found.

> The word *crocodile* has a complex etymology ("Crocodile" 139).

■ **14. Entire work** Use the author's name in a signal phrase or a parenthetical citation. There is no need to use a page number.

> Pollan explores the issues surrounding food production and consumption from a political angle.

■ **15. Selection in an anthology or a collection** Put the name of the author of the selection (not the editor of the anthology) in the signal phrase or the parentheses.

> In "Love Is a Fallacy," the narrator's logical teachings disintegrate when Polly declares that she should date Petey because "[h]e's got a raccoon coat" (Shulman 372).

In the list of works cited, the work is alphabetized under *Shulman*, the author of the story, not under the name of the editor of the anthology. (See item 29 on p. 448.)

Shulman, Max. "Love Is a Fallacy." *Current Issues and Enduring Questions*,

edited by Sylvan Barnet and Hugo Bedau, 11th ed., Bedford/

St. Martin's, 2017, pp. 365-72.

■ **16. Government document** When a government agency is the author, you will alphabetize the entry in the list of works cited under the name of the government, such as *United States* or *Great Britain* (see item 56 on p. 461). For this reason, you must name the government as well as the agency in your in-text citation.

One government agency reports that seat belt use saved an average

of more than fourteen thousand lives per year in the United States

between 2000 and 2010 (United States, Dept. of Transportation,

Natl. Highway Traffic Safety Administration 231).

■ **17. Historical document** For a historical document, such as the Constitution of the United States or the Canadian Charter of Rights and Freedoms, provide the document title, neither italicized nor in quotation marks, along with relevant article and section numbers. In parenthetical citations, use abbreviations such as "art." and "sec."

While the Constitution provides for the formation of new states

(art. 4, sec. 3), it does not explicitly allow or prohibit the secession

of states.

Cite other historical documents as you would any other work, by the first element in the works cited entry (see item 57).

■ **18. Legal source** For a legislative act (law) or court case, name the act or case either in a signal phrase or in parentheses. Italicize the names of cases but not the names of acts. (See also items 58 and 59 on pp. 461 and 462.)

The Jones Act of 1917 granted US citizenship to Puerto Ricans.

In 1857, Chief Justice Roger B. Taney declared in *Dred Scott v.*

Sandford that blacks, whether enslaved or free, could not be citizens

of the United States.

■ **19. Visual such as a table, a chart, or another graphic**   To cite a visual that has a figure number in the source, use the abbreviation "fig." and the number in place of a page number in your parenthetical citation: (Manning, fig. 4). If you refer to the figure in your text, spell out the word "figure."

To cite a visual that appears in a print source without a figure number, use the visual's title or a description in your text and cite the author and page number as for any other source.

For a visual not in a print source, identify the visual in your text and then in parentheses use the first element in the works cited entry: the artist's or photographer's name or the title of the work. (See items 51–55 on pp. 459–60.)

> Photographs such as *Woman Aircraft Worker* (Bransby) and *Women Welders* (Parks) demonstrate the US government's attempt to document the contributions of women during World War II.

■ **20. Personal communication and social media**   Cite personal letters, personal interviews, email messages, and social media posts by the name listed in the works cited entry, as you would for any other source. Identify the type of source in your text if you feel it is necessary for clarity. (See items 60–64 on pp. 462–63.)

■ **21. Web source**   Your in-text citation for a source from the web should follow the same guidelines as for other sources. If the source lacks page numbers but has numbered paragraphs, sections, or divisions, use those numbers with the appropriate abbreviation in your parenthetical citation: "par.," "sec.," "ch.," "pt.," and so on. Do not add such numbers if the source itself does not use them; simply give the author or title in your in-text citation.

> Sanjay Gupta, CNN chief medical correspondent, explains that "limited access to fresh, affordable, healthy food" is one of America's most pressing health problems.

■ **22. Indirect source (source quoted in another source)**   When a writer's or a speaker's quoted words appear in a source written by someone else, begin the parenthetical citation with the abbreviation "qtd. in." In the following example, Gostin and Gostin are the authors of the source given in the works cited list; their work contains a quotation by Beauchamp.

> Public health researcher Dan Beauchamp has said that "public health practices are communal in nature, and concerned with the

well-being of the community as a whole and not just the well-being of any particular person" (qtd. in Gostin and Gostin 217).

Literary works and sacred texts

Literary works and sacred texts are usually available in a variety of editions. Your list of works cited will specify which edition you are using, and your in-text citation will usually consist of a page number from the edition you consulted (see item 23). When possible, give enough information — such as book parts, play divisions, or line numbers — so that readers can locate the cited passage in any edition of the work (see items 24 and 25).

■ **23. Literary work without parts or line numbers**   Many literary works, such as most short stories and many novels and plays, do not have parts or line numbers. In such cases, simply cite the page number.

> At the end of Kate Chopin's "The Story of an Hour," Mrs. Mallard drops dead upon learning that her husband is alive. In the final irony of the story, doctors report that she has died of a "joy that kills" (25).

■ **24. Verse play or poem**   For verse plays, give act, scene, and line numbers that can be located in any edition of the work. Use arabic numerals and separate the numbers with periods.

> In Shakespeare's *King Lear*, Gloucester learns a profound lesson from a tragic experience: "A man may see how this world goes / with no eyes" (4.2.148-49).

For a poem, cite the part, stanza, and line numbers, if it has them, separated by periods.

> The Green Knight claims to approach King Arthur's court "because the praise of you, prince, is puffed so high, / And your manor and your men are considered so magnificent" (1.12.258-59).

For poems that are not divided into numbered parts or stanzas, use line numbers. For the first reference, use the word "lines": (lines 5-8). Thereafter use just the numbers: (12-13).

■ **25. Sacred text** When citing a sacred text such as the Bible or the Qur'an, name the edition you are using in your works cited entry (see item 33 on p. 450). In your parenthetical citation, give the book, chapter, and verse (or their equivalent), separated with periods. Common abbreviations for books of the Bible are acceptable.

> Consider the words of Solomon: "If your enemy is hungry, give him
>
> bread to eat; and if he is thirsty, give him water to drink" (*Oxford*
>
> *Annotated Bible*, Prov. 25.21).

The title of a sacred work is italicized when it refers to a specific edition of the work, as in the preceding example. If you refer to the book in a general sense in your text, neither italicize it nor put it in quotation marks.

> The Bible and the Qur'an provide allegories that help readers
>
> understand how to lead a moral life.

56b MLA list of works cited

Your list of works cited, which you will place at the end of your paper, guides readers to the sources you have quoted, summarized, and paraphrased. Ask yourself: *What would readers need to know to find this source for themselves?* Usually, you will provide basic information common to most sources, such as author, title, publisher, publication date, and location (page numbers or URL, for example).

Throughout this section of the book, you'll find models organized by type (article, book, website, multimedia source, and so on). But even if you aren't sure exactly what type of source you have (*Is this a blog post or an article?*), you can follow two general principles:

> **Gather** key publication information about the source — the citation elements.
>
> **Organize** the basic information about the source using what MLA calls "containers."

The author's name and the title of the work are needed for many (though not all) sources and are the first two pieces of information to gather. For the remaining pieces of information, you might find it helpful to think about whether the work is contained within one or more larger works. Some sources are self-contained. Others are nested in larger containers.

| ☐ | Self-contained | a *book* |
| | | a *film* |

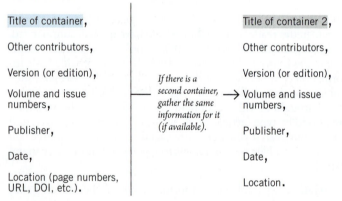	One container	an *article* in a scholarly journal
		a *poem* in a collection of poetry
		a *video* posted to YouTube
		a *fact sheet* on a government website

| | Two containers | an *article* in a journal within a database (JSTOR, etc.) |
| | | an *episode* from a TV series within a streaming service (Netflix, etc.) |

Keep in mind that most sources won't include all of the following pieces of information, so gather only those that are relevant to and available for your source.

Author.

Title of source.

Title of container,		Title of container 2,
Other contributors,		Other contributors,
Version (or edition),	*If there is a second container, gather the same information for it (if available).* →	Version (or edition),
Volume and issue numbers,		Volume and issue numbers,
Publisher,		Publisher,
Date,		Date,
Location (page numbers, URL, DOI, etc.).		Location.

WORKS CITED ENTRY, ONE CONTAINER (SELECTION IN AN ANTHOLOGY)

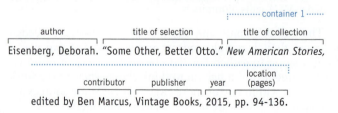

container 1

| author | title of selection | title of collection |

Eisenberg, Deborah. "Some Other, Better Otto." *New American Stories,*

| | contributor | publisher | year | location (pages) |

edited by Ben Marcus, Vintage Books, 2015, pp. 94-136.

WORKS CITED ENTRY, TWO CONTAINERS (ARTICLE IN A JOURNAL IN A DATABASE)

author   title of article

Coles, Kimberly Anne. "The Matter of Belief in John Donne's Holy Sonnets."

⋯⋯⋯⋯⋯⋯⋯⋯⋯⋯⋯ container 1 ⋯⋯⋯⋯⋯⋯⋯⋯⋯⋯⋯⋯

| journal title | volume, issue | date | location (pages) | database title |

Renaissance Quarterly, vol. 68, no. 3, Fall 2015, pp. 899-931. *JSTOR,*

⋯⋯ container 2 ⋯⋯

location (DOI)

doi:10.1086/683855.

Once you've gathered the relevant and available information about a source, you will organize the elements using the list above as your guideline. Note the punctuation after each element in that list. You will find many examples of how elements and containers are combined to create works cited entries shown in this section.

▶ List of MLA works cited models, page 419
▶ General guidelines for the works cited list, page 433

General guidelines for listing authors

The formatting of authors' names in items 1–11 applies to all sources — books, articles, websites — in print, on the web, or in other media. For more models of specific source types, see items 12–64.

■ **1. Single author**

author: last name first   title (book)   publisher   year

Bowker, Gordon. *James Joyce: A New Biography*. Farrar, Straus and Giroux, 2012.

■ **2. Two authors**

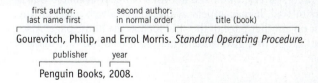

first author: last name first   second author: in normal order   title (book)

Gourevitch, Philip, and Errol Morris. *Standard Operating Procedure.*

publisher   year

Penguin Books, 2008.

■ **3. Three or more authors** Name the first author followed by "et al." (Latin for "and others"). For in-text citations, see item 7 in 56a.

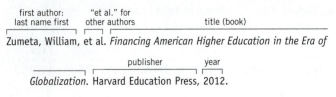

first author: last name first | "et al." for other authors | title (book)

Zumeta, William, et al. *Financing American Higher Education in the Era of*

publisher | year

Globalization. Harvard Education Press, 2012.

■ **4. Organization or company as author**

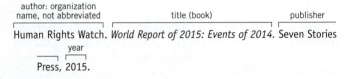

author: organization name, not abbreviated | title (book) | publisher

Human Rights Watch. *World Report of 2015: Events of 2014.* Seven Stories

year

Press, 2015.

Your in-text citation also should treat the organization as the author (see item 8 in 56a).

■ **5. No author listed**

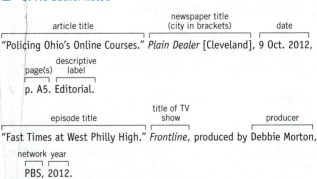

article title | newspaper title (city in brackets) | date

"Policing Ohio's Online Courses." *Plain Dealer* [Cleveland], 9 Oct. 2012,

page(s) | descriptive label

p. A5. Editorial.

episode title | title of TV show | producer

"Fast Times at West Philly High." *Frontline*, produced by Debbie Morton,

network year

PBS, 2012.

TIP: In web sources, often the author's name is available but is not easy to find. It may appear at the end of a web page, in tiny print, or on another page of the site, such as the home page. Also, an organization or a government may be the author (see items 4 and 56).

General guidelines for the works cited list

In the list of works cited, include only sources that you have quoted, summarized, or paraphrased in your paper. MLA's guidelines apply to a wide variety of sources. You can adapt the guidelines and models in this section to source types you encounter in your research.

Gathering information and organizing entries

The elements needed for a works cited entry are the following:

- The author (if a work has one)
- The title
- The title of the larger work in which the source is located, if it is contained in a larger work (MLA calls the larger work a "container"—a collection, a journal, a magazine, a website, and so on)
- As much of the following information as is available about the source and the container:

  Editor, translator, director, performer

  Version or edition

  Volume and issue numbers

  Publisher

  Date of publication

  Location of the source: page numbers, URL, DOI, and so on

Not all sources will require every element. See specific models in this section for more details.

Authors

- Arrange the list alphabetically by authors' last names or by titles for works with no authors.
- For the first author, place the last name first, a comma, and the first name. Put a second author's name in normal order (first name followed by last name). For three or more authors, use "et al." after the first author's name.
- Spell out "editor," "translator," "edited by," and so on.

Titles

- In titles of works, capitalize all words except articles (*a*, *an*, *the*), prepositions, coordinating conjunctions, and the *to* in infinitives — unless the word is first or last in the title or subtitle.

→

General guidelines for the works cited list, continued

- Use quotation marks for titles of articles and other short works. Place single quotation marks around a quoted term or a title of a short work that appears within an article title; italicize a term or title that is normally italicized.
- Italicize titles of books and other long works. If a book title contains another title that is normally italicized, neither italicize the internal title nor place it in quotation marks. If the title within the title is normally put in quotation marks, retain the quotation marks and italicize the entire book title.

Publication information

- Do not give the place of publication for a book publisher.
- Use the complete version of publishers' names, except for terms such as "Inc." and "Co."; retain terms such as "Books" and "Press." For university publishers, use "U" and "P" for "University" and "Press."
- For a book, take the name of the publisher from the title page (or from the copyright page if it is not on the title page). For a website, the publisher might be at the bottom of a page or on the "About" page. If a work has two or more publishers, separate the names with slashes.
- If the title of a website and the publisher are the same or similar, give the title of the site but omit the publisher.

Dates

- For a book, give the most recent year found on the title page or the copyright page. For a web source, use the copyright date or the most recent update date. Use the complete date as listed in the source.
- Abbreviate all months except May, June, and July and give the date in inverted form: 13 Mar. 2018.
- If the source has no date, give your date of access at the end: Accessed 24 Feb. 2018.

Page numbers

- For most articles and other short works, give page numbers when they are available, preceded by "pp." (or "p." for only one page).
- Do not use the page numbers from a printout of a web source.
- If a short work does not appear on consecutive pages, give the number of the first page followed by a plus sign: 35+.

URLs and DOIs

- Give a permalink or a DOI (digital object identifier) if a source has one.
- If a source does not have a permalink or a DOI, include the full URL for the source (omitting the protocol, such as http://).
- If a database provides only a URL that is long and complicated and if your readers are not likely to be able to use it to access the source, your instructor may allow you to use the URL for the database home page (such as go.galegroup.com). Check with your instructor.
- For open databases and archives, such as Google Books, give the complete URL for the source. (See item 25b.)
- If a URL or a DOI must be divided across lines, break it before a period or a hyphen or before or after any other mark of punctuation. Do not add a hyphen.

■ **6. Two or more works by the same author or group of authors** First alphabetize the works by title (ignoring the article *A*, *An*, or *The* at the beginning of a title). Use the author's name or authors' names for the first entry; for subsequent entries, use three hyphens and a period. The three hyphens must stand for exactly the same name or names that appear in the first entry.

García, Cristina. *Dreams of Significant Girls*. Simon and Schuster, 2011.

---. *The Lady Matador's Hotel*. Scribner, 2010.

Agha, Hussein, and Robert Malley. "The Arab Counterrevolution."
    The New York Review of Books, 29 Sept. 2011, www.nybooks.com/
    articles/2011/09/29/arab-counterrevolution.

---. "This Is Not a Revolution." The *New York Review of Books*, 8 Nov.
    2012, www.nybooks.com/articles/2012/11/08/not-revolution.

■ **7. Editor or translator** Begin with the editor's or translator's name. After the name, add "editor" or "translator." Use "editors" or "translators" for two or more (see also items 2 and 3 for how to handle multiple contributors).

first editor: second editor:
last name first   in normal order   title (book)
┌──────┐   ┌──────────┐   ┌──────────────────────────┐
Horner, Avril, and Anne Rowe, editors. *Living on Paper: Letters from Iris Murdoch,*

              publisher   year
┌──────┐ ┌──────────┐ ┌──────┐
1934-1995. Princeton UP, 2016.

HOW TO

Answer the basic question "Who is the author?"

PROBLEM: Sometimes when you need to cite a source, it's not clear who the author is. This is especially true for sources on the web and other nonprint sources, which may have been created by one person and uploaded by a different person or an organization. Whom do you cite as the author in such a case? How do you determine who *is* the author?

EXAMPLE: The video "Surfing the Web on the Job" (see below) was uploaded to YouTube by CBSNewsOnline. Is the person or organization that uploads the video the author of the video? Not necessarily.

STRATEGY: After you view or listen to the source a few times, ask yourself whether you can tell who is chiefly responsible for creating the content in the source. It could be an organization. It could be an identifiable individual. This video consists entirely of reporting by Daniel Sieberg, so in this case the author is Sieberg.

Surfing the Web on The Job

 CBSNewsOnline · 42,491 videos

▶ **Subscribe**   85,736

Uploaded on Nov 12, 2009
As the Internet continues to emerge as a critical facet of everyday life, CBS News' Daniel Sieberg reports that companies are cracking down on employees' personal Web use.

CITATION: To cite the source, you would use the basic MLA guidelines for a video found on the web (item 42).

author: last name first	title of video	website title

Sieberg, Daniel. "Surfing the Web on the Job." *YouTube*, uploaded by

upload information	upload date	URL

CBSNewsOnline, 12 Nov. 2009, www.youtube.com/watch?v=1wLhNwY-enY.

■ **8. Author with editor or translator** Begin with the name of the author. Place the editor's or translator's name after the title.

author:
last name first   title (book)   translator:
in normal order

Ullmann, Regina. *The Country Road: Stories.* Translated by Kurt Beals,

publisher   year

New Directions Publishing, 2015.

■ **9. Graphic narrative or other illustrated work** If a work has both an author and an illustrator, the order in your citation will depend on which of those persons you emphasize in your paper.

Gaiman, Neil. *The Sandman: Overture.* Illustrated by J. H. William III,

DC Comics, 2015.

Wenzel, David, illustrator. *The Hobbit.* By J. R. R. Tolkien, Ballantine

Books, 2012.

■ **10. Author using a pseudonym (pen name) or screen name** Give the author's name as it appears in the source (the pseudonym), followed by the author's real name, if available, in parentheses.

Grammar Girl (Mignon Fogarty). "Lewis Carroll: He Loved to Play with

Language." *QuickandDirtyTips.com*, 21 May 2015, www.quickanddirtytips

.com/education/grammar/lewis-carroll-he-loved-to-play-with-language.

Pauline. Comment on "Is This the End?" *The New York Times*, 25 Nov.

2012, nyti.ms/1BRUvqQ.

■ **11. Author quoted by another author (indirect source)** If one of your sources uses a quotation from another source and you'd like to use the quotation, provide a works cited entry for the source in which you found the quotation. In your in-text citation, indicate that the quoted words appear in the source (see item 22 in 56a).

Articles and other short works

► Citation at a glance: Article in an online journal, page 439
► Citation at a glance: Article from a database, page 440

■ **12. Basic format for an article or other short work**

a. Print

author:
last name first   article title   journal title   volume, issue

Tilman, David. "Food and Health of a Full Earth." *Daedalus*, vol. 144, no. 4,

date   page(s)

Fall 2015, pp. 5-7.

b. Web

author:
last name first   title of short work

Nelson, Libby. "How Schools Will Be Different without No Child Left Behind."

title of
website   date   URL

Vox, 11 Dec. 2015, www.vox.com/2015/12/11/9889350/every-student

-succeeds-act-schools.

c. Database If a database provides a DOI or a permalink, use that at the end of your citation. If it provides only a URL that is long and complicated and if your readers may not be able to access it, your instructor may allow you to use the URL for the database home page (such as go.galegroup.com). Check with your instructor.

first author:
last name first   second author:
in normal order   article title

Meyer, Michaela D. E., and Megan M. Wood. "Sexuality and Teen Television:

Emerging Adults Respond to Representations of Queer Identity on *Glee*."

journal title   volume, issue   date   page(s)

Sexuality and Culture, vol. 17, no. 3, Sept. 2013, pp. 434-48.

database
title   URL

Academic OneFile, go.galegroup.com/ps/i.do?p=PPGB&sw=w&u=

mlin_n_merrcol&v=2.1&id=GALE%7CA343054749&it=r&asid=

c78658b5b509de7c41177489da8e89ce.

CITATION AT A GLANCE
Article in an online journal (MLA)

To cite an article in an online journal in MLA style, include the following elements:

1 Author(s) of article
2 Title and subtitle of article
3 Title of journal
4 Volume and issue numbers
5 Date of publication (including month or season, if any)
6 Page number(s) of article, if given
7 Location of source (DOI, permalink, or URL)

Online journal article

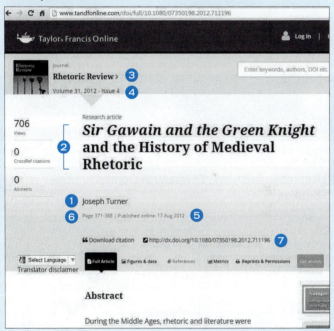

WORKS CITED ENTRY FOR AN ARTICLE IN AN ONLINE JOURNAL

Turner, Joseph. "*Sir Gawain and the Green Knight* and the History of Medieval Rhetoric." *Rhetoric Review,* vol. 31, no. 4, 17 Aug. 2012, pp. 371-88, doi:dx.doi.org/10.1080/07350198.2012.711196.

For more on citing online articles in MLA style, see item 12.

CITATION AT A GLANCE
Article from a database (MLA)

To cite an article from a database in MLA style, include the following elements:

1 Author(s) of article
2 Title and subtitle of article
3 Title of journal, magazine, or newspaper
4 Volume and issue numbers (for journal)
5 Date of publication (including month or season, if any)

6 Page number(s) of article, if any
7 Name of database
8 DOI or permalink, if available; otherwise, complete URL or shortened URL of database (see item 12c)

Database record

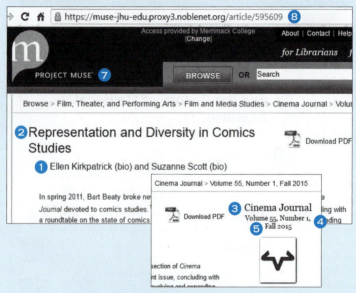

WORKS CITED ENTRY FOR AN ARTICLE FROM A DATABASE

———————— 1 ———————— ————————— 2 —————————
Kirkpatrick, Ellen, and Suzanne Scott. "Representation and Diversity

————————— 3 ———— ——— 4 ——— — 5 —
in Comics Studies." *Cinema Journal*, vol. 55, no. 1, Fall 2015.

—— 7 —— ———————————— 8 ————————————
Project Muse, muse-jhu-edu.proxy3.noblenet.org/article/595609.

For more on citing articles from a database in MLA style, see items 12 and 13.

■ 13. Article in a journal

a. Print

author: last
name first   article title   journal title

Matchie, Thomas. "Law versus Love in *The Round House*." *The Midwest*

volume,
issue   date   page(s)

    Quarterly, vol. 56, no. 4, Summer 2015, pp. 353-64.

b. Online journal

author: last
name first   article title

Butler, Janine. "Where Access Meets Multimodality: The Case of ASL Music Videos."

journal   volume,
title   issue   date   URL

    Kairos, vol. 21, no. 1, Fall 2016, kairos.technorhetoric.net/21.1/topoi

    /butler/index.html.

c. Database

author: last
name first   article title

Maier, Jessica. "A 'True Likeness': The Renaissance City Portrait."

           journal   volume,   database
           title   issue   date   page(s)   title

    Renaissance Quarterly, vol. 65, no. 3, Fall 2012, pp. 711-52. *JSTOR*,

         DOI

    doi:10.1086/668300.

■ **14. Article in a magazine**

| author: last name first | article title | magazine title | date | page(s) |

Bryan, Christy. "Ivory Worship." *National Geographic*, Oct. 2012, pp. 28-61.

| author: last name first | article title | magazine title | date | page(s) |

Vick, Karl. "The Stateless Statesman." *Time*, 15 Oct. 2012, pp. 32-37.

| author: last name first | article title | website title | date |

Leonard, Andrew. "The Surveillance State High School." *Salon*, 27 Nov. 2012,

URL

www.salon.com/2012/11/27/the_surveillance_state_high_school.

■ **15. Article in a newspaper** If the city of publication is not obvious from the title of the newspaper, include the city in brackets after the newspaper title (see item 5).

| author: last name first | article title | newspaper title |

Bray, Hiawatha. "As Toys Get Smarter, Privacy Issues Emerge." *The Boston*

| date | page(s) |

Globe, 10 Dec. 2015, p. C1.

| author: last name first | article title |

Crowell, Maddy. "How Computers Are Getting Better at Detecting Liars."

| website title | date | URL |

The Christian Science Monitor, 12 Dec. 2015, www.csmonitor.com

/Science/Science-Notebook/2015/1212/How-computers-are-getting

-better-at-detecting-liars.

■ **16. Editorial** Cite as you would a source with no author (see item 5) and use the label "Editorial" at the end (and before any database information).

"City's Blight Fight Making Difference." The *Columbus Dispatch*, 17 Nov.

2015, www.dispatch.com/content/stories/editorials/2015/11/17

/1-citys-blight-fight-making-difference.html. Editorial.

■ **17. Letter to the editor** Use the label "Letter" at the end of the entry (and before any database information). If the letter has no title, place the label directly after the author's name.

Fahey, John A. "Recalling the Cuban Missile Crisis." *The Washington*

Post, 28 Oct. 2012, p. A16. Letter. *LexisNexis Library Express*,

www.lexisnexis.com/hottopics/Inpubliclibraryexpress.

■ **18. Comment on an online article** For the use of a screen name and a real name (if known), see item 10. After the name, include "Comment on" followed by the title of the article and publication information for the article.

author:
screen name   article title

pablosharkman. Comment on "'We All Are Implicated': Wendell Berry

Laments a Disconnection from Community and the Land."

website title   date   URL

The Chronicle of Higher Education, 23 Apr. 2012, chronicle.com

/article/In-Jefferson-Lecture-Wendell/131648.

■ **19. Book review** Name the reviewer and the title of the review, if any, followed by "Review of" and the title and author of the work reviewed. Add publication information for the publication in which the review appears. If the review has no author and no title, begin with "Review of" and alphabetize the entry by the first principal word in the title of the work reviewed.

Della Subin, Anna. "It Has Burned My Heart." Review of *The Lives of*

Muhammad, by Kecia Ali. *London Review of Books*, 22 Oct. 2015,

www.lrb.co.uk/v37/n20/anna-della-subin/it-has-burned-my-heart.

Spychalski, John C. Review of *American Railroads—Decline and*

Renaissance in the Twentieth Century, by Robert E. Gallamore and

John R. Meyer. *Transportation Journal*, vol. 54, no. 4, Fall 2015,

pp. 535-38. *JSTOR*, doi:10.5325/transportationj.54.4.0535.

■ **20. Film review or other review** Name the reviewer and the title of the review, if any, followed by "Review of" and the title and the writer or director of the work reviewed. Add publication information for the publication in which the review appears. If the review has no author and no title, begin with "Review of" and alphabetize the entry by the first principal word in the title of the work reviewed.

Lane, Anthony. "Human Bondage." Review of *Spectre*, directed by Sam

Mendes. *The New Yorker*, 16 Nov. 2015, pp. 96-97.

Savage, Phil. "*Fallout 4* Review." Review of *Fallout 4*, by Bethesda Game

Studios. *PC Gamer*, Future Publishing, 8 Nov. 2015, www.pcgamer

.com/fallout-4-review.

■ **21. Performance review** Name the reviewer and the title of the review, if any, followed by "Review of" and the title of the work reviewed. After the title, add the author or director of the work, if relevant. Add publication information for the publication in which the review appears. If the review has no author and no title, begin with "Review of" and alphabetize the entry by the first principal word in the title of the work reviewed.

Stout, Gene. "The Ebullient Florence + the Machine Give KeyArena a

Workout." Review of *How Big How Blue How Beautiful Odyssey*. *The*

Seattle Times, 28 Oct. 2015, www.seattletimes.com/entertainment

/music/the-ebullient-florence-the-machine-give-keyarena-a-workout.

■ **22. Interview** Begin with the person interviewed, followed by the title of the interview (if there is one). If the interview does not have a title, include the word "Interview" after the interviewee's name. If you wish to include the name of the interviewer, put it after the title of the interview.

Weddington, Sarah. "Sarah Weddington: Still Arguing for *Roe*." Interview

by Michele Kort. *Ms.*, Winter 2013, pp. 32-35.

Putin, Vladimir. Interview. By Charlie Rose. *Charlie Rose: The Week*, PBS,

19 June 2015.

Akufo, Rosa. Personal interview. 11 Apr. 2016.

■ **23. Article in a dictionary or an encyclopedia (including a wiki)** List the author of the entry (if there is one), the title of the entry, and publication information for the reference work. Include page numbers for a print source as you would for a selection in a collection (see item 29).

Durante, Amy M. "Finn Mac Cumhail." *Encyclopedia Mythica*, 17 Apr. 2011,

www.pantheon.org/articles/f/finn_mac_cumhail.html.

"House Music." *Wikipedia*, 16 Nov. 2015, en.wikipedia.org/wiki/House_music.

■ 24. Letter in a collection

a. Print   Begin with the writer of the letter, the words "Letter to" and the recipient, and the date of the letter. Add the title of the collection and other publication information. Add the page range at the end.

Murdoch, Iris. Letter to Raymond Queneau. 7 Aug. 1946. *Living on Paper:*

Letters from Iris Murdoch, 1934-1995, edited by Avril Horner and

Anne Rowe, Princeton UP, 2016, pp. 76-78.

b. Web   After information about the letter writer, recipient, and date (if known), give the name of the website or archive, italicized; the publisher of the site; and the URL.

Oblinger, Maggie. Letter to Charlie Thomas. 31 Mar. 1895. *Prairie*

Settlement: Nebraska Photographs and Family Letters, 1862-1912,

Library of Congress / American Memory, memory.loc.gov/cgi-bin/

query/r?ammem/ps:@field(DOCID+l306)#l3060001.

Books and other long works

▶ Citation at a glance: Book, page 446

■ 25. Basic format for a book

a. Print book or e-book   If you have used an e-book, indicate "e-book" or the specific reader (using the abbreviation "ed." for "edition") before the publisher's name.

author: last
name first   book title   publisher   year

Wolfe, Tom. *Back to Blood*. Little, Brown, 2012.

Beard, Mary. *SPQR: A History of Ancient Rome*. Nook ed., Liveright

Publishing, 2015.

CITATION AT A GLANCE
Book (MLA)

To cite a print book in MLA style, include the following elements:

1 Author(s)
2 Title and subtitle

3 Publisher
4 Year of publication (latest year)

Title page

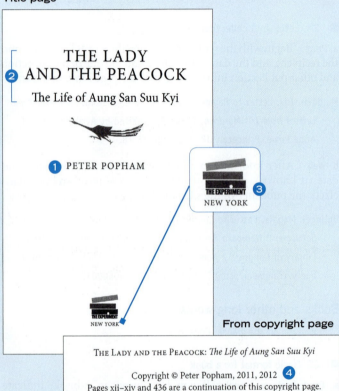

THE LADY
AND THE PEACOCK
The Life of Aung San Suu Kyi

PETER POPHAM

THE EXPERIMENT
NEW YORK

From copyright page

THE LADY AND THE PEACOCK: *The Life of Aung San Suu Kyi*

Copyright © Peter Popham, 2011, 2012
Pages xii–xiv and 436 are a continuation of this copyright page.

WORKS CITED ENTRY FOR A PRINT BOOK

Popham, Peter. *The Lady and the Peacock: The Life of Aung San Suu Kyi.*
The Experiment, 2012.

For more on citing books in MLA style, see items 25–32.

■ **25. Basic format for a book (*cont.*)**

b. Web   Give whatever print publication information is available for the work, followed by the title of the website and the URL.

author: last
name first   book title

Piketty, Thomas. *Capital in the Twenty-First Century*. Translated by

translator: in   website
normal order   publisher   year   title   URL

Arthur Goldhammer, Harvard UP, 2014. *Google Books*, books.google

.com/books?isbn=0674369556.

■ **26. Parts of a book**

a. Foreword, introduction, preface, or afterword

author of foreword: book
last name first   part   book title

Bennett, Hal Zina. Foreword. *Shimmering Images: A Handy Little Guide to*

author of book:
in normal order   publisher   year   page(s)

Writing Memoir, by Lisa Dale Norton, St. Martin's Griffin, 2008, pp. xiii-xvi.

Sullivan, John Jeremiah. "The Ill-Defined Plot." Introduction. *The*

    Best American Essays 2014, edited by Sullivan, Houghton Mifflin

    Harcourt, 2014, pp. xvii-xxvi.

b. Chapter in a book

Rizga, Kristina. "Mr. Hsu." *Mission High: One School, How Experts Tried to*

    Fail It, and the Students and Teachers Who Made It Triumph, Nation

    Books, 2015, pp. 89-114.

■ **27. Book in a language other than English**   Capitalize the title according to the conventions of the book's language. If your readers are not familiar with the language of the book, include a translation of the title in brackets.

Vargas Llosa, Mario. *El sueño del celta* [*The Dream of the Celt*]. Alfaguara

    Ediciones, 2010.

■ **28. Entire anthology or collection**   An anthology is a collection of works on a common theme, often with different authors for the selections and usually with an editor for the entire volume.

editor:
last name first   title of
anthology   publisher   year

Marcus, Ben, editor. *New American Stories*. Vintage Books, 2015.

■ **29. One selection from an anthology or a collection**

► Citation at a glance: Selection from an anthology or a collection, page 449

author of
selection   title of
selection   title of
anthology   editor(s) of
anthology

Sayrafiezadeh, Saïd. "Paranoia." *New American Stories,* edited by Ben Marcus,

publisher   year   page(s)

Vintage Books, 2015, pp. 3-29.

■ **30. Two or more selections from an anthology or a collection** Provide an entry for the entire anthology (see item 28) and a shortened entry for each selection. Alphabetize the entries by authors' or editors' last names.

author of
selection   title of
selection   editor(s) of
anthology   page(s)

Eisenberg, Deborah. "Some Other, Better Otto." Marcus, pp. 94-136.

editor of
anthology   title of
anthology   publisher   year

Marcus, Ben, editor. *New American Stories*. Vintage Books, 2015.

author of
selection   title of
selection   editor(s) of
anthology   page(s)

Sayrafiezadeh, Saïd. "Paranoia." Marcus, pp. 3-29.

■ **31. Edition other than the first**   If the book has a translator or an editor in addition to the author, give the name of the translator or editor before the edition number (see item 8 for a book with an editor or a translator).

Eagleton, Terry. *Literary Theory: An Introduction*. 3rd ed., U of Minnesota P,

2008.

CITATION AT A GLANCE
Selection from an anthology or a collection (MLA)

To cite a selection from an anthology in MLA style, include the following elements:

1 Author(s) of selection
2 Title and subtitle of selection
3 Title and subtitle of anthology
4 Editor(s) of anthology
5 Publisher
6 Year of publication
7 Page number(s) of selection

First page of selection

Title page of anthology

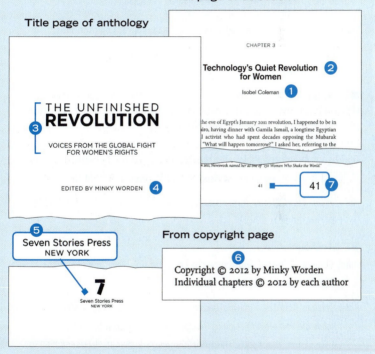

THE UNFINISHED
REVOLUTION

VOICES FROM THE GLOBAL FIGHT
FOR WOMEN'S RIGHTS

EDITED BY MINKY WORDEN

CHAPTER 3

**Technology's Quiet Revolution
for Women**

Isobel Coleman

he eve of Egypt's January 2011 revolution, I happened to be in
iro, having dinner with Gamila Ismail, a longtime Egyptian
l activist who had spent decades opposing the Mubarak
"What will happen tomorrow?" I asked her, referring to the

2011, Newsweek named her as one of "150 Women Who Shake the World."

41

Seven Stories Press
NEW YORK

From copyright page

Copyright © 2012 by Minky Worden
Individual chapters © 2012 by each author

WORKS CITED ENTRY FOR A SELECTION FROM AN ANTHOLOGY

Coleman, Isobel. "Technology's Quiet Revolution for Women." *The Unfinished Revolution: Voices from the Global Fight for Women's Rights*, edited by Minky Worden, Seven Stories Press, 2012, pp. 41-49.

For more on citing selections from anthologies in MLA style, see items 28–30.

■   **32. Multivolume work**   Include the total number of volumes at the end of the entry, using the abbreviation "vols." If the volumes were published over several years, give the inclusive dates of publication.

| author: last name first | book title | editor(s): in normal order | publisher | inclusive dates | total volumes |

Stark, Freya. *Letters*. Edited by Lucy Moorehead, Compton Press, 1974-82. 8 vols.

If you cite only one volume in your paper, include the volume number before the publisher and give the date of publication for that volume. After the date, give the total number of volumes.

| author: last name first | book title | editor(s): in normal order | volume cited | publisher |

Stark, Freya. *Letters*. Edited by Lucy Moorehead, vol. 5, Compton Press,

| date of volume | total volumes |

1978. 8 vols.

■   **33. Sacred text**   Give the title of the edition (taken from the title page), italicized; the editor's or translator's name (if any); and publication information. Add the name of the version, if there is one, before the publisher.

The Oxford Annotated Bible with the Apocrypha. Edited by Herbert G. May

and Bruce M. Metzger, Revised Standard Version, Oxford UP, 1965.

The Qur'an: Translation. Translated by Abdullah Yusuf Ali, Tahrike Tarsile

Qur'an, 2001.

■   **34. Dissertation**

Kidd, Celeste. *Rational Approaches to Learning and Development*. 2013.

U of Rochester, PhD dissertation.

Abbas, Megan Brankley. *Knowing Islam: The Entangled History of Western*

Academia and Modern Islamic Thought. 2015. Princeton U, PhD

dissertation. *DataSpace*, arks.princeton.edu/ark:/88435/dsp016682x6260.

Websites and parts of websites

■   **35. An entire website**

a. Website with author or editor

| author or editor: last name first | title of website | publisher |

Railton, Stephen. *Mark Twain in His Times*. Stephen Railton / U of Virginia

| update date | URL |

Library, 2012, twain.lib.virginia.edu.

Halsall, Paul, editor. *Internet Modern History Sourcebook*. Fordham U,

 4 Nov. 2011, legacy.fordham.edu/halsall/index.asp.

b. Website with organization as author

organization   title of website

Transparency International. *Transparency International: The Global Coalition*

date   URL

 against Corruption, 2015, www.transparency.org.

c. Website with no author   Begin with the title of the site.

The Newton Project. U of Sussex, 2016, www.newtonproject.sussex.ac.uk

 /prism.php?id=1.

d. Website with no title   Use the label "Home page" or another
appropriate description in place of a title.

Bae, Rebecca. Home page. Iowa State U, 2015, www.engl.iastate.edu

 /rebecca-bae-directory-page.

■ **36. Work from a website**   The titles of short works, such as
articles or individual web pages, are placed in quotation marks.
Titles of long works, such as books and reports, are italicized.

 ▶ Citation at a glance: Work from a website, page 452

author: last name first   title of short work   title of website

Gallagher, Sean. "The Last Nomads of the Tibetan Plateau." *Pulitzer Center on Crisis*

date   URL

 Reporting, 25 Oct. 2012, pulitzercenter.org/reporting/china-glaciers-global

 -warming-climate-change-ecosystem-tibetan-plateau-grasslands-nomads.

title of article   title of website

"Social and Historical Context: Vitality." *Arapesh Grammar and Digital Language*

publisher

 Archive Project, Institute for Advanced Technology in the Humanities,

URL

 www.arapesh.org/socio_historical_context_vitality.php. Accessed

access date for undated site

 22 Mar. 2016.

CITATION AT A GLANCE
Work from a website (MLA)

To cite a work from a website in MLA style, include the following elements:

1 Author(s) of work, if any
2 Title and subtitle
3 Title of website
4 Publisher of website (unless it is the same as the title of site)
5 Update date
6 URL of page (or of home page of site)
7 Date of access (if no update date on site)

Internal page from a website

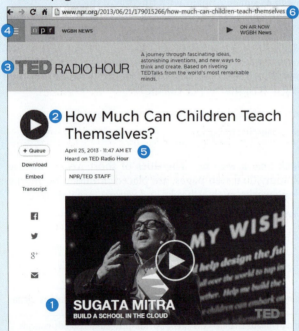

WORKS CITED ENTRY FOR A WORK FROM A WEBSITE

Mitra, Sugata. "How Much Can Children Teach Themselves?" *TED Radio Hour*, NPR, 25 Apr. 2013, www.npr.org/2013/06/21/179015266 /how-much-can-children-teach-themselves.

For more on citing sources from websites in MLA style, see item 36.

■ **36. Work from a website (*cont.*)**

first author: et al. for
last name first   other authors   title of long work

Byndloss, D. Crystal, et al. *In Search of a Match: A Guide for Helping Students*

title of   update
website   date

Make Informed College Choices. Ford Foundation, Apr. 2015,

URL

fordfoundcontentthemes.blob.core.windows.net/media/2607/

in_search_of_a_match.pdf.

■ **37. Blog post or comment** Cite a blog post or comment as you would a work from a website (see item 36), with the title of the post or comment in quotation marks. If the post or comment has no title, use the label "Blog post" or "Blog comment" (with no quotation marks). (See item 10 for the use of screen names.)

author: last   title of   update
name first   title of blog post   blog   publisher   date

Eakin, Emily. "*Cloud Atlas*'s Theory of Everything." *NYR Daily*, NYREV, 2 Nov. 2012,

URL

www.nybooks.com/daily/2012/11/02/ken-wilber-cloud-atlas.

author:
screen name   label   title of blog post

mitchellfreedman. Comment on "*Cloud Atlas*'s Theory of Everything."

title of
blog   publisher   date   URL

NYR Daily, NYREV, 3 Nov. 2012, www.nybooks.com/daily/2012/11/02/

ken-wilber-cloud-atlas.

■ **38. Academic course or department home page** Cite as a work from a website (see item 36). For a course home page, begin with the instructor and the title of the course or page, without quotation marks or italics. (Use "Course home page" if there is no title.) For a department home page, begin with the name of the department and the label "Department home page."

Masiello, Regina. 355:101: Expository Writing. *Rutgers School of Arts and Sciences*, 2016, wp.rutgers.edu/courses/55-355101.

Film Studies. Department home page. *Wayne State University, College of Liberal Arts and Sciences*, 2016, clas.wayne.edu/FilmStudies.

Audio, visual, and multimedia sources

■ **39. Podcast**

author: last
name first   podcast title   website title   publisher

Tanner, Laura. "Virtual Reality in 9/11 Fiction." *Literature Lab*, Department of English,

URL

Brandeis U, www.brandeis.edu/departments/english/literaturelab

date of access
for undated site

/tanner.html. Accessed 14 Feb. 2016.

McDougall, Christopher. "How Did Endurance Help Early Humans Survive?" *TED*

Radio Hour, NPR, 20 Nov. 2015, www.npr.org/2015/11/20/455904655

/how-did-endurance-help-early-humans-survive.

■ **40. Film**   Generally, begin the entry with the title, followed by the director and lead performers, as in the first example. If your paper emphasizes one or more people involved with the film, you may begin with those names, as in the second example.

film title   director

Birdman or (The Unexpected Virtue of Ignorance). Directed by Alejandro

major performers

González Iñárritu, performances by Michael Keaton, Emma Stone, Zach

distributor   release date

Galifianakis, Edward Norton, and Naomi Watts, Fox Searchlight, 2014.

director:
last name first   film title   major performers

Scott, Ridley, director. *The Martian*. Performances by Matt Damon, Jessica

distributor   release date

Chastain, Kristen Wiig, and Kate Mara, Twentieth Century Fox, 2015.

■ **41. Supplementary material accompanying a film**   Begin with the title of the supplementary material, in quotation marks, and the names of any important contributors, as for a film. End with information about the film, as in item 40, and about the location of the supplementary material.

"Sweeney's London." Produced by Eric Young. *Sweeney Todd: The Demon Barber of Fleet Street*, directed by Tim Burton, DreamWorks, 2007, disc 2.

■ **42. Video or audio from the web** Cite video or audio that you accessed on the web as you would a work from a website (see item 36), with the title of the video or audio in quotation marks.

author:
last name first   title of video

website
title

upload
information   date

Lewis, Paul. "Citizen Journalism." *YouTube*, uploaded by TEDx Talks, 14 May 2011,

URL

www.youtube.com/watch?v=9APO9_yNbcg.

author:
last name first

title of video

website title

Fletcher, Antoine. "The Ancient Art of the Atlatl." *Russell Cave National*

narrator

publisher

Monument, narrated by Brenton Bellomy, National Park Service,

date

URL

12 Feb. 2014, www.nps.gov/media/video/view.htm?id=C92C0D0A

-1DD8-B71C-07CBC6E8970CD73F.

author:
last name first

title of video

website
title   date

Burstein, Julie. "Four Lessons in Creativity." *TED*, Feb. 2012,

URL

www.ted.com/talks/julie_burstein_4_lessons_in_creativity.

■ **43. Video game** List the developer or author of the game (if any); the title, italicized; the version, if there is one; and the distributor and date of publication. If the game can be played on the web, add information as for a work from a website (see item 36).

Firaxis Games. *Sid Meier's Civilization Revolution*. Take-Two Interactive, 2008.

Edgeworld. Atom Entertainment, 1 May 2012, www.kabam.com/games/
edgeworld.

■ **44. Computer software or app** Cite as a video game (see item 43), giving whatever information is available about the version, distributor, and date.

Venmo. Version 7.4.0, PayPal, 2017.

■ **45. Television or radio episode or program**   If you are citing an episode of a program, begin with the title of the episode, in quotation marks. Then give the title of the program, italicized; relevant information about the program, such as the writer, director, performers, or narrator; the episode number (if any); the network; and the date of broadcast.

For a program you accessed on the web, after the information about the program give the network, the original broadcast date, and the URL. If you are citing an entire program (not an episode or a segment) or an episode that has no title, begin your entry with the title of the program, italicized.

      title of episode   program title

"Federal Role in Support of Autism." *Washington Journal,* narrated by

    narrator
  (host or speaker)   network   broadcast date

    Robb Harleston, C-SPAN, 1 Dec. 2012.

The Daily Show with Trevor Noah. Comedy Central, 18 Nov. 2015.

                program
  title of episode   title   narrator   episode

"The Cathedral." *Reply All,* narrated by Sruthi Pinnamaneni, episode 50,

                 date
    publisher   of posting   URL

    Gimlet Media, 7 Jan. 2016, gimletmedia.com/episode/50-the-cathedral.

■ **46. Transcript**   Cite the source (interview, radio or television program, video, and so on), and add the label "Transcript" at the end of the entry.

"How Long Can Florida's Citrus Industry Survive?" *All Things Considered,*

    narrated by Greg Allen, NPR, 27 Nov. 2015, www.npr.org/templates/

    transcript/transcript.php?storyId=457424528. Transcript.

"The Economics of Sleep, Part 1." *Freakonomics Radio,* narrated by

    Stephen J. Dubner, 9 July 2015, freakonomics.com/2015/07/09/

    the-economics-of-sleep-part-1-full-transcript. Transcript.

HOW TO

Cite a source reposted from another source

PROBLEM: Some sources that you find online, particularly on blogs or on video-sharing sites, did not originate with the person who uploaded or published the source online. In such a case, how do you give proper credit to the source?

EXAMPLE: Say you need to cite President John F. Kennedy's inaugural address. You have found a video on YouTube that provides footage of the address (see image). The video was uploaded by PaddyIrishMan2 on October 29, 2006. But clearly, PaddyIrishMan2 is not the author of the video or of the address.

JFK Inaugural Address 1 of 2

 PaddyIrishMan2 · 12 videos

▶ **Subscribe** ⟨ 403

Uploaded on Oct 29, 2006
President John F. Kennedy's inaugural address, January 20th 1961.

Vice President Johnson, Mr. Speaker, Mr. Chief Justice, President Eisenhower, Vice President Nixon, President Truman, reverend clergy, fellow citizens, we observe today not a victory of party, but a celebration of freedom — symbolising an end, as well as a beginning — signifying renewal, as well as change. For I have sworn before you and Almighty God the same solemn oath our forebears prescribed nearly a century and three quarters ago.

STRATEGY: Start with what you know. The source is a video that you viewed on the web. For this particular video, John F. Kennedy is the speaker and the author of the inaugural address. PaddyIrishMan2 is identified as the person who uploaded the source to YouTube.

CITATION: To cite the source, you can follow the basic MLA guidelines for a video found on the web (see item 42).

author/speaker: website
last name first   title of video   title
⌐   ⌐   ⌐   ⌐   ⌐   ⌐
Kennedy, John F. "JFK Inaugural Address: 1 of 2." *YouTube*, uploaded by

        upload   upload
     information   date   URL
  ⌐   ⌐   ⌐   ⌐   ⌐   ⌐
PaddyIrishMan2, 29 Oct. 2006, www.youtube.com/watch?v=xE0iPY7XGBo.

NOTE: If your work calls for a primary source, you should try to find the original source of the video; a reference librarian can help.

■ **47. Live performance** Begin with the title of the work performed, italicized (unless it is named by form, number, and key). Then give the author or composer of the work; relevant information such as the director, the choreographer, the conductor, or the major performers; the theater, ballet, or opera company, if any; the theater and location; and the date of the performance.

The Draft. By Peter Snoad, directed by Diego Arciniegas, Hibernian Hall,

Boston, 10 Sept. 2015.

Symphony no. 4 in G. By Gustav Mahler, conducted by Mark Wigglesworth,

performances by Juliane Banse and Boston Symphony Orchestra,

Symphony Hall, Boston, 17 Apr. 2009.

■ **48. Lecture or public address** Begin with the speaker's name, the title of the lecture, the sponsoring organization, location, and date. If you viewed the lecture on the web, cite as you would a work from a website (see item 36). Add the label "Address" or "Lecture" at the end if it is not clear from the title.

Smith, Anna Deavere. "On the Road: A Search for American Character."

National Endowment for the Humanities, John F. Kennedy Center for

the Performing Arts, Washington, 6 Apr. 2015. Address.

Khosla, Raj. "Precision Agriculture and Global Food Security." *US*

Department of State: Diplomacy in Action, 26 Mar. 2013, www.state

.gov/e/stas/series/212172.htm. Address.

■ **49. Musical score** Begin with the composer's name; the title of the work, italicized (unless it is named by form, number, and key); and the date of composition. For a print source, give the publisher and date. For an online source, give the title of the website; the publisher, the date, and the URL.

Beethoven, Ludwig van. Symphony no. 5 in C Minor, op. 67. 1807. *Center*

for Computer Assisted Research in the Humanities, Stanford U, 2000,

scores.ccarh.org/beethoven/sym/beethoven-sym5-1.pdf.

■ **50. Sound recording** Begin with the name of the person you want to emphasize: the composer, conductor, or performer. For a long work, give the title, italicized (unless it is named by form, number, and key); the names of pertinent artists; and the orchestra and conductor. End with the manufacturer and the date.

Bizet, Georges. *Carmen*. Performances by Jennifer Larmore, Thomas Moser,

Angela Gheorghiu, Samuel Ramey, and Bavarian State Orchestra and

Chorus, conducted by Giuseppe Sinopoli, Warner, 1996.

Blige, Mary J. "Don't Mind." *Life II: The Journey Continues (Act 1)*,

Geffen, 2011.

■ **51. Artwork, photograph, or other visual art** Begin with the artist and the title of the work, italicized. If you viewed the original work, give the date of composition followed by a comma and the location. If you viewed the work online, give the date of composition followed by a period and the website title, publisher (if any), and URL. If you viewed the work reproduced in a book, cite as a work in an anthology or a collection (item 29), giving the date of composition after the title. If the medium of composition is not apparent or is important for your work, you may include it at the end (as in the second example).

Bradford, Mark. *Let's Walk to the Middle of the Ocean*. 2015, Museum of

Modern Art, New York.

Lindsey, Lindsay Jones. *Fibonacci Spiral*. 2012, University of Alabama,

Tuscaloosa. Public sculpture.

Clough, Charles. *January Twenty-First*. 1988-89. *Joslyn Art Museum*,

www.joslyn.org/collections-and-exhibitions/permanent-collections/

modern-and-contemporary/charles-clough-january-twenty-first.

Kertész, André. *Meudon*. 1928. *Street Photography: From Atget to Cartier-*

Bresson, by Clive Scott, Tauris, 2011, p. 61.

■ **52. Visual such as a table, a chart, or another graphic**   Cite a visual as you would a short work within a longer work. Add a descriptive label at the end if the type of visual is not clear from the title or if it is important for your work.

"Brazilian Waxing and Waning: The Economy." *The Economist*, 1 Dec.

2015, www.economist.com/blogs/graphicdetail/2015/12/economic

-backgrounder. Graph.

"Number of Measles Cases by Year since 2010." *Centers for Disease Control and Prevention*, 2 Jan. 2016, www.cdc.gov/measles/cases-outbreaks

.html. Table.

■ **53. Cartoon**   Give the cartoonist's name; the title of the cartoon, if it has one, in quotation marks, or the label "Cartoon" without quotation marks in place of a title; and publication information. Add the label "Cartoon" at the end if it is not clear from the title. Cite an online cartoon as a work from a website (item 36).

Zyglis, Adam. "City of Light." *Buffalo News*, 8 Nov. 2015, adamzyglis

.buffalonews.com/2015/11/08/city-of-light. Cartoon.

■ **54. Advertisement**   Name the product or company being advertised and publication information for the source in which the advertisement appears. Add the label "Advertisement" at the end if it is not clear from the title.

AT&T. *National Geographic*, Dec. 2015, p. 14. Advertisement.

Toyota. *The Root*. Slate Group, 28 Nov. 2015, www.theroot.com. Advertisement.

■ **55. Map**   Cite a map as you would a short work within a longer work. If the map is published on its own, cite it as a book or another long work. Use the label "Map" at the end if it is not clear from the title or source information.

"Map of Sudan." *Global Citizen*, Citizens for Global Solutions, 2011,

globalsolutions.org/blog/bashir#.VthzNMfi_FI.

"Vote on Secession, 1861." *Perry-Castañeda Library Map Collection*, U of

Texas at Austin, 1976, www.lib.utexas.edu/maps/atlas_texas/texas_

vote_secession_1861.jpg.

Government and legal documents

■ **56. Government document**   Treat the government agency as the author, giving the name of the government followed by the name of the department and the agency, if any. For sources found on the web, follow the model for an entire website (item 35) or for a work from a website (item 36).

government · · · · · · · department · · · · · · · · · · · · · · · agency (or agencies)
United States, Department of Agriculture, Food and Nutrition Service, Child

title of work
Nutrition Programs. *Eligibility Manual for School Meals: Determining*

· website title · · · · · · · · · · · · · · · date
and Verifying Eligibility. *National School Lunch Program*, July 2015,

URL
www.fns.usda.gov/sites/default/files/cn/SP40_CACFP18

_SFSP20-2015a1.pdf.

Canada, Minister of Aboriginal Affairs and Northern Development.

2015-16 Report on Plans and Priorities. Minister of Public Works and

Government Services Canada, 2015.

■ **57. Historical document**   The titles of most historical documents, such as the US Constitution and the Canadian Charter of Rights and Freedoms, are neither italicized nor put in quotation marks.

Constitution of the United States. 1787. *The Charters of Freedom,* US

National Archives and Records Administration, www.archives.gov

/exhibits/charters.

■ **58. Legislative act (law)**   Begin with the name of the act, neither italicized nor in quotation marks. Then provide the act's Public Law number, its Statutes at Large volume and page numbers, and its date of enactment.

Electronic Freedom of Information Act Amendments of 1996. Pub. L.

104-231. 110 Stat. 3048. 2 Oct. 1996.

■ **59. Court case** Name the first plaintiff and the first defendant. Then give the volume, name, and page number of the law report; the court name; the year of the decision; and publication information. Do not italicize the name of the case. (In the text of the paper, the name of the case is italicized; see item 18 on p. 426.)

Utah v. Evans. 536 US 452. Supreme Court of the US. 2002. *Legal Information Institute*, Cornell U Law School, www.law.cornell.edu/ supremecourt/text/536/452.

Personal communication and social media

■ **60. Personal letter**

Primak, Shoshana. Letter to the author. 6 May 2016.

■ **61. Email message** Begin with the writer's name and the subject line. Then write "Received by," followed by the name of the recipient and the date of the message.

Thornbrugh, Caitlin. "Coates Lecture." Received by Rita Anderson, 20 Oct. 2015.

■ **62. Text message**

Wiley, Joanna. Message to the author. 4 Apr. 2018.

■ **63. Online discussion list post** Begin with the author's name, followed by the title or subject line, in quotation marks (use the label "Online posting," with no quotation marks, if the posting has no title). Then proceed as for a work from a website (see item 36).

Griffith, Robin. "Write for the Reading Teacher." *Developing Digital Literacies*, NCTE, 23 Oct. 2015, ncte.connectedcommunity.org/ communities/community-home/digestviewer/viewthread? GroupId=1693&MID=24520&tab=digestviewer&CommunityKey= 628d2ad6-8277-4042-a376-2b370ddceabf.

■ **64. Social media post**   Begin with the writer's screen name, followed by the real name in parentheses, if both are given. For a tweet, use the entire post as a title, in quotation marks. For other media, give a title if the post has one. If it does not, use the label "Post," without quotation marks, in place of a title. Give the date of the post, the time (if the post specifies one), and the URL.

Curiosity Rover. "Can you see me waving? How to spot #Mars in the night

sky: https://youtu.be/hv8hVvJlcJQ." *Twitter*, 5 Nov. 2015, 11:00

a.m., twitter.com/marscuriosity/status/672859022911889408.

natgeo (National Geographic). Post. *Instagram*, 22 July 2016,

www.instagram.com/p/BIKyGHtDD4W.

56c MLA information notes (optional)

Researchers who use the MLA system of parenthetical documentation may also use information notes for one of two purposes:

1. to provide additional material that is important but might interrupt the flow of the paper
2. to refer to several sources that support a single point or to provide comments on sources

Information notes may be either footnotes or endnotes. Footnotes appear at the foot of the page; endnotes appear on a separate page at the end of the paper, just before the list of works cited. For either style, the notes are numbered consecutively throughout the paper. The text of the paper contains a raised arabic numeral that corresponds to the number of the note.

TEXT

In the past several years, employees have filed a number of lawsuits

against employers because of online monitoring practices.[1]

NOTE

1. For a discussion of federal law applicable to electronic

surveillance in the workplace, see Kesan 293.

57 MLA format; sample research paper

The following guidelines are consistent with advice given in the *MLA Handbook*, 8th edition (MLA, 2016), and with typical requirements for student papers. For a sample MLA research paper, see 57b.

57a MLA format

Formatting the paper: The basics

Papers written in MLA style should be formatted as follows.

The **heading** should include the student's name, the professor's name, the course, and the date.

Use Times New Roman or another easy-to-read **font**.

For easy reading, use a **1-inch margin** on all sides of the page, and **double-space** the text.

> Harba 1
>
> Sophie Harba
>
> Professor Baros-Moon
>
> Engl 1101
>
> 9 Nov. 2017
>
> What's for Dinner? Personal Choices vs. Public Health
>
> Should the government enact laws to regulate healthy eating choices? Many Americans would answer an emphatic "No," arguing that what and how much we eat should be left to individual choice rather than unreasonable laws. Others might argue that it would be unreasonable for the government not to enact legislation, given the rise of chronic diseases that result from harmful diets. In this debate, both the definition of reasonable regulations and the role of government to legislate food choices are at stake. In the name of public health and safety, state governments have the responsibility to shape health policies and to regulate healthy eating choices, especially since doing so offers a potentially large social benefit for a relatively small cost.
>
> Debates surrounding the government's role in regulating food have a long history in the United States.

The student's last name and the **page number** appear in the right-hand corner of every page.

Center the **title**. Add no extra space above or below it, and use no quotation marks or italics.

Formatting the paper: Other concerns

Capitalization, italics, and quotation marks In titles of works, capitalize all words except articles (*a*, *an*, *the*), prepositions (*to*, *from*, *between*, and so on), coordinating conjunctions (*and*, *but*, *or*, *nor*, *for*, *so*, *yet*), and the *to* in infinitives — unless the word is first or last in the title or subtitle. Follow these guidelines in your paper even if the title appears in all capital or all lowercase letters in the source.

In the text of an MLA paper, when a complete sentence follows a colon, lowercase the first word following the colon.

Italicize the titles of books, journals, magazines, and other long works, such as websites. Use quotation marks around the titles of articles, short stories, poems, and other short works.

Long quotations When a quotation is longer than four typed lines of prose or three lines of poetry, set it off from the text by indenting the entire quotation one-half inch from the left margin. Double-space the indented quotation and do not add extra space above or below it.

Do not use quotation marks when a quotation has been set off from the text by indenting. See 55b for an example.

URLs If you need to break a URL at the end of a line in the text of a paper, break it before a period or a hyphen or before or after any other mark of punctuation. Do not add a hyphen. If you will post your project online or submit it electronically and you want your readers to click on your URLs, do not insert any line breaks.

Headings MLA neither encourages nor discourages the use of headings and provides no guidelines for their use. If you would like to insert headings in a long essay or research paper, check first with your instructor.

Visuals MLA classifies visuals as tables and figures (figures include graphs, charts, maps, photographs, and drawings). Label each table with an arabic numeral ("Table 1," "Table 2," and so on) and provide a clear title that identifies the subject. Capitalize as you would the title of an article (see 45c); do not use italics or quotation marks. Place the table number and title on separate lines above the table, flush with the left margin.

For a table that you have borrowed or adapted, give the source below the table in a note like the following:

Source: Boris Groysberg and Michael Slind, "Leadership Is a

Conversation," *Harvard Business Review*, June 2012, p. 83.

Place a figure number (using the abbreviation "Fig.") and a caption below each figure, flush left. Capitalize the caption as you would a sentence; include source information following the caption. (When referring to the figure in your paper, use the abbreviation "fig." in parenthetical citations; otherwise spell out the word.) See 57b for an example of a figure in a paper.

Place visuals in the text, as close as possible to the sentences that relate to them, unless your instructor prefers that visuals appear in an appendix.

Preparing the list of works cited

Begin the list of works cited on a new page at the end of the paper. Center the title "Works Cited" about one inch from the top of the page. Double-space throughout. See the student essays in 7h and 57b for sample lists of works cited.

Alphabetizing the list   Alphabetize the list by the last names of the authors (or editors); if a work has no author or editor, alphabetize by the first word of the title other than *A*, *An*, or *The*.

If your list includes two or more works by the same author, use the author's name for the first entry only. For subsequent entries, use three hyphens followed by a period. List the titles in alphabetical order. (See item 6 in 56b.)

Indenting   Do not indent the first line of each works cited entry, but indent any additional lines one-half inch. This technique highlights the names of the authors, making it easy for readers to scan the alphabetized list. See the works cited list in 57b.

URLs and DOIs   If a URL or a DOI in a works cited entry must be divided across lines, break it before a period or a hyphen or before or after any other mark of punctuation. Do not add a hyphen. If you will post your project online or submit it electronically and you want your readers to click on your URLs, do not insert any line breaks.

57b Sample MLA research paper

Caiaimage/Sam Edwards/
Getty Images

On the following pages is a research paper on the topic of the role of government in legislating food choices, written by Sophie Harba, a student in a composition class. Harba's paper is documented with in-text citations and a list of works cited in MLA style. Annotations in the margins of the paper draw your attention to Harba's use of MLA style and her effective writing.

Harba 1

Sophie Harba

Professor Baros-Moon

Engl 1101

9 November 2017

What's for Dinner? Personal Choices vs. Public Health

Should the government enact laws to regulate healthy
eating choices? Many Americans would answer an emphatic
"No," arguing that what and how much we eat should be
left to individual choice rather than unreasonable laws.
Others might argue that it would be unreasonable for the
government not to enact legislation, given the rise of
chronic diseases that result from harmful diets. In this
debate, both the definition of reasonable regulations
and the role of government to legislate food choices are
at stake. In the name of public health and safety, state
governments have the responsibility to shape health
policies and to regulate healthy eating choices, especially
since doing so offers a potentially large social benefit for a
relatively small cost.

Debates surrounding the government's role in
regulating food have a long history in the United States.
According to Lorine Goodwin, a food historian, nineteenth-
century reformers who sought to purify the food supply
were called "fanatics" and "radicals" by critics who argued
that consumers should be free to buy and eat what they
want (77). Thanks to regulations, though, such as the
1906 federal Pure Food and Drug Act, food, beverages, and
medicine are largely free from toxins. In addition,
to prevent contamination and the spread of disease, meat
and dairy products are now inspected by government
agents to ensure that they meet health requirements. Such
regulations can be considered reasonable because they

Marginal annotations:

Title is centered.

Opening research question engages readers.

Writer highlights the research conversation.

Thesis answers the research question and presents Harba's main point.

Signal phrase names the author. The parenthetical citation includes a page number.

Historical background provides context.

Harba explains her use of a key term, *reasonable*.

Marginal annotations indicate MLA-style formatting and effective writing.

Harba 2

protect us from harm with little, if any, noticeable consumer cost. It is not considered an unreasonable infringement on personal choice that contaminated meat or arsenic-laced cough drops are *un*available at our local supermarket. Rather, it is an important government function to stop such harmful items from entering the marketplace.

Even though our food meets current safety standards, there is a need for further regulation. Not all food dangers, for example, arise from obvious toxins like arsenic and *E. coli*. A diet that is low in nutritional value and high in sugars, fats, and refined grains—grains that have been processed to increase shelf life but that contain little fiber, iron, and B vitamins—can be damaging over time (United States, Dept. of Agriculture and Dept. of Health and Human Services 36). A graph from the government's *Dietary Guidelines for Americans, 2010* provides a visual representation of the American diet and how far off it is from the recommended nutritional standards (see fig. 1).

Michael Pollan, who has written extensively about Americans' unhealthy eating habits, notes that "[t]he Centers for Disease Control estimates that fully three quarters of US health care spending goes to treat chronic diseases, most of which are preventable and linked to diet: heart disease, stroke, type 2 diabetes, and at least a third of all cancers." In fact, the amount of money the United States spends to treat chronic illnesses is increasing so rapidly that the Centers for Disease Control has labeled chronic disease "the public health challenge of the 21st century" (United States, Dept. of Health and Human Services 1). In fighting this epidemic, the primary challenge is not the need to find a cure; the challenge is to prevent chronic diseases from striking in the first place.

Harba establishes common ground with the reader.

Transition helps readers move from one paragraph to the next.

No page number is available for this web source.

Harba emphasizes the urgency of her argument.

Harba 3

Harba uses a graph to illustrate Americans' poor nutritional choices.

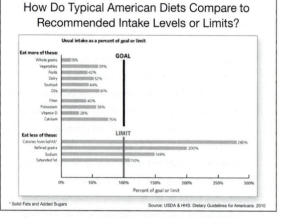

How Do Typical American Diets Compare to Recommended Intake Levels or Limits?

Usual intake as a percent of goal or limit

Eat more of these:
Whole grains 15%
Vegetables 59%
Fruits 42%
Dairy 52%
Seafood 44%
Oils 61%

Fiber 40%
Potassium 56%
Vitamin D 28%
Calcium 75%

GOAL

Eat less of these: LIMIT
Calories from SoFAS* 280%
Refined grains 200%
Sodium 149%
Saturated fat 110%

0%   50%   100%   150%   200%   250%   300%
Percent of goal or limit

* Solid Fats and Added Sugars   Source: USDA & HHS: Dietary Guidelines for Americans, 2010

The visual includes a figure number, descriptive caption, and source information.

Fig. 1. This graph shows that Americans consume about three times more fats and sugars and twice as many refined grains as is recommended but only half of the recommended foods (United States, Dept. of Agriculture and Dept. of Health and Human Services, fig. 5-1).

Harba treats both sides fairly.

Legislation, however, is not a popular solution when it comes to most Americans and the food they eat. According to a nationwide poll, 75% of Americans are opposed to laws that restrict or put limitations on access to unhealthy foods (Neergaard and Agiesta). When New York mayor Michael Bloomberg proposed a regulation in 2012 banning the sale of soft drinks in servings greater than twelve ounces in restaurants and movie theaters, he was ridiculed as "Nanny Bloomberg." In California in 2011, legislators failed to pass a law that would impose a penny-per-ounce tax on soda, which would have funded obesity

Harba 4

prevention programs. And in Mississippi, legislators passed "a ban on bans—a law that forbids . . . local restrictions on food or drink" (Conly A23).

Why is the public largely resistant to laws that would limit unhealthy choices or penalize those choices with so-called fat taxes? Many consumers and civil rights advocates find such laws to be an unreasonable restriction on individual freedom of choice. As health policy experts Mello and others point out, opposition to food and beverage regulation is similar to the opposition to early tobacco legislation: the public views the issue as one of personal responsibility rather than one requiring government intervention (2602). In other words, if a person eats unhealthy food and becomes ill as a result, that is his or her choice. But those who favor legislation claim that freedom of choice is a myth because of the strong influence of food and beverage industry marketing on consumers' dietary habits. According to one nonprofit health advocacy group, food and beverage companies spend roughly two billion dollars per year marketing directly to children. As a result, kids see nearly four thousand ads per year encouraging them to eat unhealthy food and drinks ("Facts"). As was the case with antismoking laws passed in recent decades, taxes and legal restrictions on junk food sales could help to counter the strong marketing messages that promote unhealthy products.

The United States has a history of state and local public health laws that have successfully promoted a particular behavior by punishing an undesirable behavior. The decline in tobacco use as a result of antismoking taxes and laws is perhaps the most obvious example. Another example is legislation requiring the use of seat belts,

Harba anticipates objections to her idea. She counters opposing views and provides support for her argument.

An analogy extends Harba's argument.

Harba 5

which have significantly reduced fatalities in car crashes. One government agency reports that seat belt use saved an average of more than fourteen thousand lives per year in the United States between 2000 and 2010 (United States, Dept. of Transportation, Natl. Highway Traffic Safety Administration 231). Perhaps seat belt laws have public support because the cost of wearing a seat belt is small, especially when compared with the benefit of saving fourteen thousand lives per year.

Laws designed to prevent chronic disease by promoting healthier food and beverage consumption also have potentially enormous benefits. To give just one example, Marion Nestle, New York University professor of nutrition and public health, notes that "a 1% reduction in intake of saturated fat across the population would prevent more than 30,000 cases of coronary heart disease annually and save more than a billion dollars in health care costs" (7). Few would argue that saving lives and dollars is not an enormous benefit. But three-quarters of Americans say they would object to the costs needed to achieve this benefit—the regulations needed to reduce saturated fat intake.

Why do so many Americans believe there is a degree of personal choice lost when regulations such as taxes, bans, or portion limits on unhealthy foods are proposed? Some critics of anti-junk-food laws believe that even if state and local laws were successful in curbing chronic diseases, they would still be unacceptable. Bioethicist David Resnik emphasizes that such policies, despite their potential to make our society healthier, "open the door to excessive government control over food, which could restrict dietary choices, interfere with cultural, ethnic, and religious

Harba introduces a direct quotation with a signal phrase and follows with a comment that shows readers why she chose to use the source.

Harba acknowledges critics and counter-arguments.

traditions, and exacerbate socioeconomic inequalities" (31). Resnik acknowledges that his argument relies on "slippery slope" thinking, but he insists that "social and political pressures" regarding food regulation make his concerns valid (31). Yet the social and political pressures that Resnik cites are really just the desire to improve public health, and limiting access to unhealthy, artificial ingredients seems a small price to pay. As legal scholars L. O. Gostin and K. G. Gostin explain, "[I]nterventions that do not pose a truly significant burden on individual liberty" are justified if they "go a long way towards safeguarding the health and well-being of the populace" (214).

To improve public health, advocates such as Bowdoin College philosophy professor Sarah Conly contend that it is the government's duty to prevent people from making harmful choices whenever feasible and whenever public benefits outweigh the costs. In response to critics who claim that laws aimed at stopping us from eating whatever we want are an assault on our freedom of choice, Conly offers a persuasive counterargument:

> [L]aws aren't designed for each one of us individually.
> Some of us can drive safely at 90 miles per hour, but
> we're bound by the same laws as the people who can't,
> because individual speeding laws aren't practical.
> Giving up a little liberty is something we agree to
> when we agree to live in a democratic society that is
> governed by laws. (A23)

As Conly suggests, we need to change our either/or thinking (either we have complete freedom of choice *or* we have government regulations and lose our freedom) and instead need to see health as a matter of public good, not individual liberty. Proposals such as Mayor Bloomberg's that seek to limit portions of unhealthy beverages aren't about

Including the source's credentials makes Harba more credible.

A signal phrase names the author.

Long quotation is set off from the text. Quotation marks are omitted.

Long quotation is followed with comments that connect the source to Harba's argument.

Harba 7

giving up liberty; they are about asking individuals to choose substantial public health benefits at a very small cost.

Despite arguments in favor of regulating unhealthy food as a means to improve public health, public opposition has stood in the way of legislation. Americans freely eat as much unhealthy food as they want, and manufacturers and sellers of these foods have nearly unlimited freedom to promote such products and drive increased consumption, without any requirements to warn the public of potential hazards. Yet mounting scientific evidence points to unhealthy food as a significant contributing factor to chronic disease, which we know is straining our health care system, decreasing Americans' quality of life, and leading to unnecessary premature deaths. Americans must consider whether to allow the costly trend of rising chronic disease to continue in the name of personal choice or whether to support the regulatory changes and public health policies that will reverse that trend.

Conclusion sums up Harba's argument and provides closure.

Harba 8

Works Cited

Conly, Sarah. "Three Cheers for the Nanny State." *The New York Times*, 25 Mar. 2013, p. A23.

"The Facts on Junk Food Marketing and Kids." *Prevention Institute*, www.preventioninstitute.org/focus-areas/ were-not-buying-it-get-involved/were-not-buying-it -the-facts-on-junk-food-marketing-and-kids. Accessed 16 Oct. 2017.

Goodwin, Lorine Swainston. *The Pure Food, Drink, and Drug Crusaders, 1879-1914*. McFarland, 2006.

Gostin, L. O., and K. G. Gostin. "A Broader Liberty: J. S. Mill, Paternalism, and the Public's Health." *Public Health*, vol. 123, no. 3, 2009, pp. 214-21, doi:10.1016 /j.puhe.2008.12.024.

Mello, Michelle M., et al. "Obesity—the New Frontier of Public Health Law." *The New England Journal of Medicine,* vol. 354, no. 24, 2006, pp. 2601-10, www.nejm.org/doi/pdf/10.1056/NEJMhpr060227.

Neergaard, Lauran, and Jennifer Agiesta. "Obesity's a Crisis but We Want Our Junk Food, Poll Shows." *The Huffington Post*, 4 Jan. 2013, www.huffingtonpost .com/2013/01/04/obesity-junk-food-government -intervention-poll_n_2410376.html.

Nestle, Marion. *Food Politics: How the Food Industry Influences Nutrition and Health*. U of California P, 2013.

Pollan, Michael. "The Food Movement, Rising." *The New York Review of Books*, 10 June 2010, www.nybooks.com/ articles/2010/06/10/food-movement-rising.

Resnik, David. "Trans Fat Bans and Human Freedom." *The American Journal of Bioethics*, vol. 10, no. 3, Mar. 2010, pp. 27-32.

Heading is centered.

List is alphabetized by authors' last names (or by title if no author).

Access date used for an online source that has no update date.

First line of each entry is at the left margin; extra lines are indented ½".

Double-spacing is used throughout.

The government agency is used as the author of a government document.

United States, Department of Agriculture and Department
of Health and Human Services. *Dietary Guidelines
for Americans, 2010*, health.gov/dietaryguidelines/
dga2010/dietaryguidelines2010.pdf.

United States, Department of Health and Human Services,
Centers for Disease Control and Prevention. *The Power
of Prevention*. National Center for Chronic Disease
Prevention and Health Promotion, 2009, www.cdc.gov/
chronicdisease/pdf/2009-Power-of-Prevention.pdf.

United States, Department of Transportation, National
Highway Traffic Safety Administration. *Traffic Safety
Facts 2010: A Compilation of Motor Vehicle Crash Data
from the Fatality Analysis Reporting System and the
General Estimates System*. 2010, www.nrd.nhtsa.dot
.gov/Pubs/811659.pdf.

WRITING PAPERS IN APA STYLE

Note: An in-text citation is a reference to a source that you place within your paper. A reference list entry is a reference to a source that you include at the end of your paper.

Most instructors in the social sciences and some instructors in other disciplines will ask you to document your sources using the American Psychological Association (APA) system of in-text citations and references described in chapter 61. When writing an APA-style paper that draws on sources, you face three main challenges: (1) supporting a thesis, (2) citing your sources and avoiding plagiarism, and (3) integrating source material effectively.

Examples in chapters 58–60 are drawn from one student's research for a review of the literature on technology's role in the shift to student-centered learning. April Wang's paper appears in 62b.

58 Supporting a thesis

Most research assignments ask you to form a thesis, or main idea, and to support that thesis with well-organized evidence. In a paper reviewing the literature on a topic, the thesis analyzes conclusions drawn by a variety of researchers.

58a Form a working thesis.

Once you have read a range of sources, considered your issue from different perspectives, and chosen an entry point in the research conversation (see 50b), you are ready to form a working thesis: a one-sentence (or occasionally two-sentence) statement of your central idea. (See also 1c.)

The working thesis expresses more than your opinion; it expresses your informed, reasoned answer to your research question. As you learn more about your subject, your ideas may change, and you can revise your thesis as you draft. Here, for example, is a research question posed by April Wang, a student in an education class, followed by her working thesis in response.

RESEARCH QUESTION

Can educational technology improve student learning and solve the problem of teacher shortages?

WORKING THESIS

Educational technology can help solve teacher shortages by shifting the focus from teachers to students.

The thesis usually appears at the end of the introductory paragraph. To read April Wang's thesis in the context of her introduction, see 62b.

For questions that you can use to test a working thesis, see 53a.

58b Organize your ideas.

The American Psychological Association (APA) encourages the use of headings to help readers follow the organization of a paper. For an original research report, the major headings often follow a standard model: "Method," "Results," "Discussion." The introduction does not have a heading; it consists of the material between the title of the paper and the first heading.

For a literature review, headings will vary. Student writer April Wang used three questions to focus her research (see her final paper in 62b); the questions then became headings in her paper:

- In what ways is student-centered learning effective?
- Can educational technology help students drive their own learning?
- How can public schools effectively combine teacher talent and educational technology?

58c Use sources to inform and support your argument.

The source materials you have gathered can play many different roles and will help you support and develop your argument.

Providing background information or context

Readers often need some background information and context to anchor their understanding of your topic. Describing a research study or offering facts and statistics, as student writer April Wang does, can help readers grasp your topic's significance.

> In the United States, most public school systems are struggling with teacher shortages, which are projected to worsen as the number of applicants to education schools decreases (Donitsa-Schmidt & Zuzovsky, 2014, p. 420). Citing federal data, *The New York Times* reported a 30% drop in "people entering teacher preparation programs" between 2010 and 2014 (Rich, 2015, para. 10).

Explaining terms or concepts

If readers are unfamiliar with a term or concept important to your topic, you will want to define or explain it; or if your argument depends on a term with multiple meanings, you will want to explain your use of the term. Quoting or paraphrasing a source can help you define terms and concepts in accessible language. April Wang uses a source to define a key concept, student-centered learning.

> According to the International Society for Technology in Education (2016), "student-centered learning moves students from passive receivers of information to active participants in their own discovery process" (What Is It? section).

Supporting your claims

As you draft, make sure to back up your assertions with facts, examples, and other evidence from your research (see also 7e). April Wang, for example, uses one source's findings to support her claim that a combination of certified teachers and educational technology can promote student-centered learning.

> Many schools have already effectively paired a reduced faculty with educational technology to support successful student-centered learning. For example, Watson (2008) offered a case study of the Cincinnati Public Schools Virtual High School, which brought students together in a physical school building to work with an assortment of online learning programs. Although there were only 10 certified teachers in the building, students were able to engage in highly individualized instruction according to their own needs, strengths, and learning styles, using the 10 teachers as support (p. 7).

Lending authority to your argument

Expert opinion can add credibility to your argument (see also 7e). But don't rely on experts to make your points for you. State your ideas in your own words and, when appropriate, cite the judgment of an authority in the field to support your position.

Horn and Staker (2011) concluded that the chief benefit of technological learning was that it could adapt to the individual student in a way that whole-class delivery by a single teacher could not. Their study examined various schools where technology enabled student-centered learning.

Anticipating and countering alternative interpretations

Do not ignore sources that seem contrary to your position. Instead, use them to state potential objections to your argument before you counter them (see 7f). Readers often have objections in mind already, whether or not they agree with you. Wang uses a source to acknowledge that some teachers oppose student instruction driven by technology.

Some researchers have expressed doubt that schools are ready for student-centered learning—or any type of instruction—that is driven by technology. In a recent survey conducted by the Nellie Mae Education Foundation, Moeller and Rietzes (2011) reported not only that many teachers lacked confidence in their ability to incorporate technology in the classroom but that 43% of polled high school students said that they lacked confidence in their technological proficiency going into college and careers.

59 Citing sources; avoiding plagiarism

In a research paper, you will draw on the work of other researchers and writers, and you must document their contributions by citing your sources. Sources are cited for two reasons:

(1) to tell readers where your information comes from — so that they can assess its reliability and, if interested, find and read the original source

(2) to give credit to the writers from whom you have borrowed words and ideas

You must cite anything you borrow from a source, including direct quotations; statistics and other specific facts; visuals such as tables, graphs, and diagrams; and summaries and paraphrases. Borrowing without proper acknowledgment is a form of dishonesty known as plagiarism. The only exception is common knowledge — information that your readers may know or could easily locate in any number of reference sources.

59a Understand how the APA system works.

The American Psychological Association (APA) recommends an author-date system of citations. Here, briefly, is how the APA citation system works.

IN-TEXT CITATION

A signal phrase names the author and gives the publication date. Fields that use APA style value current research.

Bell (2010) reported that students engaged in this kind of learning performed better on both project-based assessments and standardized tests (pp. 39–40).

The cited material is followed by a page number or other section locator in parentheses.

ENTRY IN THE LIST OF REFERENCES

Bell, S. (2010). Project-based learning for the 21st century: Skills for the future. *The Clearing House, 83*(2), 39–43.

At the end of the paper, a list of references gives complete publication information.

NOTE: This basic APA format varies for different types of sources. For a detailed discussion and other models, see 61.

59b Understand what plagiarism is.

In a research paper, you draw on the work of other writers. To be fair and responsible, you must document their contributions by citing your sources. When you acknowledge and document your sources, you avoid plagiarism, a form of academic dishonesty.

Three different acts are considered plagiarism:

(1) failing to cite quotations and borrowed ideas
(2) failing to enclose borrowed language in quotation marks
(3) failing to put summaries and paraphrases in your own words

Definitions of plagiarism vary; it's a good idea to find out how your school defines academic dishonesty.

59c Use quotation marks around borrowed language.

To indicate that you are using a source's exact phrases or sentences, you must enclose them in quotation marks unless they have been set off from the text by indenting (see 60b). To omit the quotation marks is to claim — falsely — that the language is your own. Such an omission is plagiarism even if you have cited the source.

ORIGINAL SOURCE

Student-centered learning, or student centeredness, is a model which puts the student in the center of the learning process.

— Z. Çubukçu, "Teachers' Evaluation of Student-Centered Learning Environments" (2012), p. 50

PLAGIARISM

The shaded words are directly from the original.

According to Professor Zuhal Çubukçu (2012), student-centered learning . . . is a model which puts the student in the center of the learning process (p. 50).

BORROWED LANGUAGE IN QUOTATION MARKS

According to Professor Zuhal Çubukçu (2012), "student-centered learning . . . is a model which puts the student in the center of the learning process" (p. 50).

NOTE: A page number, paragraph number, or other locator is required when you cite direct quotations.

59d Put summaries and paraphrases in your own words.

A summary condenses information from a source; a paraphrase conveys the information using roughly the same number of words as the original source. When you summarize or paraphrase, you must present the source's meaning using your own words and sentence structure. (See also 51c and 60a.)

You commit plagiarism if you "patchwrite"—half-copy the author's sentences, either by mixing the author's phrases with your own without using quotation marks or by plugging synonyms into the author's sentence structure.

The following paraphrases are plagiarism—even though the source is cited—because their language and sentence structure are too close to those of the source.

ORIGINAL SOURCE

Student-centered teaching focuses on the student. Decision-making, organization and content are determined for most by taking individual students' needs and interests into consideration. Student-centered teaching provides opportunities to develop students' skills of transferring knowledge to other situations, triggering retention, and adapting a high motivation for learning.

— Z. Çubukçu, "Teachers' Evaluation of Student-Centered Learning Environments" (2012), p. 52

UNACCEPTABLE BORROWING OF PHRASES

The paraphrase borrows too much language from the original.

According to Professor Zuhal Çubukçu (2012), student-centered teaching takes into account the needs and interests of each student, making it possible to foster students' skills of transferring knowledge to new situations and triggering retention (p. 52).

UNACCEPTABLE BORROWING OF STRUCTURE

The paraphrase follows the structure of the original too closely.

According to Zuhal Çubukçu (2012), this new model of teaching centers on the student. The material and flow of the course are chosen by considering the students' individual requirements. Student-centered teaching gives a chance for students to develop useful, transferable skills, ensuring they'll remember material and stay motivated (p. 52).

To avoid plagiarizing an author's language, resist the temptation to look at the source while you are summarizing or paraphrasing. After you have read the passage you want to paraphrase, set the source aside. Ask yourself, "What is the author's meaning?" In your own words, state your understanding of the author's basic point.

Then return to the source and check that you haven't used the author's language or sentence structure or misrepresented the author's ideas. When you understand another writer's meaning, you can more easily present those ideas in your own words.

ACCEPTABLE PARAPHRASE

The writer understands the ideas in the text and uses original language and structure to present them.

In his research, Çubukçu (2012) documents the numerous benefits of student-centered teaching in putting the student at the center of teaching and learning. When students are given the option of deciding what they learn, and how they learn, they are motivated to apply their learning to new settings and to retain the content of their learning (p. 52).

APA does not require page numbers for paraphrases, but writers can choose to include page numbers to help a reader locate a passage in the source.

60 Integrating sources

Your research draws on and borrows from the work of others to help you develop and support your ideas, but readers should always know who is speaking in your paper — you or your source. You can use several strategies to integrate research sources into your paper while maintaining your own voice.

- Use sources as concisely as possible so that your own thinking and voice aren't lost (60a and 60b).
- Use signal phrases to indicate the boundary between your words and the source's words (60c).
- Discuss and analyze your sources to show readers how each source supports your points and how the sources relate to one another (60d).

60a Summarize and paraphrase effectively.

In your academic writing, keep the emphasis on your ideas and your language; use your own words to summarize and to paraphrase your sources and to explain your points. How you choose to use a source — through summary or paraphrase — depends on your purpose.

LaunchPad Solo macmillan learning **Activities for Chapter 60**
7 Exercises

Summarizing

When you summarize a source, you express another writer's ideas in your own words, condensing the author's key points and using fewer words than the author. Even though a summary is in your own words, the original ideas remain the intellectual property of the author, so you must include a citation. Summarizing allows you to state the source's main idea simply before you respond to or counter it. See "When to use a summary" (pp. 403–04) for more advice.

Paraphrasing

When you paraphrase, you express an author's ideas in your own words and sentence structure, using approximately the same number of words and details as in the source. Even though the words are your own, the original ideas are the author's intellectual property, so you must give a citation. Paraphrasing allows you to capture a source's ideas but perhaps simplify or reorder them. See "When to use a paraphrase" (p. 404) for more advice.

For a step-by-step guide to paraphrasing effectively, see 55a.

60b Use quotations effectively.

When you quote a source, you borrow some of the author's exact words and enclose them in quotation marks. Quotation marks show your readers that both the idea and the words belong to the author. Use quotations when your source's language is especially vivid or when exact wording is needed for technical accuracy. See "When to use quotations" (p. 406) for more advice.

Limiting your use of quotations

Although it is tempting to insert many quotations in your paper and to use your own words only for connecting passages, do not quote excessively.

You can often integrate phrases from a source into your own sentence structure.

Citing federal data, *The New York Times* reported a 30-percent drop in "people entering teacher preparation programs" between 2010 and 2014 (Rich, 2015, para. 10).

Bell (2010) has argued that the chief benefit of student-centered learning is that it connects students with "real-world tasks," thus making learning more engaging as well as more comprehensive (p. 39).

Using the ellipsis mark

To condense a quoted passage, you can use the ellipsis mark (three periods, with spaces between) to indicate that you have left words out. What remains must be grammatically complete.

> Demski (2012) noted that "personalized learning . . . acknowledges and accommodates the range of abilities, prior experiences, needs and interests of each student" (p. 33).

The writer has omitted the phrase "a student-centered teaching and learning model that" from the source.

If you leave out one or more full sentences, use a period before the three ellipsis dots.

> According to Demski (2012), "In any personalized learning model, the student—not the teacher—is the central figure. . . . Personalized learning may finally allow individualization and differentiation to actually happen in the classroom" (p. 34).

Ordinarily, do not use an ellipsis mark at the beginning or at the end of a quotation. Readers will understand that you have taken the quoted material from a longer passage. The only exception occurs when you feel it is necessary, for clarity, to indicate that your quotation begins or ends in the middle of a sentence.

★ **Using sources responsibly**   Make sure that omissions and ellipsis marks do not distort the meaning of your source.

Using brackets

Brackets allow you to insert your own words into quoted material to clarify a confusing reference or to keep a sentence grammatical in the context of your own writing.

> Demski's (2012) research confirms that "implement[ing] a true personalized learning model on a national level" is difficult for a number of reasons (p. 36).

To indicate an error such as a misspelling in a quotation, insert "[*sic*]," italicized and in brackets, right after the error.

Setting off long quotations

When you quote forty or more words from a source, set off the quotation by indenting it one-half inch from the left margin. Use the normal right margin and do not single-space the quotation.

Long quotations should be introduced by an informative sentence, often followed by a colon. Quotation marks are unnecessary because the indented format tells readers that the passage is taken word for word from the source.

> According to Svokos (2015), some educational technology resources entertain students while supporting student-centered learning:
>
>> GlassLab, a nonprofit that was launched with grants from the Bill & Melinda Gates and MacArthur Foundations, creates educational games that are now being used in more than 6,000 classrooms across the country. Some of the company's games are education versions of existing ones—for example, its first release was SimCity EDU—while others are originals. Teachers get real-time updates on students' progress as well as suggestions on what subjects they need to spend more time perfecting. (5. Educational Games section)

NOTE: The parenthetical citation with a locator (page number, paragraph number, or section title) goes outside the final mark of punctuation. (When a quotation is run into your text, the opposite is true. See the sample citations on p. 487.)

60c Use signal phrases to integrate sources.

Whenever you include a paraphrase, summary, or direct quotation of another writer's work in your paper, prepare your readers for it with a signal phrase. A signal phrase usually names the author of the source, gives the publication year in parentheses, and often provides some context. It is generally acceptable in APA style to call authors by their last name only, even on a first mention. If your paper refers to two authors with the same last name, use initials as well.

When you write a signal phrase, choose a verb that fits with the way you are using the source (see 58c). Are you providing

Using signal phrases in APA papers

To avoid monotony, try to vary both the language and the placement of your signal phrases.

Model signal phrases

In the words of Mitra (2013), ". . ."

As Bell (2010) has noted, ". . ."

Donista-Schmidt and Zuzovsky (2014) pointed out that ". . ."

". . .," claimed Çubukçu (2012, Introduction section).

". . .," explained Demski (2012), ". . ."

Horn and Staker (2011) have offered a compelling argument for this view: ". . ."

Moeller and Rietzes (2011) answered objections with the following analysis: ". . ."

Verbs in signal phrases

admitted	contended	pointed out
agreed	declared	reasoned
argued	denied	refuted
asserted	emphasized	rejected
believed	explained	reported
claimed	insisted	responded
compared	noted	suggested
confirmed	observed	wrote

background, explaining a concept, supporting a claim, lending authority, or refuting an argument? See the chart above for a list of verbs commonly used in signal phrases.

NOTE: APA style calls for using verbs in the past tense or present perfect tense ("explained" or "has explained") to introduce source material. Use the present tense only for discussing the applications or effects of your own results ("the data suggest") or knowledge that has been clearly established ("researchers agree").

Marking boundaries

Readers need to move from your words to the words of a source without feeling a jolt. Avoid dropping direct quotations into your text without warning. Instead, provide clear signal phrases, including at least the author's name and the year of publication. A signal phrase marks the boundary between source material and your own words and can also tell readers why a source is worth quoting. (The signal phrase is highlighted in the second example.)

DROPPED QUOTATION

Many educators have been intrigued by the concept of blended learning but have been unsure how to define it. "Blended learning is a formal education program in which a student learns at least in part through online delivery of content and instruction with some element of student control over time, place, and pace" (Horn & Staker, 2011, p. 4).

QUOTATION WITH SIGNAL PHRASE

Many educators have been intrigued by the concept of blended learning but have been unsure how to define it. As researchers Horn and Staker (2011) have argued, "blended learning is a formal education program in which a student learns at least in part through online delivery of content and instruction with some element of student control over time, place, and pace" (p. 4).

Introducing summaries and paraphrases

As with quotations, you should introduce most summaries and paraphrases with a signal phrase that mentions the author and the year and places the material in the context of your own writing. Readers will then understand where the summary or paraphrase begins.

Without the signal phrase (highlighted) in the following example, readers might think that only the last sentence was being cited, when in fact the whole paragraph is based on the source.

Watson (2008) reported that for American post-secondary students, technology is integral to their academic lives. Nearly three-quarters own their own laptops, and 83% have used a course management system for an online component of a class. Watson pointed out that online and blended learning models are even more widespread outside of the United States (p. 15).

There are times, however, when a summary or a paraphrase does not require a signal phrase naming the author. When the context makes clear where the cited material begins, you may omit the signal phrase and include the author's name and the year in parentheses.

Integrating statistics and other data

When you are citing a statistic or another specific fact, a signal phrase is often not necessary. In most cases, readers will understand that the citation refers to the data (not the whole paragraph).

> Of polled high school students, 43% said that they lacked confidence in their technological proficiency going into college and careers (Moeller & Rietzes, 2011).

There is nothing wrong, however, with using a signal phrase to introduce a statistic or other data.

Putting source material in context

Readers should not have to guess why source material appears in your paper; you must put the source in context. If you use another writer's words, you must explain how they relate to your point. It is a good idea to sandwich a quotation between sentences of your own, introducing it with a signal phrase and following it with interpretive comments that link the quotation to your paper's argument. (See also 60d.)

> **QUOTATION WITH EFFECTIVE CONTEXT (QUOTATION SANDWICH)**
>
> According to the International Society for Technology in Education (2016), "student-centered learning moves students from passive receivers of information to active participants in their own discovery process" (What Is It? section). The results of student-centered learning have been positive, not only for academic achievement but also for student self-esteem. In this model of instruction, the teacher acts as a facilitator, and the students actively participate in the process of learning and teaching.

60d Synthesize sources.

When you synthesize multiple sources in a research paper, you create a conversation about your research topic. You show readers how the ideas of one source relate to those of another by connecting and analyzing the ideas in the context of your argument. Keep the emphasis on your own writing. The thread of your argument should be easy to identify and to understand, with or without your sources.

SAMPLE SYNTHESIS

Student writer begins with a claim that needs support.

A signal phrase indicates how the source contributes to Wang's paper and shows that the ideas that follow are not her own.

It is clear that educational technology will continue to play a role in student and school performance. Horn and Staker (2011) acknowledged that they focused on programs in which integration of educational technology led to improved student performance. In other schools, technological learning is simply distance learning—watching a remote teacher—and not student-centered learning that allows students to partner with teachers to develop enriching learning experiences.

That said, many educators seem convinced that educational technology has the potential to help them transition from traditional teacher-driven learning to student-centered learning.

Wang extends the argument and sets up two additional sources.

All four schools in the Stanford study heavily relied on technology (Friedlaender et al., 2014). And indeed, Demski (2012) argued that technology is not supplemental but instead is "central" to student-centered learning (p. 33).

Wang closes the paragraph by interpreting the source and connecting it to her claim.

Rather than turning to a teacher as the source of information, students are sent to investigate solutions to problems by searching online, emailing experts, collaborating with one another in a wiki space, or completing online practice. Rather than turning to a teacher for the answer to a question, students are driven to perform—driven to use technology to find those answers themselves.

Student writer

Source 1

Student writer

Source 2

Source 3

Student writer

In this synthesis, Wang uses her own analysis to shape the conversation among her sources. She does not simply string quotations and statistics together or allow her sources to overwhelm her writing. The final sentence, written in her own voice, gives her an opportunity to explain to readers how her sources support and extend her argument.

When synthesizing sources, ask yourself these questions:

- How do your sources address your research question?
- How do your sources respond to one another's ideas?
- Have you varied the functions of sources — to provide background, explain concepts, lend authority, and anticipate counterarguments? Do your signal phrases indicate these functions?
- Do you connect and analyze sources in your own voice?
- Is your own argument easy to identify and to understand, with or without your sources?

61 Documenting sources in APA style

In most social science classes, you will be asked to use the APA system for documenting sources, which is set forth in the *Publication Manual of the American Psychological Association*, 7th ed. (2010).

APA recommends in-text citations that refer readers to a list of references. An in-text citation gives the author of the source (often in a signal phrase), the year of publication, and often a page number in parentheses. At the end of the paper, a list of references provides publication information about the source; the list is alphabetized by authors' last names (or by titles for works with no authors). The direct link between the in-text citation and the entry in the reference list is highlighted in the following example.

IN-TEXT CITATION

Bell (2010) reported that students engaged in this kind of learning performed better on both project-based assessments and standardized tests (pp. 39–40).

ENTRY IN THE LIST OF REFERENCES

Bell, S. (2010). Project-based learning for the 21st century: Skills for the future. *The Clearing House, 83*(2), 39–43.

For a reference list that includes this entry, see 62b.

List of APA in-text citation models

List of APA reference list models

General guidelines for listing authors

Articles and other short works

Books and other long works

List of APA reference list models, continued

61a APA in-text citations

APA's in-text citations provide the author's last name and the year of publication, usually before the cited material, and a page number in parentheses directly after the cited material. In the following models, the elements of the in-text citation are highlighted.

NOTE: APA style requires the use of the past tense or the present perfect tense in signal phrases introducing cited material: Smith (2020) reported; Smith (2020) has argued.

■ **1. Basic format for a quotation**   Ordinarily, introduce the quotation with a signal phrase that includes the author's last name followed by the year of publication in parentheses. Put the page number (preceded by "p." or "pp." for more than one page) in parentheses after the quotation. For sources from the web without page numbers, see item 11a.

> Çubukçu (2012) argued that for a student-centered approach
>
> to work, students must maintain "ownership for their goals and
>
> activities" (p. 64).

If the author is not named in the signal phrase, place the author's name, the year, and the page number in parentheses after the quotation: (Çubukçu, 2012, p. 64). (See items 5 and 11 for citing sources that lack authors; item 11 also explains how to handle sources without dates or page numbers.)

NOTE: Do not include a month in an in-text citation, even if the entry in the reference list includes the month.

■ **2. Basic format for a summary or a paraphrase**   As for a quotation (see item 1), include the author's last name and the year either in a signal phrase introducing the material or in parentheses following it. A page number is not required for a summary or a paraphrase, but include one if it would help readers locate the information or if your instructor requires it. For sources from the web without page numbers, see item 11a in this section.

> Watson (2008) offered a case study of the Cincinnati Public Schools
>
> Virtual High School, in which students were able to engage in highly
>
> individualized instruction according to their own needs, strengths,
>
> and learning styles, using 10 teachers as support (p. 7).

The Cincinnati Public Schools Virtual High School brought students together to engage in highly individualized instruction according to their own needs, strengths, and learning styles, using 10 teachers as support (Watson, 2008, p. 7).

■ **3. Work with two authors**   Name both authors in the signal phrase or in parentheses each time you cite the work. In the parentheses, use "&" between the authors' names; in the signal phrase, use "and."

According to Donitsa-Schmidt and Zuzovsky (2014), "demographic growth in the school population" can lead to teacher shortages (p. 426).

In the United States, most public school systems are struggling with teacher shortages, which are projected to worsen as the number of applicants to education schools decreases (Donitsa-Schmidt & Zuzovsky, 2014, p. 420).

■ **4. Work with three or more authors**   Use the first author's name followed by "et al." (Latin for "and others") in either a signal phrase or a parenthetical citation.

In 2013, Harper et al. studied teachers' perceptions of project-based learning (PBL) before and after participating in a PBL pilot program.

Researchers studied teachers' perceptions of project-based learning (PBL) before and after participating in a PBL pilot program (Harper et al., 2013).

■ **5. Work with unknown or anonymous author**   If the author is unknown, include the work's title (shortened if more than a few words) in the in-text citation.

Collaboration increases significantly among students who own or have regular access to a laptop ("Tech Seeds," 2015).

In in-text citations, capitalize the first and last words of a title and subtitle, all significant words, and any words of four letters or more. For books and most stand-alone works (except web-sites), italicize the title; for most articles and other parts of larger works, set the title in quotation marks. In the rare case when "Anonymous" is specified as the author, treat it as if it were a real name: (Anonymous, 2011). In the list of references, also use the name Anonymous as author.

■ **6. Organization as author**   If the author is an organization or a government agency, name the organization in the signal phrase or in the parentheses the first time you cite the source.

> According to the International Society for Technology in Education (2016), "student-centered learning moves students from passive receivers of information to active participants in their own discovery process" (What Is It? section).

For an organization with a long name, you may abbreviate the name of the organization in citations after the first.

> **FIRST CITATION**   (Texas Higher Education Coordinating
> Board [THECB], 2012)
>
> **LATER CITATIONS**   (THECB, 2012)

■ **7. Authors with the same last name**   To avoid confusion, use initials with the last names in your in-text citations. If authors share the same initials, spell out each author's first name.

> Research by E. Smith (2019) revealed that . . .
>
> One 2018 study contradicted . . . (R. Smith, p. 234).

■ **8. Two or more works by the same author in the same year**   In your reference list, you will use lowercase letters ("a," "b," and so on) with the year to order the entries (see item 8 in 61b). Use those same letters with the year in the in-text citation.

> Research by Durgin (2013b) has yielded new findings about the role of smartphones in the classroom.

■ **9. Two or more works in the same parentheses**   Put the works in the order in which they appear in the reference list, separated with semicolons: (Nazer, 2015; Serrao et al., 2014).

■ **10. Multiple citations to the same work in one paragraph**   If you give the author's name in the text of your paper (not in parentheses) and you mention that source again in the text of the same paragraph, give only the author's name, not the date, in the later citation. If any subsequent reference in the same paragraph is in parentheses, include both the author and the date in the parentheses.

> Bell (2010) has argued that the chief benefit of student-centered
> learning is that it can connect students with "real-world tasks," thus
> making learning more engaging as well as more comprehensive (p. 42).
> For example, Bell observed a group of middle-school students who
> wanted to build a social justice monument for their school. Students
> engaged in this kind of learning performed better on both project-
> based assessments and standardized tests (Bell, 2010).

■ **11. Web source**   Cite sources from the web as you would cite any other source, giving the author and the year when they are available.

> Atkinson (2011) found that children who spent at least four hours
> a day engaged in online activities in an academic environment were
> less likely to want to play video games or watch TV after school.

Usually a page number is not available; occasionally a web source will lack an author or a date (see 11a, 11b, and 11c).

a. No page numbers   When a web source lacks stable numbered pages, include a paragraph number, section heading, or both to help readers locate the passage being cited. If a heading is long, use a shortened version of the heading in quotation marks.

If a source lacks numbered paragraphs or headings, count the paragraphs manually. When quoting audio and video sources, use a time stamp to indicate the start of the quotation.

> Crush and Jayasingh (2015) pointed out that school districts in
> low-income areas had "jump-started their distance learning
> initiatives with available grant funds" (Funding Change section,
> para. 6).

b. Unknown author   If no author is named in the source, mention the title of the source in a signal phrase or give the first word or two of the title in parentheses (see also item 5). (If an organization serves as the author, see item 6.)

> A student's IEP may, in fact, recommend the use of mobile
> technology ("Considerations," 2012).

c. Unknown date   When the source does not give a date, use the abbreviation "n.d." (for "no date").

> Administrators believe 1-to-1 programs boost learner engagement (Magnus, n.d.).

■   **12. An entire website**   If you mention an entire website from which you did not pull specific information, give the URL in the text of your paper but do not include it in the reference list.

> The Berkeley Center for Teaching and Learning website (https://teaching.berkeley.edu/) shares ideas for using mobile technology in the classroom.

■   **13. Personal communication**   Interviews that you conduct, letters, email messages, and similar communications that would be difficult for your readers to retrieve should be cited in the text only, not in the reference list. (Use the first initial with the last name either in your text sentence or in parentheses.)

> One of Yim's colleagues has contended that the benefits of this technology for children under 12 years old are few (F. Johnson, personal communication, October 20, 2013).

■   **14. Course materials**   Cite lecture notes from your instructor or your own class notes as personal communication (see item 13). If your instructor's material contains publication information, cite it as you would the appropriate source. See also item 52 in section 61b.

■   **15. Part of a source (chapter, figure)**   To cite a specific part of a source, such as a whole chapter or a figure or table, identify the element in parentheses. Don't abbreviate terms such as "Figure," "Chapter," and "Section."

> The data support the finding that peer relationships are difficult to replicate in a completely online environment (Hanniman, 2010, Figure 8-3).

■   **16. Indirect source (source quoted in another source)**   When a published source is quoted in a source written by someone else, cite the original source first; include "as cited in" before the author and date of the source you read. In the following example, Chow is the author of the source in the reference list; that source contains a quotation by Brailsford.

Brailsford (1990) commended the writer and educator's "sure understanding of the thoughts of young people" (as cited in Chow, 2019, para. 9).

■ **17. Sacred or classical text** Identify the book (specifying the version or edition you used), the publication date(s), and the relevant part (chapter, verse, line). It is not necessary to include the source in the reference list.

Peace activists have long cited the biblical prophet's vision of a world without war: "And . . . nation shall not lift up sword against nation, neither shall they learn war any more" (*Holy Bible Revised Standard Edition*, 1952/2004, Isaiah 2:4).

■ **18. Quotation from a source without page numbers** If your source does not include page numbers, include a locator—other information from the source, such as a section heading, paragraph number, figure or table number, slide number, or time stamp—to help readers find the cited passage:

Lopez (2020) has noted that ". . ." (Symptoms section).

Myers (2019) explained the benefits of humility (para. 5).

The American Immigration Council has recommended that ". . ." (Slide 5).

In a recent TED Talk, Gould (2019) argued that ". . ." (13:27).

If you shorten a long heading, place it in quotation marks: ("How to Apply" section).

61b APA list of references

The information you will need for the reference list at the end of your paper will differ slightly depending on the source, but the main principles apply to all sources: identify an author, a creator, or a producer whenever possible; give a title; and provide the date on which the source was produced. In most cases, you will provide page numbers or other locator or retrieval information.

▶ General guidelines for the reference list, page 503

Section 61b provides specific requirements for and examples of many of the sources you are likely to encounter. When you cite sources, your goals are to provide your readers with enough information so that they can find your sources easily and to provide that information in a consistent way according to APA conventions.

In the list of references, include only sources that you have quoted, summarized, or paraphrased in your paper.

General guidelines for listing authors

The formatting of authors' names in items 1–10 applies to all sources in print and on the web — books, articles, websites, and so on. For more models of specific source types, see items 11–55.

■ 1. Single author

author: last name + initial(s) / year (book) / title (book) / publisher

Yanagihara, H. (2015). *A little life.* Doubleday.

■ 2. Two to twenty authors

List up to twenty authors by last names followed by initials. Use an ampersand (&) before the name of the last author. (See items 3–4 in 61a for citing works with multiple authors in the text of your paper.)

all authors: last name + initial(s) / year (journal) / title (article)

Kim, E. H., Hollon, S. D., & Olatunji, B. O. (2016). Clinical errors in

journal title / volume / pages

cognitive-behavior therapy. *Psychotherapy, 53*(3), 325–330.

DOI

https://doi.org/10.1037/pst0000074

■ 3. Twenty-one or more authors

List the first nineteen, followed by an ellipsis mark (. . .) and the last author's name. Then proceed as in item 2.

Sharon, G., Cruz, N. J., Kang, D.-W., Gandal, M. J., Wang, B., Kim, Y.-M.,

Zink, E. M., Casey, C. P., Taylor, B. C., Lane, C. J., Bramer, L. M.,

Isern, N. G., Hoyt, D. W., Noecker, C., Sweredoski, M. J., Moradian,

A., Borenstein, E., Jansson, J. K., Knight, R., . . . Mazmanian, S. K.

General guidelines for the reference list

In APA style, the alphabetical list of works cited, which appears at the end of the paper, is titled "References."

Authors and dates

- Alphabetize entries in the list of references by authors' last names; if a work has no author, alphabetize it by its title.
- For all authors' names, put the last name first, followed by a comma; use initials for the first and middle names.
- With two or more authors, separate the names with commas. Include names for up to twenty authors, with an ampersand (&) before the last author's name. For twenty-one or more authors, list the first nineteen authors, three ellipsis dots, and the last author.
- If the author is a company or an organization, give the name in normal order.
- Put the date of publication immediately after the first element of the citation. Enclose the date in parentheses, followed by a period (outside the parentheses).
- Use the date as given in the publication. Generally, give the year for books and journals; the year and month for monthly magazines; and the year, month, and day for weekly magazines and for newspapers. Use the season when a publication gives the season. For web sources, use the date of posting, if it is available. Use "(n.d.)" if no date is given.

Titles

- Italicize the titles and subtitles of books, journals, and other stand-alone works. If a book title contains another book title or an article title, do not italicize the internal title and do not put quotation marks around it.
- Use no italics or quotation marks for the titles of articles. If an article title contains another article title or a term usually placed in quotation marks, use quotation marks around the internal title or term. If an article title contains a title or term usually italicized, use italics for that title or term.
- For books and articles, capitalize only the first word of the title and subtitle and all proper nouns.
- For the titles of journals, magazines, and newspapers, capitalize all words of four letters or more (and all nouns, pronouns, verbs, adjectives, and adverbs of any length).

General guidelines for the reference list, continued

Source information

- In publishers' names, omit business designations such as Inc. or Ltd. Otherwise, write the publisher's name exactly how it appears in the source.

- For online sources, list the name of the website in the publisher position: Twitter; YouTube; U.S. Census Bureau.

- If the publisher is the same as the author, do not repeat the name in the publisher position.

- Provide locations only for works associated with a single location (such as a conference presentation).

- Include the volume and issue numbers for any journals, magazines, or other periodicals that have them. Italicize the volume number and put the issue number, not italicized, in parentheses: *26*(2).

- When an article appears on consecutive pages, provide the range of pages. When an article does not appear on consecutive pages, give all page numbers: A1, A17.

- Use "p." and "pp." before page numbers only with selections in edited books. Do not use "p." and "pp." with magazines, journals, and newspapers.

URLs, DOIs, and other retrieval information

- For articles and books from the web, use the DOI (digital object identifier), if available. If a source does not have a DOI, give the URL. Do not insert a period after a DOI or URL.

- If a URL or DOI is long, you can create a permalink using a shortening service such as shortdoi.org or bitly.com.

- Use a retrieval date for a web source only if the content is likely to change (such as content on a website's home page or in a social media profile).

■ **4. Organization as author**

author:
organization name   year   title (book)

American Psychiatric Association. (2013). *Diagnostic and statistical manual*

edition

of mental disorders (5th ed.).

■ **5. Unknown author**   Begin the entry with the work's title.

title (article)   year + month + day (weekly publication)   magazine title

The rise of the sharing economy. (2013, March 9). *The Economist,*

volume, issue   page(s)

406(8826), 14.

■ **6. Author using a screen name, pen name, or stage name**   Use the author's real name, if known, and give the screen name or pen name in brackets exactly as it appears in the source. If only the screen name is known, begin with that name and do not use brackets. (See also items 36 and 54 on citing screen names in social media.)

screen name   year + month + day (daily publication)   text of comment

dr.zachary.smith. (2019, October 3). What problem are they trying to solve?

label

[Comment on the article "Georgia is purging voter rolls again"].

title of publication   shortened URL

Slate. https://fyre.it/sjSPFyza.4

If the author uses just a single name ("Sophocles") or a two-part name in which the two parts are essential ("Cardi B"), list the name with no abbreviations or alterations.

■ **7. Two or more works by the same author**   Use the author's name for all entries. List the entries by year, the earliest first.

Coates, T. (2008). *The beautiful struggle*. Spiegel & Grau.

Coates, T. (2015). *Between the world and me*. Spiegel & Grau.

■ **8. Two or more works by the same author in the same year** List the works alphabetically by title. In the parentheses, following the year, add "a," "b," and so on. Use these same letters when giving the year in the in-text citation.

Bower, B. (2012a, December 15). Families in flux. *Science News, 182*(12), 16.

Bower, B. (2012b, November 3). Human-Neandertal mating gets a new

date. *Science News, 182*(9), 8.

■ **9. Editor** Begin with the name of the editor or editors; place the abbreviation "Ed." (or "Eds." for more than one editor) in parentheses following the name.

```
    editor          year                    title (book)
```
Yeh, K.-H. (Ed.). (2019). *Asian indigenous psychologies in the global context.*

```
        publisher
```
Palgrave Macmillan.

■ **10. Translator** Begin with the name of the author. After the title, in parentheses, place the name of the translator (in normal order) and the abbreviation "Trans." (for "Translator"). Add the original date of publication at the end of the entry.

Calasso, R. (2019). *The unnamable present* (R. Dixon, Trans.). Farrar,

Straus and Giroux. (Original work published 2017).

Articles and other short works

▶ Citation at a glance: Online article in a journal or magazine, page 509
▶ Citation at a glance: Article from a database, page 510

■ **11. Article in a journal** For an article from the web, give the DOI if available or include the URL for the article. If an article from a database has no DOI, do not include a URL.

a. Print

authors: last name + initial(s) year article title

Terry, C. P., & Terry, D. L. (2015). Cell phone-related near accidents among

journal title

young drivers: Associations with mindfulness. *The Journal of Psychology,*

volume,
issue page(s)

149(7), 665–683.

b. Web

all authors:
last name
+ initial(s) year article title

Bruns, A. (2019). The third shift: Multiple job holding and the incarceration of

journal title volume,
issue page(s)

women's partners. *Social Science Research, 80*(1), 202–215.

DOI

http://doi.org/dfgj

all authors:
last name + initial(s) year article title

Vicary, A. M., & Larsen, A. (2018). Potential factors influencing attitudes

toward veterans who commit crimes: An experimental investigation of

journal title (no volume available)

PTSD in the legal system. *Current Research in Social Psychology.*

URL for article

https://www.uiowa.edu/crisp/sites/uiowa.edu.crisp/files/crisp_vol_26_2.pdf

c. Database

author year article title

Maftsir, S. (2019). Emotional change: Romantic love and the university in

journal title volume,
issue page(s)

postcolonial Egypt. *Journal of Social History, 52*(3), 831–859.

DOI

https://doi.org/10.1093/jsh/shx155

■ **12. Article in a magazine** If an article from the web has no DOI, use the URL for the article. If an article from a database has no DOI, do not include a URL.

a. Print

author | year + month (monthly magazine) | article title | magazine title | volume, issue

Paris, W. (2015, March/April). The new survivors. *Psychology Today, 48*(2),

page(s)

66–73, 82.

b. Web

author | date of posting (when available) | article title

Srinivasan, D. (2019, June 4). How digital advertising markets really work.

magazine title | URL for article

The American Prospect. https://prospect.org/article/how-digital

-advertising-markets-really-work

c. Database

author | year + month (monthly magazine) | article title

Greengard, S. (2019, August). The algorithm that changed quantum

magazine title | volume, issue | page(s)

machine learning. *Communications of the ACM, 62*(8), 15–17.

DOI

http://doi.org/10.1145/3339458

■ **13. Article in a newspaper**

a. Print

author | year + month + day | article title

Finucane, M. (2019, September 25). Americans still eating too many

newspaper title | page

low-quality carbs. *The Boston Globe,* B2.

b. Web

author | year + month + day | article title

Daly, J. (2019, August 2). Duquesne's med school plan part of national

newspaper title | Shortened URL

trend to train more doctors. *Pittsburgh Post-Gazette.* http://bit.ly/2CbUZOX

CITATION AT A GLANCE

Online article in a journal or magazine (APA)

To cite an online article in a journal or magazine in APA style, include the following elements:

1 Author(s)
2 Year of publication for journal; complete date for magazine
3 Title and subtitle of article
4 Name of journal or magazine
5 Volume and issue numbers
6 DOI (digital object identifier), if article has one; otherwise, URL for article

Online article

REFERENCE LIST ENTRY FOR AN ONLINE ARTICLE IN A JOURNAL OR MAGAZINE

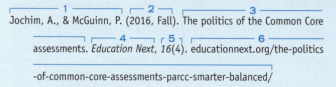

Jochim, A., & McGuinn, P. (2016, Fall). The politics of the Common Core assessments. *Education Next, 16*(4). educationnext.org/the-politics-of-common-core-assessments-parcc-smarter-balanced/

For more on citing online articles in APA style, see items 11–13.

CITATION AT A GLANCE
Article from a database (APA)

To cite an article from a database in APA style, include the following elements:

1 Author(s)
2 Year of publication for journal; complete date for magazine or newspaper
3 Title and subtitle of article
4 Name of periodical
5 Volume and issue numbers
6 Page number(s)
7 DOI (digital object identifier)

Database record

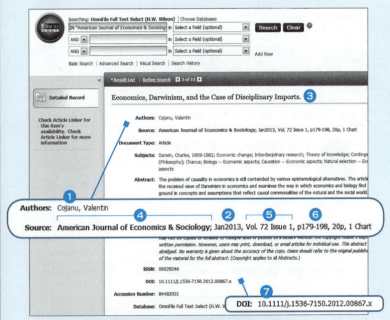

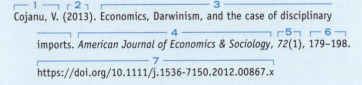

REFERENCE LIST ENTRY FOR AN ARTICLE FROM A DATABASE

┌─1─┐ ┌2┐ ┌─────────────── 3 ───────────────
Cojanu, V. (2013). Economics, Darwinism, and the case of disciplinary

┌──────────────── 4 ────────────────┐ ┌5┐ ┌─6─┐
imports. *American Journal of Economics & Sociology*, *72*(1), 179–198.

┌─────────────── 7 ───────────────┐
https://doi.org/10.1111/j.1536-7150.2012.00867.x

For more on citing articles from a database in APA style, see items 11–12.

■ **14. Supplemental material** If an article on the web contains supplemental material that is not part of the main article, cite the material as you would an article and add the label "Supplemental material" in brackets following the title.

Hansen, J. D., & Reich, J. (2015). Democratizing education? Examining

access and usage patterns in massive open online courses

[Supplemental material]. *Science, 350*(6265), 1245–1248.

https://doi.org/10.1126/science.290.5494.1148

■ **15. Letter to the editor** Insert the words "Letter to the editor" in brackets after the title of the letter. If the letter has no title, use the bracketed words as the title.

Doran, K. (2019, October 11). When the homeless look like grandma or

grandpa [Letter to the editor]. *The New York Times*. https://nyti.

ms/33foDOK

■ **16. Editorial or other unsigned article**

The business case for transit dollars [Editorial]. (2012, December 9). *Star

Tribune*. http://m.startribune.com/editorial-the-business-case-for

-transit-dollars/182608311/

■ **17. Review** In brackets, give the type of work reviewed, the title, and the director for a film or the author for a book.

author of review | year + month + day (magazine) | review title

Douthat, R. (2019, October 14). A hustle gone wrong [Review of the film

film title | magazine | volume, issue | page(s)

Hustlers, by L. Scafaria, Dir.]. *National Review, 71*(18), 47.

Hall, W. (2019). [Review of the book *How to change your mind: The

new science of psychedelics*, by M. Pollan]. *Addiction, 114*(10),

1892–1893. https://doi.org/10.1111/add.14702

■ **18. Published interview**

Remnick, D. (2019, July 1). Robert Caro reflects on Robert Moses, L.B.J.,
  and his own career in nonfiction. *The New Yorker*. https://bit.
  ly/2Lukm3X

■ **19. Article in a dictionary or an encyclopedia (including a wiki)**
When referencing an online, undated reference work entry, include the retrieval date. When referencing a work with archived
versions, like Wikipedia, use the date and URL of the archived
version you read.

Brue, A. W., & Wilmshurst, L. (2018). Adaptive behavior assessments.
  In B. B. Frey (Ed.), *The SAGE encyclopedia of educational research,
  measurement, and evaluation* (pp. 40–44). SAGE Publications.
  https://doi.org/10.4135/9781506326139.n21

Merriam-Webster. (n.d.). Adscititious. In *Merriam-Webster.com dictionary*.
  Retrieved September 5, 2019, from https://www.merriam-webster.
  com/dictionaryadscititious

■ **20. Comment on an online article**   Include the first 20 words of
the comment followed by the source article in brackets.

lollyl2. (2019, September 25). My husband works in IT in a major city down
  South. He is a permanent employee now, but for years [Comment on
  the article "The Google workers who voted to unionize in Pittsburgh
  are part of tech's huge contractor workforce"]. *Slate*. https://fyre.it
  /0RT8HmeL.4

■ **21. Paper or poster presented at a conference (unpublished)**

Wood, M. (2019, January 3–6). *The effects of an adult development course
  on students' perceptions of aging* [Poster session]. Forty-First Annual
  National Institute on the Teaching of Psychology, St. Pete Beach,
  FL, United States. https://nitop.org/resources/Documents/2019%20
  Poster%20Session%20II.pdf

Books and other long works

▶ Citation at a glance: Book, page 514

■ 22. Basic format for a book

a. Print

author(s):
last name
+ initial(s)   year   book title   publisher

Southard, S. (2015). *Nagasaki: Life after nuclear war.* Viking.

b. Web (or online library) Give the URL for the page where you accessed the book.

author(s) or
editor(s)   year   book title publisher   URL

Obama, M. (2018). *Becoming.* Crown. https://books.google.com/books

?id=YbtNDwAAQBAJ

c. E-book Include the DOI or, if a DOI is not available, the URL for the page from which you downloaded the book.

author(s) or
editor(s)   year   book title

Coates, T.-N. (2017). *We were eight years in power: An American tragedy.*

publisher   URL

One World. https://www.amazon.com/dp/B01MT734OD/

d. Database If the book has a DOI, include it. If not, do not list a URL or database name.

Dessler, A. E., & Parson, E. A. (2019). *The science and politics of*
    global climate change: A guide to the debate (3rd ed.). Cambridge
    University Press.

CITATION AT A GLANCE
Book (APA)

To cite a print book in APA style, include the following elements:

1 Author(s)
2 Year of publication
3 Title and subtitle
4 Publisher

Title page

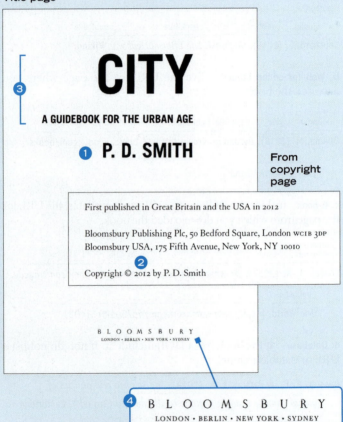

CITY

A GUIDEBOOK FOR THE URBAN AGE

❶ **P. D. SMITH**

From copyright page

First published in Great Britain and the USA in 2012

Bloomsbury Publishing Plc, 50 Bedford Square, London WC1B 3DP
Bloomsbury USA, 175 Fifth Avenue, New York, NY 10010

❷ Copyright © 2012 by P. D. Smith

BLOOMSBURY
LONDON · BERLIN · NEW YORK · SYDNEY

❹ BLOOMSBURY
LONDON · BERLIN · NEW YORK · SYDNEY

REFERENCE LIST ENTRY FOR A PRINT BOOK

┌── 1 ──┐ ┌─ 2 ─┐ ┌──────── 3 ────────┐ ┌── 4 ──┐
Smith, P. D. (2012). *City: A guidebook for the urban age*. Bloomsbury.

For more on citing books in APA style, see items 22–26.

514

■ **23. Edition other than the first**   Include the edition number (abbreviated) in parentheses after the title.

Harvey, P. (2013). *An introduction to Buddhism: Teachings, history, and practices* (2nd ed.). Cambridge University Press.

■ **24. Selection in an anthology or a collection**   An anthology is a collection of works on a common theme, often with different authors for the selections and usually with an editor for the entire volume.

a. Entire anthology

editor(s)   year

Amelina, A., Horvath, K., & Meeus, B. (Eds.). (2016). *An anthology of migration*

title of anthology   publisher

and social transformation: European perspectives. Springer.

b. Selection in an anthology

author of
selection   year   title of selection

Abdou, L. H. (2016). The Europeanization of immigration policies.

editors of anthology   title of anthology

In A. Amelina, K. Horvath, & B. Meeus (Eds.), *An anthology of*

migration and social transformation: European perspectives

page numbers
of selection   publisher

(pp. 105–119). Springer.

■ **25. Multivolume work**   If you have used only one volume of a multivolume work, indicate the volume number after the title of the complete work; if the volume has its own title, add that title after the volume number.

a. All volumes

Zeigler-Hill, V., & Shackelford, T. K. (Eds.). (2018). *The SAGE handbook of personality and individual differences* (Vols. I–III). SAGE Publications.

b. One volume, with title

Zeigler-Hill, V., & Shackelford, T. K. (Eds.). (2018). *The SAGE handbook of personality and individual differences: Vol. II. Origins of personality and individual differences*. SAGE Publications.

■ **26. Dictionary or other reference work**

Leong, F. T. L. (Ed.). (2008). *Encyclopedia of counseling* (Vols. 1–4). SAGE Publications.

■ **27. Dissertation**

Bacaksizlar, N. G. (2019). *Understanding social movements through simulations of anger contagion in social media* [Doctoral dissertation, University of North Carolina at Charlotte]. ProQuest Dissertations & Theses.

■ **28. Government document** If no author is listed, begin with the department that produced the document. Any broader organization listed can be included as the publisher of the document, as in the first example below. If a specific report number is provided, include it after the title.

National Park Service. (2019, April 11). *Travel where women made history: Ordinary and extraordinary places of American women*. U.S. Department of the Interior. https://www.nps.gov/subjects /travelwomenshistory/index.htm

Berchick, E. R., Barnett, J. C., & Upton, R. D. (2019, September 10). *Health insurance coverage in the United States: 2018* (Report No. P60-267). U.S. Census Bureau. https://www.census.gov/library /publications/2019/demo/p60-267.html

■ 29. Report from a private organization

Ford Foundation International Fellowships Program. (2019). *Leveraging higher education to promote social justice: Evidence from the IFP alumni tracking study.* https://p.widencdn.net/kei61u/IFP-Alumni -Tracking-Study-Report-5

■ 30. Legal source   The title of a court case is italicized in an in-text citation, but it is not italicized in the reference list.

Sweatt v. Painter, 339 U.S. 629 (1950). http://www.law.cornell.edu /supct/html/historics/USSC_CR_0339_0629_ZS.html

■ 31. Sacred or classical text

The Holy Bible 1611 edition: King James version. (2006). Hendrickson Publishers. (Original work published 1611)

Homer. (2018). *The odyssey* (E. Wilson, Trans.). W. W. Norton & Company. (Original work published ca. 675–725 B.C.E.)

Websites and parts of websites

► Citation at a glance: Page from a website, page 519

■ 32. Entire website   If you retrieved specific information from the home page of a website, include the website name, retrieval date, and URL in your reference list entry. If you mention the website in only a general way in the body of your paper, do not include it in your reference list. See item 12 in 61a.

■ 33. Page from a website   Use one of the models that follow only when your source doesn't fit into any other category. The following models are for content found on an interior page of a website and not published elsewhere. The website name follows the page title unless the author and website name are the same.

National Institute of Mental Health. (2016, March). *Seasonal affective disorder.* National Institutes of Health. https://www.nimh.nih.gov /health/topics/seasonal-affective-disorder/index.shtml

BBC News. (2019, October 31). *Goats help save Ronald Reagan Presidential Library*. bbc.com/news/world-us-canada-50248549

■ **34. Document on a website** Most documents published on websites fall into other categories, such as an article, a government document, or a report from an organization (items 11, 28, and 29).

author(s): last name + initials — year — document title
Tahseen, M., Ahmed, S., & Ahmed, S. (2018). *Bullying of Muslim youth:*

website
A review of research and recommendations. The Family and Youth

URL
Institute. http://www.thefyi.org/wp-content/uploads/2018/10

/FYI-Bullying-Report.pdf

■ **35. Blog post** Cite a blog post as you would an article in a periodical.

Fister, B. (2019, February 14). Information literacy's third wave. *Library Babel Fish*. https://www.insidehighered.com/blogs/library-babel -fish/information-literacy%E2%80%99s-third-wave

■ **36. Blog comment** Use a screen name if the writer's real name is not given. Give the comment title, if any, or up to the first twenty words of the comment.

Mollie F. (2019, February 14). It's a daunting task, isn't it? Last year, I got a course on Scholarly Communication and Information Literacy approved for [Comment on the blog post "Information literacy's third wave"]. *Library Babel Fish*. http://disq.us/p/1zr92uc

CITATION AT A GLANCE
Page from a website (APA)

To cite a page from a website in APA style, include the following elements:

1 Author(s)
2 Date of publication or most recent update ("n.d." if there is no date)
3 Title of web page
4 Name of website (if not the same as the author)
5 URL of web page

Page from a website

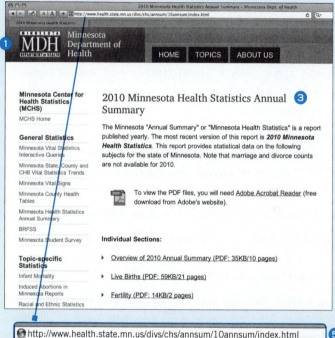

519

REFERENCE LIST ENTRY FOR A PAGE FROM A WEBSITE

———— 1 ———— ⌐2⌐ ———— 3 ————
Minnesota Department of Health. (n.d.). *2010 Minnesota health*

————————————————⌐ ⌐———— 5 ————————
statistics annual summary. http://www.health.state.mn.us

————————————————————⌐
/divs/chs/annsum/10annsum/index.html

For more on citing websites in APA style, see items 32–34.

Audio, visual, and multimedia sources

■ **37. Podcast**

Abumrad, J., & Krulwich, R. (Hosts). (2002–present). *Radiolab* [Audio
podcast]. WNYC Studios. https://www.wnycstudios.org/podcasts/
radiolab/podcasts

Longoria, J. (Host & Producer). (2019, April 19). Americanish [Audio
podcast episode]. In J. Abumrad & R. Krulwich (Hosts), *Radiolab*.
WNYC Studios. https://www.wnycstudios.org/podcasts/radiolab/
articles/americanish

■ **38. Video or audio on the web (YouTube, TED Talk)**

The New York Times. (2018, January 9). *Taking a knee and taking
down a monument* [Video]. YouTube. https://www.youtube.com
/watch?v=qY34DQCdUvQ

Wray, B. (2019, May). *How climate change affects your mental health*
[Video]. TED. https://www.ted.com/talks/britt_wray_how_climate
_change_affects_your_mental_health

■ **39. Transcript of an audio or video file**

Gopnik, A. (2019, July 10). *A separate kind of intelligence* [Video
transcript]. Edge. https://www.edge.org/conversation/
alison_gopnik-a-separate-kind-of-intelligence

■ **40. Film (DVD, BD, or other format)**   If the film is a special version, like an extended cut, include that information in brackets
after the title.

Peele, J. (Director). (2017). *Get out* [Film]. Universal Pictures.

Hitchcock, A. (Director). (1959). *The essentials collection: North by northwest* [Film; special ed. on DVD]. Metro-Goldwyn-Mayer; Universal Pictures Home Entertainment.

■ 41. TV or radio series or episode

Waller-Bridge, P., Williams, H., & Williams, J. (Executive Producers). (2016–2019). *Fleabag* [TV series]. Two Brothers Pictures; BBC.

Waller-Bridge, P. (Writer), & Bradbeer, H. (Director). (2019, March 18). The provocative request (Season 2, Episode 3) [TV series episode]. In P. Waller-Bridge, H. Williams, & J. Williams (Executive Producers), *Fleabag*. Two Brothers Pictures; BBC.

■ 42. Music recording

Nielsen, C. (2014). *Carl Nielsen: Symphonies 1 & 4* [Album recorded by New York Philharmonic Orchestra]. Dacapo Records. (Original work published 1892–1916)

Carlile, B. (2018). The mother [Song]. On *By the way, I forgive you*. Low Country Sound; Elektra.

■ 43. Lecture, speech, address, or recorded interview Cite the speaker or interviewee as the author.

Warren, E. (2019, September 16). *Senator Elizabeth Warren speech in Washington Square Park* [Speech video recording]. C-SPAN. https://www.c-span.org/video/?464314-1/ senator-elizabeth-warren-campaigns-york-city

■ 44. Data set or graphic representation of data (chart, table)

Reid, L. (2019). *Smarter homes: Experiences of living in low carbon homes 2013–2018* [Data set]. UK Data Service. http://doi.org/10.5255 /UKDA-SN-853485

Pew Research Center. (2018, November 15). *U.S. public is closely divided about overall health risk from food additives* [Chart]. https://www.pewresearch.org/science/2018/11/19/public-perspectives-on-food-risks/

■ **45. Mobile app** Begin with the developer of the app, if known.

Google. (2019). *Google Earth* (Version 9.3.3) [Mobile app]. App Store. https://apps.apple.com/us/app/google-earth/id293622097

■ **46. Video game**

ConcernedApe. (2016). *Stardew Valley* [Video game]. Chucklefish.

■ **47. Map**

Desjardins, J. (2017, November 17). *Walmart nation: Mapping the largest employers in the U.S.* [Map]. Visual Capitalist. https://www.visualcapitalist.com/walmart-nation-mapping-largest-employers-u-s/

■ **48. Advertisement**

Wieden+Kennedy. (2018, September). Nike: Dream crazy [Advertisement]. https://www.wk.com/work/nike-dream-crazy/

■ **49. Work of art or photograph**

O'Keeffe, G. (1931). *Cow's skull: Red, white, and blue* [Painting]. Metropolitan Museum of Art, New York, NY, United States. https://www.metmuseum.org/art/collection/search/488694

Browne, M. (1963). *The burning monk* [Photograph]. Time. http://100photos.time.com/photos/malcolm-browne-burning-monk

■ **50. Brochure or fact sheet**

National Council of State Boards of Nursing. (2014). *A nurse's guide to professional boundaries* [Brochure]. https://www.ncsbn.org/

World Health Organization. (2015, December). *Food safety* (No. 399) [Fact sheet]. http://www.who.int/mediacentre/factsheets/fs399/en/

■ **51. Press release**

New York University. (2019, September 5). *NYU Oral Cancer Center awarded*
    $2.5 million NIH grant to study cancer pain [Press release]. https://
    www.nyu.edu/about/news-publications/news/2019/september/nyu
    -oral-cancer-center-awarded—2-5-million-nih-grant-to-study-c.html

■ **52. Lecture notes or other course materials**   Cite posted materials as you would a web page or document on a website (see items 33–34). Cite material from your instructor that is not available to others as personal communication in the text of your paper (see item 13 in 61a).

Chatterjee, S., Constenla, D., Kinghorn, A., & Mayora, C. (2018).
    Teaching vaccine economics everywhere: Costing in vaccine planning
    and programming [Lecture notes and slides]. Department of
    Population, Family, and Reproductive Health, Johns Hopkins
    University. http://ocw.jhsph.edu/index.cfm/go/viewCourse/course
    /TeachVaccEconCosting/coursePage/lectureNotes/

Social media

■ **53. Email**   Email messages, letters, and other personal communication are not included in the list of references. See item 13 in 61a for citing these sources in the text of your paper.

■ **54. Social media post**   If the writer's real name and screen name are given, put the real name first, followed by the screen name in brackets. If only the screen name is known, begin with the screen name, not in brackets. For the title, include up to twenty words (including hashtags or emojis) of the title or caption. After the title, list any attachments (such as a photo or link) and the type of post in separate brackets. List the website or app in the publisher position. Include the URL for the post. Cite posts that are not accessible to all readers as personal communication in the text of your paper.

National Science Foundation [@NSF]. (2019, October 13). *Understanding*
    how forest structure drives carbon sequestration is important for
    ecologists, climate modelers and forest managers, who are working
    on [Thumbnail with link attached] [Tweet]. Twitter. https://twitter.
    com/NSF/status/1183388649263652864

Georgia Aquarium. (2019, June 25). *True love* [[two hearts emoj]] *Charlie and Lizzy are a bonded pair of African penguins who have been together for more than* [Image attached] [Status update]. Facebook. https://www.facebook.com/GeorgiaAquarium/photos/a.163898398123 /10156900637543124/?type=3&theater

Smithsonian [@smithsonian]. (2019, October 7). *You're looking at a ureilite meteorite under a microscope. When illuminated with polarized light, they appear in dazzling colors, influenced* [Photograph]. Instagram. https://www.instagram.com/p /B3VI27yHLQG/

■ **55. Social media profile or highlight** Because profiles are designed to change over time, include the date you viewed the webpage.

National Science Foundation [@NSF]. (n.d.). *Tweets* [Twitter profile]. Twitter. Retrieved October 15, 2019, from https://twitter.com/NSF

Smithsonian [@smithsonian]. (n.d.). *#Apollo50* [Highlight]. Instagram. Retrieved October 15, 2019, from https://www.instagram.com/ stories/highlights/17902787752343364/

62 APA format; sample research paper

The guidelines in this section are consistent with advice given in the *Publication Manual of the American Psychological Association*, 7th ed. (2020), and with typical requirements for undergraduate papers.

62a APA format

Formatting the paper: The basics

The guidelines in 62a describe APA's recommendations for a paper written for an undergraduate college course and for preparing the reference list. A title page appears here; the full paper appears in section 62b.

Sample title page for an undergraduate paper

**Technology and the Shift From Teacher-Delivered to
Student-Centered Learning: A Review of the Literature**

April Bo Wang

Department of Education, Glen County Community College

EDU 107: Education, Technology, and Media

Dr. Julien Gomez

October 29, XXXX

Formatting the paper: Other concerns

Capitalization, italics, and quotation marks   In headings and in titles of works that appear in the text of the paper, capitalize all words of four letters or more (and all nouns, pronouns, verbs, adjectives, and adverbs of any length). Capitalize the first word following a colon in a title or a heading. Capitalize the first word following a colon if the word begins a complete sentence.

In the body of your paper, italicize the titles of books, journals, magazines, and other long works, including websites. Use quotation marks around the titles of articles, short stories, and other short works named in the body of your paper.

NOTE: APA has different requirements for titles in the reference list. See "Preparing the list of references" later in this section.

Long quotations   When a quotation is forty or more words, indent it one-half inch from the left margin. Double-space the quotation. Do not use quotation marks around it. (See 62b for an example.)

Footnotes   Insert footnotes using the footnote function of your word processing program. The number in the text should immediately follow a word or any mark of punctuation except a dash. The text of the footnote should be single-spaced.

Abstract and keywords (typically not required for an undergraduate paper)   If your assignment requires an abstract—a 150-to-250-word summary paragraph—include it on a new page after the title page. Center the word "Abstract" (in bold) one inch from the top of the page. Double-space the abstract and do not indent the first line. See the end of 62b for an example of an abstract.

An optional list of keywords may follow the abstract; the keywords help readers search for a published paper on the web or in a database.

Headings   Although headings are not always necessary, their use is encouraged in the social sciences. For most undergraduate papers, one level of heading is usually sufficient. (See 62b.)

First-level headings are centered and boldface. In research papers and laboratory reports, the major headings are "Method," "Results," and "Discussion." In other types of papers, the major headings should be informative and concise, conveying the structure of the paper.

Second-level headings are left-aligned and boldface. Third-level headings are left-aligned, italic, and boldface.

In first- and second-level headings, capitalize the first and last words and all words of four or more letters (and nouns, pronouns, verbs, adjectives, and adverbs of any length). In third-level headings, capitalize only the first word, any proper nouns, and the first word after a colon.

First-Level Heading Centered

Second-Level Heading Aligned Left

Third-level Heading Aligned Left

Visuals (tables and figures)

APA classifies visuals as tables and figures (figures include graphs, charts, drawings, and photographs). Place each visual after the paragraph in which it is called out, or on the following page if it does not fit on the same page as the callout.

Tables   Number each table (Table 1, Table 2) and provide a clear title. The label and title should appear on separate lines above the table, flush left and double-spaced. Type the table number in bold font; italicize the table title.

Table 2

Effect of Nifedipine (Procardia) on Blood Pressure in Women

If you have used data from an outside source or have taken or adapted the table from a source, give the source information in a note below the table. Begin with the word "Note," italicized and followed by a period. If you use lettered footnotes to explain specific data in the table, those footnotes begin on a new line after the source information.

Figures Like tables, number each figure in bold and include a title in italic font. If you have taken or adapted the figure from an outside source, give the source information in a note underneath the figure, starting with the word "Note" in italic and followed by a period. Use the term "From" or "Adapted from" before the source information. Notes can also give additional information or context for the figure.

Preparing the list of references

Begin your list of references on a new page at the end of the paper. Center the title "References" in bold one inch from the top of the page. Double-space throughout. For a sample reference list, see 62b.

Indenting entries Type the first line of each entry at the left margin and indent any additional lines one-half inch.

Alphabetizing the list Alphabetize the reference list by the last names of the authors (or editors) or by the first word of an organization name (if the author is an organization). When a work has no author or editor, alphabetize by the first word of the title other than "A," "An," or "The."

If your list includes two or more works by the same author, arrange the entries by year, the earliest first. If your list includes two or more works by the same author in the same year, arrange the works alphabetically by title. Add the letters "a," "b," and so on within the parentheses after the year. For journal articles, use only the year and the letter: (2012a). For articles in magazines and newspapers, use the full date and the letter in the reference list: (2012a, July 7); use only the year and the letter in the in-text citation.

Authors' names Invert all authors' names and use initials instead of first names. Separate the names with commas. For two to twenty authors, use an ampersand (&) before the last author's name. For twenty-one or more authors, give the first nineteen authors, three ellipsis dots, and the last author (see item 3 in 61b).

Titles of books and articles In the reference list, italicize the titles and subtitles of books. Do not italicize or use quotation marks around the titles of articles and other stand-alone works. For both books and articles, capitalize only the first word of the title and subtitle (and all proper nouns). Capitalize names of journals, magazines, and newspapers as you would normally (see 45c).

APA

Abbreviations for page numbers Abbreviations for "page" and "pages" ("p." and "pp.") are used before page numbers of selections in anthologies (see item 24 on p. 515). Do not use "p." or "pp." before page numbers of articles in journals and magazines (see items 11 and 12 on pp. 506–08).

Breaking a URL or DOI Do not insert any line breaks into URLs or DOIs (digital object identifier). Any line breaks that your word processor makes automatically are acceptable. Do not add a period at the end of the URL or DOI.

62b Sample APA research paper

Courtesy April Bo Wang

On the following pages is a research paper on the use of educational technology in the shift to student-centered learning, written by April Wang, a student in an education class. Wang's assignment was to write a literature review paper documented with APA-style citations and references.

1

Technology and the Shift From Teacher-Delivered to
Student-Centered Learning: A Review of the Literature

April Bo Wang

Department of Education, Glen County Community College

EDU 107: Education, Technology, and Media

Dr. Julien Gomez

October 29, XXXX

2

Technology and the Shift From Teacher-Delivered to Student-Centered Learning: A Review of the Literature

In the United States, most public school systems are struggling with teacher shortages, which are projected to worsen as the number of applicants to education schools decreases (Donitsa-Schmidt & Zuzovsky, 2014, p. 420). Citing federal data, *The New York Times* reported a 30% drop in "people entering teacher preparation programs" between 2010 and 2014 (Rich, 2015, para. 10). Especially in science and math fields, the teacher shortage is projected to escalate in the next 10 years (Hutchison, 2012). In recent decades, instructors and administrators have viewed the practice of student-centered learning as one promising solution. Unlike traditional teacher-delivered (also called "transmissive") instruction, student-centered learning allows students to help direct their own education by setting their own goals and selecting appropriate resources for achieving those goals. Though student-centered learning might once have been viewed as an experimental solution in understaffed schools, it is gaining credibility as an effective pedagogical practice. What is also gaining momentum is the idea that technology might play a significant role in fostering student-centered learning. This literature review will examine three key questions:

1. In what ways is student-centered learning effective?
2. Can educational technology help students drive their own learning?
3. How can public schools effectively combine teacher talent and educational technology?

Sources provide background information and context.

An in-text citation includes a paragraph number or other locator for a quotation from a source without page numbers.

Wang sets up her organization by posing three questions.

3

In the face of mounting teacher shortages, public schools should embrace educational technology that promotes student-centered learning in order to help all students become engaged and successful learners.

In What Ways Is Student-Centered Learning Effective?

According to the International Society for Technology in Education (2016), "Student-centered learning moves students from passive receivers of information to active participants in their own discovery process. What students learn, how they learn it, and how their learning is assessed are all driven by each individual student's needs and abilities" (What Is It? section). The results of student-centered learning have been positive, not only for academic achievement but also for student self-esteem. In this model of instruction, the teacher acts as a facilitator, and the students actively participate in the process of learning and teaching. With guidance, students decide on the learning goals most pertinent to themselves, they devise a learning plan that will most likely help them achieve those goals, they direct themselves in carrying out that learning plan, and they assess how much they learned (Çubukçu, 2012, Introduction section). The major differences between student-centered learning and instructor-centered learning are summarized in Table 1.

Bell (2010) has argued that the chief benefit of student-centered learning is that it can connect students with "real-world tasks," thus making learning more engaging as well as more comprehensive (p. 42). For example, Bell observed a group of middle-school students who wanted to build a social justice monument

---

Wang states her thesis.

Headings, centered and boldface, help readers follow the organization.

Wang uses a source to define the key term "student-centered learning."

A locator (section title) is included for a paraphrase to help readers find the source in a long article without page numbers.

4

Table 1

Comparison of Two Approaches to Teaching and Learning

Teaching and learning period	Instructor-centered approach	Student-centered approach
Before class	• Instructor prepares a lecture/instruction on new topic. • Students complete homework on previous topic.	• Students read and view new material, practice new concepts, and prepare questions ahead of class. • Instructor views student practice and questions, identifies learning opportunities.
During class	• Instructor delivers new material in a lecture or prepared discussion. • Students—unprepared—listen, watch, take notes, and try to follow along with the new material.	• Students lead discussions of the new material or practice applying the concepts or skills in an active environment. • Instructor answers student questions and provides immediate feedback.
After class	• Instructor grades homework and gives feedback about the previous lesson. • Students work independently to practice or apply the new concepts.	• Students apply concepts/skills to more complex tasks, some of their own choosing, individually and in groups. • Instructor posts additional resources to help students.

Note. Adapted from *The Flipped Class Demystified*, by New York University, n.d. (https://www.nyu.edu/faculty/teaching-and-learning-resources/instructional-technology-support/instructional-design-assessment/flipped-classes/the-flipped-class-demystified.html).

Wang creates a table to compare and contrast two key concepts for her readers.

5

for their school. They researched social justice issues, selected several to focus on, and then designed a three-dimensional playground to represent those issues. In doing so, they achieved learning goals in the areas of social studies, physics, and mathematics and practiced research and teamwork. Students engaged in this kind of learning performed better on both project-based assessments and standardized tests (Bell, 2010).

A Stanford study came to a similar conclusion; researchers examined four schools that had moved from teacher-driven instruction to student-centered learning (Friedlaender et al., 2014). The study focused on students from a mix of racial, cultural, and socioeconomic backgrounds, with varying levels of English-language proficiency. The researchers predicted that this mix of students, representing differing levels of academic ability, would benefit from a student-centered approach. Through interviews, surveys, and classroom observations, the researchers identified key characteristics of the new student-centered learning environments at the four schools:

- teachers who prioritized building relationships with students
- support structures for teachers to improve and collaborate on instruction
- a shift in classroom activity from lectures and tests to projects and performance-based assessments (pp. 5–7)

After the schools designed their curriculum to be personalized to individual students rather than standardized

A page number or other locator is not necessary for a paraphrase from a short article.

In a citation of a work with three or more authors, the first author's name is given followed by "et al." in parentheses or in a text sentence.

The author's name and year of publication are given in a signal phrase, so page numbers are provided at the end of the paraphrase.

6

across a diverse student body and to be inclusive of
skills such as persistence as well as traditional academic
skills, students outperformed peers on state tests and
increased their rates of high school and college graduation
(Friedlaender et al., 2014, p. 3).

Can Educational Technology Help Students Drive Their Own Learning?

When students engage in self-directed learning, they
rely less on teachers to deliver information and require less
face-to-face time with teachers. For content delivery, many
school districts have begun to use educational technology
resources that, in recent years, have become more available,
more affordable, and easier to use. For the purposes of
this paper, the term "educational technology resources"
encompasses the following: distance learning, by which
students learn from a remote instructor online; other online
education programming such as slide shows and video or
audio lectures; interactive online activities, such as quizzing
or games; and the use of computers, tablets, smartphones,
SMART Boards, or other such devices for coursework.

Much like student-centered learning, the use of
educational technology began in many places as a temporary
measure to keep classes running despite teacher shortages.
A Horn and Staker study (2011) examined the major patterns
over time for students who subscribed to distance learning,
for example. A decade ago, students who enrolled in distance
learning often fell into one of the following categories:
They lived in a rural community that had no alternative
for learning; they attended a school where there were
not enough qualified teachers to teach certain subjects;

Wang develops her thesis.

In a signal phrase, the word "and" links the names of two authors; the date is given in parentheses.

7

or they were homeschooled or homebound. But faced with tighter budgets, teacher shortages, increasingly diverse student populations, and rigorous state standards, schools recognized the need and the potential for distance learning across the board.

As the teacher shortage has intensified, educational technology resources have become more tailored to student needs and more affordable. Pens that convert handwritten notes to digital text and organize them, backpacks that charge electronic devices, and apps that create audiovisual flash cards are just a few of the more recent innovations. According to Svokos (2015), some educational technology resources entertain students while supporting student-centered learning:

> GlassLab, a nonprofit that was launched with grants from the Bill & Melinda Gates and MacArthur Foundations, creates educational games that are now being used in more than 6,000 classrooms across the country. Some of the company's games are education versions of existing ones—for example, its first release was SimCity EDU—while others are originals. Teachers get real-time updates on students' progress as well as suggestions on what subjects they need to spend more time perfecting. (5. Educational Games section)

Many of the companies behind these products offer institutional discounts to schools where such devices are used widely by students and teachers.

Horn and Staker (2011) concluded that the chief benefit of technological learning was that it could adapt to the individual

A quotation of 40 or more words is indented without quotation marks.

A locator (section title) is used for a direct quotation from an online source with no page numbers.

student in a way that whole-class delivery by a single teacher could not. Their study examined various schools where technology enabled student-centered learning. For example, Carpe Diem High School in Yuma, Arizona, hired only six certified subject teachers and then outfitted its classrooms with 280 computers connected to online learning programs. The programs included software that offered "continual feedback, assessment, and incremental victory in a way that a face-to-face teacher with a class of 30 students never could. After each win, students continue to move forward at their own pace" (p. 9). Students alternated between personalized 55-minute courses online and 55-minute courses with one of the six teachers. The academic outcomes were promising. Carpe Diem ranked first in its county for student math and reading scores. Similarly, Rocketship Education, a charter network that serves low-income, predominantly Latino students, created a digital learning lab, reducing the need to hire more teachers. Rocketship's academic scores ranked in the top 15 of all California low-income public schools.

It is clear that educational technology will continue to play a role in student and school performance. Horn and Staker (2011) acknowledged that they focused on programs in which integration of educational technology led to improved student performance. In other schools, technological learning is simply distance learning—watching a remote teacher—and not student-centered learning that allows students to partner with teachers to develop enriching learning experiences. That said, many educators seem convinced that educational technology has the potential to help them transition from traditional teacher-driven learning to student-centered learning.

Wang uses her own analysis to shape the conversation among her sources in this synthesis paragraph.

9

All four schools in the Stanford study heavily relied on technology (Friedlaender et al., 2014). And indeed, Demski (2012) argued that technology is not supplemental but instead is "central" to student-centered learning (p. 33). Rather than turning to a teacher as the source of information, students are sent to investigate solutions to problems by searching online, emailing experts, collaborating with one another in a wiki space, or completing online practice. Rather than turning to a teacher for the answer to a question, students are driven to perform—driven to use technology to find those answers themselves.

How Can Public Schools Effectively Combine Teacher Talent and Educational Technology?

Some researchers have expressed doubt that schools are ready for student-centered learning—or any type of instruction—that is driven by technology. In a recent survey conducted by the Nellie Mae Education Foundation, Moeller and Reitzes (2011) reported not only that many teachers lacked confidence in their ability to incorporate technology in the classroom but that 43% of polled high school students said that they lacked confidence in their technological proficiency going into college and careers. The study concluded that technology alone would not improve learning environments. Yet others argued that students adapt quickly to even unfamiliar technology and use it to further their own learning. For example, Mitra (2013) caught the attention of the education world with his study of how to educate students in the slums of India. He installed an Internet-accessible computer in a wall in a New Delhi urban slum and left it there with no instructions. Over a few months, many of the children had learned how to use

Wang uses a source to introduce a counterargument.

the computer, how to access information over the Internet, how to interpret information, and how to communicate this information to one another. Mitra's experiment was "not about making learning happen. [It was] about letting it happen" (16:31). He concluded that in the absence of teachers, even in developing countries less inundated by technology, a tool that allowed access to an organized database of knowledge (such as a search engine) was sufficient to provide students with a rewarding learning experience.

> Brackets indicate Wang's change in the quoted material.

> For a direct quotation from a video, a time stamp indicates the start of the quotation.

According to the Stanford study, however, the presence of teachers is still crucial (Friedlaender et al., 2014). Their roles will simply change from distributors of knowledge to facilitators and supporters of self-directed student-centered learning. The researchers asserted that teacher education and professional development programs can no longer prepare their teachers in a single instructional mode, such as teacher-delivered learning; they must instead equip teachers with a wide repertoire of skills to support a wide variety of student learning experiences. The Stanford study argued that since teachers would be partnering with students to shape the learning experience, rather than designing and delivering a curriculum on their own, the main job of a teacher would become relationship building. The teacher would establish a relationship with each student so that the teacher could support whatever learning the student pursues.

Many schools have already effectively paired a reduced faculty with educational technology to support successful student-centered learning. For example, Watson (2008) offered a case study of the Cincinnati Public Schools Virtual High School, which brought students together in a physical school building to work with an assortment of

11

online learning programs. Although there were only 10 certified teachers in the building, students were able to engage in highly individualized instruction according to their own needs, strengths, and learning styles, using the 10 teachers as support (p. 7). Commonwealth Connections Academy (CCA), a public school in Pennsylvania, also brings students into a physical school building to engage in digital curriculum. However, rather than having students identify their own learning goals and design their own curriculum around those goals, CCA uses educational technology as an assessment tool to identify areas of student weakness. It then partners students with teachers to address those areas (pp. 8–9).

Conclusion

The tone of the conclusion is objective and presents answers to Wang's three organizational questions.

Public education faces the opportunity for a shift from the model of teacher-delivered instruction that has characterized American public schools since their foundation to a student-centered learning model. Not only has student-centered learning proved effective in improving student academic and developmental outcomes, but it can also synchronize with technological learning for widespread adaptability across schools. Because it relies on student direction rather than an established curriculum, student-centered learning supported by educational technology can adapt to the different needs of individual students and a variety of learning environments—urban and rural, well funded and underfunded. Similarly, when student-centered learning relies on technology rather than a corps of uniformly trained teachers, it holds promise for schools that would otherwise suffer from a lack of human or financial resources.

12

References

Bell, S. (2010). Project-based learning for the 21st century: Skills for the future. *The Clearing House, 83*(2), 39–43.

Çubukçu, Z. (2012). Teachers' evaluation of student-centered learning environments. *Education, 133*(1).

Demski, J. (2012, January). This time it's personal. *THE Journal (Technological Horizons in Education), 39*(1), 32–36.

Donitsa-Schmidt, S., & Zuzovsky, R. (2014). Teacher supply and demand: The school level perspective. *American Journal of Educational Research, 2*(6), 420–429. https://doi.org/10.12691/education-2-6-14

Friedlaender, D., Burns, D., Lewis-Charp, H., Cook-Harvey, C. M., & Darling-Hammond, L. (2014). *Student-centered schools: Closing the opportunity gap* [Research brief]. Stanford Center for Opportunity Policy in Education. https://edpolicy.stanford.edu/sites/default/files /scope-pub-student-centered-research-brief.pdf

Horn, M. B., & Staker, H. (2011). *The rise of K-12 blended learning.* Innosight Institute. http:// www .christenseninstitute.org/wp-content/uploads/2013/04 /The-rise-of-K-12-blended-learning.pdf

Hutchison, L. F. (2012). Addressing the STEM teacher shortage in American schools: Ways to recruit and retain effective STEM teachers. *Action in Teacher Education, 34*(5/6), 541–550. https://doi.org/10.1080 /01626620.2012.729483

International Society for Technology in Education. (2016). *Student-centered learning.* http://www.iste.org /connected/standards/essential-conditions/student -centered-learning

List of references begins on a new page. Heading is centered and boldface.

List is alphabetized by authors' last names. All authors' names are inverted.

The first line of an entry is at the left margin; subsequent lines indent ½″.

Double-spacing is used throughout.

13

Mitra, S. (2013, February). *Build a school in the cloud* [Video]. TED. https://www.ted.com/talks/sugata_mitra _build_a_school_in_the_cloud?language=en

Moeller, B., & Reitzes, T. (2011, July). *Integrating technology with student-centered learning.* Nellie Mae Education Foundation. http://www.nmefoundation .org/research/personalization/integrating-technology -with-student-centered-learn

Rich, M. (2015, August 9). Teacher shortages spur a nationwide hiring scramble (credentials optional). *The New York Times.* https://nyti.ms/1WaaV7a

Svokos, A. (2015, May 7). 5 innovations from the past decade that aim to change the American classroom. *Huffpost.* https://www.huffpost.com/entry/ technology-changes-classrooms_n_7190910

Watson, J. (2008, January). *Blended learning: The convergence of online and face-to-face education.* North American Council for Online Learning. http:// www .inacol.org/wp-content/uploads/2015/02/NACOL_PP -BlendedLearning-lr.pdf

Abstract and running head (for professional papers)

For professional papers: running head (short form of the title; 50 characters or fewer) in all capital letters on every page; title "Abstract" centered and boldface

Abstract

In recent decades, instructors and administrators have viewed student-centered learning as a promising pedagogical practice that offers both the hope of increasing academic performance and a solution for teacher shortages. Differing from the traditional model of instruction in which a teacher delivers content from the front of a classroom, student-centered learning puts the students at the center of teaching and learning. Students set their own learning goals, select appropriate resources, and progress at their own pace. Student-centered learning has produced both positive results and increases in students' self-esteem. Given the recent proliferation of technology in classrooms, school districts are poised for success in making the shift to student-centered learning. The question for district leaders, however, is how to effectively balance existing teacher talent with educational technology.

Keywords: digital learning, student-centered learning, personalized learning, education technology, transmissive, blended

An abstract is required for professional papers submitted for publication.

Keywords help readers search for a paper online or in a database.

APPENDIX

Models of professional writing

Good document design promotes readability and increases the chances that you will achieve your purpose for writing and reach your readers. How you design a document — how you format it for the printed page or for a computer screen, for example — affects your readers' response to it. Most readers have expectations about document design and format, usually depending on the context and the purpose of the piece of writing.

This gallery features pages from business documents. The annotations on the sides of the pages point out design choices as well as important features of the writing.

- ▶ Page from a business report (showing a visual), 546
- ▶ Business letter, 547
- ▶ Résumé, 548
- ▶ Professional memo, 549

Standard academic formatting

Use the manuscript format that is recommended for your academic discipline. In most English and some other humanities classes, you will be asked to use MLA (Modern Language Association) format (see 57). In most social science classes, such as psychology and sociology, and in most business, education, and health-related classes, you'll be asked to use APA (American Psychological Association) format (see 62).

Standard professional formatting

It helps to look at examples when you are preparing to write a professional document such as a letter, a memo, or a résumé. In general, business and professional writing is direct, clear, and courteous, and documents are designed to be read easily and quickly. When writing less formal documents such as email messages in academic contexts, it is just as important to craft the document for easy readability.

Business report with a visual

Report formatted in typical business style, with citations in APA style.

Doug Ames, manager of operations for OAISYS, noted that some of these issues keep the company from outperforming expectations: "Communication is not timely or uniform, expectations are not clear and consistent, and some employees do not contribute significantly yet nothing is done" (personal communication, February 28, 2006).

Recommendations

It appears that a combination of steps can be used to unlock greater performance for OAISYS. Most important, steps can be taken to strengthen the corporate culture in key areas such as communication, accountability, and appreciation. Employee feedback indicates that these are areas of weakness or motivators that can be improved. This feedback is summarized in Figure 1.

Visual referred to in body of report.

A plan to use communication effectively to set expectations, share results in a timely fashion, and publicly offer appreciation to specific contributors will likely go a long way toward aligning individual motivation with corporate goals. Additionally, holding individuals accountable for results will bring parity to the workplace.

Figure, a bar graph, appears at bottom of page on which it is mentioned. Figure number and caption are placed below figure.

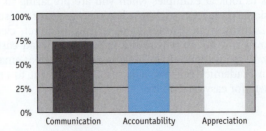

Figure 1. Areas of greatest need for improvements in motivation.

Business letter in full block style

LatinoVoice

March 16, 2017 ————— Date

Jonathan Ríos
Managing Editor   Inside
Latino World Today   address
2971 East Oak Avenue
Baltimore, MD 21201

Dear Mr. Ríos: ————— Salutation

Thank you very much for taking the time yesterday to speak to the   Paragraphs
University of Maryland's Latino Club. A number of students have   single-spaced,
told me that they enjoyed your presentation and found your job   not indented;
search suggestions to be extremely helpful.   double-spacing
                                between
As I mentioned to you, the club publishes a monthly newsletter,   paragraphs.
Latino Voice. Our purpose is to share up-to-date information and
expert advice with members of the university's Latino population.
Considering how much students benefited from your talk, I would
like to publish excerpts from it in our newsletter.   Body

I have transcribed parts of your presentation and organized them
into a question-and-answer format for our readers. Would you mind
looking through the enclosed article and letting me know if I may
have your permission to print it? I'm hoping to include this article
in our next newsletter, so I would need your response by April 4.

Once again, Mr. Ríos, thank you for sharing your experiences with
us. I would love to be able to share your thoughts with students
who couldn't hear you in person.

Sincerely, ————————— Close

Jeffrey Richardson

Jeffrey Richardson   Signature
Associate Editor

                          Indicates
Enc. ————————————— something
                          enclosed
                          with letter.

210 Student Center University of Maryland College Park MD 20742

Résumé

Limit résumé to one page if possible, two pages at most.

Alexis A. Smith

404 Ponce de Leon NE, #B7   404-231-1234
Atlanta, GA 30308   asmith@smith.localhost

SKILLS SUMMARY

- Writing: competent communicating to different audiences, using a range of written forms (articles, reports, flyers, pamphlets, memos, letters)
- Design: capable of creating visually appealing, audience-appropriate documents; skilled at taking and editing photographs
- Technical: proficient in Microsoft Office; comfortable with Dreamweaver, Photoshop, InDesign
- Language: fluent in spoken and written Spanish

EDUCATION

Bachelor of Arts, English   expected May 2017
Georgia State University, Atlanta, GA

- Emphasis areas: journalism and communication
- Study Abroad, Ecuador (Fall 2012)
- Dean's List (Fall 2012, Fall 2013, Spring 2014)

EXPERIENCE

Copyeditor   Sept. 2016-present
The Signal, Atlanta, GA

- copyedit articles for spelling, grammar, and style
- fact-check articles
- prepare copy for web publication in Dreamweaver

Writing Tutor   Oct. 2014-present
Georgia State University Writing Studio, Atlanta, GA

- work with undergraduate and graduate students on writing projects in all subject areas
- provide technical support for multimedia projects

OUTREACH AND ACTIVITIES

- Publicity Director, English Department
  Student Organization   Aug. 2016-present
- Coordinator, Georgia State University
  Relay for Life Student Team   April 2016, 2017

Annotations (left margin):

Information organized into clear categories — Skills Summary, Education, Experience, etc. — and formatted for easy scanning.

Information presented in reverse chronological order.

Bulleted lists organize information.

Present-tense verbs (*work*) used for current activities.

Professional memo

COMMONWEALTH PRESS

MEMORANDUM

February 26, 2018

To: Editorial assistants, Advertising Department

cc: Stephen Chapman

From: Helen Brown

Subject: Training for new database software

The new database software will be installed on your computers next week. I have scheduled a training program to help you become familiar with the software and with our new procedures for data entry and retrieval.

Training program

A member of our IT staff will teach in-house workshops on how to use the new software. If you try the software before the workshop, please be prepared to discuss any problems you encounter.

We will keep the training groups small to encourage hands-on participation and to provide individual attention. The workshops will take place in the training room on the third floor from 10:00 a.m. to 2:00 p.m.

Lunch will be provided in the cafeteria.

Sign-up

Please sign up by March 2 for one of the following dates by adding your name in the department's online calendar:

- Monday, March 5
- Wednesday, March 7
- Friday, March 9

If you will not be in the office on any of those dates, please let me know by March 2.

Date, name of recipient, name of sender on separate lines.

Subject line describes topic concisely.

Introduction states point of memo.

Headings guide readers and promote quick scanning of document.

List calls attention to important information.

APPENDIX

Glossary of usage

This glossary includes words commonly confused (such as *accept* and *except*), words commonly misused (such as *aggravate*), and words that are nonstandard (such as *hisself*). It also lists colloquialisms and jargon. Colloquialisms are casual expressions that may be appropriate in informal speech but are inappropriate in formal writing. Jargon is needlessly technical or pretentious language that is inappropriate in most contexts. If an item is not listed here, consult the index. For irregular verbs (such as *sing*, *sang*, *sung*), see 27a. For idiomatic use of prepositions, see 18d.

a, an Use *an* before a vowel sound, *a* before a consonant sound: *an apple*, *a peach*. Problems sometimes arise with words beginning with *h* or *u*. If the *h* is silent, the word begins with a vowel sound, so use *an*: *an hour*, *an honorable deed*. If the *h* is pronounced, the word begins with a consonant sound, so use *a*: *a hospital*, *a historian*, *a hotel*. Words such as *university* and *union* begin with a consonant sound (a *y* sound), so use *a*: *a union*. Words such as *uncle* and *umbrella* begin with a vowel sound, so use *an*: *an underground well*. When an abbreviation or an acronym begins with a vowel sound, use *an*: *an EKG*, *an MRI*, *an AIDS prevention program*.

accept, except *Accept* is a verb meaning "to receive." *Except* is usually a preposition meaning "excluding." *I will accept all the packages except that one. Except* is also a verb meaning "to exclude." *Please except that item from the list.*

adapt, adopt *Adapt* means "to adjust or become accustomed"; it is usually followed by *to. Adopt* means "to take as one's own." *Our family adopted a Vietnamese child, who quickly adapted to his new life.*

adverse, averse *Adverse* means "unfavorable." *Averse* means "opposed" or "reluctant"; it is usually followed by *to. I am averse to your proposal because it could have an adverse impact on the economy.*

advice, advise *Advice* is a noun, *advise* a verb. *We advise you to follow John's advice.*

affect, effect *Affect* is usually a verb meaning "to influence." *Effect* is usually a noun meaning "result." *The drug did not affect the disease, and it had adverse side effects. Effect* can also be a verb meaning "to bring about." *Only the president can effect such a dramatic change.*

aggravate *Aggravate* means "to make worse or more troublesome." *Overgrazing aggravated the soil erosion.* In formal writing, avoid the use of *aggravate* meaning "to annoy or irritate." *Her babbling annoyed* (not *aggravated*) *me.*

agree to, agree with *Agree to* means "to give consent to." *Agree with* means "to be in accord with" or "to come to an understanding with." *He agrees with me about the need for change, but he won't agree to my plan.*

ain't *Ain't* is nonstandard. Use *am not, are not* (*aren't*), or *is not* (*isn't*). *I am not* (not *ain't*) *going home for spring break.*

all ready, already *All ready* means "completely prepared." *Already* means "previously." *Susan was all ready for the concert, but her friends had already left.*

all right *All right,* written as two words, is correct. *Alright* is nonstandard.

all together, altogether *All together* means "everyone or everything in one place." *Altogether* means "entirely." *We were not altogether certain that we could bring the family all together for the reunion.*

allude To *allude* to something is to make an indirect reference to it. Do not use *allude* to mean "to refer directly." *In his lecture, the professor referred* (not *alluded*) *to several pre-Socratic philosophers.*

allusion, illusion An *allusion* is an indirect reference. An *illusion* is a misconception or false impression. *Did you catch my allusion to Shakespeare? Mirrors give the room an illusion of depth.*

a lot *A lot* is two words. Do not write *alot. Sam lost a lot of weight.* See also *lots, lots of.*

among, between See *between, among.*

amongst In American English, *among* is preferred.

amoral, immoral *Amoral* means "neither moral nor immoral"; it also means "not caring about moral judgments." *Immoral* means "morally wrong." *Until recently, most business courses were taught from an amoral perspective. Murder is immoral.*

amount, number Use *amount* with quantities that cannot be counted; use *number* with those that can. *This recipe calls for a large amount of sugar. We have a large number of toads in our garden.*

an See *a, an.*

and etc. *Et cetera* (*etc.*) means "and so forth"; *and etc.* is redundant. See also *etc.*

and/or Avoid the awkward construction *and/or* except in technical or legal documents.

angry at, angry with Use *angry with,* not *angry at,* when referring to a person. *The coach was angry with the referee.*

ante-, anti- The prefix *ante-* means "earlier" or "in front of"; the prefix *anti-* means "against" or "opposed to." *William Lloyd Garrison was a* *leader of the antislavery movement during the antebellum period. Anti-* should be used with a hyphen when it is followed by a capital letter (*anti-Semitic*) or a word beginning with *i* (*anti-intellectual*).

anxious *Anxious* means "worried" or "apprehensive." In formal writing, avoid using *anxious* to mean "eager." *We are eager* (not *anxious*) *to see your new house.*

anybody, anyone *Anybody* and *anyone* are singular. (See 21e and 22a.)

anymore Use the adverb *anymore* in a negative context to mean "any longer" or "now." *The factory isn't producing shoes anymore.* Using *anymore* in a positive context is colloquial; in formal writing, use *now* instead. *We order all our food online now* (not *anymore*).

anyone See *anybody, anyone.*

anyone, any one *Anyone*, an indefinite pronoun, means "any person at all." *Any one*, the pronoun *one* preceded by the adjective *any*, refers to a particular person or thing in a group. *Anyone from the winning team may choose any one of the games on display.*

anyplace *Anyplace* is colloquial. In formal writing, use *anywhere.*

anyways, anywheres *Anyways* and *anywheres* are nonstandard. Use *anyway* and *anywhere.*

as Do not use *as* to mean "because" if there is any chance of ambiguity. *We canceled the picnic because* (not *as*) *it began raining. As* here could mean either "because" or "when."

as, like See *like, as.*

as to *As to* is jargon for *about. He inquired about* (not *as to*) *the job.*

averse See *adverse, averse.*

awful The adjective *awful* and the adverb *awfully* are not appropriate in formal writing.

awhile, a while *Awhile* is an adverb; it can modify a verb, but it cannot be the object of a preposition such as *for*. The two-word form *a while* is a noun preceded by an article and therefore can be the object of a preposition. *Stay awhile. Stay for a while.*

back up, backup *Back up* is a verb phrase. *Back up the car carefully. Be sure to back up your hard drive. Backup* is a noun meaning "a copy of electronically stored data." *Keep your backup in a safe place. Backup* can also be used as an adjective. *I regularly create backup disks.*

bad, badly *Bad* is an adjective, *badly* an adverb. *They felt bad about ruining the surprise. Her arm hurt badly after she slid into second base.* (See 26a, 26b, and 26c.)

being as, being that Both *being as* and *being that* are nonstandard expressions. Write *because* instead. *Because* (not *Being as*) *I slept late, I had to skip breakfast.*

beside, besides *Beside* is a preposition meaning "at the side of" or "next to." *Annie sleeps with a flashlight beside her bed. Besides* is a preposition meaning "except" or "in addition to." *No one besides Terrie can have that ice cream. Besides* is also an adverb meaning "in addition." *I'm not hungry; besides, I don't like ice cream.*

between, among Ordinarily, use *among* with three or more entities, *between* with two. *The prize was divided among several contestants. You have a choice between carrots and beans.*

bring, take Use *bring* when an object is being transported toward you, *take* when it is being moved away. *Please bring me a glass of water. Please take these forms to Mr. Scott.*

burst, bursted; bust, busted *Burst* is an irregular verb meaning "to come open or fly apart suddenly or violently." Its past tense is *burst.* The past-tense form *bursted* is nonstandard. *Bust* and *busted* are slang for *burst* and, along with *bursted*, should not be used in formal writing.

can, may The distinction between *can* and *may* is fading, but some writers still observe it in formal writing. *Can* is traditionally reserved for ability, *may* for permission. *Can you speak French? May I help you?*

capital, capitol *Capital* refers to a city, *capitol* to a building where lawmakers meet. *Capital* also refers to wealth or resources. *The residents of the state capital protested plans to close the streets surrounding the capitol.*

censor, censure *Censor* means "to remove or suppress material considered objectionable." *Censure* means "to criticize severely." *The administration's policy of censoring books has been censured by the media.*

cite, site *Cite* means "to quote as an authority or example." *Site* is usually a noun meaning "a particular place." *He cited the zoning law in his argument against the proposed site of the gas station.* Locations on the Internet are usually referred to as *sites. The library's website improves every week.*

climactic, climatic *Climactic* is derived from *climax*, the point of greatest intensity in a series or progression of events. *Climatic* is derived from *climate* and refers to meteorological conditions. *The climactic period in the dinosaurs' reign was reached just before severe climatic conditions brought on an ice age.*

coarse, course *Coarse* means "crude" or "rough in texture." *The coarse weave of the wall hanging gave it a three-dimensional quality. Course* usually refers to a path, a playing field, or a unit of study; the expression *of course* means "certainly." *I plan to take a course in car repair this summer. Of course, you are welcome to join me.*

compare to, compare with *Compare to* means "to represent as similar." *She compared him to a wild stallion. Compare with* means "to examine similarities and differences." *The study compared the language ability of apes with that of dolphins.*

complement, compliment *Complement* is a verb meaning "to go with or complete" or a noun meaning "something that completes." As a verb, *compliment* means "to flatter"; as a noun, it means "flattering remark." *Her skill at rushing the net complements his skill at volleying. Martha's flower arrangements receive many compliments.*

conscience, conscious *Conscience* is a noun meaning "moral principles." *Conscious* is an adjective meaning "aware or alert." *Let your conscience be your guide. Were you conscious of his love for you?*

continual, continuous *Continual* means "repeated regularly and frequently." *She grew weary of the continual telephone calls. Continuous* means "extended or prolonged without interruption." *The broken siren made a continuous wail.*

could care less *Could care less* is nonstandard. Write *couldn't care less* instead. *He couldn't* (not *could*) *care less about his psychology final.*

could of *Could of* is nonstandard for *could have*. *We could have* (not *could of*) *taken the train.*

council, counsel A *council* is a deliberative body, and a *councilor* is a member of such a body. *Counsel* usually means "advice" and can also mean "lawyer"; a *counselor* is one who gives advice or guidance. *The councilors met to draft the council's position paper. The pastor offered wise counsel to the troubled teenager.*

criteria *Criteria* is the plural of *criterion*, which means "a standard or rule or test on which a judgment or decision can be based." *The only criterion for the scholarship is ability.*

data *Data* is a plural noun technically meaning "facts or propositions." But *data* is increasingly being accepted as a singular noun. *The new data suggest* (or *suggests*) *that our theory is correct.* (The singular *datum* is rarely used.)

different from, different than Ordinarily, write *different from*. *Your sense of style is different from Jim's.* However, *different than* is acceptable to avoid an awkward construction. *Please let me know if your plans are different than* (to avoid *from what*) *they were six weeks ago.*

differ from, differ with *Differ from* means "to be unlike"; *differ with* means "to disagree with." *My approach to the problem differed from hers. She differed with me about the wording of the agreement.*

disinterested, uninterested *Disinterested* means "impartial, objective"; *uninterested* means "not interested." *We sought the advice of a disinterested counselor to help us solve our problem. Mark was uninterested in anyone's opinion but his own.*

don't *Don't* is the contraction for *do not. I don't want any. Don't* should not be used as the contraction for *does not*, which is *doesn't*. *He doesn't* (not *don't*) *want any.*

due to *Due to* is an adjective phrase and should not be used as a preposition meaning "because of." *The trip was canceled because of* (not *due to*) *lack of interest. Due to* is acceptable as a subject complement and usually follows a form of the verb *be. His success was due to hard work.*

each *Each* is singular. (See 21e and 22a.)

effect See *affect, effect.*

e.g. In formal writing, replace the Latin abbreviation *e.g.* with its English equivalent: *for example* or *for instance.*

either *Either* is singular. (See 21e and 22a.) For *either . . . or* constructions, see 21d and 22a.

elicit, illicit *Elicit* is a verb meaning "to bring out" or "to evoke." *Illicit* is an adjective meaning "unlawful." *The reporter was unable to elicit any information from the police about illicit drug traffic.*

emigrate from, immigrate to *Emigrate* means "to leave one country or region to settle in another." *In 1903, my great-grandfather emigrated from Russia to escape the religious pogroms. Immigrate* means "to enter another country and reside there." *More than fifty thousand Bosnians immigrated to the United States in the 1990s.*

eminent, imminent *Eminent* means "outstanding" or "distinguished." *We met an eminent professor of Greek history. Imminent* means "about to happen." *The snowstorm is imminent.*

enthused Avoid using *enthused* as an adjective. Use *enthusiastic* instead. *The children were enthusiastic* (not *enthused*) *about baking.*

etc. Avoid ending a list with *etc.* It is more emphatic to end with an example, and in most contexts readers will understand that the list is not exhaustive. When you don't wish to end with an example, *and so on* is more graceful than *etc.* (See also *and etc.*)

eventually, ultimately Often used interchangeably, *eventually* is the better choice to mean "at an unspecified time in the future," and *ultimately* is better to mean "the furthest possible extent or greatest extreme." *He knew that eventually he would complete his degree. The existentialists considered suicide the ultimately rational act.*

everybody, everyone *Everybody* and *everyone* are singular. (See 21e and 22a.)

everyone, every one *Everyone* is an indefinite pronoun. *Every one,* the pronoun *one* preceded by the adjective *every,* means "each individual or thing in a particular group." *Every one* is usually followed by *of. Everyone wanted to go. Every one of the missing books was found.*

except See *accept, except.*

expect Avoid the informal use of *expect* meaning "to believe, think, or suppose." *I think* (not *expect*) *it will rain tonight.*

explicit, implicit *Explicit* means "expressed directly" or "clearly defined"; *implicit* means "implied, unstated." *I gave him explicit instructions not to go swimming. My mother's silence indicated her implicit approval.*

farther, further *Farther* usually describes distances. *Further* usually suggests quantity or degree. *Chicago is farther from Miami than I thought. I would be grateful for further suggestions.*

fewer, less Use *fewer* for items that can be counted; use *less* for items that cannot be counted. *Fewer people are living in the city. Please put less sugar in my tea.*

finalize *Finalize* is jargon meaning "to make final or complete." Use ordinary English instead. *The architect prepared final drawings* (not *finalized the drawings*).

firstly *Firstly* sounds pretentious, and it leads to the ungainly series *firstly, secondly, thirdly,* and so on. Write *first, second, third* instead.

further See *farther, further.*

get *Get* has many colloquial uses. In writing, avoid using *get* to mean the following: "to evoke an emotional response" (*That music always gets to me*); "to annoy" (*After a while, his sulking got to me*); "to take revenge on" (*I got back at her by leaving the room*); "to become" (*He got sick*); "to start or begin" (*Let's get going*). Avoid using *have got to* in place of *must. I must* (not *have got to*) *finish this paper tonight.*

good, well *Good* is an adjective, *well* an adverb. (See 26a, 26b, and 26c.) *He hasn't felt good about his game since he sprained his wrist last season. She performed well on the uneven parallel bars.*

graduate Both of the following uses of *graduate* are standard: *My sister was graduated from UCLA last year. My sister graduated from UCLA last year.* It is nonstandard, however, to drop the word *from: My sister graduated UCLA last year.* Though this usage is common in informal English, many readers object to it.

grow Phrases such as *to grow the economy* and *to grow a business* are jargon. Usually the verb *grow* is intransitive (it does not take a direct object). *Our business has grown very quickly.* Use *grow* in a transitive sense, with a direct object, to mean "to cultivate" or "to allow to grow." *We plan to grow tomatoes this year. John is growing a beard.*

hanged, hung *Hanged* is the past-tense and past-participle form of the verb *hang* meaning "to execute." *The prisoner was hanged at dawn. Hung* is the past-tense and past-participle form of the verb *hang* meaning "to fasten or suspend." *The stockings were hung by the chimney with care.*

hardly Avoid expressions such as *can't hardly* and *not hardly,* which are considered double negatives. *I can* (not *can't*) *hardly describe my surprise at getting the job.* (See 26e.)

has got, have got The word *got* is unnecessary and awkward in such constructions. It should be dropped. *We have* (not *have got*) *three days to prepare for the opening.*

he At one time *he* was commonly used to mean "he or she." Today such usage is inappropriate. (See 17e and 22a.)

he/she, his/her In formal writing, use *he or she* or *his or her*. For alternatives to these wordy constructions, see 17e and 22a.

hisself *Hisself* is nonstandard. Use *himself*.

hopefully *Hopefully* means "in a hopeful manner." *We looked hopefully to the future.* Some usage experts object to the use of *hopefully* as a sentence adverb, apparently on grounds of clarity. To be safe, avoid using *hopefully* in sentences such as the following: *Hopefully, your son will recover soon.* Instead, indicate who is doing the hoping: *I hope that your son will recover soon.*

however In the past, some writers objected to the conjunctive adverb *however* at the beginning of a sentence, but current experts allow placing the word according to the intended meaning and emphasis. All of the following sentences are correct. *Pam decided, however, to attend the lecture. However, Pam decided to attend the lecture.* (She had been considering other activities.) *Pam, however, decided to attend the lecture.* (Unlike someone else, Pam chose to attend the lecture.) (See 32f.)

hung See *hanged, hung*.

i.e. In formal writing, use "in other words" or "that is" rather than the Latin abbreviation *i.e.* to introduce a clarifying statement. *Exposure to borax usually causes only mild skin irritation; in other words* (not *i.e.*), *it's not especially toxic.*

if, whether Use *if* to express a condition and *whether* to express alternatives. *If you go on a trip, whether to Nebraska or Italy, remember to bring traveler's checks.*

illusion See *allusion, illusion*.

immigrate See *emigrate from, immigrate to*.

imminent See *eminent, imminent*.

immoral See *amoral, immoral*.

implement *Implement* is a pretentious way of saying "do," "carry out," or "accomplish." Use ordinary language instead. *We carried out* (not *implemented*) *the director's orders.*

implicit See *explicit, implicit*.

imply, infer *Imply* means "to suggest or state indirectly"; *infer* means "to draw a conclusion." *John implied that he knew all about computers, but the interviewer inferred that John was inexperienced.*

in, into *In* indicates location or condition; *into* indicates movement or a change in condition. *They found the lost letters in a box after moving into the house.*

in regards to *In regards to* confuses two different phrases: *in regard to* and *as regards*. Use one or the other. *In regard to* (or *As regards*) *the contract, ignore the first clause.*

irregardless *Irregardless* is nonstandard. Use *regardless*.

is when, is where These constructions are often incorrectly used in definitions. *A runoff election is a second election held to break a tie* (not *is when a second election is held to break a tie*). (See 11c.)

its, it's *Its* is a possessive pronoun; *it's* is a contraction of *it is*. (See 36c and 36e.) *It's always fun to watch a dog chase its tail.*

kind, kinds *Kind* is singular and should be treated as such. Don't write *These kind of chairs are rare*. Write instead *This kind of chair is rare*. *Kinds* is plural and should be used only when you mean more than one kind. *These kinds of chairs are rare.*

kind of, sort of Avoid using *kind of* or *sort of* to mean "somewhat." *The movie was somewhat* (not *sort of*) *boring*. Do not put *a* after either phrase. *That kind of* (not *kind of a*) *salesclerk annoys me.*

lay, lie See *lie, lay*.

lead, led *Lead* is a metallic element; it is a noun. *Led* is the past tense of the verb *lead*. *He led me to the treasure.*

learn, teach *Learn* means "to gain knowledge"; *teach* means "to impart knowledge." *I must teach* (not *learn*) *my sister to read.*

leave, let *Leave* means "to exit." Avoid using it with the nonstandard meaning "to permit." *Let* (not *Leave*) *me help you with the dishes.*

led See *lead, led*.

less See *fewer, less*.

let, leave See *leave, let*.

liable *Liable* means "obligated" or "responsible." Do not use it to mean "likely." *You're likely* (not *liable*) *to trip if you don't tie your shoelaces.*

lie, lay *Lie* is an intransitive verb meaning "to recline or rest on a surface." Its forms are *lie, lay, lain*. *Lay* is a transitive verb meaning "to put or place." Its forms are *lay, laid, laid*. (See 27b.)

like, as *Like* is a preposition, not a subordinating conjunction. It can be followed only by a noun or a noun phrase. *As* is a subordinating conjunction that introduces a subordinate clause. In casual speech, you may say *She looks like she hasn't slept* or *You don't know her like I do*. But in formal writing, use *as*. *She looks as if she hasn't slept. You don't know her as I do.* (See also 46f and 46g.)

loose, lose *Loose* is an adjective meaning "not securely fastened." *Lose* is a verb meaning "to misplace" or "to not win." *Did you lose your only loose pair of work pants?*

lots, lots of *Lots* and *lots of* are informal substitutes for *many*, *much*, or *a lot*. Avoid using them in formal writing.

mankind Avoid *mankind* whenever possible. It offends many readers because it excludes women. Use *humanity, humans, the human race,* or *humankind* instead. (See 17e.)

may See *can, may.*

maybe, may be *Maybe* is an adverb meaning "possibly." *Maybe the sun will shine tomorrow. May be* is a verb phrase. *Tomorrow may be brighter.*

may of, might of *May of* and *might of* are nonstandard for *may have* and *might have. We might have* (not *might of*) *had too many cookies.*

media, medium *Media* is the plural of *medium. Of all the media that cover the Olympics, television is the medium that best captures the spectacle of the events.*

might of See *may of, might of.*

most *Most* is informal when used to mean "almost" and should be avoided. *Almost* (not *Most*) *everyone went to the parade.*

must of See *may of, might of. Must of* is nonstandard for *must have.*

myself *Myself* is a reflexive or intensive pronoun. Reflexive: *I cut myself.* Intensive: *I will drive you myself.* Do not use *myself* in place of *I* or *me. He gave the pie to Ed and me* (not *myself*). (See also 24a and 24b.)

neither *Neither* is singular. For *neither . . . nor* constructions, see 21d, 22a, and 22d.

none *None* may be singular or plural. (See 21e.)

nowheres *Nowheres* is nonstandard. Use *nowhere* instead.

number See *amount, number.*

of Use the verb *have*, not the preposition *of*, after the verbs *could, should, would, may, might,* and *must. They must have* (not *must of*) *left early.*

off of *Off* is sufficient. Omit *of. The ball rolled off* (not *off of*) *the table.*

OK, O.K., okay All three spellings are acceptable, but avoid these expressions in formal speech and writing.

parameters *Parameter* is a mathematical term that has become jargon for "boundary" or "guideline." Use ordinary English instead. *The task force worked within certain guidelines* (not *parameters*).

passed, past *Passed* is the past tense of the verb *pass. Ann passed me another slice of cake. Past* usually means "belonging to a former time" or "beyond a time or place." *Our past president spoke until past midnight. The hotel is just past the next intersection.*

percent, per cent, percentage *Percent* (also spelled *per cent*) is always used with a specific number. *Percentage* is used with a descriptive term such as *large* or *small*, not with a specific number. *The candidate won 80 percent of the primary vote. A large percentage of registered voters turned out for the election.*

phenomena *Phenomena* is the plural of *phenomenon*, which means "an observable occurrence or fact." *Strange phenomena occur at all hours of the night in that house, but last night's phenomenon was the strangest of all.*

plus *Plus* should not be used to join independent clauses. *This raincoat is dirty; moreover* (not *plus*), *it has a hole in it.*

precede, proceed *Precede* means "to come before." *Proceed* means "to go forward." *As we proceeded up the mountain path, we noticed fresh tracks in the mud, evidence that a group of hikers had preceded us.*

principal, principle *Principal* is a noun meaning "the head of a school or an organization" or "a sum of money." It is also an adjective meaning "most important." *Principle* is a noun meaning "a basic truth or law." *The principal expelled her for three principal reasons. We believe in the principle of equal justice for all.*

proceed, precede See *precede, proceed.*

quote, quotation *Quote* is a verb; *quotation* is a noun. Avoid using *quote* as a shortened form of *quotation*. *Her quotations* (not *quotes*) *from current movies intrigued us.* Also avoid shortening *quotation marks* to *quotes*. *Put quotation marks* (not *quotes*) *around exact language from a source.*

raise, rise *Raise* is a transitive verb meaning "to move or cause to move upward." It takes a direct object. *I raised the shades. Rise* is an intransitive verb meaning "to go up." *Heat rises.*

real, really *Real* is an adjective; *really* is an adverb. *Real* is sometimes used informally as an adverb, but avoid this use in formal writing. *She was really* (not *real*) *angry.* (See 26a and 26b.)

reason . . . is because Use *that* instead of *because*. *The reason she's cranky is that* (not *because*) *she didn't sleep last night.* (See 11c.)

reason why The expression *reason why* is redundant. *The reason* (not *The reason why*) *Jones lost the election is clear.*

respectfully, respectively *Respectfully* means "showing or marked by respect." *Respectively* means "each in the order given." *He respectfully submitted his opinion to the judge. John, Tom, and Larry were a butcher, a baker, and a lawyer, respectively.*

rise See *raise, rise.*

sensual, sensuous *Sensual* means "gratifying the physical senses," especially those associated with sexual pleasure. *Sensuous* means "pleasing to the senses," especially those involved in the experience of art, music, and nature. *The sensuous music and balmy air led the dancers to more sensual movements.*

set, sit *Set* is a transitive verb meaning "to put" or "to place." Its past tense is *set. She set the dough in a warm corner of the kitchen. Sit* is an intransitive verb meaning "to be seated." Its past tense is *sat. The cat sat in the doorway.*

shall, will *Shall* was once used in place of the helping verb *will* with *I* or *we: I shall, we shall.* Today, however, *will* is generally accepted even when the subject is *I* or *we.* The word *shall* occurs primarily in polite questions (*Shall I find you a pillow?*) and in legalistic sentences suggesting duty or obligation (*The applicant shall file form A by December 31*).

should of *Should of* is nonstandard for *should have. They should have* (not *should of*) *been home an hour ago.*

since Do not use *since* to mean "because" if there is any chance of ambiguity. *Because* (not *Since*) *we won the game, we have been celebrating with a pitcher of root beer. Since* here could mean "because" or "from the time that."

sit See *set, sit.*

site See *cite, site.*

somebody, someone *Somebody* and *someone* are singular. (See 21e and 22a.)

something *Something* is singular. (See 21e.)

sometime, some time, sometimes *Sometime* is an adverb meaning "at an indefinite time." *Some time* is the adjective *some* modifying the noun *time* and means "a period of time." *Sometimes* is an adverb meaning "at times, now and then." *I'll see you sometime soon. I haven't lived there for some time. Sometimes I see him at work.*

suppose to *Suppose to* is nonstandard for *supposed to. I was supposed to* (not *suppose to*) *be there by noon.*

sure and Write *sure to. We were all taught to be sure to* (not *sure and*) *look both ways before crossing a street.*

take See *bring, take.*

than, then *Than* is a conjunction used in comparisons; *then* is an adverb denoting time. *That pizza is more than I can eat. Tom laughed, and then we recognized him.*

that See *who, which, that.*

that, which Many writers reserve *that* for restrictive clauses, *which* for nonrestrictive clauses. (See 32e.)

theirselves *Theirselves* is nonstandard for *themselves. The crash victims pushed the car out of the way themselves* (not *theirselves*).

them The use of *them* in place of *those* is nonstandard. *Please take those* (not *them*) *flowers to the patient in room 220.*

then, than See *than, then.*

there, their, they're *There* is an adverb specifying place; it is also an expletive (placeholder). Adverb: *Sylvia is sitting there patiently.* Expletive: *There are two plums left. Their* is a possessive pronoun: *Fred and Jane finally washed their car. They're* is a contraction of *they are*: *They're later than usual today.*

they The use of *they* to indicate possession is nonstandard. Use *their* instead. *Cindy and Sam decided to sell their* (not *they*) *1975 Corvette.*

they, their The use of the plural pronouns *they* and *their* to refer to singular nouns or pronouns has traditionally been considered nonstandard. Now such usage is becoming increasingly acceptable. *No one handed in his or her draft on time.* Also acceptable in most cases: *No one handed in their draft on time.* (See 22a.)

this kind See *kind, kinds.*

to, too, two *To* is a preposition; *too* is an adverb; *two* is a number. *Too many of your shots slice to the left, but the last two were just right.*

toward, towards *Toward* and *towards* are generally interchangeable, although *toward* is preferred in American English.

try and *Try and* is nonstandard for *try to. The teacher asked us all to try to* (not *try and*) *write an original haiku.*

ultimately, eventually See *eventually, ultimately.*

unique Avoid expressions such as *most unique, more straight, less perfect, very round.* Either something is unique or it isn't. It is illogical to suggest degrees of uniqueness. (See 26d.)

usage The noun *usage* should not be substituted for *use* when the meaning is "employment of." *The use* (not *usage*) *of insulated shades has cut fuel costs dramatically.*

use to *Use to* is nonstandard for *used to. I used to* (not *use to*) *take the bus to work.*

utilize *Utilize* means "to make use of." It often sounds pretentious; in most cases, *use* is sufficient. *I used* (not *utilized*) *the laser printer.*

wait for, wait on *Wait for* means "to be in readiness for" or "to await." *Wait on* means "to serve." *We're waiting for* (not *waiting on*) *Ruth to take us to the museum.*

ways *Ways* is nonstandard when used to mean "distance." *The city is a long way* (not *ways*) *from here.*

weather, whether The noun *weather* refers to the state of the atmosphere. *Whether* is a conjunction referring to a choice between alternatives. *We wondered whether the weather would clear.*

well, good See *good, well.*

where Do not use *where* in place of *that. I heard that* (not *where*) *the crime rate is increasing.*

whether See *if, whether* and *weather, whether.*

which See *that, which* and *who, which, that*.

while Avoid using *while* to mean "although" or "whereas" if there is any chance of ambiguity. *Although* (not *While*) *Gloria lost money in the slot machine, Tom won it at roulette.* Here *While* could mean either "although" or "at the same time that."

who, which, that Do not use *which* to refer to persons. Use *who* instead. *That*, though generally used to refer to things, may be used to refer to a group or class of people. *The player who* (not *that* or *which*) *made the basket at the buzzer was named MVP. The team that scores the most points in this game will win the tournament.*

who, whom *Who* is used for subjects and subject complements; *whom* is used for objects. (See 25.)

who's, whose *Who's* is a contraction of *who is*; *whose* is a possessive pronoun. *Who's ready for more popcorn? Whose coat is this?* (See 36c and 36e.)

will See *shall, will*.

would of *Would of* is nonstandard for *would have*. *She would have* (not *would of*) *had a chance to play if she had arrived on time.*

you In formal writing, avoid *you* in an indefinite sense meaning "anyone." (See 23d.) *Any spectator* (not *You*) *could tell by the way John caught the ball that his throw would be too late.*

your, you're *Your* is a possessive pronoun; *you're* is a contraction of *you are*. *Is that your new bike? You're in the finals.* (See 36c and 46b.)

Answers to lettered exercises

SCAVENGER HUNT, page xxx

1. 1c; 2. 2i, 4e, 7h, 57b; 3. 61b; 4. 7h; 5. 52c; 6. 2c; 7. A verb has to agree with its subject. 8. Commas are useful but are generally overused.
9. Academic writers should avoid sentence fragments. 10. I plan to lie down for a nap before my shift begins. 11. Professor, will you accept late papers?
12. The city felt the effects of the hurricane for months afterward.

EXERCISE 6–2, page 89

a. hasty generalization; b. false analogy; c. *either . . . or* fallacy; d. biased language; e. faulty cause-and-effect reasoning

EXERCISE 8–1, page 111   *Possible revisions:*

a. The Prussians defeated the Saxons in 1745.
b. Ahmed, the producer, manages the entire operation.
c. The tour guides expertly paddled the sea kayaks.
d. Emphatic and active; no change
e. Protesters were shouting on the courthouse steps.

EXERCISE 8–2, page 111

a. passive; b. active; c. passive; d. active; e. active

EXERCISE 9–1, page 114   *Possible revisions:*

a. Police dogs are used for finding lost children, tracking criminals, and detecting bombs and illegal drugs.
b. Hannah told her rock-climbing partner that she bought a new harness and that she wanted to climb Otter Cliffs.
c. It is more difficult to sustain an exercise program than to start one.
d. During basic training, I was told not only what to do but also what to think.
e. Jan wanted to drive to the wine country or at least to Sausalito.

EXERCISE 10–1, page 118   *Possible revisions:*

a. A grapefruit or an orange is a good source of vitamin C.
b. The women entering the military academy can expect haircuts as short as those of the male cadets.
c. Looking out the family room window, Sarah saw that her favorite tree, which she had climbed as a child, was gone.
d. The graphic designers are interested in and knowledgeable about producing posters for the balloon race.
e. The Great Barrier Reef is larger than any other coral reef in the world.

EXERCISE 11–1, page 121   *Possible revisions:*

a. Using surgical gloves is a precaution now taken by dentists to prevent contact with patients' blood and saliva.
b. A career in medicine, which my brother is pursuing, requires at least ten years of challenging work.

c. The pharaohs had bad teeth because tiny particles of sand found their way into Egyptian bread.
d. Recurring bouts of flu caused the team to forfeit a record number of games.
e. This box contains the key to your future.

EXERCISE 12–1, page 124   *Possible revisions:*

a. More research is needed to evaluate effectively the risks posed by volcanoes in the Pacific Northwest.
b. Many students graduate from college with debt totaling more than fifty thousand dollars.
c. It is a myth that humans use only 10 percent of their brains.
d. A coolhunter is a person who can find the next wave of fashion in the unnoticed corners of modern society.
e. Not all geese fly beyond Narragansett for the winter.

EXERCISE 12–2, page 127   *Possible revisions:*

a. To complete an online purchase with a credit card, you must enter the expiration date and the security code.
b. Though Martha was only sixteen, UCLA accepted her application.
c. As I settled in the cockpit, the pounding of the engine was muffled only slightly by my helmet.
d. After studying polymer chemistry, Phuong found computer games less complex.
e. When I was a young man, my mother enrolled me in ballet and tap dance classes.

EXERCISE 13–3, page 132   *Possible revisions:*

a. An incredibly talented musician, Ray Charles mastered R&B, soul, and gospel styles. He even performed country music well.
b. Environmentalists point out that shrimp farming in Southeast Asia is polluting water and making farmlands useless. They warn that governments must act before it is too late.
c. We observed the samples for five days before we detected any growth. *Or* The samples were observed for five days before any growth was detected.
d. In his famous soliloquy, Hamlet contemplates whether death would be preferable to his difficult life and, if so, whether he is capable of committing suicide.
e. The lawyer told the judge that Miranda Hale was innocent and asked that she be allowed to prove the allegations false. *Or* The lawyer told the judge, "Miranda Hale is innocent. Please allow her to prove the allegations false."

EXERCISE 13–4, page 133   *Possible revisions:*

a. Courtroom lawyers need to have more than a touch of theater in their blood.
b. The interviewer asked if we had brought our proof of citizenship and our passports.
c. Experienced reconnaissance scouts know how to make fast decisions and use sophisticated equipment to keep their teams from being detected.
d. After the animators finish their scenes, the production designer arranges the clips according to the storyboard and makes synchronization notes for the sound editor and the composer.
e. Madame Defarge is a sinister figure in Dickens's *A Tale of Two Cities*. On a symbolic level, she represents fate; like the Greek Fates, she knits the fabric of individual destiny.

EXERCISE 14–1, page 136 *Possible revisions:*

a. Williams played for the Boston Red Sox from 1939 to 1960, and he managed the Washington Senators and Texas Rangers for several years after retiring as a player.
b. In 1941, Williams finished the season with a batting average of .406; no player has hit over .400 for a season since then.
c. Although he acknowledged that Joe DiMaggio was a better all-around player, Williams felt that he was a better hitter than DiMaggio.
d. Williams was a stubborn man; for example, he always refused to tip his cap to the crowd after a home run because he claimed that fans were fickle.
e. Williams's relationship with the media was unfriendly at best; he sarcastically called baseball writers the "knights of the keyboard" in his memoir.

EXERCISE 14–2, page 138 *Possible revisions:*

a. The X-Men comic books and Japanese woodcuts of kabuki dancers, all part of Marlena's research project on popular culture, covered the tabletop and the chairs.
b. Our waitress, costumed in a kimono, had painted her face white and arranged her hair in a lacquered beehive.
c. Students can apply for a spot in the leadership program, which teaches thinking and communication skills.
d. Shore houses were flooded up to the first floor, beaches were washed away, and Brant's Lighthouse was swallowed by the sea.
e. Laura Thackray, an engineer at Volvo Car Corporation, addressed women's safety needs by designing a pregnant crash-test dummy.

EXERCISE 14–3, page 140 *Possible revisions:*

a. These particles, known as "stealth liposomes," can hide in the body for a long time without detection.
b. Irena, a competitive gymnast majoring in biochemistry, intends to apply her athletic experience and her science degree to a career in sports medicine.
c. Because students, textile workers, and labor unions have loudly protested sweatshop abuses, apparel makers have been forced to examine their labor practices.
d. Developed in a European university, IRC (Internet relay chat) was created as a way for a group of graduate students to talk from their dorm rooms about projects.
e. The cafeteria's new menu, which has an international flavor, includes everything from pizza to pad thai.

EXERCISE 14–4, page 141 *Possible revisions:*

a. To help the relief effort, Gina distributed food and medical supplies.
b. Janbir, who spent every Saturday learning tabla drumming, noticed that with each hour of practice his memory for complex patterns was growing stronger.
c. When the rotor hit, it gouged a hole about an eighth of an inch deep in my helmet.
d. My grandfather, who was born eighty years ago in Puerto Rico, raised his daughters the old-fashioned way.
e. By reversing the depressive effect of the drug, the Narcan saved the patient's life.

EXERCISE 15–1, page 144   *Possible revisions:*

a. Across the hall from the fossils exhibit are the exhibits for insects and spiders.
b. After growing up desperately poor, Sayuri becomes a successful geisha.
c. Researchers who have been studying Mount St. Helens for years believe that earthquakes may have caused the 1980 eruption.
d. Ice cream typically contains 10 percent milk fat, but premium ice cream may contain up to 16 percent milk fat and has less air in it.
e. If home values climb, the economy may recover quickly.

EXERCISE 16–1, page 148   *Possible revisions:*

a. Martin Luther King Jr. set a high standard for future leaders.
b. Alice has loved cooking since she could first peek over a kitchen tabletop.
c. Bloom's race for the governorship is futile.
d. A successful graphic designer must have technical knowledge and an eye for color and balance.
e. You will set up email for all employees.

EXERCISE 17–1, page 152   *Possible revisions:*

a. When I was young, my family was poor.
b. This conference will help me serve my clients better.
c. The meteorologist warned the public about the possible dangers of the coming storm.
d. Government studies show a need for after-school programs.
e. Passengers should try to complete the customs declaration form before leaving the plane.

EXERCISE 17–4, page 157   *Possible revisions:*

a. Dr. Geralyn Farmer is the chief surgeon at University Hospital. Dr. Paul Green is her assistant.
b. All applicants want to know how much they will earn.
c. Elementary school teachers should understand the concept of nurturing if they intend to be effective.
d. Obstetricians need to be available to their patients at all hours.
e. If we do not stop polluting our environment, we will perish.
NOTE: Since it is becoming increasingly acceptable to use the plural pronoun *they* to refer to an indefinite pronoun or a generic noun, sentences b, c, and d could have alternative revisions. For example, this sentence could be considered acceptable: *Every applicant wants to know how much they will earn.*

EXERCISE 18–2, page 161   *Possible revisions:*

a. We regret this delay; thank you for your patience.
b. Ada's plan is to acquire education and experience to prepare herself for a position as property manager.
c. Serena Williams, the ultimate competitor, has earned millions of dollars just in endorsements.
d. Many people take for granted that public libraries have up-to-date computer systems.
e. The effect of Gao Xingjian's novels on Chinese exiles is hard to gauge.

EXERCISE 18–3, page 162   *Possible revisions:*

a. Queen Anne was so angry with Sarah Churchill that she refused to see her again.
b. Correct
c. The parade moved off the street and onto the beach.
d. The frightened refugees intend to make the dangerous trek across the mountains.
e. What type of wedding are you planning?

EXERCISE 18–4, page 164   *Possible revisions:*

a. John stormed into the room like a hurricane.
b. Some people insist that they'll always be available to help, even when they haven't been before.
c. The Cubs easily beat the Mets, who were in trouble early in the game today at Wrigley Field.
d. We worked out the problems in our relationship.
e. My mother accused me of evading her questions when in fact I was just saying the first thing that came to mind.

EXERCISE 19–1, page 172   *Possible revisions:*

a. Listening to the CD her sister had sent, Mia was overcome with a mix of emotions: happiness, homesickness, and nostalgia.
b. Cortés and his soldiers were astonished when they looked down from the mountains and saw Tenochtitlán, the magnificent capital of the Aztecs.
c. Although my spoken Spanish is not very good, I can read the language with ease.
d. There are several reasons for not eating meat. One reason is that dangerous chemicals are used throughout the various stages of meat production.
e. To learn how to sculpt beauty from everyday life is my intention in studying art and archaeology.

EXERCISE 20–1, page 178   *Possible revisions:*

a. The city had one public swimming pool that stayed packed with children all summer long.
b. The building is being renovated, so at times we have no heat, water, or electricity.
c. The view was not what the travel agent had described. Where were the rolling hills and the shimmering rivers?
d. Walker's coming-of-age novel is set against a gloomy scientific backdrop; the earth's rotation has begun to slow down.
e. City officials had good reason to fear a major earthquake: Most [*or* most] of the business district was built on landfill.

EXERCISE 20–2, page 178   *Possible revisions:*

a. Wind power for the home is a supplementary source of energy that can be combined with electricity, gas, or solar energy.
b. Correct
c. In the Middle Ages, when the streets of London were dangerous places, it was safer to travel by boat along the Thames.
d. "He's not drunk," I said. "He's in a state of diabetic shock."

e. Are you able to endure extreme angle turns, high speeds, frequent jumps, and occasional crashes? Then supermoto racing may be a sport for you.

EXERCISE 21–1, page 189

a. One of the main reasons for elephant poaching is the profits received from selling the ivory tusks.
b. Correct
c. A number of students in the seminar were aware of the importance of joining the discussion.
d. Batik cloth from Bali, blue and white ceramics from Delft, and a bocce ball from Turin have made Angelie's room the talk of the dorm.
e. Correct

EXERCISE 22–1, page 194   *Possible revisions:*

a. Every presidential candidate must appeal to a wide variety of ethnic and social groups to win the election.
b. Either Tom Hanks or Harrison Ford will win an award for his lifetime achievement in cinema.
c. The aerobics teacher motioned for all the students to move their arms in wide, slow circles.
d. Correct
e. Applicants should be bilingual if they want to qualify for this position.
NOTE: Since it is becoming increasingly acceptable to use the plural pronoun *they* to refer to an indefinite pronoun or a generic noun, sentences a, c, and e could be labeled correct as written.

EXERCISE 23–1, page 198   *Possible revisions:*

a. Some professors say that engineering students should have hands-on experience with dismantling and reassembling machines.
b. Because she had decorated her living room with posters from chamber music festivals, her date thought that she was interested in classical music. Actually, she preferred rock.
c. In my high school, students didn't need to get all A's to be considered a success; they just needed to work to their ability.
d. Marianne told Jenny, "I am worried about your mother's illness." [*or* ". . . about my mother's illness."]
e. Though Lewis cried for several minutes after scraping his knee, eventually his crying subsided.

EXERCISE 24–1, page 203

a. Correct [But the writer could change the end of the sentence: . . . *than he was.*]
b. Correct [But the writer could change the end of the sentence: . . . *that she was the coach.*]
c. She appreciated his telling the truth in such a difficult situation.
d. The director has asked you and me to draft a proposal for a new recycling plan.
e. Five close friends and I rented a station wagon, packed it with food, and drove two hundred miles to Mardi Gras.

EXERCISE 25–1, page 206

a. Correct
b. The environmental policy conference featured scholars whom I had never heard of. [*or* . . . scholars I had never heard of.]
c. Correct
d. Daniel always gives a holiday donation to whoever needs it.
e. So many singers came to the audition that Natalia had trouble deciding whom to select for the choir.

EXERCISE 26–1, page 211

a. Do you expect to perform well on the exam next week?
b. With the budget deadline approaching, our office has hardly had time to handle routine correspondence.
c. Correct
d. The customer complained that he hadn't been treated nicely by the agent on the phone.
e. Of all the smart people in my family, Aunt Ida is the cleverest. [*or* . . . most clever.]

EXERCISE 27–1, page 217

a. When I get the urge to exercise, I lie down until it passes.
b. Grandmother had driven our new hybrid to the sunrise church service, so we were left with the station wagon.
c. A pile of dirty rags was lying at the bottom of the stairs.
d. How did the game know that the player had gone from the room with the blue ogre to the hall where the gold was heaped?
e. Abraham Lincoln took good care of his legal clients; the contracts he drew for the Illinois Central Railroad could never be broken.

EXERCISE 27–2, page 222

a. The glass sculptures of the Swan Boats were prominent in the brightly lit lobby.
b. Visitors to the glass museum were not supposed to touch the exhibits.
c. Our church has all the latest technology, even a closed-circuit TV.
d. Christos didn't know about Marlo's promotion because he never listens. He is [*or* He's] always talking.
e. Correct

EXERCISE 27–3, page 228   *Possible revisions:*

a. Correct
b. Watson and Crick discovered the mechanism that controls inheritance in all life: the workings of the DNA molecule.
c. When city planners proposed rezoning the waterfront, did they know that the mayor had promised to curb development in that neighborhood?
d. Tonight's concert begins at 9:30. If it were earlier, I'd consider going.
e. Correct

EXERCISE 28–1, page 235

a. In the past, tobacco companies denied any connection between smoking and health problems.
b. The volunteer's compassion has touched many lives.
c. I want to register for a summer tutoring session.
d. By the end of the year, the state will have tested 139 birds for avian flu.
e. The golfers were prepared for all weather conditions.

EXERCISE 28–2, page 237

a. A major league pitcher can throw a baseball more than ninety-five miles per hour.
b. The writing center tutor will help you revise your essay.
c. A reptile must adjust its body temperature to its environment.
d. Correct
e. My uncle, a cartoonist, could sketch a face in less than two minutes.

EXERCISE 28–3, page 241   *Possible revisions:*

a. The electrician might have discovered the broken circuit if she had gone through the modules one at a time.
b. If Verena wins a scholarship, she will go to graduate school.
c. Whenever a rainbow appears after a storm, everybody comes out to see it.
d. Sarah did not understand the terms of her internship.
e. If I lived in Budapest with my cousin Szusza, she would teach me Hungarian cooking.

EXERCISE 28–4, page 244   *Possible answers:*

a. I enjoy riding my motorcycle.
b. The tutor told Samantha to come to the writing center.
c. The team hopes to work hard and win the championship.
d. Ricardo and his brothers miss surfing during the winter.
e. Jon remembered to lock the door. *Or* Jon remembered seeing that movie years ago.

EXERCISE 29–1, page 253

a. Doing volunteer work often brings satisfaction.
b. As I looked out the window of the plane, I could see Cape Cod.
c. Melina likes to drink her coffee with lots of cream.
d. Correct
e. I completed my homework assignment quickly. *Or* I completed the homework assignment quickly.

EXERCISE 30–1, page 257

a. There are some cartons of ice cream in the freezer.
b. I don't use the subway because I am afraid.
c. The prime minister is the most popular leader in my country.
d. We tried to get in touch with the same manager whom we spoke to earlier.
e. Recently there have been a number of earthquakes in Turkey.

EXERCISE 30–2, page 258   *Possible revisions:*

a. Although freshwater freezes at 32 degrees Fahrenheit, ocean water freezes at 28 degrees Fahrenheit.
b. Because we switched cable packages, our channel lineup has changed.
c. The competitor confidently mounted his skateboard.
d. My sister performs the *legong*, a Balinese dance, well.
e. Correct

EXERCISE 30–3, page 260

a. Listening to everyone's complaints all day was irritating.
b. The long flight to Singapore was exhausting.
c. Correct
d. After a great deal of research, the scientist made a fascinating discovery.
e. Surviving that tornado was one of the most frightening experiences I've ever had.

EXERCISE 30–4, page 261

a. an intelligent young Vietnamese sculptor
b. a dedicated Catholic priest
c. her old blue wool sweater
d. Joe's delicious Scandinavian bread
e. many beautiful antique jewelry boxes

EXERCISE 31–1, page 263

a. Whenever we eat at the Centerville Café, we sit at a small table in the corner of the room.
b. Correct
c. On Thursday, Nancy will attend her first home repair class at the community center.
d. Correct
e. We decided to go to a restaurant because there was no fresh food in the refrigerator.

EXERCISE 32–1, page 270

a. Alisa brought the injured bird home and fashioned a splint out of Popsicle sticks for its wing.
b. Considered a classic of early animation, *The Adventures of Prince Achmed* used hand-cut silhouettes against colored backgrounds.
c. If you complete the evaluation form and return it within two weeks, you will receive a free breakfast during your next stay.
d. Correct
e. Roger had always wanted a handmade violin, but he couldn't afford one.

EXERCISE 32–2, page 270

a. J. R. R. Tolkien finished writing his draft of *The Lord of the Rings* trilogy in 1949, but the first book in the series wasn't published until 1954.
b. In the first two minutes of its ascent, the space shuttle had broken the sound barrier and reached a height of over twenty-five miles.
c. German shepherds can be gentle guide dogs, or they can be fierce attack dogs.

d. Some former professional cyclists admit that the use of performance-enhancing drugs is widespread in cycling, and they argue that no rider can be competitive without doping.
e. As an intern, I learned most aspects of the broadcasting industry, but I never learned about fundraising.

EXERCISE 32–3, page 272

a. The cold, impersonal atmosphere of the university was unbearable.
b. An ambulance cut through police cars, fire trucks, and bystanders.
c. Correct
d. After two broken arms, three cracked ribs, and one concussion, Ken quit the varsity football team.
e. Correct

EXERCISE 32–4, page 272

a. NASA's rovers on Mars are equipped with special cameras that can take close-up, high-resolution pictures of the terrain.
b. Correct
c. Correct
d. Love, greed, and betrayal are common themes in fiction.
e. Sharks often mistake surfboards for small injured seals.

EXERCISE 32–5, page 276

a. Choreographer Alvin Ailey's best-known work, *Revelations*, is more than just a crowd-pleaser.
b. Correct
c. Correct
d. A member of an organization that provides job training for teens was also appointed to the education commission.
e. Brian Eno, who began his career as a rock musician, turned to meditative compositions in the late 1970s.

EXERCISE 32–6, page 280

a. Cricket, which originated in England, is also popular in Australia, South Africa, and India.
b. At the sound of the starting pistol, the horses surged forward toward the first obstacle, a sharp incline three feet high.
c. After seeing an exhibition of Western art, Gerhard Richter escaped from East Berlin and smuggled out many of his notebooks.
d. Corrie's new wet suit has an intricate blue pattern.
e. We replaced the rickety old spiral staircase with a sturdy new ladder.

EXERCISE 32–8, page 280

a. On January 16, 2017, our office moved to 29 Commonwealth Avenue, Mechanicsville, VA 23111.
b. Correct
c. Ms. Carlson, you are a valued customer whose satisfaction is very important to us.
d. Mr. Mundy was born on July 22, 1939, in Arkansas, where his family had lived for four generations.
e. Correct

EXERCISE 33–1, page 285

a. Correct
b. Tricia's first artwork was a bright blue clay dolphin.
c. Some modern musicians (trumpeter John Hassell is an example) blend several cultural traditions into a unique sound.
d. Myra liked hot, spicy foods such as chili, kung pao chicken, and buffalo wings.
e. On the display screen was a soothing pattern of light and shadow.

EXERCISE 34–1, page 289

a. Do not ask me to be kind; just ask me to act as though I were.
b. When men talk about defense, they always claim to be protecting women and children, but they never ask the women and children what they think.
c. When I get a little money, I buy books; if any is left, I buy food and clothes.
d. Correct
e. Wit has truth in it; wisecracking is simply calisthenics with words.

EXERCISE 34–2, page 289

a. Strong black coffee will not sober you up; the truth is that time is the only way to get alcohol out of your system.
b. Margaret was not surprised to see hail and vivid lightning; conditions had been right for violent weather all day.
c. There is often a fine line between right and wrong, good and bad, truth and deception.
d. Correct
e. Severe, unremitting pain is a ravaging force, especially when the patient tries to hide it from others.

EXERCISE 35–1, page 291

a. Correct [Either *It* or *it* is correct.]
b. If we have come to fight, we are far too few; if we have come to die, we are far too many.
c. The travel package includes a round-trip ticket to Athens, a cruise through the Cyclades, and all hotel accommodations.
d. The news article portrays the land use proposal as reckless, although 62 percent of the town's residents support it.
e. Psychologists Kindlon and Thompson (2000) offer parents a simple starting point for raising male children: "Teach boys that there are many ways to be a man" (p. 256).

EXERCISE 36–1, page 295

a. Correct
b. The innovative shoe fastener was inspired by the designer's young son.
c. Each day's menu features a different European country's dish.
d. Sue worked overtime to increase her family's earnings.
e. Ms. Jacobs is unwilling to listen to students' complaints about computer failures.

EXERCISE 37–1, page 301

a. As for the advertisement "Sailors have more fun," if you consider chipping paint and swabbing decks fun, then you will have plenty of it.
b. Correct
c. After winning the lottery, Juanita said that she would give half the money to charity.
d. After the movie, Vicki said, "The reviewer called this flick 'trash of the first order.' I guess you can't believe everything you read."
e. Correct

EXERCISE 39–1, page 308

a. A client left his or her [*or* a] cell phone in our conference room after the meeting.
b. The films we made of Kilauea on our trip to Hawaii Volcanoes National Park illustrate a typical spatter cone eruption.
c. Correct
d. Of three engineering fields — chemical, mechanical, and materials — Keegan chose materials engineering for its application to toy manufacturing.
e. Correct

EXERCISE 40–1, page 313

a. Correct
b. Some combat soldiers are trained by government diplomats to be sensitive to issues of culture, history, and religion.
c. Correct
d. A gluten-free diet is not always the best strategy for shedding pounds.
e. The work of Dr. Khan, a psychology professor and researcher, has helped practitioners better understand post-traumatic stress.

EXERCISE 41–1, page 314

a. *MLA style:* The carpenters located three maple timbers, twenty-one sheets of cherry, and ten oblongs of polished ebony for the theater set. *APA style:* The carpenters located three maple timbers, 21 sheets of cherry, and 10 oblongs of polished ebony for the theater set.
b. Correct
c. Correct
d. Eight students in the class had been labeled "learning disabled."
e. The Vietnam Veterans Memorial in Washington, DC, had 58,132 names inscribed on it when it was dedicated in 1982.

EXERCISE 42–1, page 317

a. Howard Hughes commissioned the *Spruce Goose*, a beautifully built but thoroughly impractical wooden aircraft.
b. The old man screamed his anger, shouting to all of us, "I will not leave my money to you worthless layabouts!"
c. I learned the Latin term *ad infinitum* from an old nursery rhyme about fleas: "Great fleas have little fleas upon their back to bite 'em, / Little fleas have lesser fleas and so on *ad infinitum*."

d. Correct
e. Neve Campbell's lifelong interest in ballet inspired her involvement in the film *The Company*, which portrays a season with the Joffrey Ballet.

EXERCISE 44–1, page 324

a. Correct
b. The swiftly moving tugboat pulled alongside the barge and directed it away from the oil spill in the harbor.
c. Correct
d. Your dog is well known in our neighborhood.
e. Roadblocks were set up along all the major highways leading out of the city.

EXERCISE 45–1, page 328

a. Assistant Dean Shirin Ahmadi recommended offering more world language courses.
b. Correct
c. Kalindi has an ambitious semester, studying differential calculus, classical Hebrew, brochure design, and Greek literature.
d. Lydia's aunt and uncle make modular houses as beautiful as modernist works of art.
e. We amused ourselves on the long flight by discussing how spring in Kyoto stacks up against summer in London.

EXERCISE 46–1, page 331

a. stage, confrontation, proportions; b. courage, hiker, inspiration, rescuers; c. need, guest, honor, fog; d. defense (noun/adjective), attorney, appeal, jury; e. museum, women (noun/adjective), artists, 1987

EXERCISE 46–2, page 333

a. his; b. that, our (pronoun/adjective); c. he, himself, some, his (pronoun/adjective); d. I, my (pronoun/adjective), you, one; e. no one, her

EXERCISE 46–3, page 335

a. told; b. were, killed; c. brought down; d. Stay, 'll [will] arrive; e. struggled, was trapped

EXERCISE 46–4, page 336

a. Adjectives: weak, unfocused; b. Adjectives: The (article), Spanish, flexible; adverb: wonderfully; c. Adjectives: The (article), fragrant, the (article), steady; adverb: especially; d. Adjectives: hot, cold; adverbs: rather, slightly, bitterly; e. Adjectives: The (article), its (pronoun/adjective), wicker (noun/adjective); adverb: soundly

EXERCISE 47–1, page 341

a. Complete subjects: The hills and mountains, the snow atop them; simple subjects: hills, mountains, snow; b. Complete subject: points; simple subject: points; c. Complete subject: (You); d. Complete subject: hundreds of fireflies; simple subject: hundreds; e. Complete subject: The evidence against the defendant; simple subject: evidence

EXERCISE 47–2, page 344

a. Subject complement: expensive; b. Direct object: death; c. Direct object: their players' efforts; d. Subject complement: the capital of the Russian Empire; e. Subject complement: bitter

EXERCISE 47–3, page 344

a. Direct objects: adults and children; object complement: weary; b. Indirect object: students; direct object: healthy meal choices; c. Direct object: the work; object complement: finished; d. Indirect objects: the agent, us; direct objects: our tickets, boarding passes; e. Direct object: community service; object complement: her priority

EXERCISE 48–1, page 346

a. In northern Italy (adverb phrase modifying *met*); as their first language (adverb phrase modifying *speak*); b. through the thick forest (adjective phrase modifying *hike*); with ease (adverb phrase modifying *completed*); c. To my boss's dismay (adverb phrase modifying *was*); for work (adverb phrase modifying *late*); d. of Mayan artifacts (adjective phrase modifying *exhibit*); into pre-Columbian culture (adjective phrase modifying *insight*); e. In 2002, in twelve European countries (adverb phrases modifying *became*)

EXERCISE 48–2, page 349

a. Updating your software (gerund phrase used as subject); b. decreasing the town budget (gerund phrase used as object of the preposition *in*); identifying nonessential services (gerund phrase used as subject complement); c. to help her mother by raking the lawn (infinitive phrase used as direct object); raking the lawn (gerund phrase used as object of the preposition *by*); d. Understanding little (participial phrase modifying *I*); passing my biology final (gerund phrase used as object of the preposition *of*); e. Working with animals (gerund phrase used as subject)

EXERCISE 48–3, page 352

a. so that every vote would count (adverb clause modifying *adjusted*); b. that targets baby boomers (adjective clause modifying *campaign*); c. After the Tambora volcano erupted in the southern Pacific in 1815 (adverb clause modifying *realized*); that it would contribute to the "year without a summer" in Europe and North America (noun clause used as direct object of *realized*); d. that at a certain point there will be no more oil to extract from the earth (noun clause used as direct object of *implies*); e. when you are rushing (adverb clause modifying *are overlooked*)

EXERCISE 49–1, page 355

a. Complex; that are ignited in dry areas (adjective clause); b. Compound; c. Simple; d. Complex; Before we leave for the station (adverb clause); e. Compound-complex; when you want to leave (noun clause)

Index

N

Multilingual Menu

A complete section for multilingual writers:

Multilingual and Academic English notes in other sections:

Revision Symbols

Boldface numbers refer to sections of the handbook.

abbr	faulty abbreviation **40**
adj/adv	misuse of adjective or adverb **26**
add	add needed word **10**
agr	faulty agreement **21, 22**
appr	inappropriate language **17**
art	article (*a, an, the*) **29**
awk	awkward
cap	capital letter **45**
case	error in case **24, 25**
cliché	cliché **18e**
coh	coherence **3d**
coord	faulty coordination **14a**
cs	comma splice **20**
dev	inadequate development **3b, 6h**
dm	dangling modifier **12e**
-ed	*-ed* ending **27d**
emph	emphasis **14**
ESL	English as a second language, multilingual **28–31**
exact	inexact language **18**
frag	sentence fragment **19**
fs	fused sentence **20**
gl/us	see glossary of usage
hyph	hyphen **44**
idiom	idiom **18d**
inc	incomplete construction **10**
irreg	irregular verb **27a**
ital	italics **42**
jarg	jargon **17a**
lc	lowercase letter **45**
mix	mixed construction **11**
mm	misplaced modifier **12a–d**
mood	mood **27g**
nonst	nonstandard usage **17c, 27**
num	use of numbers **41**
om	omitted word **10, 30b**

p	error in punctuation
^;	comma **32**
no ,	no comma **33**
;	semicolon **34**
:	colon **35**
˅	apostrophe **36**
" "	quotation marks **37**
. ?	period, question mark **38a–b**
!	exclamation point **38c**
— ( )	dash, parentheses **39a–b**
[ ] . . .	brackets, ellipsis mark **39c–d**
/	slash **39e**
¶	new paragraph **4e**
pass	ineffective passive **8**
pn agr	pronoun agreement **22**
proof	proofreading problem **3c**
ref	pronoun reference **23**
run-on	run-on sentence **20**
-s	*-s* ending **21, 27c**
sexist	sexist language **17e, 22a**
shift	distracting shift **13**
sl	slang **17c**
sp	misspelled word **43**
sub	subordination **14a**
sv agr	subject-verb agreement **21, 27c**
t	verb tense **27f**
trans	transition needed **3d**
usage	see glossary of usage
v	voice **8a**
var	lack of variety in sentence structure **14, 15**
vb	verb problem **27, 28**
w	wordy **16**
//	faulty parallelism **9**
^	insert
#	insert space
⌒	close up space

Detailed Menu